Money, Finance and Crises in Economic History

T0270728

Recently, students and scholars have expressed dissatisfaction with the current state of economics and have called for the reintroduction of historical perspectives into economic thinking.

Supporting the idea that fruitful lessons can be drawn from the work of past economists, this volume brings together an international cross section of leading economists and historians of economic thought to reflect on the crucial role that money, crises and finance play in the economy. The book draws on the work of economists throughout history to consider afresh themes such as financial and real explanations of economic crises, the role of central banks, and the design of macro-economic policies. These themes are all central to the work of Maria Cristina Marcuzzo, and the contributions both reflect on and further her research agenda.

This book will be of interest to researchers in the history of economic thought, and those who wish to gain a deeper understanding of the variety and diversity in approaches to economic ideas throughout history.

Annalisa Rosselli is professor of History of Economic Thought at the University of Rome Tor Vergata, Italy.

Nerio Naldi is associate professor of Economics at the University of Rome La Sapienza, Italy.

Eleonora Sanfilippo is associate professor of Economics at the University of Cassino and Southern Lazio, Italy.

Routledge Studies in the History of Economics

For more information about this series, please visit www.routledge.com/series/ SE0341

Money, Finance and Crises in Economic History

The Long-Term Impact of Economic Ideas

Essays in Honour of Maria Cristina Marcuzzo

Edited by Annalisa Rosselli, Nerio Naldi and Eleonora Sanfilippo

Routledge
Taylor & Francis Group

LONDON AND NEW YORK

First published 2019
by Routledge
2 Park Square, Milton Park, Abingdon, Oxon OX14 4RN

and by Routledge
52 Vanderbilt Avenue, New York, NY 10017, USA

First issued in paperback 2020

Routledge is an imprint of the Taylor & Francis Group, an informa business

© 2019 selection and editorial matter, Annalisa Rosselli, Nerio Naldi and
Eleonora Sanfilippo; individual chapters, the contributors

The right of Annalisa Rosselli, Nerio Naldi and Eleonora Sanfilippo to be
identified as the authors of the editorial material, and of the authors for
their individual chapters, has been asserted in accordance with sections 77
and 78 of the Copyright, Designs and Patents Act 1988.

All rights reserved. No part of this book may be reprinted or reproduced or
utilised in any form or by any electronic, mechanical, or other means, now
known or hereafter invented, including photocopying and recording, or in
any information storage or retrieval system, without permission in writing
from the publishers.

Trademark notice: Product or corporate names may be trademarks or
registered trademarks and are used only for identification and explanation
without intent to infringe.

British Library Cataloguing-in-Publication Data
A catalogue record for this book is available from the British Library

Library of Congress Cataloging-in-Publication Data
Names: Naldi, Nerio, editor. | Rosselli, Annalisa, editor. | Sanfilippo,
Eleonora.
Title: Money, finance and crises in economic history : the long-term
impact of economic ideas / edited by Nerio Naldi, Annalisa Rosselli and
Eleonora Sanfilippo.
Description: 1 Edition. | New York : Routledge, [2018] |
Series: Routledge studies in the history of economics ; 214
Identifiers: LCCN 2018024315| ISBN 9781138089815 (hardback) |
ISBN 9781315108971 (ebook) | ISBN 9781351611664 (pdf) |
ISBN 9781351611657 (epub) | ISBN 9781351611640 (mobi)
Subjects: LCSH: Economic history. | Money. | Finance. |
Financial crises.
Classification: LCC HC21 .M746 2018 | DDC 330.9–dc23
LC record available at https://lccn.loc.gov/2018024315

ISBN 13: 978-0-367-66543-2 (pbk)
ISBN 13: 978-1-138-08981-5 (hbk)

Typeset in Bembo
by Integra Software Services Pvt. Ltd.

Contents

Figures

Tables

Contributors

Editors

Annalisa Rosselli is professor of History of Economic Thought at the University of Rome Tor Vergata, Italy

Nerio Naldi is associate professor of Economics at the University of Rome La Sapienza, Italy

Eleonora Sanfilippo is associate professor of Economics at the University of Cassino and Southern Lazio, Italy

Contributors

Carlo Benetti is emeritus professor at the University of Paris Nanterre, France

Daniele Besomi is senior research fellow at the Centre Walras-Pareto, University of Lausanne, Switzerland

Pascal Bridel is emeritus professor at Centre Walras-Pareto, University of Lausanne, Switzerland

Fernando J. Cardim de Carvalho† was emeritus professor of Economics at the Federal University of Rio de Janeiro, Brazil

Mario Cedrini is research fellow in Economics at the University of Turin, Italy

Marcella Corsi is professor of Economics at the University of Rome La Sapienza, Italy

Carlo Cristiano is research fellow in Economics at the University of Pisa, Italy

Marco Dardi is professor of Economics at the University of Florence, Italy

Elisabetta De Antoni is lecturer in Macroeconomics and Monetary Economics at the University of Trento, Italy

Ghislain Deleplace is emeritus professor of Economics, University of Paris 8, France

Luca Fantacci is lecturer at Bocconi University, Milan, Italy

Christian Gehrke is associate professor at the University of Graz, Austria

Alberto Giacomin is former associate professor of History of Economic Thought at the University of Venice, Italy

Harald Hagemann is emeritus professor of Economic Theory at the University of Hohenheim, Germany

Toshiaki Hirai is emeritus professor at Sophia University, Tokyo, Japan and President of the Keynes Society Japan

Jan Kregel is director of research at the Levy Economics Institute, New York, USA

Heinz D. Kurz is emeritus professor at the University of Graz, Austria

Julio López G. is former associate professor at the Universidad Nacional Autónoma de México, Mexico

Perry Mehrling is professor of International Political Economy at the Pardee School of Global Studies, Boston University, USA

Carlo Panico is professor of Economics at Universidad Nacional Autonoma de Mexico, Mexico

Marco Piccioni is research fellow in Economics at the University Federico II of Naples, Italy

Alessandro Roncaglia is a member of the Accademia Nazionale dei Lincei, Rome, Italy

Neri Salvadori is professor of Economics at the University of Pisa, Italy

Bertram Schefold is senior professor at the Faculty of Economics and Business Administration, Goethe-University, Frankfurt am Main, Germany

Annamaria Simonazzi is professor of Economics at the University of Rome La Sapienza, Italy

Giulia Zacchia is research fellow in Economics at the University of Rome La Sapienza, Italy

Acknowledgements

This volume would never have seen the light of day without the help and commitment of many people.

Our thanks go to the contributors, who responded promptly and enthusiastically to our invitation to pay homage to Cristina Marcuzzo on her retirement, and moreover in such a number as to accept confining the length of the chapters within the set limits and, in some cases, also to co-author some of the contributions rather than be absent on this special occasion.

Thanks are also due to Graham Sells and Iolanda Sanfilippo, who have provided Cristina with support in her work over the years, respectively with revision of the English and editorial preparation of the texts. They, too, have gladly collaborated on this book dedicated to her, offering the usual contribution of professionalism, precision and competence.

The editors
Rome, July 2018

Introduction

Annalisa Rosselli, Nerio Naldi and Eleonora Sanfilippo

This volume is a tribute to the long academic career of Cristina Marcuzzo and to her commitment to promoting the history of economic thought and pluralism in economics throughout the world. It brings together essays written by authors who, in various periods and continents, shared in her scientific initiatives, research projects and cultural exchanges.

However, this is not the only feature that these essays have in common, both among themselves and also with the vast scientific production of Cristina Marcuzzo. First and foremost, they are based on the belief that economics still needs to study its own history and reflect on it. It has recently been argued (Weintraub, 2016) that, subsequent to WWII and in the United States, economics has become a serious science by shedding any remnant of political interpretation. Serious sciences progress from darkness to light building ever better theories grounded on ever sounder evidence and do not investigate past mistakes. According to this view, the history of economics, like the history of physics, is not devoid of interest because it helps us reconstruct one of the many aspects of human past, but it does not bring any valuable addition in terms of knowledge to the economist of the twenty-first century. The history of economic thought, then, should accept its place in the history of sciences, and not claim any special attention from practicing economists. The times when economists mastered history and analysis are deemed to be gone forever, belonging to an early and rude stage of the science. None of the essays in this volume shares this view. On the contrary, they all move from the idea that economists can deepen their understanding through awareness of the evolution of economic ideas. Some essays focus on the plurality of methods and tools available to address economic issues, others recover forgotten ideas and approaches, while yet others employ the insights of economists of the past to explain past or present economic events. None accepts the divorce between economics and history, be this history of ideas or history of facts.

Secondly, all or nearly all the essays in this volume share a particular attention towards money and crises. This is not only suggested by recent events, important as they have been in opening some cracks in the faith in the equilibrating power of market forces – cracks now appearing after decades of almost universal consensus. Explaining the role played by money (and finance) in the working of the economy has always been one of the most fascinating but difficult tasks facing economists since the dawn of their discipline. Money is a serious challenge to many assumptions on which economics has rested over the centuries. Being based on a social convention, backed by political authority, it makes it difficult to represent the economy as a sum of individuals. Being the medium in which prices are expressed, it is sometimes represented as a prerequisite for market exchanges to the effect that markets could not exist without money, sometimes as an inessential means to facilitate exchanges. Being an asset with little or no intrinsic value, money calls for explanations as to why rational agents should demand it. Some of the best minds in economics have exercised their powers grappling with these puzzles. Cristina Marcuzzo has devoted much of her research to studying them: Keynes, of course, who placed money at the centre of his analysis, but also Ricardo, who was too far ahead of his time and proposed monetary reforms that were to be adopted only a hundred years later. And together with Keynes and Ricardo, Galiani, Marx and Hicks, the great monetary economists, also figure as protagonists in this book.

We have divided the volume into two parts. The first part has a more theoretical character and deals with time-honoured issues in the field of value and money. History of economic thought serves its function helping us deepen our understanding of economic concepts by reconstructing their development over time and the different meanings they acquire in different authors. In this vein, the first part of the volume opens with a chapter by Bertram Schefold, which contrasts the idea of natural prices conceived by Smith and his successors with neoclassicals' equilibrium prices. Schefold argues that, in spite of the dramatic change of paradigm that long excluded some of Smith's most interesting insights from economic analysis (growth, increasing returns, endogenous technical change), the "old" or early neoclassicals retained the classical conception of "normal" prices of production based on a uniform rate of profit. He supports his argument with reference to Böhm-Bawerk and his critique of Fisher. Of course, the differences between the two approaches were great. In neoclassical theory market conditions were represented by supply and demand schedules based on consumers' preferences while for the classical economists supply and demand were forces which reflected the strength of competition on the market and played no role in the determination of normal prices. Nevertheless, the idea of long-period positions persisted in neoclassical theory and was abandoned only with the advent of intertemporal equilibrium, which released the condition of uniformity of the profit rate on all capital goods.

Böhm-Bawerk – Schefold reminds us – explained how relative prices change with distribution using Ricardo's invariable measure of value. And Ricardo and his theory of money and value are the focus of three more chapters in Part I. Ghislain Deleplace does not accept that the distinction between temporary and permanent causes of changes of prices be extended to changes in the value of money. In the case of commodities, permanent causes are hierarchically superior to temporary causes, since the former affect the determination of normal prices while the latter concern only their gravitation. On the contrary, in the case of changes in the value of money, the important distinction is between real causes, which are related to changes in the value of gold, and monetary causes, which depend on variations in the quantity of money. In both cases, a market mechanism is at work, which will bring the quantity of money back to its normal level, provided that a suitable institutional arrangement has been established for the market price of gold bullion to be kept at its legal price.

This was the core of Ricardo's proposal for an efficient monetary system which limited to a minimum the need for gold reserves, as reconstructed by Jan Kregel in his chapter. Against the background of modern-day monetary proposals, ranging from a return to the gold standard to the wholesale abolition of currency, this chapter draws implications from David Ricardo's *Proposals for an Economical and Secure Currency* for plans to reform the operation of central banks and for extraordinary monetary policy. Although 200 years old, the "Ingot plan" appears to be applicable to modern monetary conditions and suggests possible avenues of reform.

The theoretical foundation of Ricardo's Ingot plan lay in the belief that the value of gold was the least variable among the values of commodities. Linking the value of money to that of gold would minimise the sources of monetary disturbances in the economy. For this reason, Ricardo's search for an invariable measure of value was a search for a real commodity to be used as standard of money and its role, Ricardo believed, could not be performed by a composite commodity. From this point of view it differs from Sraffa's "standard commodity", as reconstructed by Christian Gerkhe, Heinz Kurz and Neri Salvadori in their chapter. They revisit their previous work on Ricardo and Sraffa in the light of the material now available in the Sraffa archive, showing how reflections on the measure of value led Sraffa to his famous critique of marginalist theory of the rate of interest based on a notion of capital measurable independently of prices and distribution. At the same time, they show that both Ricardo's invariable measure and Sraffa's standard commodity shared a common destiny: conceived as a device to arrive at a correct theory of value and distribution, they ended up as a by-product of it, since their precise specification was possible only after the theory sought was eventually found.

Ricardo is also the central figure in the chapter by Pascal Bridel – in this case, he is compared with one of his contemporaries. Bridel, one of the editors of Sismondi's *Œuvres économiques complètes*, reconstructs Sismondi's critique of Ricardo, focussing on the theory of rent and the Corn Laws debate. Sismondi's attacks on Ricardo were based on a different theory of prices and rejection of all the assumptions on which the method of long-period positions rests: mobility of capital and labour, uniform rate of profit in all sectors, zero rent on the marginal land. Sismondi also criticises Ricardo for assuming as universal the English capitalist organisation of production in agriculture, disregarding other forms existing outside England. In this way, even more interestingly,

Sismondi's criticisms opens a debate which is still in progress, representing one of the 'first critical appraisals of rigorous abstract theory not in terms of its internal logic but in terms of what is seen as its relevance to solve real-world issues'.

The remaining chapters of Part I investigate the relation between the role played by money in the economy and the genesis of crises. Daniele Besomi and Harald Hagemann guide us in reading the theory of crises through the metaphors of economic physiology and pathology employed by Wilhelm Roscher. Pathology – i.e. crisis – is a disturbance where small disequilibria between sales and purchases allowed for by the monetary medium can grow larger, as in a living organism, due to the interconnectedness between the components of the economic system. Therapeutics can rely on the natural course of the healing process, but governments should put in a helping hand in both prevention and relief.

Economists associate crisis and disequilibrium, because economic theory deals with equilibrium prices, be they classical prices of production or the outcome of neoclassical curves of supply and demand. However, trade at disequilibrium prices should be considered the normal condition for a decentralised economy with division of labour, as Carlo Benetti argues in his chapter where he contrasts Galiani and Marx. Both see money as the condition for the very existence of prices, and not the means to eliminate the difficulties of the "double coincidence of wants" of a barter economy. From this point of view, Galiani's analysis is more convincing than Marx's theory of the genesis of money, because Marx fails to show that money emerges as "universal equivalent" from a social process and, in the end, he can only assume the existence of money as a datum. Unlike Galiani, however, Marx endeavours to address disequilibrium prices, although unsuccessfully. Benetti suggests an alternative solution to his problem.

From Galiani and Marx, two of the most original pre-twentieth-century monetary thinkers, we move on to the two – perhaps most original – monetary theorists of the last century, Hicks and Keynes. Perry Mehrling's chapter deals with Hicks's representation of the working of a monetary economy, and in particular with the alleged contradiction to be seen, according to secondary literature, between monetary theory in his early writings and in his later works in the same area. Reinterpreting Hicks's writings on the role of liquidity and the characteristics of monetary systems, Mehrling convincingly demonstrates that this contradiction is only apparent since there is an essential continuity in Hicks's approach to monetary matters. The main element of this continuity lies, in the author's view, in Hicks's deep conviction of the importance of extending banking theory to every agent in the economy in order to explain (and, eventually, counteract) the inherent instability of credit in contemporary monetary systems. This is an aspect which Hicks also developed in his last work (Hicks, 1989), bringing in the crucial role of dealers in supplying liquidity.

Carlo Cristiano's chapter deals with the relation between Keynes's theory of investment (both real and financial) and his practice as an investor in the stock markets. Recalling the fundamental tenets of Keynes's theory of choice in a context of radical uncertainty, grounded on the notions of "logical probability" and the "weight of arguments", considered as reasonable bases to make decisions in an environment where the amount of knowledge possessed by economic agents is necessarily small, Cristiano underlines Keynes's eventual distrust of any sort of long-term approach to investment. As for his practice, on the other hand, Keynes operated in financial markets on a very large scale, in general showing long-term rather than purely speculative behaviour, especially during the 1930s. Cristiano insightfully explains the reasons for this apparent contrast.

Part I ends with a chapter which establishes a direct link between Quesnay – at the beginning of classical Political Economy – and Keynes. Alberto Giacomin's chapter examines schemes proposed as from the 1950s interpreting Quesnay's *Tableau économique* by means of input-output models. Giacomin highlights their weaknesses and presents an alternative interpretation built on Leontief's open model and on the idea that Quesnay's analysis is based on a conception of effective demand where landowners' expenditure on luxury goods plays a crucial role as leading force in the process of income determination. It is an interesting interpretation of Quesnay which combines elements of Leontief and Keynes and brings us back from Classical political economy to our own times.

The second part of the book opens with two chapters dealing with Keynes's proposal for an international monetary system, the Clearing Union plan. The first essay, by Mario Cedrini and Luca Fantacci, focuses on its theoretical aspects and investigates the role that this scheme, based on an international monetary unit (the bancor), had in the entire corpus of Keynes's theoretical views. Dissenting from the received view, the authors underline the substantial coherence between Keynes's prescriptions for managing the domestic economy and his proposals for an international monetary order, provided that the importance of the interconnectedness of national economies is duly acknowledged as well as the supportive role that supranational institutions can play in attaining domestic targets.

The second chapter, by Toshiaki Hirai, also looks at the Clearing Union but from a different perspective. Having reconstructed in detail the process through which it came to light, and analysed the main differences in terms of economic implications and political vision between the architecture of Keynes's Plan and its US counterpart, the White Plan, the author focuses on Keynes's attitude during the negotiations with the US delegation, highlighting his pragmatic approach to policy. Notwithstanding his personal conviction in favour of internationalism, which permeated his proposal in its first versions, Keynes gave up his "ideal" plan as soon as he realised that it would have had no chance of being accepted by the US government. He opted for a down-to-earth strategy, finalised to include some features of his plan within the US scheme, thus avoiding the risk of jeopardising US financial assistance to Great Britain in the second part of the war. In the final phases of the negotiations, he also showed a considerable degree of flexibility on technical aspects, giving priority to feasibility and reaching agreement on every other consideration.

Both reconstructions help cast light on some important features of Keynes's personality and approach to economic policy, his pragmatism and realism, as well as his deep awareness of the complexity of political and economic processes, and indeed of the real world in general. This attitude is illustrated by another episode in Keynes's career as economic commentator, reconstructed by Carlo Panico and Marco Piccioni. Their chapter addresses the issue of central bank independence from the viewpoint of a debate which took place in Britain after WWI, in the wake of transformations in the size of the debt supplied to finance the war, as well as the dimension and complexity of financial markets and the functions assumed by banks of issue. In this new context, the relationship between central bank independence and democratic powers came to be fiercely disputed within the Labour Party, and in 1932 Keynes intervened in the debate with a proposal on how to organise relations between the central bank and the other private and public institutions. Panico and Piccioni's reconstruction of the above-mentioned developments, of the overall debate and of Keynes's intervention stresses the relevance of Keynes's views to current debate. Keynes considerate attitude towards the political authorities can still stand as a guiding spirit in the design of satisfactory institutional arrangements. Moreover, in the face of the disappointing results achieved by an approach based on extending the powers of the central banks and restraining those of the other authorities, notably with regard to fiscal policies, Keynes powerful advocacy of an institutional setting promoting coordination between monetary and fiscal policies is particularly timely.

The theme of private and public interest is also at the core of Marco Dardi's chapter. He analyses how the formation of a revised liberal doctrine capable of contending with socialism for political space and the dissociation of liberalism as a political doctrine from economic liberalism ("liberismo" in the Italian lexicon) occurred in Italy, somewhat paradoxically, in 1918–1947, in spite of the fact that for a large part of the period freedom of expression and political debate were suffocated by the anti-liberal fascist regime. Even more paradoxically, in those years, anti-fascist "new-liberal" movements and a minority of "left-wing fascists" came to occupy strikingly close positions. Furthermore, strictly economic arguments were kept on the sidelines of this process – the main issue being not just where to place the boundary that divides private from public interest, but how to draw it. Dardi's chapter may then be read as a case study on the complexity of the relations linking philosophy, political theory and economic theory, and of the forms they actually assume entering into the fields of cultural, political and social history.

The chapter by Julio López and Fernando Cardim de Carvalho (very sadly, Fernando passed away before this book was published) brings us from the first to the second half of the twentieth century, but once again the importance of cultural, historical and political awareness comes to the fore. The authors argue that the triumph of neoliberalism by the turn of this century had caused severe selective memory loss, erasing from the record successful episodes of large-scale state interventions in the economy. They consider two of the many experiences of successful democratic planning – untainted by authoritarian political methods – in the Western world: the National Industrial Recovery Act, passed by the Roosevelt administration in 1933, which created the National Recovery Administration and lasted until 1935, and post-war French indicative planning, inaugurated by De Gaulle immediately after WWII to remain in force until the early 1970s. The chapter singles out the lines of force of each initiative, where government planning in democratic societies tackled such formidable situations as the Great Depression and the challenge of post-war reconstruction.

Another case where long-forgotten theories once more show their vitality and their capacity to prompt policy indications competing with mainstream proposals lies at the core of the chapter by Annamaria Simonazzi. Here we see that, after the liberal phase of the last few decades, the long Eurozone crisis and the spectre of "secular stagnation" have brought industry back into fashion as an engine for growth, and reindustrialisation as a strategic goal. However, agreement on the premise does not imply uniformity of views on potential remedies. In the mainstream approach, the problem of development is mostly one of achieving static efficiency: how to better allocate resources by countering market failures caused by monopolies, asymmetric information and externalities. Conversely, the network theory of development stresses the need for multilevel analysis to capture the interactions between firms and institutions, and the interdependence between aggregate demand and the supply of products and capabilities. Government policy once again has an important role to play: it is called upon to coordinate the dispersed actions of firms, help them identify new opportunities for differentiation and upgrading, and contribute to developing the capabilities needed for the production of more complex products.

Elisabetta De Antoni provides an insightful reconstruction of the evolution of macroeconomics in the twentieth century. Her analysis starts with a critical review of the Swedish Flag, a metaphor introduced by Axel Leijonhufvud to describe the course of macroeconomic analysis since Keynes (Leijonhufvud 1983). The Swedish Flag, adopting an "impulse plus propagation mechanism scheme" to explain economic fluctuations – considered as deviations from the "ideal" framework of competitive general equilibrium – distinguishes the different major schools of thought according to the binomial nature, real/ monetary, of shocks and maladjustments, alternatively associated. De Antoni then critically discusses the pervasive and attractive role played by the general equilibrium paradigm, with its unrealistic assumptions, as the sole theoretical benchmark of all mainstream approaches of the last century, including the Swedish Flag representation itself. According to De Antoni, this is the main reason why, in the twentieth century, standard macroeconomics proved substantially unable to explain the recurrent crises of modern monetary and financial systems, negatively influencing the evolution of the discipline in terms of both relevance and richness.

After so many chapters stressing the variety of approaches to economic theory and policies, the book concludes with a chapter by Marcella Corsi, Alessandro Roncaglia and Giulia Zacchia addressing the issue of the general impoverishment of economic analysis due to the lack of pluralism. In the authors' view, an important role in fostering this negative tendency is played by the distorting mechanisms through which the quality of research is currently assessed. After a brief introduction reaffirming the close link between history of economic thought and economics, the chapter shows – through aggregate data analysis of the Italian case – how bibliometric indicators applied to economics tend to discriminate against journals and articles in the former subfield, and non-mainstream approaches in general. Indicators such as journal impact factors and citation counts are mainly of a quantitative and not qualitative nature. Indeed, the authors stress the risk that excessive reliance on them implies both in terms of lack of theoretical richness and fruitful competition between different schools of thought within the discipline. This assertion of the rights of alternative "voices" in the interests of healthy development in economic science brings the volume fittingly to a close. Cristina Marcuzzo has devoted great efforts to counteracting the negative long-term impact of the current trend in the system to evaluate scientific research in our field. It has been one of the many cultural battles in her long career and, we are sure, also one of the many that will see her on the front line for many years to come.

References

Hicks, J.R. (1989). *A market theory of money*. Oxford: Clarendon Press.

Leijonhufvud, A. (1983), "What would Keynes have thought of rational expectations?", in Worswick G., Trevithick J. (eds), *Keynes And The Modern World*, Cambridge: Cambridge University Press, pp. 179–204.

Weintraub, R.E. (2016). Paul Samuelson's historiography: more wag than Whig. *History of Political Economy*, 48 (2), 349–363.

Part I

The working of a monetary economy

1 Continuity and change in the transition from the classical to the neoclassical theory of normal prices

Bertram Schefold

1. Introduction[1]

Adam Smith (1776) possessed a tool in his approach to the theory of value which, in his hands and in the hands of his classical successors, led to a theory of growth and accumulation that became the foundation block of political economy. However, it lost its most fruitful application when the neoclassicals replaced growth and accumulation with equilibrium analysis, focused on full employment and the marginal productivity theory of distribution with its questionable claims to justice, and when the classical concept of competition, based on the tendency to (not the achievement of) the uniform rate of profit was replaced by the new concept of competition, in which firms were simply price-takers. The result was that increasing returns, external effects and the analysis of the causes of technical process were lost and out of sight for a long time. However, this paradigmatic change, also associated with the less important shift from an "objective" theory of value to a "subjective" theory – did not at once entail the abandonment of the concept of natural or "normal prices" of production, i.e. the use of prices based on a uniform rate of profit. Only the explanation of the level of this rate changed with the change in the perspective on distribution and employment. Normal prices ceased to be the central concept of the analysis of long-period positions or long-term equilibria much later with the advent of intertemporal equilibrium theory, based on the dating of commodities and factors, and the introduction of futures markets (Garegnani, 1976). Intertemporal theory takes the quantities of capital goods produced in the past and available as inputs (endowments) at the beginning of the first period of the intertemporal equilibrium as given. They are scarce in different degrees; therefore their relative prices will change as more of the initially scarce endowment is produced, hence the rate of profit in the classical sense is not uniform and prices are usually not normal in the beginning. However they will tend towards normality in later periods, if there are no obstacles to the convergence of rates of profit such as sudden changes in endowments and if the time horizon is sufficiently far away. The "old" neoclassicals, prior to this change in the method of analysis, had, with the exception of Walras, assumed instead that the relative quantities of capital goods were adjusted to future production from the start, and future production to demand, so that prices could be normal.

Before we turn to the neoclassical analysis of normal prices, we want to show in what follows how Smith used the concept of natural price and we shall recall briefly how the concept was modified by his classical successors (Section 2 – readers well acquainted with the modern revival of classical theory may skip this section). We then turn to our main contribution, the discussion of how this concept of natural price was still present among the early neoclassicals or "old" neoclassicals, as I prefer to call them (to distinguish them from the later neoclassicals) who used the modern concept of intertemporal equilibrium (Böhm-Bawerk's use of intertemporal equilibrium was different, as we shall see). We mainly focus on Böhm-Bawerk (Section 3) and conclude with shorter remarks on Marshall and Walras (Section 4).

2. Essentials of the classical theory of value

At the origin of the Smithian theory of value, there is the distinction between market price and natural price. The natural price results from the pressure of competition in the long run, which reduces the price to the cost of production. This consists of the cost of the means of production, including a normal profit. Effectual demand is the quantity of the commodity demanded at the natural price by consumers who are ready, and able, to pay it. It is therefore a point in the modern diagram for the curves of supply and demand, but these curves did not exist yet at the time of Smith. If the supply deviated temporarily from the natural level, or was short or excessive, and similarly, if demand deviated given the supply, then the market price would tend to rise or fall. This obvious mechanism was not described in a formal manner, but illustrated by anecdotes (the black cloth, which rose in price when the subjects mourned their king and showed their loyalty by displaying black flags, or the price of bread, which rose in a beleaguered city). The price would return to its natural level after the elimination of these disturbing causes; the price "gravitated" to its normal level, and the analogy with astronomy suggested oscillations of the market price around the natural price according to "forces" of supply and demand. We shall later explain the difference between this traditional notion and the explanation of supply and demand in terms of curves in more detail. We are used to associating supply and demand curves with Marshall, but the difference between them and the classical notion was best illustrated by Böhm-Bawerk (Section 3).

We are now concerned with the natural price. Smith approached it in two ways, which seemed to involve a contradiction in the eyes of Karl Marx, but this is not the case, at least in principle (there were ambiguous formulations in Smith's text). On the one hand, Smith developed the model of a society where land is free and capital is insignificant, so that commodities are produced by labour alone. The examples of beaver and deer suggested that he was thinking of barter among the members of a tribe of Native Americans but Smith knew that he would then have had to discuss gift-giving rather than barter. The example really is a model, based on abstractions from reality. The barter goes on as if a modern commercial rationality prevailed and the hunters calculated the time spent on each prey, hence abstraction is made from the traditions of an Indian tribe which might regulate exchange according to conventions. On the other hand, abstraction is also created from modern complications, which derive from the production with capital and land. Under the circumstances, it is clear that commodities will exchange according to labour values. Since no other factors besides labour are involved in production, the labour value – here the direct labour embodied in a commodity – will be equal to the labour commanded by (or needed for the purchase of) the same commodity. This measure in terms of labour commanded was also used by Smith when he turned to the production by means of labour, land and capital. But then prices, although still expressed in terms of labour by being measured in terms of labour commanded, will stand above labour values, and this would lead to confusion as long as an adequate terminology was not reached.

The problem here was not the contradiction between two different princi-ples for determining the price of a commodity (labour embodied versus the adding up of all the cost components), but the inadequate formalisation of the process of adding up, which led to two difficulties: as Ricardo would observe, adding up suggested that the components could move independently of each other. But if the system had a given surplus, and if we abstract from land, the rise of wages would entail a fall in profits, with given techniques of produc-tion. Hence, the conflict of distribution was not properly visible in Smith. Moreover, the procedure created the mistaken impression that the cost of the commodity could always be resolved into a series of past and present costs in terms of labour, capital and land, but Sraffa showed by means of his reduction to dated quantities of labour that this was not possible in a system with circular production (e.g. given the existence of at least a basic commodity), unless the rate of profit was lower than the maximum rate of profit, where the wage rate would have reached zero; moreover, the reduction became impossible with joint production.

The details of Sraffa's analysis need not be reproduced here (see Sraffa, 1960; Schefold, 1989). But we shall write down the main formulas when we shall have discussed Ricardo. As regards Smith, it suffices to recall his theory of the natural prices of the factors. The wage of labour is a subsistence wage, regarded by Smith as quite variable according to historical circumstances. The rate of profit is uniform, but the level is not well explained. Smith believed that it would gradually fall with competition, but Ricardo would point out that, if the techniques were the same, the level of the rate of profit depended on the surplus left after the payment of wages so that profits were a residual. Smith characterised rent as derived from a monopoly, and it is in fact clear that the landlord could not demand a rent, if he had not the soil in his sole possession, but this is only a restatement of the distribution of property and not sufficient to explain the level of rents.

Ricardo, when discussing value, got rid of rent by introducing his differential theory of it and by looking at the cost of production on the marginal land, where rent was zero. By "value" he really meant the natural price, which would ultimately prevail, and this was equal to labour cost or labour embodied (taking account of the produced means of production) if the rate of profit was zero. Ricardo was fascinated by the influence changes of distribution had on relative prices, although he knew that the corresponding deviation of prices from labour values (to use the Marxian term) was only of a limited extent. If there were, described in modern terminology, two industries, one capital-intensive and one labour-intensive, and if the rate of profit rose, the natural price of the capital-intensive commodity had to rise, because more profits had to be earned on the capital. At the same time the cost would be reduced, to the extent that labour was used, in that the rise in the rate of profit implied, with given methods of production in the economy as a whole, a fall in the rate of wages. In the capital-intensive industry the effect of the rise of profit could be expected to prevail. The surprising implication was that the price of the commodity produced in the labour-intensive industry fell. For there, the fall of the wage rate would be of greater importance than the rise in the rate of profit so that the relatively bigger component of cost was reduced.

The consideration was not exact, insofar as the extent to which the wage rate would fall in consequence of the rise in the rate of profit, given unchanged methods of production, had not been determined in the first place. For that purpose, a standard had to be fixed in terms of which prices were expressed. Without such a standard, all that one could say was that the price of the capital-intensive commodity would rise *relative* to that of the labour-intensive commodity. Ricardo concluded that this mechanism would become most perspicuous, if a commodity of intermediate capital composition was chosen as the numéraire. He spoke of an "invariable" measure of value, which was inept, for all measures of value are invariable by definition. He meant that the ideal numéraire was one where the fundamental causes for deviations of its price from its original value, in consequence of the change in the rate of profit, were *absent*. This consideration can be rendered precise, following Sraffa, and I gave my account of the reasoning many years ago (Schefold, 1989, 2014).

In order to measure capital, Ricardo would speak of "the time it takes to bring a commodity to market." If nuts are collected by two workers, the value of the nuts will be equal to two units of labour. If a worker produces a machine and another worker then uses the machine to produce cloth, the value of the cloth will also be equal to two units of labour if the rate of profit is zero, but if it is positive and if wages have to be advanced, the cost of cloth will rise because profit has to be earned on the wage advanced for the first worker two periods ago and on the wage of the second worker which was advanced one period ago, so that the wage rate has to be multiplied in the case of cloth by $(1 + r)^2 + (1 + r)$, whereas the wage rate in the case of nut production has to be multiplied by $2(1 + r)$; the difference in price is to be derived from the difference between these two factors which is $r + r^2$.

The modern formalisation in terms of Sraffa's dated quantities of labour may be considered known; it demonstrates that Smith was wrong when he thought that prices could always be expressed as sums of past wages and profits, for the reduction does represent a resolution into past wages and profits, but the series converges only if $0 \leq r < R$ and it makes plain that prices do not simply rise with the rate of profit, for the rise in the rate of profit implies a fall in the wage. The series also shows how prices deviate from labour values under the influence of the change in distribution, for if $r = 0$, prices are equal to labour values, being equal to the sum of all past labour inputs.

With this we come to Marx. He tried to face the problem of the change in relative prices induced by changes in distribution for given techniques of production, although he thought that the influence of technical change on prices was more important. Since he did not have a mathematical expression to determine normal prices, he followed Ricardo and determined prices by regarding them as modifications of labour values, but his tool to calculate the modifications was not the time it takes to bring a commodity to market but the organic composition of capital, the relation of the value of capital goods used up in production (circulating capital plus depreciation, expressed in labour time) divided by the labour value of the real wage, which in his case, as in Ricardo's, was advanced: this was variable capital. He assumed that prices were equal to labour values in the first two volumes of *Das Kapital*, but he had already announced in the first volume that this was only an assumption to be overcome in the third volume. The challenge posed was that the theory of exploitation should hold also if normal prices (he called them "prices of production") deviated from values. Marx took account of this in the so-called transformation of values into prices. The prices of production resulted from a redistribution of the total surplus value earned by all capitalists. Where the organic composition was higher, surplus value had to be obtained through a transfer from sectors where the organic composition of capital was lower. Marx thought that this transfer would result from the process of competition, which was therefore interpreted as a redistribution of total surplus value in such a way that total profits were equal to it, and profits were in each sector proportional to capital advanced. Marx measured prices by assuming that the total price of capital and profit was equal to the value of total capital and surplus value, so that the rate of profit in price terms was equal to the rate of profit in value terms.

This solution to the problem of the transformation of values into prices was contested by Marx's critics, in particular the neoclassicals. It was pointed out that this transformation did not take into account that the values of the capital goods should also have been transformed from values into prices, for profit is earned on capital measured in prices, not in values. Marx had seen this point, but thought that, on average, this correction would not matter. It can be shown that Marx was right in special cases, but wrong in general (Schefold, 1894/2004). One special case obtains if the economy is in standard proportions and if the workers and the capitalists also receive shares which are proportional to the standard commodity. Another special case obtains if the activity levels are general, but if the structure of production of the economy is random. The labour theory of value then holds on average, in that the average of the deviations of labour values from prices of production disappears so that total profits are equal to total surplus value on average, and the rates of profit in value and in price terms coincide (Schefold, 2016a). But these modern solutions were not known to the economists of the nineteenth century and to the neoclassical authors to whom we now turn.

3. Normal prices in the analysis of neoclassical economists

An initial difference between neoclassical and classical theory concerns market prices. Smith was not interested in determining the market price theoretically; he was content with stating the gravitation to the natural price. But the terms "supply" and "demand" along with similar expressions were used much earlier, and so the question is what people who reflected seriously on economic matters meant by them. Supply and demand *curves* appear as geometric figures first in a German textbook by Rau (1826),[2] but mercantilist authors such as James Steuart (1767) thought of supply and demand as *forces* that could be stronger or weaker depending on the market situation (Schefold, 2016c, p. 251). This was characterised not via the preferences of the consumers, but the competitive conditions. Example: if only one ship with provisions arrived in the harbour of a colony, the supplier was in a strong position, especially if a long time had elapsed since the last supplier had anchored there, but his position was weaker if the colonists knew that other supply ships would follow soon. The characteristic difference between Rau's concept and that of other authors consists in the fact, that Rau, like all the authors who used demand and supply curves later, thought that something definite could be said about the desire to buy or sell in conditions other than those actually prevailing so that, for instance, a definite quantity could be indicated as the "demand" at a price other than the one which would be realised in the market. Even today, it is difficult for a beginner in economics to think of this quantity as something definite so long as one is unfamiliar with the theory of ordered preferences and the derivation of indifference curves on that basis. And yet it seems that such curves were conceived by several authors independently of one other. Cournot had a demand curve as a formula; he spoke of a "loi de la demande." He did not draw it (Cournot, 1838, p. 50), but described its properties and then proceeded to an analysis much richer than that provided by Rau.

Karl Marx, probably without knowing either Rau or Cournot, thought like Steuart of supply and demand as forces generating a trend. If demand was stronger than supply the price would rise, and it would fall in the converse case. But what if they were of equal magnitude? Then, Marx proclaimed, the price would be indifferent; the forces would stop determining anything and one would have to resort to the theory of prices of production, which for him was inseparable from the labour theory of value.

This was regarded as absurd by Böhm-Bawerk who thought that this concept was a specifically Marxian idea (Böhm-Bawerk, 1896, p. 409). Böhm-Bawerk suggested that the forces would by no means cease to operate in equilibrium. His example was that of a balloon which rises in the air up to the level where the lift, due to the gas in the hull of the balloon being lighter than air, is just compensated by the weight of the balloon. In other words, the definite equilibrium is determined because there is a definite relationship between the "strength" of supply and demand and the level of price. The strict conceptual difference between market price and natural price encountered in Smith and his classical successors disappears, because the "forces" of demand and supply reign both in and out of equilibrium.

Marx may have thought of a different physical analogue. Imagine two weights, attached to the ends of a rope which runs over a wheel that can turn without noticeable friction. If the weight on the left is heavier than that on the right, the weight on the left will sink, the one on the right will rise and the wheel will turn. But if the weights are exactly equal, there will be no such movement, and if the weight of the rope can be neglected, the weights can stand still in any position.

If the Marxian interpretation of supply and demand as forces is accepted, a special theory is required to determine the normal price. By contrast, Böhm-Bawerk's example points the way towards a theory, in which the difference between market price and natural or normal price is gradual. The new concept of supply and demand was so simple and suggestive that most authors to this day tend to reason in terms of supply and demand as explained by the familiar intersecting curves. Curiously, however, the old neoclassicals, as defined in the Introduction above, retained the idea of the normal price with its complexity and its dependence on the level of distribution.

The most obvious proof of this consists in the discussions of Ricardo's invariable standard of value, which continued to come up even in neoclassical reasonings, although they violate the methodology of the analysis of equilibria in terms of supply and demand. A remarkable instance of this can be found in Böhm-Bawerk's *Exkurse* (Böhm-Bawerk, 1884/1889, Part 2, Vol. II). Irving Fisher had argued in a controversy with Böhm-Bawerk that prices would fall, if the rate of interest rose. His reasoning was that prices of goods depended on the utility generated by the goods, hence, in the case of capital goods, the price of the goods had to be equal to the discounted future returns to be ascribed to these capital goods (see also Fisher, 1907). This argument was taken up by John Maynard Keynes (1936) with his concept of the marginal efficiency of capital. It was correct in Keynes, to the extent that Keynes here kept the expectations of the returns as constant by assumption, while the rate of interest was, also by assumption, varied in the short run. But, as has been pointed out by authors familiar with the literature on capital theory, the change in the rate of interest will affect the returns in a long-period equilibrium and reflect the change in distribution of prices in general (Petri, 2004, criticises the Keynesian investment function; Schefold, 1980, p. 157, shows how the normal price of the same machine can be represented as cost of production *and* as discounted return).

This is precisely the answer Böhm-Bawerk gave Irving Fisher. As we saw in our discussion on Ricardo, the price of a commodity produced in a capital-intensive industry will tend to rise with the rate of profit, that of a commodity produced in a labour-intensive industry will tend to fall, because the rise in the rate of profit causes the wage rate to fall. Hence, there are two opposite influences on the price; which influence prevails depends on the intensity of capital (we here exclude indirect effects discussed by Sraffa: the direction of the movement of the relative price may be reversed if the capital goods used in the capital-intensive industry are produced in labour-intensive industries etc.).

With his critique of Fisher, Böhm-Bawerk argued outside the context of supply and demand, on the basis of the classical theory of a determination of prices by costs including normal profits. An isolated movement of the rate of interest is not possible in a general equilibrium with given data, as it would affect not only cost relationships in terms of the theory of supply and demand, hence prices, but also the quantities used and produced in the system as a whole. Nevertheless, Böhm-Bawerk argued in a thought experiment, as in the classical tradition and in Sraffa, on the basis of a change in distribution with the quantities in the input–output structure of the system remaining unchanged.

Böhm-Bawerk thus seemed to identify value with cost of production. He justified this in an exchange with Karl Dietzel of 1892 (Böhm-Bawerk, 1892) by underlining that the defenders of marginal utility theory also recognised the "law of costs" (*Kostengesetz*) in the case of reproducible goods. Costs had to be recognised as an "intermediate cause" (*Zwischenursache*, Böhm-Bawerk, 1892, p. 319). The difference was that the identification of the cost of the good as the cause of its value did not represent the end of the investigation:

> For we supplement the theory of the value of the products by a theory of the value of the means of production or cost goods, where we arrive at the result that this value in turn eventually is rooted in marginal utility.
>
> (Böhm-Bawerk, 1892, p. 321)

We here recognise *first* the analogy with Adam Smith's resolution of the elements of the normal price into its components added up, *second* the Austrian explanation of the value of the factors from the demand side in terms of the utility of the product going "backwards" (Böhm-Bawerk, 1892, p. 326), and *third* the explanation of the utility of the factors on the supply side. On the one hand, workers must be compensated for the disutility of labour and for leisure forgone, on the other, capital accrues interest (and this is Böhm-Bawerk's main contribution) because capitalists have a low time preference and are willing to wait for their compensation. Böhm-Bawerk's *explanandum* is not total profit (interest plus entrepreneurial profit), but only interest. Entrepreneurial profit is primarily a matter of risk. Böhm-Bawerk thought that Anglo-Saxon economists erred when they primarily set out to explain the rate of total profit instead of interest (Böhm-Bawerk, 1911, p. 27).

Böhm-Bawerk, the neoclassical, later corrects Dietzel, the Ricardian, for a mistake in his Ricardianism. In a second controversy, Böhm-Bawerk notes Dietzel's belief that a rise in wages will have the same effect on the prices of all commodities (Böhm-Bawerk, 1898, p. 399). Böhm-Bawerk replies, in a manner similar to that in his response to Irving Fisher, that products, in the cost of which the factor labour is represented more than on average, will rise in price, while those products, in which the factor time ("or however else one wants to call it," p. 400) is represented above average, will fall in value:

> Finally, a certain intermediate layer of products, the composition of costs of which corresponds to the average, will remain unchanged in value and hence fall in relative value with respect to the first group and rise relative to the second.
>
> (ibid.)

Böhm-Bawerk here clearly talks about Ricardo's "invariable measure of value." Surprisingly, he adds: "By the way, this is not only abstract deduction, but an empirically confirmed fact which has long been accepted in theory and also by the economic textbook" (ibid.). The textbook, it turns out, is Roscher's *Die Grundlagen der Nationalökonomie* (Roscher, 1854). In fact, we find that Roscher (1854, p. 448, Book III, Ch. 6, §197) considers eleven industries. Number one shall use machines almost exclusively, number two a few workers more and less fixed capital and so on until, finally, number eleven uses its entire capital to pay for workers. Number six then is thought to be the one where the opposed influences are of equal magnitude. Roscher suggests that if producers of gold belong to this sixth group, "then one could see the entire complex of the relations of cost of production of several commodities in a very simple manner in the gold prices" (Roscher, 1854, p. 400). And this is the empirical confirmation for the founder of the Historical School: the black death in the fourteenth century rendered all products made primarily from labour more expensive, but leather and wool became cheaper. And the same effect could be observed in Latin America in more recent times. Leather producers must first elevate cattle, we may add, and the time it takes to bring these products to market is long. This is the curious state of economics in the German speaking area in the late nineteenth century: the Austrian theorist seeks the support of the German historical economist in order to convince the Ricardian of Freiburg of his mistake in classical economics!

We now turn to the use made of the theory of normal prices in Böhm-Bawerk's theory of interest. He had first conceived of it as a student in Karl Knies's seminar at Heidelberg (Yagi, 1983), but did not use it in his early lecture courses (Tomo, 1987). Interest had nothing to do with abstinence, as it was a result of waiting. He explained this in one of the controversies which followed upon the publication of his book:

> He who saves restricts only his desire for present means of gratification, by no means his demand for goods . . . one fully agrees nowadays that the abstinence displayed by the saver is no true abstinence . . . but a mere waiting. The saver does not want to give his saving without compensation but wants to get it back, as a rule increased by interest for himself or his heirs.
>
> (Böhm-Bawerk, 1901, p. 316)

To assume an intertemporal exchange seems an innocuous assumption, as long as two people formulate an explicit contract, but if markets are not complete in a competitive anonymous process, uncertain future demand must be anticipated. Unlike modern intertemporal general equilibrium theory, Böhm-Bawerk's approach does not involve a complete exchange of promises to deliver and buy and therefore does not include the corresponding futures markets. To know what savers will demand in the future seems to be an immense problem, to which he replies simply: "The producers know this of the special demand of the savers neither better, nor less well than of the demand of consumers in general." He concedes (Böhm-Bawerk, 1901, p. 316): "The producers can in this be gravely in error, and if they are, they must pay for their errors through the known sufferings in crises."

The means of production in Böhm-Bawerk's theory of capital and distribution (Böhm-Bawerk, 1910) are represented as a subsistence fund for the labourers producing those means. The fund consists of the goods made available by those prepared to wait for future goods. It can be interpreted as what used to be called the wage fund for the workers, plus the means of production which the workers need in the labour process as instruments: fuel, other raw materials etc. But these materials in turn had to be produced in the past, by labourers who needed subsistence. Böhm-Bawerk here returns to a consideration familiar from Smithian and Ricardian economics. The subsistence fund resolves into wage goods for present *and* past (indirect) labour. The structure of the subsistence fund can be represented by the labour inputs distributed over previous periods, as in the labour theory of value. Given Böhm-Bawerk's Ricardian background, it is less of a surprise that his average period of production turns out to be essentially the same thing as the capital coefficient. A similar transformation has led von Weizsäcker to equate the average period of production to the ratio of interest earning capital to the wage bill (Weizsäcker, 1971, p. 35). The average period of production T is a weighted average of the past periods $t = 0, 1, 2, 3, ...$, during which labour was indirectly expended for present production. The average period of production is − using usual notation − an average of all periods t, taking the indirect labour input of period t, $\mathbf{A}^t\mathbf{1}$, as the weight to form the average and dividing by the sum of all these weights:

$$T = \frac{\sum_{t=0}^{\infty} t\mathbf{y}\mathbf{A}^t\mathbf{1}}{\sum_{t=0}^{\infty} \mathbf{y}\mathbf{A}^t\mathbf{1}}$$

The vector $\mathbf{y}$ is a vector of activity levels. One can show easily that T equals the capital-output ratio K/Y precisely,

$$\frac{K}{Y} = \frac{\mathbf{y}\mathbf{A}\mathbf{p}}{\mathbf{y}(\mathbf{I} - \mathbf{A})\mathbf{p}}$$

provided certain conditions are met. (The vector $\mathbf{p}$ is here the vector of normal prices.) This precise coincidence of the average period of production with the capital-output ratio is obtained in three and only three distinct cases: if $\mathbf{y}$ is in standard proportions, that is proportional to Sraffa's standard commodity, if the labour theory of value holds, that means, if one has the familiar condition for a pure labour theory of value $(1 + R)\mathbf{A}\mathbf{l} = \mathbf{l}$ or if matrix $\mathbf{A}$ is of special composition, that is, if $\mathbf{A} = \mathbf{c}\mathbf{e}$, where $\mathbf{c}$ is a column vector of intensities and $\mathbf{e} = (1, ..., 1)$. Such a matrix represents the structure towards which random matrices tend if the number of commodities and industries grows large. It is ironic that we get the simple coincidence $T = K/Y$ under the same conditions under which the Marxian $P = M$ holds, as discussed above. These matters are explained in more detail in Schefold (2013, 2016b, 2017, pp. 199, 223). The importance of the observation is that the average period of production is, except in these special cases, not exactly equal to the capital-output ratio, but actual systems can be looked upon as systems for which the deviations from the labour theory of value are not necessarily large, where the activity levels are not strongly different from the standard commodity, and they are not far from random systems, as is indicated by empirical observations. This means that the average period of production is not a bad indicator of the capital-output ratio after all and intuitively easy to understand.

Böhm-Bawerk used the average period of production to illustrate how the economy would adapt to the time preference of consumers and to changes in the wage rate. Techniques with a longer average period of production indicated a higher intensity of capital. They were to be used if the consumers were prepared to defer consumption and also if labour was relatively scarce. The wage rate would adapt so that the subsistence fund was adequate, given the amount of labour available, and the average period of production would be lengthened according to time preference. This, at least, is the simplified picture; for a more detailed account, ultimately based on Wicksell, see Blaug (1962) and Schefold (2017).

Böhm-Bawerk's Ricardianism in the use of normal prices did not extend to the theory of distribution. Here we come to our most important point. Against Ricardo's treatment of profits as a residual in the surplus, after the deduction of wages, he would argue that there was not only a determination of wages via the condition of subsistence but that there were *also* forces determining profits – without interest, production would not be forthcoming (Böhm-Bawerk, 1884/1889, Part 2, Vol. I, pp. 80–81). Does this mean that there was an overdetermination, if the rate of wages resulted from conditions in the labour market – e.g. from a subsistence wage – *and* if interest resulted from time-preference? There would indeed be overdetermination, if the structure of production was given as in a Sraffa system with only one technique and hence only one degree of freedom for the determination of distribution and prices after the fixation of a numéraire. But there would not be overdetermination, according to Böhm-Bawerk, if the technique – the methods of production and the levels at which they were operated – was regarded as variable and not as a datum as in the Ricardian consideration of the given surplus. There could be supply and demand operating in the labour market *and* supply and demand operating in the market for capital without a resulting overdetermination, if there was not a given surplus, but one that was variable, thanks to the variability of the technique, to accommodate both *w* and *r*, and therefore thanks to the possibility of substitution. This then is the function of the period of production in Böhm-Bawerk: to characterise the technique at which *both* the labour market and that for capital can *simultaneously* be in equilibrium at full employment.

The concept of equilibrium in Böhm-Bawerk implies that crises can only be seen as deviations from a long-term position. On the one hand, there are the monetary disturbances. The rate of interest, reflecting the scarcity of capital through time preference, is susceptible of being influenced by monetary factors. This line of thought was pursued not so much by Böhm-Bawerk himself as by his followers, first of all Wicksell and then the later Austrian writers like von Mises and Hayek. What Böhm-Bawerk had established now became a "natural" rate of interest, to be confronted by a "monetary" rate. This could deviate from the natural rate because of expectations, but primarily because of a disturbing influence by the state and the Central Bank.

In a late publication "Macht oder ökonomisches Gesetz" (literally: "power or economic law"), Böhm-Bawerk (1914) himself looked at another disturbance, caused by trade unions. Various economists under the influence of the Historical School believed in the possibility of permanently influencing distribution through political means, as part of their reformist programs. One thought that labour unions could, within limits, influence the wage by means of industrial action and if supported by the state. Böhm-Bawerk showed how this would lead to a lengthening of the average period of production and hence to unemployment, how it would cause the members of the trade unions to defect and how equilibrium would be re-established in the long run, when the power of the trade unions was exhausted. This action therefore was wasteful, but he did not deny that a pressure for high wages could foster growth to some extent by inducing innovations.

Böhm-Bawerk may have been the most influential economist of his time. His position was so strong because he had provided – or seemed to have provided – a firm foundation for the concept of capital. The endowments of labour and capital defined the level of production which could be reached, if competition was allowed to run its course. This gave an intellectual orientation at a time when socialism and the Historical School proposed to interfere in the economy to different degrees and with different intentions, but always questioning the existence of a "natural" course of events.

4. Other neoclassicals – epilogue

It would be a task for a book, not for a chapter, to look into all the important neoclassical economists prior to the transition of modern intertemporal equilibrium in order to see how they used the classical theory of normal prices in the new context of the neoclassical theory of distribution. I here confine myself to a few remarks on Marshall and Walras.

The continuity with the classical theory is best known in the case of Marshall who emphasised it himself. His theory of the short run, with prices given to the individual producer by market conditions and with the individual producer adapting production of his firm until the equality of marginal cost and price is achieved, is a special explanation of how a market price in the sense of Adam Smith may be formed, and it has the merit of showing how it leads to the formation of a uniform rate of profit in the long run, in that the quasi-rents, if they are positive, attract producers from other sectors to invest where conditions are favourable, until competition has reduced the price to the minimum of average cost, equal to marginal cost. In consequence, the supply curve is in the short run a rising curve obtained from aggregating the marginal cost curves, in the long run a horizontal curve, if the firms are all alike. It illustrates how normal prices are determined by cost. In 1925, Sraffa showed how this analysis could be extended, if external effects led to a reduction of cost with the expansion of the market, and this has become one of the leading ideas of modern growth theory. If diminishing costs are due not to external effects, but to returns to scale under the control of the firm, imperfect competition results, and this may be considered a heritage of Adam Smith's theory of the division of labour.

The case of Walras is less well known and technically more complex. I have dealt with it in Schefold (2016b). Walras wanted to represent the process of accumulation by means of a determination of long-period positions, that is, with a uniform rate of profit, in a long-term equilibrium referring to one period, for he did not believe in futures markets. He distinguished between consumption goods and capital goods. Given distribution, the maximisation of utility resulted in demand functions for all consumers, and there was also saving. Given any level of distribution, the optimum technique could be determined; given the optimum technique, prices were determined, given prices and distribution, demand for consumption goods resulted and also the activity levels for production and the requirements for capital goods in current production. On the other hand, pre-existing capital goods were supplied by the consumers as owners of the endowments, and it seemed plausible that a solution would exist, in which the demand for capital equipment for consumption goods production was inferior to the gross savings supplied, so that capacity was left to produce new capital goods (investment) of a total value equal to the savings. An analysis of the corresponding equations demonstrates that the number of equations is sufficient to determine the unknowns, but the production of the new capital goods is arbitrary in that the potential for producing them depends on the capacities left after the demand for capital for consumer goods production has been satisfied. As it turns out, it is by no means certain that the solutions for the quantities of new capital goods will be semi-positive, hence economically meaningful, *and* adequate for future reproduction. The possibilities of substitution with varying levels of distribution are not sufficient to guarantee a full employment equilibrium with positive production of the new capital goods – a requirement necessary for the future survival of the economy. As Garegnani (1960) and several followers have argued, this combination of the theory of normal prices with the neoclassical theory of distribution could not really work. In Walras's model of capital formation, it is not possible to adapt the prices of capital goods, so as to steer the supply of old capital goods, in order to have adequate capacities for the production of new capital goods in proportions guaranteeing reproduction since relative prices are determined by the cost of production, including normal profits. In order to overcome the difficulty encountered by Walras, it became necessary to conceive of capital as a value magnitude for the economy as a whole and to regard the endowments of capital goods in a long period as endogenous variables, not as givens (Petri, 2004; Schefold, 2016b).

But what did this aggregate of capital mean prior to the determination of prices? There followed the great debates about the theory of capital in which it became clear that objections could be raised against not only the Walrasian formulation of the matter, but also against Böhm-Bawerk's, while Marshall was confined to partial equilibrium analysis in the textbook versions. So it appeared that a choice had to be made between a return to the classical Ricardian approach or to modern intertemporal equilibrium, which was, however, not immune to the critique of capital either. While the scope of this critique is still being debated, we have here tried to trace its origins. The history of economic thought turns out to be indispensable for the understanding of modern economic theory, as Cristina Marcuzzo, to whom this chapter is dedicated, has shown in her many contributions, which invariably are both of great topical *and* historical interest.

Notes

1 This paper was first given at the International Conference on "The dissemination and practice of market economic thought in China and the Commemoration of the 240th anniversary of the publication of *An inquiry into the nature and causes of the wealth of nations,*" held in September, 2016, in Shanghai, China, at the Institute of Economics, Shanghai Academy of Social Sciences. I should like to thank the participants for the comments I received on that occasion. The translations from German texts are mine.

2 Rau spoke of "offer" and "desire" ("Angebot" and "Begehr"). The curves first appear in the fourth edition of 1841 (repr. in Rau, 1826, in the Appendix, vol. III.2, pp. 475–477).

References

Blaug, M. (1962). *Economic theory in retrospect.* 3rd edition 1978. Cambridge: Cambridge University Press.

Böhm-Bawerk, E. von. (1884/1889). *Kapital und Kapitalzins.* Part 1: *Geschichte und Kritik der Kapitalzinstheorien.* Part 2: *Positive Theorie des Kapitales.* Vol. I: *Buch I–IV.* Vol. II: *Exkurse.* 4th edition 1921. Jena: G. Fischer.

Böhm-Bawerk, E. von. (1892). Wert, Kosten und Grenznutzen. As reprinted in: (1924). *Vol. I of: Gesammelte Schriften von Eugen von Böhm-Bawerk* (F.X. Weiß, ed.). Wien: Hölder, 309–374.

Böhm-Bawerk, E. von. (1896). Zum Abschluss des Marxschen Systems. As reprinted in: (1926). *Vol. II of: Gesammelte Schriften von Eugen von Böhm-Bawerk* (F.X. Weiß ed.). Reprint 1968. Frankfurt am Main: Sauer und Auvermann, 321–435.

Böhm-Bawerk, E. von. (1898). Kostenwert und Nutzwert. As reprinted in: (1926). *Vol. II of: Gesammelte Schriften von Eugen von Böhm-Bawerk* (F.X. Weiß, ed.). Reprint 1968. Frankfurt am Main: Sauer und Auvermann, 375–403.

Böhm-Bawerk, E. von. (1901). Wesen und Bedeutung des Sparens. As reprinted in: (1926). *Vol. II of: Gesammelte Schriften von Eugen von Böhm-Bawerk* (F.X. Weiß, ed.). Reprint 1968. Frankfurt am Main: Sauer und Auvermann, 307–318.

Böhm-Bawerk, E. von. (1910). Kapital. As reprinted in: (1926). *Vol. II of: Gesammelte Schriften von Eugen von Böhm-Bawerk* (F.X. Weiß, ed.). Reprint 1968. Frankfurt am Main: Sauer und Auvermann, 3–20.

Böhm-Bawerk, E. von. (1911). Zins. As reprinted in: (1926). *Vol. II of: Gesammelte Schriften von Eugen von Böhm-Bawerk* (F.X. Weiß ed.). Reprint 1968. Frankfurt am Main: Sauer und Auvermann, 21–51.

Böhm-Bawerk, E. von. (1914). *Macht oder ökonomisches Gesetz?* Reprint 1975 (with an introduction by H.-H. Barnikel). Darmstadt: WBG.

Cournot, A.A. (1838). *Recherches sur les principes mathématiques de la théorie des richesses.* Reprint 1991. Düsseldorf: Verlag Wirtschaft und Finanzen.

Fisher, I. (1907). *The rate of interest.* Reprint 1994. Düsseldorf: Verlag Wirtschaft und Finanzen.

Garegnani, P. (1960). *Il capitale nelle teorie della distribuzione.* Milano: Giuffrè.

Garegnani, P. (1976). On a change in the notion of equilibrium in recent work on value and distribution. In: N. Brown, K. Sato and P. Zarembka (eds.) *Essays in modern capital theory.* Amsterdam: North Holland, 25–45.

Keynes, J.M. (1936). *The general theory of employment, interest and money.* London: Macmillan.

Petri, F. (2004). *General equilibrium, capital and macroeconomics.* Cheltenham: Edward Elgar.

Rau, K.H. (1826). *Lehrbuch der politischen Oekonomie.* Reprint 1997 (B. Schefold ed.). Vols I, II, III.1 and III.2. Hildesheim: Olms.

Roscher, W. (1854). *Die Grundlagen der Nationalökonmie. Ein Hand- und Lesebuch für Geschäftsmänner und Studierende.* 10th revised edition 1873. Stuttgart: Cotta.

Schefold, B. (1980). Fixed capital, accumulation and technical process. In: L.L. Pasinetti (ed.) *Essays on the theory of joint production.* London: Macmillan, 138–217.

Schefold, B. (1989). *Mr. Sraffa on joint production and other essays.* London: Unwin & Hyman.

Schefold, B. (1894/2004). Einführung. Der dritte Band: Herkunft und Wirkung. In: K. Marx (ed.). *Das Kapital. Kritik der politischen Ökonomie.* Vol. III. Berlin: Akademie Verlag, 871–910.

Schefold, B. (2013). Approximate surrogate production functions. *Cambridge Journal of Economics*, 37 (5), 1161–1184.

Schefold, B. (2014). Nachworte. In: P. Sraffa (ed.). *Warenproduktion mittels Waren, Einleitung zu einer Kritik der ökonomischen Theorie*. Reprint of 1976 edition. Marburg: Metropolis.

Schefold, B. (2016a). Profits equal surplus value on average and the significance of this result for the Marxian theory of accumulation. *Cambridge Journal of Economics*, 40 (1), 165–199.

Schefold, B. (2016b). Marx, the production function and the old neoclassical equilibrium: workable under the same assumptions? With an appendix on the likelihood of reswitching and of Wicksell effects. Centro Sraffa Working Paper. n. 19, April. Available at: http://www.centrosraffa.org/cswp_details.aspx?id=20.

Schefold, B. (2016c). *Great economic thinkers from antiquity to the Historical School.* New York: Routledge.

Schefold, B. (2017). *Great economic thinkers from the classicals to the moderns.* New York: Routledge.

Smith, A. (1776). *An inquiry into the nature and causes of the wealth of nations.* Glasgow edition 1976. Oxford: Oxford University Press.

Sraffa, P. (1960). *Production of commodities by means of commodities.* Cambridge: Cambridge University Press.

Steuart, J. (1767). *An inquiry into the principles of political oeconomy.* Reprint 1993. Düsseldorf: Verlag Wirtschaft und Finanzen.

Tomo, S. (ed.). (1987). *Earlier lectures on economics by Böhm-Bawerk.* Tokyo: Center for Historical Social Science Literature, Hitotsubashi University.

Weiß, F.X. (ed.). (1924). *Gesammelte Schriften von Eugen von Böhm-Bawerk.* Wien: Hölder.

Weiß, F.X. (ed.). (1926). Eugen von Böhm-Bawerks Kleinere Abhandlungen über Kapital und Zins. In: *Gesammelte Schriften von Eugen von Böhm-Bawerk.* Vol. II. Reprint 1968. Frankfurt am Main: Sauer und Auvermann.

Weizsäcker, C.C. von. (1971). *Steady state capital theory.* Berlin: Springer.

Yagi, K. (ed.). (1983). *Böhm-Bawerk's first interest theory.* Tokyo: Center for Historical Social Science Literature, Hitotsubashi University.

2 Money, value and the division of labour

Galiani and Marx

Carlo Benetti

This chapter[1] aims at showing how a comparative analysis of some selected writings by Galiani and Marx, more than a century apart, provides unconventional and fruitful theoretical insights about money and prices in equilibrium and in disequilibrium as well.

As Smith clearly showed, the social division of labour (as distinct from its technical division inside the factory) implies a systematic exchange relationship, by creating interdependent relationships between producers. Individual wealth thus depends both on production decision and on prices out of individual control. Following a long tradition since the middle of the eighteenth century, both issues about prices and exchange relations are treated separately. The main achievement of the theories of value, classical prices of production and neoclassical general equilibrium, is the determination, under suitable hypotheses, of equilibrium prices. Then it can be shown that individuals can only reach their equilibrium allocation by a centralised procedure (see Ostroy and Starr, 1974). Money is then introduced as the means of eliminating the well-known condition of 'double coincidence of wants' so that decentralised exchanges at exogenous equilibrium prices can be carried out. On such a basis, the 'integration of money into the theory of value' as a research program of monetary theory has been implemented.

Section 1 shows the similarities and the differences between Galiani's and Marx's approaches. As a common unit of account (Marx) and as a means of exchange (Galiani), money is the condition at which prices, determined by the theory of value, are also the exchange values on markets. Contrary to tradition, money is not a remedy to the difficulties of barter trades at equilibrium prices. On the other hand, we highlight the originality and theoretical relevance of Galiani's analysis of money and prices, and contrast it with Marx's theory of the genesis of money.

Section 2 deals with the limits of the methodology of equilibrium, common to both modern Neoclassical and Classical theories of value, according to which prices are only determined at equilibrium. This method discards disequilibrium as a field of research and somehow expresses a faith in the automatic equilibrium of markets. Galiani is a forerunner of such an approach whereas Marx moved aside from that tradition. He constructed a theory of value in disequilibrium, which is conceived as a necessary consequence of the social division of labour and not as a departure from an equilibrium position due to 'accidental causes' *à la* Ricardo (1821, p. 91). The main analytical tool is an original, non-classical, labour theory of value. We highlight the weakness of that theory and propose a monetary determination of prices in disequilibrium, based on Marx's remarkable study of the division of labour.

1. Money and exchange values

Both authors dealt with the monetary question after building a general theory of value, shared the same position on the nature of money, in essence metallic,[2] and pointed out that money is the necessary condition of exchange values. Notwithstanding these theoretical similarities, their conception of money is radically different. According to Marx's theory of the logical genesis of money he so proudly put forth,[3] money is a particular commodity which is derived from exchanges.[4] We propose a critique of that theory. On the contrary, in Galiani's original analysis of the issuance of the means of exchange, money is conceived as an institution or social device. We show that his method provides worthwhile insights in monetary theory.

1.1. Marx: the logical genesis of money

For the time being, we accept Marx's determination of values by the amount of social labour bestowed on the production of commodities (see Section 2.1). In the first chapter of *Capital*, Marx asserted that 'the value of commodities has a purely social reality, . . . it follows as a matter of course, that value can only manifest itself in the social relation of commodity to commodity' (1867, p. 32), i.e. as exchange value, which is possible only if values are expressed in a suitable way.

In the section on 'The form of value or exchange-value' such an issue is dealt with. Marx analysed four expressions or 'forms' of value, logically related, which are four analytical stages towards the monetary form of value. The starting point is the simplest form of value, called 'elementary or accidental' which, using Marx's notation, is written: x commodity $A = y$ commodity B. Note that the equality sign is misleading. Marx lengthily explained that the relation is not reversible since the value of commodity A is expressed as a relative value and commodity B is its particular equivalent. The elementary form is then generalised by considering more than two commodities. The outcome is the 'total or expanded' form of value. Special attention must be given to its writing, which is crucial for the rest of the analysis: the value of commodity A is expressed in terms of all the other $n - 1$ commodities, each of them being a particular equivalent of A (Marx, 1867, pp. 41–42). This is not a suitable expression of the value of commodity A. Marx obtained his central result by 'reversing' the series x commodity $A = y$ commodity B or $= z$ commodity C, etc. (p. 42). All commodities express now their value in terms of the same commodity A which is the general equivalent (i.e. the common unit of account.) This third stage is named 'the general form of value', in which 'commodities are, for the first time, effectively brought into relation with one another as values, or made to appear as exchange values'. (p. 43). The expression of values does not change in the fourth and last form of value, named 'the money form' in which gold is the general equivalent instead of commodity A. The main theoretical point is the transition from the second to the third form of value and it is here that the fatal weakness of Marx's analysis lies. The general equivalent is obtained by reversing the expanded form of value only because, in this form, A is the unique commodity expressing its value in terms of all the other $n - 1$ commodities. But this is a flawed reasoning. Not only commodity A, but every commodity expresses its value in terms of all the others so that there are $n(n - 1)$ expressions of relative values (and $n(n - 1)$ particular equivalents) and not $n - 1$ as stated by Marx. It follows that the outcome of the reversal of the expanded form of value is the expanded form itself and not the general form. Consequently, the general equivalent cannot be obtained as the result of the generalisation of exchange relationships. In Chapter 2 on 'exchanges', Marx clearly addressed the real issue:

> To the owner of a commodity, every other commodity is, in regard to his own, a particular equivalent, and consequently his own commodity is the universal equivalent for all the others. But since this applies to every owner, there is, in fact, no commodity acting as universal equivalent, and the relative value of commodities possesses no general form under which they can be equated as values and have the magnitude of their values compared. So far, therefore, they do not confront each other as commodities, but only as products or use-values.
>
> Marx (1867, p. 60)

In a nutshell, as we saw, the general equivalent is a necessary condition for the existence of exchange values but it cannot be obtained by reverting the expanded form of value in which use-values only exist. Marx's answer is nothing but a loophole: 'In their difficulties our commodity owners think like Faust: ... 'In the beginning was the deed' ... They therefore acted and transacted before they thought' (ibid.). The only solution we see is to give up Marx's theory of the genesis of money, and to presuppose the existence of the general equivalent as a datum of the theory of the exchange values.

1.2. Galiani: the issuance of the means of exchange

Galiani's (1751) analysis in Chapter 1 of Book II of *Della moneta* is centred on individual economic constraints necessary to a viable exchange system when barter is replaced by monetary trade. Let us consider an economy with social division of labour. The difficulty of barter trades is self-evident (Galiani, 1751, p. 158). As goods are both means of exchange and useful things, trades are only possible if the condition of the double coincidence of wants is verified. Galiani imagined an original solution, which plays a strategic role in his analysis. As in the theory of barter, it is assumed that equilibrium prices in terms of a common unit of account are determined and known by everybody. Production is carried out by specialised producers. Each of them puts down his net product in an appropriate warehouse and gets a voucher on which the warehouseman writes down its equilibrium value. Vouchers are a general means of exchange, the value of which gradually decreases by the amount equal to the value of each purchase and circulation ends when the value of all the vouchers and the quantities of goods in all the warehouses are simultaneously nil (clearly, these two conditions are only met in equilibrium). Goods are not means of exchange anymore: the double coincidence of wants is eliminated and consequently the difficulties of barter disappear.

Galiani only saw one shortcoming: the lack of virtue makes the fraudulent issue of vouchers inescapable (p. 162). Let us consider this matter more closely. The nominal value of a fraudulent voucher is greater than its equilibrium value so that individual budget constraint at equilibrium prices (verified in barter trades) is removed. Why is fraud possible and what are its consequences? The basic point is that producer and warehouseman have no exchange relationship. Like any sale, by putting down his commodity in the warehouse, the producer gets a means of payment. But the warehouseman does not buy anything. He creates a means of payment. The economic relation between them is a sale without purchase.[5] In this system the warehouseman is not subject to any economic constraint since his fraud does not give rise to any deficit (real or nominal) in his accounts. In a world without virtue, the inescapable outcome is a widespread fraud. Actually, the relation between producer and warehouseman is purely fictitious. Everything happens as if the producer himself issues the voucher on which he writes down the nominal value of his supply. His own claim on the social product is then arbitrarily fixed. By eliminating the budget constraint at equilibrium prices, the fraudster modifies the relative prices to his own benefit. Fraud being widespread, there are as many relative price systems as there are possible structures of fraud: i.e. an indefinite number. Thus, the relative prices are meaningless and such a system of exchange is obviously not viable.

Galiani's solution is to grant the 'Prince' exclusive rights on the issuing of the means of exchange. The vouchers, 'tutti di uno stesso prezzo' [all of the same value] are signed by the Prince and 'convenienti somme' [appropriate amounts] are allocated to the warehousemen. The means of exchange is now real money. The warehouses are true markets and the warehousemen are tradesmen who have an exchange relationship with producers to whom they buy and sell goods. They are subject to the monetary constraint of having, at the closure of markets, the same amount of money as the initial one. This constraint makes the working of the exchange system possible. The difficulties of both barter and voucher systems are eliminated and the 'utility' of money (p. 158) is demonstrated.

It is clear that Galiani's 'Prince' is nothing but a Central Bank through which the equilibrium values of individual products are monetised. As we saw, warehousemen can easily be removed. Producers get money directly from the Bank, make trades and must give back the same amount of money at the closure of markets. Such a monetary system will be generalised to disequilibrium states in Section 2.2.

Contrary to a generally admitted idea, money is not the remedy to the difficulties of barter trades, the voucher system is all that is needed. Money is a necessary condition for the existence of economically meaningful prices. Our analysis of Galiani's theory confirms the conclusion of our critique of Marx's theory of the forms of value. Money must be present from the beginning of the analysis and we can now go further: the quantity of money is endogenous and a monetary institution must be added to the initial data of the price theory.

Let us go back to Galiani's last stage of his analysis. As in the previous exchange system a similar difficulty arises, which is due to the lack of virtue of the warehousemen in the voucher system and of the Prince in the monetary system which only works if money is not refused 'per timore di frode' [for fear of some fraud] (Galiani, 1751, p. 162). Galiani's solution is based on his remarkable theory of value.[6] His theoretical strategy was 'sviluppare i principi del valore di tutte le cose in generale, ed adattargli all'oro e all'argento' [to develop the principles of the value of all things and to adapt them to gold and silver] (p. 116). Like all other commodities, the physical matter of metallic money has 'il suo naturale valore, da principi certi, generali e costanti derivato; che né il capriccio, né la legge, né il principe e né altra cosa può far violenza a questi principi e al loro effetto' [its natural value which stems from undoubted, general and constant principles; neither whim, law, Prince nor any other thing can do violence to these principles and to their effect] (p. 64 and 66).

Galiani and Marx have the same position on metallic money. But that similarity hides a deep theoretical difference. In Marx's theory, money is a particular commodity (i.e. gold) which 'has been excluded from the rest of commodities, as their equivalent' (1867, p. 45) through a mysterious 'social process' (p. 60). On the contrary, in Galiani's system money is conceived as the remedy to the difficulties of the voucher system and it appears simultaneously with its issuance by a Central Bank. Expressed in Marx's framework, it can be said that money is a particular voucher and not a particular commodity. We just saw that, according to Galiani, such a voucher must be made of a precious metal (i.e. a particular commodity) only because the value of metallic money is independent of any will and thus, the Prince's fraud can be prevented. It is clear that such a task of gold can theoretically be fulfilled by some appropriate legal regulations of the issuance of paper money.

2. Money and prices out of equilibrium

Galiani's theory of value is explicitly based on the equilibrium methodology which will be adopted by the subsequent economic theory. He certainly is one of the first authors who argued for restricting the theory to equilibrium states.

After explaining the principles by which the values of commodities are regulated, Galiani showed how changes in demands and supplies spontaneously rule out the gap between prices and 'intrinsic values' and he concluded: 'non bisogna de' primi movimenti in alcuna cosa tener conto, ma degli stati permanenti e fissi … come se in un vaso d'acqua si fa alcuna mutazione dopo un confuso e irregolare sbattimento, siegue il regolato livello' [in every field, only permanent and fixed states are to be taken into account and not the initial movements … some changes appear after shaking a glass of water, then the normal level is back in its proper place] (1751, p. 100), and 'sono vari i valori ma non capricciosi' [values are varied but not whimsical] (p. 92).

Values are only determined in equilibrium, so that disequilibrium states are only considered in order to establish a property of equilibrium, viz. its (global) stability. Let us mention that this property is far from being demonstrated as it is shown by the difficulties of the Classical theory of gravitation and the failure of the Walrasian theory which has been generally admitted since the 1970s. The main point is that the equilibrium methodology rules out disequilibrium states as a field of research. Yet, as Marx pointed out, the necessity of the determination of prices out of equilibrium is a logical consequence of the social division of labour, which is at the basis of market economies.

2.1. The social division of labour and the failure of Marx's theory of value

According to Marx, in an economy with social division of labour 'As a general rule, articles of utility become commodities, only because they are products of the labour of private individuals or groups of individuals who carry on their work independently of each other' (1867, Book I, Ch. 1, p. 47; see also p. 30). In such a society, each agent decides his production independently of the others, without knowing their decisions, whereas the result of his action depends on the others. Individual freedom and interdependencies are two sides of the same coin: 'The seeming mutual independence of the individuals is supplemented by a system of general and mutual dependence through or by means of the products' (pp. 72–73). The consequence is what, in his colourful language, Marx designated as 'the salto mortale of the commodity' when it is sold (1867, p. 71, 1859, p. 47), resulting from the ignorance of exchange values, itself a direct consequence of the division of labour. Disequilibrium occurs because actual prices differ from those on which the agents decided their actions. The amounts of goods obtained after trade, as well as the prices, are not those that had been foreseen. An analysis restricted to market equilibrium states does not address that issue: any contradiction between private and social evaluations (viz. expected and market prices) disappears and the economy behaves as if it was centralised or, in Marx's words, as 'the patriarchal industries of a peasant family' or 'a community of free individuals, carrying on their work with the means of production in common' (1867, p. 50).

Marx's economic analysis relies on an original labour theory of value which is based on the 'twofold character of the labour embodied in commodities'.

Labour is both private and social. What is 'private' is the concrete and heterogeneous labour expent by the producers of use-values, the quantities of which result from individual decisions taken independently from each other. Social labour, which is homogeneous and abstract, is the substance of value, and its quantity determines the exchange values. Marx stressed the importance of that distinction: 'I was the first to point out and to examine critically this twofold nature of the labour contained in commodities. ... this point is the pivot on which a clear comprehension of political economy turns' (1867, p. 29). He explained the relationship between these two notions of labour in the following terms:

> The point of departure is not the labour of individuals considered as social labour, but on the contrary the particular kinds of labour of private individuals, i.e., labour which proves that it is universal social labour only by the supersession of its original character in the exchange process. Universal social labour is consequently not a ready-made prerequisite but an emerging result.
>
> Marx (1859, p. 16)

The question is then to determine values inside the unity of production and circulation, viz. the amounts of social labour, which are formed through exchanges by starting from given quantities of private labours. The basic weakness of his theory was noticed by Marx himself: 'Thus a new difficulty arises: on the one hand, commodities must enter the exchange process as materialised universal labour-time, on the other hand, the labour-time of individuals becomes materialised universal labour-time only as the result of the exchange process' (ibid.). Hence a contradiction: the 'universal social labour' is simultaneously the condition and the result of exchange. In other words, concrete labour and social labour are clearly not commensurable magnitudes and it is not surprising that Marx did not succeed in converting given quantities of the first one[7] in determined quantities of the second one by means of the exchange relations.

As far as we know, neither Marx nor the Marxists have ever solved that problem. In the canonical model, labour values v are determined as the solution $v = (I - A)^{-1} l$ of a system of linear equations. But that formalisation is not acceptable as it contradicts the whole of Marx's analysis of the division of labour: vector l cannot represent heterogeneous private labours when v is a vector of values and therefore of social homogeneous labour, and l cannot be a vector of social labour either since, as Marx clearly showed, that vector is not a datum analogous to the matrix A of technical coefficients.

Marx's labour theory of value fails in determining exchange values in an economy with division of labour in which the agents are generally in disequilibrium. That failure deprives Marx's analysis of 'commodities' (1867, Ch. 1) of its indispensable theoretical ground that neither philosophy nor history can provide.

2.2. A monetary solution to Marx's problem

Our starting point is Marx's opposition between the 'private' and the 'social' evaluations of commodities, which is at the very basis of market economies. But we discard Marx's method of dealing with such evaluations in terms of private and social labour. In short, we propose a non-Marxist solution to Marx's problem, without any reference to the labour theory of value. Our answer introduces two devices inseparable from the division of labour itself: one is money, the other is a market mechanism by which market prices are determined (but not the actual allocation, as we will see later on). As pointed out in the conclusion of the analysis of Galiani's approach, money is the institutional expression of the division of labour. Like Galiani, we highlight money as a universal means of exchange.[8] The market mechanism uses the notion of the 'twofold character of price', which is inspired by the 'twofold character of labour' we have seen in Marx. We distinguish between two notions, the 'expected prices' and the 'market prices'.

Let us consider the economy with division of labour as described by Marx. We assume that during the previous period individuals have produced given quantities of commodities which are available at the beginning of the current period t. We seek their social evaluation starting from their private evaluation. At date t (which denotes the beginning of the current period) and before the opening of markets, each producer owns the product obtained at the end of period $t-1$ and has to decide the amount he will produce during period t without knowing the market prices of his product and of the inputs (including his consumption) which he requires. His plan of production is determined on the unsound basis of expected prices, which result from his personal opinion on the evaluation, by the other agents (i.e. society), of his own product and of the other goods he needs. Note that it doesn't matter what theory on individual economic rationality is chosen.

Before the opening of the market, each producer is assumed to take irrevocable decisions on his expenses, which lead him to ask a bank for some amount of money and to bring his product to the market. The amount of money required by each agent is equal to the expected value of his supply, given by the amount he produced during period $t-1$, which itself is equal to the expected value of his purchases. Each agent commits himself to reimburse the money he received from the bank and money is destroyed after having accomplished its circular flow. As we assume that the creation of money, its circulation and its destruction take place within a very short time interval, the rate of interest is ignored.

At date t individual productions are socially evaluated on the market. What are the prices resulting from the whole set of individual actions governed by expected prices?

'Market' is conceived as the set of places of exchanges, or trading posts, one for each commodity. We follow Cantillon (1755) by assuming that the market price of commodity i is equal to the ratio between the aggregated monetary expense and the quantity of the commodity brought to that market.[9] Thus, the social evaluation of commodity i results from the whole set of private evaluations. Let us outline the working of the market mechanism in an economy with n commodities ($i = 1, 2, ..., n$) and H producers ($h = 1, 2, ..., H$). There exist $n(n-1)/2$ trading posts. Consider producer h. Let s_{hi} be the quantity of commodity i he produced during the previous period and brought to the market at date t, d_{hi} be the quantity of commodity i he demands, and let p_i^h be his personal expected price of i. At date t his total monetary expense is $m_h = \sum_i p_i^h d_{hi}$ and his expense on market i is $m_{hi} = p_i^h d_{hi}$. The monetary market price of commodity i, denoted v_i, is given by $\sum_h m_{hi} / \sum_h s_{hi}$. The same rule applies on each market so that all money prices are determined and relative prices can be derived from them.

Except by a fluke, expected prices differ from market prices. The production plans are not fulfilled so that both monetary and real disequilibria appear. They are defined for each producer by the positive or negative monetary balance (their algebraic sum being zero) and the positive or negative differences $(m_{hi}/p_i^h) - (m_{hi}/v_i)$ between quantities respectively demanded and obtained on markets.

To sum up, money takes the place which labour had in Marx's theory and individual (real and monetary) disequilibria express Marx's 'salto mortale of the commodity'. Private evaluations of production are made in monetary terms (at expected prices), and not in terms of concrete labour. As in Marx, commodities are socially evaluated through the exchange process but, contrary to Marx, in monetary terms and not in those of social labour. The crucial issue of the incommensurability between heterogeneous private labours and homogenous social labour, which is the source of difficulties in Marx's approach, disappears since the monetary magnitudes associated with private and social evaluations are of the same nature.

We stop here our discussion of Marx's approach of value. However the subject is not exhausted yet. There is still the central issue of determining the allocation of commodities in disequilibrium which, in turn, is related to the monetary disequilibrium. Since the availability of a means of exchange allows each agent to buy goods independently of his sales, monetary imbalances also appear and must be settled. The amount of money that an agent spends at a given date is the total expected value of his product $\sum_i p_i^h s_{hi}$, whereas the amount he actually receives is the value of that product at market prices $\sum_i v_i s_{hi}$. These two amounts result from distinct evaluations (the first is private, the second is social) of the same physical product and their difference gives a positive or negative balance. The cause of an agent's negative balance is that the price he expected was higher than the market price: the total value of purchases exceeds the sales.[10] The budget constraint, which is met *ex ante* when calculations are made at expected prices, is violated *ex post* at market prices. An agent who has not financed the whole of his purchases is not the actual owner of the goods he has obtained on the market. Different institutional rules might be considered for the settlements of the monetary imbalances. Some of them rely on an agreement between agents with a positive and agents with a negative monetary balance, about transfers of money in one direction and of real goods in the other. According to other rules, money transfers might be made through the bank. After the balance settlement, all magnitudes defining the disequilibrium state are determined. The commodities available at date *t* are now allocated; the real individual disequilibrium and the effective productions during period *t* are known.

Such disequilibrium is temporary since monetary values and produced quantities necessarily change from one period to the next. Thus, the dynamical analysis is the last issue to be addressed. We do not embark on this difficult matter which, furthermore, is irrelevant here.[11]

3. Conclusion

Several lessons can be drawn from the comparison of some of Galiani's and Marx's writings. Both authors move aside from the tradition by conceiving of money as a necessary condition of exchange values and not as a remedy for difficulties of trades at exogenous (equilibrium) prices. On the other hand, their notion of money is radically different. By seeking the logical genesis of money and conceiving of it as a particular commodity derived from trades, surprisingly enough Marx is closer to the orthodoxy than Galiani. We have shown that Galiani's voucher system allows us to understand why money is inseparable from a social institution like the Mint or more generally a Central Bank, the primary function of which is monetising some agents' real assets, for instance the equilibrium value of individual products in Galiani's system. Using Galiani's notion of money but moving away from his equilibrium methodology and adopting Marx's approach to value (but not his theory), it is possible to introduce a monetary market mechanism allowing for the determination of prices in disequilibrium. Adding some institutional rules for the settlements of individual monetary imbalances, allocations (and thus effective productions) are also determined. In a nutshell, the analysis of Galiani's and Marx's writings and the market mechanism for the determination of prices in disequilibrium lead to an unconventional notion of money: it is not defined as a particular commodity, but as a complex object formed of a unit of account and two institutions, a Central Bank for monetisation of individual assets and a legal rule for the settlements of individual imbalances in disequilibrium.

Notes

1 While writing this chapter we made use of some parts of previous works: Benetti et al. (2015), Benetti and Cartelier (1999), and Benetti (1994).
2 For instance see Marx: 'The difficulty lies, not in comprehending that money is a commodity, but in discovering how, why, and by what means a commodity becomes money' (Marx, 1867, p. 62) and Galiani according to whom metallic money is 'una necessità che alla natura stessa dei metalli e a' requisiti della moneta era congiunta' [a necessity due to the very nature of metals and the requirements

of money] (Galiani, 1751, p. 114). Obviously, both authors also studied paper money but that analysis is not the purpose of this paper.

3 As a task 'which has never yet even been attempted by *bourgeois* economy, the task of tracing the genesis of this money form' (Marx, 1867, p. 33).

4 In a sense, Marx is a forerunner. His idea is also found in Menger's contribution (Menger, 1892) on 'the origin of money' and the 'Menger problem' has become the cornerstone of the main neoclassical line of research on money as means of exchange, known as 'monetary search' (see Iwai, 1988; Kiyotaki and Wright, 1993). For a critique of this theory, see Cartelier (2018, Part I, Ch. 2).

5 Note Marx's analysis of a similar case: 'sales (by the owners of commodities) without purchases (by the owners of gold and silver)' (Marx, 1867, p. 84).

6 See also Dmitriev's excellent presentation (Dmitriev, 1904/1974).

7 Notice that it is not clear either how the labour time of independent workers could be known.

8 See Wicksell (1906, p. 7): 'Of the three main functions, only the last [medium of exchange] is in a true sense characteristic of money.'

9 The notion of 'trading post' was introduced in the modern theory of strategic market games by Shapley and Shubik (1977) who determine the market price by using a rule similar to Cantillon's.

10 By contrast with the so-called 'monetary economy' in disequilibrium as described by Arrow and Hahn (1971, p. 337ff.), monetary imbalances occur because the means of exchange is not an initial endowment.

11 A bisector reproduction model is proposed in Benetti et al. (2014). It is shown that the dynamics of the economy are those of a sequence of temporary disequilibria. There are several possibilities (local or global stability, cycles) depending on the values of the parameters. These dynamics are never explosive.

References

Arrow, K. and Hahn, F. (1971). *General competitive analysis.* San Francisco: Holden-Day.

Benetti, C. (1994). Troc, bons d'achat et monnaie: la conception de Ferdinando Galiani. *Revue Économique,* 45 (5), 1177–1187.

Benetti, C., Bidard, C., Klimovsky, E. and Rebeyrol, A. (2014). Disequilibrium, reproduction and money: a Classical approach. *Metroeconomica,* 65 (3), 524–540.

Benetti, C., Bidard, C., Klimovsky, E. and Rebeyrol, A. (2015). Temporary disequilibrium and money in a Classical approach. *Cahiers d'Economie Politique,* 69 (2), 159–184.

Benetti, C. and Cartelier, J. (1999). Market and division of labour: a critical reformulation of Marx's view. *Rivista di Politica Economica,* 89 (4–5), 117–139.

Cantillon, R. (1755). *Essai sur la nature du commerce en général* (H. Higgs ed. and trans. into English). Reprint of the 1931 edition by Macmillan for the Royal Economic Society, 1959. London: Frank Cass.

Cartelier, J. (2018). *Money, markets and capital: the case for a monetary analysis.* London: Routledge.

Dmitriev, V.K. (1904/1974). The evolution of 'marginal utility theory' (1750–1854). In: *Economic essays on value, competition and utility* (D.M. Nuti ed. and D. Fry trans.). Cambridge: Cambridge University Press, 181–199.

Galiani, F. (1751). *De la monnaie/Della moneta.* Reprint 2005 (bilingual edition A. Tiran ed. and trans.). Paris: Economica.

Iwai, K. (1988). *The evolution of money: a search-theoretic foundation of monetary economics.* University of Pennsylvania CARESS Working Paper, no. 88-03.

Kiyotaki, N. and Wright, R. (1993). A search-theoretic approach to monetary economics. *The American Review*, 83 (1), 63–77.

Marx, K. (1859). *A contribution to the critique of political economy*. Moscow: Progress Publishers. Online Version: Marx.org, 1993.

Marx, K. (1867). *Capital: a critique of political economy* (Translation into English 1887, F. Engels, ed., S. Moore and E. Aveling trans.). Reprint 1954. Moscow: Progress Publishers.

Menger, K. (1892). On the origin of money. *Economic Journal*, 2 (6), 239–255.

Ostroy, J.M. and Starr, R. (1974). Money and the decentralization of exchange. *Econometrica*, 42 (6), 1093–1113.

Ricardo, D. (1821). On the principles of political economy and taxation. As reprinted in: (1951). In: P. Sraffa (ed.). *Vol. I of: the works and correspondence of David Ricardo*. Cambridge: Cambridge University Press.

Shapley, L. and Shubik, M. (1977). Trading using one commodity as a means of payment. *Journal of Political Economy*, 85 (5), 937–968.

Wicksell, K. (1906/1935). Money. In: E. Classen (trans.) *Lectures on political economy*, Vol. II. London: Routledge. Reprint 1967. New York: A.M. Kelley.

3 "Hierarchy of causes" and theory of money in Ricardo and Keynes

Ghislain Deleplace

In a paper published in the December 2014 issue of *Journal of the History of Economic Thought*, Cristina Marcuzzo concludes:

> Notwithstanding these profound epistemological differences, Ricardo's quest for a theory in which the hierarchy of causes is detectable in the structure of the arguments was also pursued by Keynes, who shared with Ricardo the recognition of its relevance and usefulness.
>
> Marcuzzo (2014, p. 433)

This suggestion that Ricardo and Keynes – two authors with whom Marcuzzo shared a lifelong intellectual companionship – might be bedfellows on methodological issues is all the more surprising since it relies on a distinction made by Ricardo between "permanent" and "temporary" causes, which Marcuzzo illustrates with the notion of "natural quantity of money" – that is, a notion which could hardly be found in Keynes's *General Theory*. Nevertheless, the "profound epistemological differences" acknowledged by Marcuzzo do not, according to her, preclude a common quest by both authors for a "hierarchy of causes". It may then be worthwhile inquiring whether Ricardo's and Keynes's theories of money are consistent with such a common methodological approach. This is the aim of my contribution to Cristina Marcuzzo's *Festschrift*.

In Section 1, I distinguish between two meanings of "permanent" in Ricardo's monetary writings, before discussing, in Section 2, how Marcuzzo derives her idea of "hierarchy of causes" from the relation between "permanent" and "natural" in Ricardo. Section 3 questions the "analogy" made by Marcuzzo between the natural prices of commodities and what she calls "the natural quantity of money," and contends that the idea of "hierarchy of causes," duly reformulated, should be restricted to Ricardo's theory of money. Section 4 suggests that a "hierarchy of causes" may indeed be detected in Chapter 17 of Keynes's *General Theory* but this leads, in Section 5, to another methodological resemblance between Ricardo and Keynes on money.

1. The two meanings of "permanent" in Ricardo's monetary writings

In relation to money, the distinction between a permanent and a temporary phenomenon appears in Ricardo with two different meanings. The first was borrowed from common language: something is permanent if it lasts for a long time, as opposed to something temporary which does not. Permanent is then synonymous with durable, and temporary with provisional. An illustration of such a distinction is to be found in Ricardo's contention in 1819 that his Ingot Plan should be applied permanently, in contrast with the position adopted in Peel's bill, according to which convertibility of the Bank of England note into bullion would, after three years, give way to the pre-1797 convertibility into specie. Already in 1811, after the return to convertibility proposed by the Bullion Committee had been rejected by Parliament, Ricardo had outlined this plan in the Appendix to the fourth edition of *High Price of Bullion*, stressing that it should be permanent:

> This privilege of paying their notes as above described [in bullion] might be extended to the Bank for three or four years after such payments commenced, and if found advantageous, might be continued as a permanent measure.
>
> Ricardo (1811, p. 125)

After his plan had been partly adopted in 1819 by Peel's bill and discontinued two years later, Ricardo contended that, if it had been fairly tried, it could have been adopted permanently. In a speech before the House of Commons on 12 June 1822, he declared:

> That bill [of 1819] he had always considered as an experiment, to try whether a bank could not be carried on with advantage to the general interests of the country, upon the principle of not being called upon to pay their notes in coin, but in bullion; and he had not the least doubt that, if the Bank had gone on wisely in their preliminary arrangements – if, in fact, they had done nothing but watch the exchanges and the price of gold, and had regulated their issues accordingly, the years 1819, 1820, 1821 and 1822 would have passed off so well with the working of the bullion part of the plan, that parliament would have continued it for a number of years beyond the time originally stipulated for its operation. Such, he was convinced, would have been the course, had the Bank refrained from making those unnecessary purchases of gold which had led to so many unpleasant consequences.
>
> Ricardo (1952, p. 200)

Ricardo's consistent position from 1811 until his death in 1823 thus shows that in his mind, the Ingot Plan should lead to "the euthanasia of metal currency," as James Bonar wrote one century later (Bonar, 1923, p. 298). In other words, it amounted to a demonetisation of gold in circulation: gold would remain the standard of money, but no longer money. In his *Proposals* of 1816, Ricardo considered this achievement to be a major progress in civilisation:

> A well regulated paper currency is so great an improvement in commerce, that I should greatly regret, if prejudice should induce us to return to a system of less utility. The introduction of the precious metals for the purposes of money may with truth be considered as one of the most important steps towards the improvement of commerce, and the arts of civilised life; but it is no less true that, with the advancement of knowledge and science, we discover that it would be another improvement to banish them again from the employment to which, during a less enlightened period, they had been so advantageously applied.
>
> Ricardo (1816, p. 65)

A system of payments exclusively based on the circulation of notes convertible into bullion opened thus a new age in "the arts of civilised life". The reason for adopting it permanently – and not as a transitory device for facilitating the return to the pre-1797 system – was to be found in its two properties summed up in the title of the 1816 pamphlet: *Proposals for an Economical and Secure Currency*. Apart from its "economical" character – the possibility of keeping low the level of gold reserves of the issuing bank – the main advantage of this system was that it provided the exact amount of currency required by the "wants of commerce"; in other words, the supply of money was endogenously self-adjusting (see Deleplace, 2017, Ch. 7).

This leads to a second meaning – more analytical – of the distinction between "permanent" and "temporary". The payments system advocated by Ricardo was to be permanently applied because it created the appropriate quantity of money permanently, thanks to the following policy rule: the contraction of the note issue whenever the market price of bullion was above the legal price at which the note was convertible into bullion, and the expansion of the note issue whenever the market price of bullion was below the legal price (slightly inferior to the other one) at which bullion was convertible into the note:

> We should possess all these advantages by subjecting the Bank to the delivery of uncoined gold or silver at the mint standard and price, in exchange for their notes, instead of the delivery of guineas; by which means paper would never fall below the value of bullion, without being followed by a reduction of its quantity. To prevent the rise of paper above the value of bullion, the Bank should be also obliged to give their paper in exchange for standard gold at the price of 3*l*. 17*s*. per ounce. [...] In other words, the Bank should be obliged to purchase any quantity of gold that

was offered them, not less than twenty ounces, at 3*l*. 17*s*. per ounce, and to sell any quantity that might be demanded at 3*l*. 17*s*. 10½*d*. While they have the power of regulating the quantity of their paper, there is no possible inconvenience that could result to them from such a regulation.

Ricardo (1816, pp. 66–67; 1819–1821, p. 357)

Combining the convertibility of the note into bullion and the management of the note issue in accordance with the divergence between the market price of the standard and a legal norm, the Ingot Plan provided a self-adjustment of the quantity of money that prevented the value of the currency in terms of commodities from varying more than the value of the standard itself:

> Besides, then, all the other advantages attending the use of paper money; by the judicious management of the quantity, a degree of uniformity, which is by no other means attainable, is secured to the value of the circulating medium in which all payments are made.

Ricardo (1816, pp. 57–58)

> To secure the public against any other variations in the value of the currency than those to which the standard itself is subject, and, at the same time, to carry on the circulation with a medium the least expensive, is to attain the most perfect state to which a currency can be brought.

Ricardo (1816, p. 66; 1819–1821, pp. 356–357)

In a book co-authored with Annalisa Rosselli (Marcuzzo and Rosselli, 1991), Cristina Marcuzzo had already emphasised this self-adjusting property of the quantity of money, on the basis of an analysis of the international payments mechanism. In her 2014 paper, she uses it as an illustration of the meaning given by Ricardo to the word "permanent".

2. Marcuzzo on "permanent" and "natural" in Ricardo

According to Marcuzzo, Ricardo's use of the word "permanent" may be related to the existence of a market mechanism, in contrast with the time dimension (long term *versus* short term) usually ascribed to it. In this sense, the "permanent" level of the quantity of money may be called "natural":

> Ricardo's definition of the natural quantity of money is given by analogy with the definition of natural wages and natural prices. [...] The word "analogy" is used to indicate the similarity, rather than the identity, of the meaning "natural" when applied to a quantity, rather than to a price. It is the idea of a benchmark that market mechanisms tend to establish whenever temporary or accidental causes make prices (or wages) or the quantity of money deviate from it.

Marcuzzo (2014, p. 423 and fn. 4)

This market mechanism is implemented in the international bullion market and it adjusts the quantity of money to its "natural level," making it "permanent":

> Thus, changes in the quantity of money involving changes in its purchasing power in terms of gold at home and abroad are "temporary," because market mechanisms will bring the quantity of money to its natural level, thereby restoring the equality of the purchasing power of money at home and abroad. Changes in the quantity of money deriving from a change in the condition of production of gold, on the other hand, are permanent, because they cause a change in its natural level.
>
> (ibid., p. 424)

From this understanding of the distinction between "permanent" and "temporary" in Ricardo on money, Marcuzzo derives a conclusion on what she calls "the hierarchy of causes" (ibid., p. 432) in Ricardo's theory in general:

> In conclusion, the question in Ricardo's theory is, then, not one of measuring "for how long" or "to what extent" an observed consequence follows from a given cause, before deciding whether it is a temporary or permanent effect. The question is one of deciding which causes can be made the object of a theory; whether, from a given cause, consequences can be derived that are certain. For Ricardo, the distinction between temporary and permanent pertains to the question of which *causes* are eligible to become part of a theory, and not to the question of which *effects* endure or fail to endure. Ricardo takes permanency as a property independent of the length of time during which causes exercise their influence because the definition of a permanent cause is given not by the length of the duration of its effects but by its place in the structure of the theory.
>
> (ibid., p. 425, Marcuzzo's emphasis)

By emphasising that in Ricardo the analytical distinction between "permanent" and "temporary" is not a matter of time but of forces at work in the determination of the economic variables, Marcuzzo convincingly discards the usual interpretation (long term *versus* short term) which is also commonly applied to the distinction between "natural" and "market" magnitudes. This denial of the conventional view on Ricardo is in line with other critical reappraisals of this view, such as Depoortère (2008, 2013). However, Marcuzzo's analysis raises a difficulty. Her conclusion that temporary causes of disturbance are hierarchically ranked by Ricardo below permanent causes "in the structure of the theory" is derived from the "analogy" she makes on this point between commodities, labour, and money:

> We have seen that Ricardo's temporary situations are defined relative to the nature of the causes occasioning them: in the case of prices, these are the changes in the quantities supplied and demanded; in the case of wages,

they are the supply and demand of labor; while, in the case of the natural quantity of money, they consist of deviations in the market price from the official price of gold. These causes will produce temporary, not permanent, effects, like those produced by a change in the cost of production in the case of the prices of commodities, the price of necessities in the case of wages, and the value of gold in the case of the natural quantity of money.

Marcuzzo (2014, p. 432)

It is of secondary importance to inquire whether Marcuzzo's analysis of money and the gold standard in Ricardo has led her to a general conclusion on "the hierarchy of causes" or whether her methodological preconception of the latter is responsible for an "analogy" illustrated by the notion of a "natural quantity of money". The point is that they must stand or fall together. Let me concentrate on the "analogy" between the prices of commodities and the quantity of money as to "the hierarchy of causes," leaving aside labour, which raises additional difficulties.

3. "Hierarchy of causes" for commodities, gold, and money in Ricardo

As quoted above, the "analogy" between the prices of commodities and the quantity of money is based by Marcuzzo on "the idea of a benchmark that market mechanisms tend to establish whenever temporary or accidental causes make prices (or wages) or the quantity of money deviate from it" (2014, p. 423, fn. 4). However, it is one thing to say that the adjustment of the quantity of money is market-driven because it responds to profitability conditions in the bullion market; it is another thing to draw an analogy with the adjustment in the markets for all other commodities. As will be seen below, arbitrage in the domestic market for gold bullion is permitted by the existence of an institutional set-up (convertibility at a legal price) which transforms this particular commodity into the standard of money and has no equivalent for any other commodity.

But there is more. As far as competitively produced commodities are concerned, it is well known that such "market mechanisms" – usually called "gravitation" after Adam Smith's use of the word – raise a disturbing problem in the Ricardo-Sraffa line of the Classical tradition: they have no role in the determination of natural prices. In the modern Classical theory of prices to be found in Sraffa (1960) and derived from Ricardo, the determination of the price system requires the knowledge of the technical methods of production and of one exogenous distribution variable, under the assumption of a uniform rate of profit, but no particular theory of the market prices: the only assumption is that the system of (natural) prices is "adopted by the market," (Sraffa, 1960, p. 3), whatever the market process that causes it to be so.

In such a framework, the distinction between "permanent" and "temporary" causes, if based on Marcuzzo's above-mentioned "idea of a benchmark," amounts to a distinction between those producing their effects independently of the market process, and those which, because their effects trigger a market mechanism, do not interact with the other, "permanent," causes. However, it is then difficult to reconcile this distinction with the common idea that in a market economy a change in the cost of production of a commodity actually affects its market. Strictly speaking, "permanent" can thus only be consistently distinguished from "temporary" if it is understood as "constant," so that the expression "permanent cause of change" is deprived of any meaning.

In contrast, there are no such disturbing analytical consequences of "the hierarchy of causes" (between "permanent" and "temporary" ones), when applied to money in Ricardo, for two reasons: the market for the standard (gold bullion) plays a central role in the determination of the quantity of money, and the working of this market is specific, as compared with that of the markets for commodities. According to my interpretation of Ricardo's theory of money (in Deleplace, 2017), the integration of the value of money in Ricardo's general theory of value relies on the distinction between a real cause of change – when the relative value of the standard in terms of all other commodities varies for exogenous reasons – and a monetary cause of change – when the actual quantity of money departs from its conformable level (which equalises the value of money with that of the standard and makes money "conform" to the standard, in Ricardo's parlance) and affects the market price of the standard. Whatever the cause of change in the value of money a self-adjusting process is at work. If the cause is real (such as a change in the difficulty of production of gold bullion), the value of money settles permanently at a new level and the prices of all commodities except the standard adjust accordingly in the same proportion. If the cause is monetary (such as a discretionary change in the note issue, not required by "the wants of commerce"), the value of money departs temporarily from its initial (conformable) level, before returning to it after the excess or deficiency in the quantity of money has been endogenously eliminated.

The self-adjusting process of the quantity, hence of the value, of money depends on the working of the market for gold bullion, but because gold bullion is the standard of money, its market is very peculiar. Arbitrage is practiced on it as on every other market, but the conditions of this practice are unique, because arbitrage is not only with foreign markets but also with domestic monetary institutions: the mint, where bullion is converted at a legal price into coin, and the Bank of England, where notes are converted at par into coins to be melted into bullion (in Ricardo's Ingot Plan, the issuing bank provides convertibility both ways between bullion and the note). The outcome of this domestic arbitrage is the equalisation of the market price of bullion with the fixed legal price at which bullion and money are convertible into each other (taking into account the costs of this convertibility). This means that the market price of the standard is affected by the laws governing these monetary institutions and by their behaviour, independently of what happens to the market prices of all other commodities. In other words, as soon as gold bullion becomes the standard of money, its market price does *not* gravitate around its natural price – as is the case for all commodities to which the competition of capitals applies – but is stabilised thanks to an adjustment process *sui generis*. As Ricardo declared in 1819 before the Commons' Committee on Resumption, "in a sound state of the currency the value of gold may vary, but its price cannot" (Ricardo, 1952, p. 392).

In contrast with the natural price of any commodity, which can be determined independently of the market process, the legal price of the standard of money only acquires an economic meaning because of a specific process which adjusts the market price to it. Far from being of secondary importance, the adjustment process of the market price of gold bullion makes the legal price effective and therefore constitutes it as an economic magnitude: for want of such adjustment, this institutional datum would simply remain outside of economic theory, and money with it. In modern parlance, one would say that for any other commodity produced in competitive conditions the question of the existence of the price system can be solved in the absence of a definite analysis of its stability – the price system in Sraffa (1960) is an example of this method – while for the commodity acting as the standard of money, the existence of its legal price as an economic magnitude depends on a specific analysis of its stability. In other words, the Ricardo-Sraffa tradition on the price question leaves stability (the determination of price in disequilibrium) outside the theory, while Ricardo's theory of money puts it centre-stage: the legal price of the standard actually regulates the quantity of money insofar as its market price is subject to a definite adjustment process.

While, as seen above, the distinction between a "permanent" and a "temporary" cause of change in the price of any commodity cannot be based in Ricardo on the working of the market-adjustment process, Ricardo's theory of money provides a clear and coherent foundation for such a distinction, when applied to the value of money. A permanent cause of change in the value of money is one that triggers an adjustment in the market for the standard which sets a new value for it and consequently a new value of money conforming to this new value of the standard, hence a new quantity of money consistent with this new value of money. This is the case when the value of money is lowered permanently after the discovery of a new gold mine more productive than at least some of those previously worked, or when the value of money is permanently raised after the issuing bank increases its demand for gold reserve in the perspective of the implementation of a new monetary system, as it happened with the return to the convertibility of the Bank of England note into specie in 1820–1821 (see Deleplace, 2017, Ch. 5). In contrast, a temporary cause of change in the value of money is one that triggers an adjustment in the market for the standard which does not affect its value but only generates a change in the quantity of money that brings back the value of money to the unchanged value of the standard. This is the case when the value of money is lowered temporarily ("depreciated," in Ricardo's parlance) after the issuing bank has discretionarily increased the quantity of notes (that is, in the absence of any increase in "the wants of commerce"), or when the value of money is raised temporarily ("appreciated") after the issuing bank has failed to respond to an increase in "the wants of commerce" (whether durable, as when trade is continuously expanding, or provisional, as when notes are required to fill the void occasioned by a want of confidence between merchants in the credit market) (see Deleplace, 2017, Ch. 7).

Strictly speaking, Marcuzzo's notion of "hierarchy of causes," duly reformulated, should thus be restricted in Ricardo to his theory of money. One may now ask what happens to it when it is tested on Keynes – as suggested by Marcuzzo herself – provided this test is made on his theory of money.

4. A "hierarchy of causes" in Chapter 17 of *General Theory*

It would be too long to list the differences between Ricardo's and Keynes's theories of money, which are not less "profound" than the "epistemological differences" mentioned by Marcuzzo (2014, p. 433). Nevertheless one may inquire whether, as suggested by her about the relation between effective demand and employment in Keynes, "Ricardo's quest for a theory in which the hierarchy of causes is detectable in the structure of the arguments" (ibid.) also applies to Keynes's theory of money.

The only place where market adjustments are analysed in *General Theory* in relation to money is Chapter 17, entitled "The essential properties of interest and money," where, as is well known, Keynes studies the adjustment process that generates the equilibrium level of the production of all capital-assets (hence the level of aggregate investment) for a given money-rate of interest. The question of such adjustment is raised by Keynes as follows:

> Let us suppose (as a mere hypothesis at this stage of the argument) that there is some asset (*e.g.* money) of which the rate of interest is fixed (or declines more slowly as output increases than does any other commodity's rate of interest); how is the position adjusted?
>
> Keynes (1936, p. 228)

And the answer is:

> As the stock of the assets, which begin by having a marginal efficiency at least equal to the rate of interest, is increased, their marginal efficiency (for reasons, sufficiently obvious, already given) tends to fall. Thus a point will come at which it no longer pays to produce them, *unless the rate of interest falls* pari passu. When there is *no* asset of which the marginal efficiency reaches the rate of interest, the further production of capital-assets will come to a standstill.
>
> (ibid., Keynes's emphasis)

The role of the money-rate of interest in the determination of the equilibrium level of aggregate investment (hence in the determination of the equilibrium level of aggregate output and employment) thus seems a good candidate to illustrate Marcuzzo's point that, like Ricardo with his "hierarchy of causes," Keynes "also holds that there are some causes which are more "important" than others" (Marcuzzo, 2014, p. 432; inverted commas hers). The rest of Chapter 17 of *General Theory* is devoted to the analysis of the reasons why this cause has, in Keynes's parlance, "a peculiar significance". The analysis of these "peculiarities" – which justify what was just "a mere hypothesis" in the quotation above – opens with the summing-up of the method used previously by Keynes to answer the question "how is the position adjusted?":

> In attributing, therefore, a peculiar significance to the money-rate of interest, we have been tacitly assuming that the kind of money to which we are accustomed has some special characteristics which lead to its own-rate of interest in terms of itself as standard being more reluctant to fall as output increases than the own-rates of interest of any other assets in terms of themselves. Is this assumption justified? Reflection shows, I think, that the following peculiarities, which commonly characterise money as we know it, are capable of justifying it.
>
> Keynes (1936, pp. 229–230)

This method is to use *both* for every asset *and* for money the notion of "own-rate of interest [of an asset] in terms of itself" (see ibid., pp. 225–227). Comparing this method with Marcuzzo's interpretation of the "natural quantity of money" in Ricardo suggests that the resemblance between Ricardo and Keynes on money should be looked for somewhere else.

5. A methodological resemblance between Ricardo and Keynes on money

There is a striking parallelism between Marcuzzo's methodological interpretation of Ricardo on the one hand, and Keynes's methodological stance in Chapter 17 of *General Theory* on the other hand. Marcuzzo uses the same adjective "natural" both for the prices of commodities and for the quantity of money and she concludes that in both cases, a "hierarchy of causes" operates, in which the cost of production (of each commodity or of gold, respectively) is "more 'important'" than accidental causes, such as "changes in the quantities [of each commodity] supplied and demanded," or "deviations in the market price from the official price of gold," respectively (Marcuzzo, 2014, p. 432). Keynes uses the same substantive "own-rate of interest" both for every capital-asset and for money and he concludes that the "peculiarities" of money as compared with all capital-assets explain that the own-rate of interest of money hierarchically dominates the own-rates of interest of capital-assets as the main determinant of the equilibrium level of aggregate investment:

> For it may be that it is the *greatest* of the own-rates of interest (as we may call them) which rules the roost (because it is the greatest of these rates

that the marginal efficiency of a capital-asset must attain if it is to be newly produced); and that there are reasons why it is the money-rate of interest which is often the greatest (because, as we shall find, certain forces, which operate to reduce the own-rates of interest of other assets, do not operate in the case of money).

Keynes (1936, pp. 223–224, Keynes's emphasis)

Unfortunately, there is also a parallelism in that Marcuzzo's use of "natural" for commodities *and* for money and Keynes's use of "own-rate of interest" for capital-assets *and* for money face logical difficulties which undermine the generality of "the hierarchy of causes". For both authors, the problem lies in the very nature of the market adjustment. In the case of Keynes, two logical difficulties were raised by Sraffa in his manuscript notes on Chapter 17 (Sraffa, 1936). First, what Keynes called the "own-rate of interest" of a capital-asset was simply a marginal efficiency of capital, not a commodity-rate of interest (as Sraffa called it). Second, contrary to what he wrote, Keynes should have understood that in his analysis the role of the money-rate of interest in the limitation of aggregate investment is consequent upon the specific nature of money as standard of value, and not upon the supposed fact that forces which reduce the marginal efficiencies of capital-assets do not apply to money (on these two logical difficulties, see Deleplace, 2014). In the case of Marcuzzo on Ricardo, as shown above, the extension of the adjective "natural" to the quantity of money is at odds with Ricardo's analysis of the working of the market for gold bullion as dependent upon an institutional set-up (convertibility at a legal price) which transforms this particular commodity into the standard of money and has no equivalent for any other commodity.

There is thus something common to Ricardo's and Keynes's theories of money: the notion of standard – understood differently by the two authors – implies that a specific magnitude – the legal price of gold in Ricardo or the money-rate of interest with a central bank "under public control" in Keynes (1936, p. 235) – regulates the quantity of money. But this conclusion requires recognising that the central role of this magnitude in the market adjustment (for gold bullion in Ricardo or for capital-assets in Keynes) stems from its specific nature as an institutional datum. This is the condition to pinpoint a "hierarchy of causes" in Ricardo's and Keynes's theories of money and, more unexpectedly, to suggest a methodological resemblance between the role of the legal price of gold in Ricardo and the post-Keynesian emphasis on the rate of interest being fixed by the monetary authorities.

References

Bonar, J. (1923). Ricardo's Ingot Plan. A centenary tribute. *The Economic Journal*, 33 (131), 281–304. Reprinted in: J. Cunningham Wood, ed. (1991). *David Ricardo: critical assessments*, vol. IV. London: Routledge, 25–43.

Deleplace, G. (2014). The essentiality of money in the Sraffa Papers. In: R. Bellofiore and S. Carter (eds.) *Towards a new understanding of Sraffa: insights from archival research*. Houndmills: Palgrave Macmillan, 139–166.

Deleplace, G. (2017). *Ricardo on money. A reappraisal*. Abingdon: Routledge.

Depoortère, C. (2008). Quel modèle d'accumulation du capital chez Ricardo? *Cahiers d'économie politique*, 55, 141–154.

Depoortère, C. (2013). William Nassau Senior and David Ricardo on the method of political economy. *Journal of the History of Economic Thought*, 35 (1), 19–42.

Keynes, J.M. (1936). *The general theory of employment, interest and money*. As reprinted in: (1973). *Vol. VII of: The Collected Writings of John Maynard Keynes*. London: Macmillan.

Marcuzzo, M.C. (2014). On the notion of permanent and temporary causes: the legacy of Ricardo. *Journal of the History of Economic Thought*, 36 (4), 421–434.

Marcuzzo, M.C. and Rosselli, A. (1991). *Ricardo and the Gold Standard. The foundations of the international monetary order*. London: Macmillan.

Ricardo, D. (1811). Appendix to *The high price of bullion. A proof of the depreciation of bank notes*. As reprinted in: P. Sraffa (ed.) with the collaboration of M.H. Dobb, *Pamphlets and papers 1809–1811. Vol. III of: The works and correspondence of David Ricardo*. Cambridge: Cambridge University Press, 99–127.

Ricardo, D. (1816). Proposals for an economical and secure currency. As reprinted in: P. Sraffa (ed.) with the collaboration of M.H. Dobb, *Pamphlets and papers 1815–1823. Vol. IV of: The works and correspondence of David Ricardo*. Cambridge: Cambridge University Press, 49–141.

Ricardo, D. (1819–1821). On the principles of political economy and taxation. 2nd and 3rd edition. As reprinted in: P. Sraffa (ed.) with the collaboration of M.H. Dobb, *Vol. I of: The works and correspondence of David Ricardo*. Cambridge: Cambridge University Press.

Ricardo, D. (1952). *Speeches and evidence*. As reprinted in: P. Sraffa, (ed)., with the collaboration of M.H. Dobb. *Vol. V of: The works and correspondence of David Ricardo*. Cambridge: Cambridge University Press.

Sraffa, P. (1936). Manuscript notes on *General Theory*. In: *Sraffa Papers*. Cambridge: Trinity College, SP I 100.

Sraffa, P. (1960). *Production of commodities by means of commodities. Prelude to a critique of economic theory*. Cambridge: Cambridge University Press.

4 Financial stability and secure currency in a modern context

Jan Kregel

1. Introduction

It is hard to assess the role of money in the economy these days. Larry Summers (2016) and Willem Buiter (Buiter and Rahbari 2015) (among others) have recommended the abolition of currency, while Lord Turner (2013) has proposed a helicopter drop of the very bank notes that Summers and Buiter want to eliminate.

Clearly we have need of a straightforward, logical proposal, such as David Ricardo presented in his so-called "Ingot Plan" for the return to gold convertibility in his *Proposals for an Economical and Secure Currency* (Ricardo 1951–1973, IV, 43–141, hereafter *Proposals*[1]).

Revisiting Ricardo's monetary *Proposals* is also timely because it is based on his concerns for the impact of the monetary system on the distribution of income. While Ricardo's unsuccessful search for an invariable measure of value (and Sraffa's solution) are now well known, it is perhaps less-widely recognised that his monetary proposals were driven by his concerns, as an active participant in financial markets,[2] that variations in the value of the currency in which time contracts are denominated would produce changes in the distribution of income between creditors and debtors. However, it is now generally accepted that the invariable standard proposed by Sraffa could not provide the measure of value sought to preserve the sanctity of financial contracts.[3]

This modern assessment of Ricardo's monetary proposal will reflect on two different frameworks. The first relates to the specific economic and institutional conditions that served as its background. Monetary measures can never be considered outside the particular historical and institutional context in which they take place, and Ricardo's proposal cannot be understood outside that context. The second will place the proposal in the framework of the historical evolution of the theory of monetary systems, using the work of James Steuart and Luigi Einaudi, which highlights the distinction between what we will call "dual" and "mono" monetary systems. Finally, a closing section will attempt an analysis of the relevance of the modern proposals elicited above against the background of Ricardo's analysis.

2. Ricardo as revolutionary

Indeed, Ricardo's proposal was considered as unorthodox and revolutionary[4] as any of the modern-day proposals mentioned above, for he went against the historical and traditional view, arguing that the Bank of England could restore the gold standard by eliminating payment in specie, suggesting that Bank of England notes should fully displace minted gold coin. The paradox, indeed heresy, of a gold standard without gold money!

It is also appropriate to note the similarity between the context of these various modern proposals and financial conditions of Ricardo's proposal in the aftermath of the financial crisis of 1793–1794 that led to the 1797 Bank Restriction Act, which suspended specie payment of Bank of England notes. The proximate cause of the British government's instruction to the Bank of England to suspend payment is generally believed to have been the widespread failure of country banks to redeem their notes in 1794, aggravated by increasing government demands for finance of the war with France, the collapse of the French Assignat, and then the general panic caused by an apparently staged French invasion of Wales.[5] Thus the main issue to be faced was that of the resumption of specie payments against a background of frequent suspension in periods of crisis. While Ricardo supported resumption, he recognised the inherent risks in backing the note issue with specie and thus sought a system that might avoid the frequent suspensions and crises. The historical background thus suggests concerns about the stability of the currency and measures to meet the recognised fragility of the pre-restriction system of specie payments.

To the modern reader (or modern currency abolitionist), the *Proposals* is hard to understand, so some linguistic interpretation may be useful. It is certainly not current to define a currency regime as "economical." In Section V of the *Proposals*, Ricardo refers to '[t]he very great perfection to which our system of economising the use of money has arrived, by the various operations of banking' (IV,75). He indicates that

> those who are well acquainted with the economical system, now adopted in London, throughout the whole banking concern, will readily understand that the plan here proposed is merely the extension of this economical system to a species of payments to which it has not yet been applied.

> (IV, 76)

For Ricardo this economical system is effectuated by means of 'payments … made by checks on bankers; by means of which money is merely written off one account and added to another, and that to the amount of millions daily, with few or no bank notes or coin passing' (IV, 58). It is through the use of what Keynes would call "bank money" via bank clearing houses that payments are made without the need of currency, thus making payments in a more "economical" way than through either the use of specie or paper notes.

Note that Ricardo here appears to conflate two means of effectuating "economy" in the currency. One is the process of the offsetting of debts and credits via the clearing house, which requires 'few or no bank notes or coin passing,' (IV, 58) and the other a substitution of bank notes rather than coin in effectuating payments. Indeed, as we shall see below, he was more interested in the savings in the use of gold to make payments than in the use of notes, but the distinction is not made at this stage of his analysis since it was implicitly assumed that notes would simply substitute for minted coin.

In the first definition of economical, Ricardo would seem to be in concert with the modern currency abolitionists, suggesting that most payments could be made without the presence of currency. It is interesting that had he followed this approach, he might have been led back to the analysis of money as a unit of account and institutions such as the Bank of Amsterdam, but this is an approach that he rejects. More on this below.

Ricardo only pursues the second definition, and the problem then becomes how to maximise the role of bank notes in substituting for gold coin, but on the condition that the issue of paper does not have an impact on the value of the currency, however composed as notes or coin. Here we see an announcement of the currency versus banking school debates. Thus, Ricardo's economy problem is to discover a monetary regime in which notes can provide a substitute for specie without this producing any change in the "value of the whole currency."

As historical context, it is important to note that Ricardo believed that the suspension of redemption had caused a change (depreciation) in the value of the "whole currency." While we might today be tempted to refer to this as an inflation of prices, this was not the way Ricardo or any other economist of the time would have viewed the matter, as it was sometime later that a change in the value of money would have been presented as the purchasing power of money over goods or the inverse of some appropriate price index. Today we are not accustomed to reason in terms of monetary standards, but it is impossible to understand these debates without them.

Thus for Ricardo, the value of money was measured against a standard of value. In this case the standard was gold (which meant gold bullion, a commodity, not minted gold coin), so that the measure of the depreciation of the currency was represented by the appreciation of gold bullion in terms of the paper notes. If the price of bullion had risen, then the currency had depreciated, independently of the behaviour of the prices of other commodities. It is also to be noted that the causes of this condition were the subject of heated debate. In Ricardo's view, it was clear it is the excessive issue of notes by the Bank of England as it pursued its own interests in maximising its profit, rather than pursuing monetary stability.

Thus to return to the problem of instituting an economical currency whose value is stable: 'A currency, to be perfect, should be absolutely invariable in value' (IV, 58). After noting that it is not possible to stabilise the value of the currency absolutely, because fixing to any standard will always be subject to variations caused by possible variations in the standard itself, the instability (Ricardo calls it the "variation") in the currency since the Restriction Act was to be found in the absence of a specific standard for the currency in the form of convertibility into gold coin, which has removed any limitation on the issue of currency to insure stability in its value. The problem is thus to formulate appropriate policy in order,

> [t]o secure the public against any other variations in the value of the currency than those to which the standard itself is subject, and, at the same time, to carry on the circulation with a medium the least expensive, is to attain the most perfect state to which a currency can be brought.
>
> (IV, 66)

This also creates an arbitrage differential to advantage redemption in bullion rather than coin by creating a price differential that produced a stabilising arbitrage by private-sector traders.[6] Whenever there is a discrepancy between the value of bullion and currency there would be an incentive to sell the overvalued item against the undervalued and convert at the mint, taking a profit. This would reduce the quantity of the overvalued item and increase the demand for the undervalued, leading to a convergence in their values.

This market arbitrage is also the system that produces the second characteristic of the "secure" currency:

> Under such a system, and with a currency so regulated, the Bank would never be liable to any embarrassments whatever, excepting on those extraordinary occasions, when a general panic seizes the country, and when everyone is desirous of possessing the precious metals as the most convenient mode of realizing or concealing his property. Against, such panics, Banks have no security *on any system*; from their very nature they are subject to them, as at no time can there be in a Bank, or in a country, so much specie or bullion as the money individuals of such a country have the right to demand. A panic of this kind was the cause of the crisis in 1797.
>
> (IV, 68)

Thus the plan for the "perfect," "economical," and "secure" system results in a currency that is not quite so perfect, it is a sort of second best – since it will have variable value given that the standard cannot be guaranteed to be invariable over time and on occasion it may be subject to panic, since there will never be enough specie or bullion available to cover the entire note issue if the public chooses to "run" from the currency. While Ricardo concedes that there is nothing that can be done about the first imperfection, he does offer a rather novel approach to the second.

In the current context of imposing increasing capital requirements to ensure bank solvency, Ricardo rejects this remedy, at least in the case of

Bank of England notes. In Ricardo's view, bank profits result primarily from the note issue, rather than from employing bank capital:

> There is this material difference between a Bank and all other trades: A Bank would never be established, if it obtained no other profits but those from the employment of its own capital: its real advantage commences only when it employs the capital of others.
>
> (IV, 108)

Thus, for Ricardo an addition to bank capital will have only a marginal impact on bank profits and he argues that if the Bank was forced to meet its contractual commitment to pay dividends to its shareholders (which it was not doing) the reduction in bank capital would not have a negative impact on the stability of its notes or the overall profitability of the Bank.

Symmetrically, it thus follows that:

> [n]either would such an addition [to bank capital by refraining from paying dividends] contribute towards the *security* of the Bank; for the Bank can never be called upon for more than the payment of their notes, and the public and private deposits; these constituting at all times, the whole of their debts. After paying away their cash and bullion, their remaining securities, consisting of merchants acceptances and Exchequer bills, must be at least equal to the value of their debts; and in no case can these securities be deficient, even without any surplus capital, excepting the Bank could lose all that which constitutes their growing dividend; and even then they could not be distressed, unless we suppose that at the same time payment were demanded for every note in circulation, and for the whole of their deposits, both public and private.
>
> (ibid.)

And this is the case of a systemic run from the currency[7] rather than a classic run on the liabilities of an individual institution, and, as Ricardo has noted, cannot be prevented by any amount of capital.

Ricardo points out, regulating the capital of banks would have no impact on the size of the note issue since

> [t]he amount of notes in circulation depends in no degree on the amount of capital possessed by the issuers of notes, but on the amount required for the circulation of the country, which is regulated, as I have before attempted to shew, by the value of the standard, the amount of payments and the economy practiced in effecting them.
>
> (IV, 109)

Thus, the current emphasis on capital requirements must rest on a rejection of the proposition that 'their remaining securities, consisting of merchants acceptances and Exchequer bills, must be at least equal to the value of their debts; and in no case can these securities be deficient.' No securitised subprime mortgages for the asset portfolio of the Bank!

However, when it came to the note issue of the country banks, Ricardo took a different approach to stability; indeed, it was the instability of the country banks that he considered to have been the cause of the crisis that led to the restriction in the first place. Here he again makes a distinction between the incentives that generate bank profits and those of commercial enterprise; while defending the principle of free trade for the latter, he makes an exception for government interference in the provision of paper currency, noting that while the quality of gold minted in coin:

> is obtained by means of a government stamp ... how much more necessary is such protection when paper money forms the whole, or almost the whole, of the circulating medium of the country?
>
> (IV, 73)

In an often-overlooked aspect of the *Proposals*, Ricardo recommended a system in which stamps would be given in exchange for reserves against the note issue, with the faculty of recovering reserves on the return of the stamps, i.e., when the notes had been paid. Because of their doubtful fraudulent practices, he also notes that the country bankers should support such a system since it 'would prevent the competition of those, who are at present so little entitled to appear in the market against them' (ibid.). Ricardo thus clearly comes out in favour of reserves, rather than higher capital requirements, to ensure the stability of the value of the perfect currency system.

3. Ricardo and the monetary standard: dual vs. mono frameworks

In his famous essay on "imaginary money," Einaudi (1953) points out that for modern readers it is virtually impossible to correctly interpret "monetary treatises written prior to the eighteenth century" without being aware of the distinction between:

> a monetary unit used only as a standard of value and of deferred payments and another monetary unit used only as a medium of exchange. There was, then, a monetary unit used only a standard of deferred payments (promises to pay) or for the purpose of keeping accounts. This was the function of a money of account, and imaginary or ideal money. ... Although it was possible to make contracts or to keep account in imaginary money – that is, in pounds, shillings and pence – it was impossible to make actual payments in these monetary units, since they had not been coined [for several centuries]. Payment was made in real currency, that is, gold coins ...
>
> Einaudi (1953, pp. 235–266)

Since there was no coin equivalent to the money of account, but there was a plethora of circulating metal coins of varying weight and quality, the role of the unit of account was to allow payments to be made in any currency by converting it into standard money or money of account. This was done by specifying the metallic content of the standard unit and producing tables providing conversion factors for all the various coins in common circulation. Einaudi notes 'no less than 22 different gold coins and 29 silver coins, most of which were foreign' circulating in Milan in 1762. The existence of the unit of account allowed any of these coins to be used as a medium of exchange.

However, this "dual" system had a basic drawback, which Einaudi illustrates by reference to the relative rates of exchange of gold for silver. If the tables were based on a gold:silver ratio of 1:12 and the market value of silver fell to 1:12.5 or rose to 1:11.5, then all the conversion factors for silver coins would have to be rewritten. And in practice this was what was done, but usually with some delay. The effect of this adjustment was that the money of account remained stable over time, but its equivalent in amounts of real money (circulating minted metal coin) changed according to the market price of the metal (NB, not the quantity) in the coins. This process was called an "enhancement of the currency." As Einaudi notes, this could be very confusing, for the price of bread could remain stable in unit of account, but require either more or fewer real coins to be purchased. It was thus possible to have price stability and inflation or deflation at the same time! And since contracts were denominated in unit of account, it would represent a *de facto* change in the real value of debts and credits, depending on the change in the metal market.

Einaudi notes two implications of this method of adjustment. First, it would be impossible for banks to issue notes stipulating payment in money of account, since they might be redeemed under a different conversion table, producing either a gain or loss to the holder. Nonetheless, this system remained in place, Einaudi argues, because of the overwhelming desire for monetary stability. This is in contrast to the modern system in which the response to a change in prices in the metal market is to adjust the amount of circulating coin or notes – reducing to counter inflation, increasing to counter deflation, or changing the metal content of coins through a recoinage. He believes that the use of imaginary money was a more efficient way of providing stability of the price level than these alternatives.

One implication of this approach, which Einaudi emphasises, is that suspension of convertibility is of little importance in such a system. It is not the metallic content of the coins that may be converted into notes that is fixed, but the metallic content of the unit of account, which since it is notional (imaginary) is independent of whether notes are convertible into a specific quantity of metal. The problem is the weight of the metal contained in the coins that are the equivalent of the weight of metal established for the unit of account:

[B]ecause of the existence of money of account, men every day set the price [on the various circulating coins,] which they received and paid out. Every day, in every single transaction it was made clear to their minds that the money with which they paid even bank money or paper money, was a commodity like any other, that its price was governed by the market and, like any other price, was the result of an infinite number of economic and noneconomic forces which determine the general equilibrium of all prices.

Einaudi (1953, p. 273)

Sir James Steuart (1767), in Book III, Part I, Chapter 1 of *An Inquiry into the Principles of Political Oeconomy*, starts by defining[8] money of account as 'quite a different thing from money-coin' and that it 'preserves itself invariable amidst the fluctuations, not only of the value of things themselves, but of the metals which are commonly considered measures of their value' (p. 408). With respect to measures of value, he noted 'the moment any measure begins to be measured by another, the proportion of which it is not physically, perpetually, and invariably the same, all the usefulness of such a measure is lost' (p. 416), finally noting the

> circumstance which incapacitates the metals from performing the office of money; the substance of which the coin is made, is a commodity, which rises and sinks in its value with respect to other commodities, according to the wants, competition, and caprices of mankind. ... What regards the paper is foreign to our purpose, and belongs to the doctrine of credit.
>
> Steuart (1767, p. 420)

which he analyses by distinguishing banks of circulation and banks of deposit in Book IV, "Of Credit and Debts."

Einaudi notes that this system was eventually replaced when the monetary unit (coin or paper) became the money of account with a specified content. And thus the problem of whether the paper notes could be converted into the specified metallic content. Ricardo's financial experience would have taken place at period in which European monetary systems were in transition from dual to mono currency systems so that he was faced with the problem of the intertemporal stability of the imaginary unit of account in specie producing variation in its value and in the income redistributions that were the result. Whether this was from his business experience or not, he does note and criticise Steuart's description of the unit of account system (citing Book III, Chapter 1, "Of Money of Accompt"), in particular the importance of the dual system and the stability of the money of account.

In his discussion of Steuart, Ricardo defines it as 'a system without a specific standard,' noting that after suspension, 'a pound note did not and ought not to vary with a given quantity of gold, more than with a given quantity of any other commodity.' He then goes on to criticise the absence of a standard as 'no one has yet been able to offer any test by which we could ascertain the uniformity in the value of money so constituted. Those who supported this opinion did not see, that such a currency, instead of being invariable, was subject to the greatest variation' and goes on to criticise this view because 'the only use of a standard is to regulate the quantity, and by the quantity the value of the currency' (*Proposals*, IV, 59).

Thus, Ricardo seems to represent, at least partially, those Einaudi believed unable to understand the system based on the unit of account. Ricardo does identify correctly the fact that the unit will not be invariable in terms of any commodity standard, yet fails to accept that this will be true of any money linked directly to a commodity standard. Yet, one might interpret Ricardo's proposal as seeking to avoid the problem of the variation in the official tables converting multiple currencies into the single unit of account by substituting bullion and replacing minted coin by Bank of England notes. Thus, Ricardo sought a replacement for the unit of account that avoids its variation in terms of means of payment and thus the impact on the distribution of income.

Thus if we try to situate Ricardo's *Proposals*, it is necessary to place them at the transition from the Steuart/Einaudi dual monetary system to the single (mono) monetary system, and the recent experience of the suspension of convertibility and financial crisis. Ricardo's rupture with this prior dual currency approach is evident from the first line of Section 1 of the *Proposals*: 'All writers on the subject of money have agreed that uniformity in the value of the circulating medium is an object greatly to be desired,' rejecting the non-circulating unit of account as being the target of uniformity. The 'approximation to that object' is to find a means of 'diminishing the causes of variation,' even though Ricardo admits that 'no plan can possibly be devised which will maintain money at an absolutely uniform value . . .' (*Proposals*, IV, 54). Here it is important to note that Ricardo is not in search of an invariable standard of value, but of a plan, what Ghislain Deleplace has called a "monetary regime," which minimises variation in the value of the currency.

Ricardo takes as given the British monetary system in which gold and silver have been "the standard of our currency" and the "standard by which to measure the value of other things" (p. 55). Again, note the identity of standard and minted metal coin. He opines that this tradition is based on the "comparative steadiness in the value of the precious metals," that is of the market price of bullion, recognising that this may not be a permanent state of affairs.[9]

This reflects Einaudi's definition of monetary systems after the turn of the century; he refers to the legislators of the French Revolution unifying the weight and standard with the means of payment:

> What they wanted to make clear to the public was that the monetary unit was a disc of silver weighing 4.5 grams, or a disc of gold of 0.29 grams. Thereby they erroneously assumed people would never again fall into the error of looking at the monetary unit as perpetually endowed with a fixed value of its own.
>
> Einaudi (1953, p. 256)

Ricardo's plan is designed to perpetuate this error through a plan to achieve a "perfect currency" that he defines as one whose (metallic) standard is invariable, that always conforms to the standard, and "the utmost economy is practiced" in its use. He goes on to note that there are advantages of paper over coin minted in the standard, given by 'the facility with which it may be altered in quantity, as the wants of commerce and temporary circumstances may require' (IV, 55).

As already noted, Ricardo's interest was in finding a way to prevent the inequitable impact on the relation between creditors and debtors. Recognising that nothing could be done to influence changes in prices resulting from real forces (what would eventually become the neoclassical distinction between relative prices and nominal prices), it was necessary to find a way to identify independent changes in the value of money. Writing to James Mill during the drafting of the *Proposals* he noted:

> I know I shall be soon stopped by the word price, and then I must apply to you for advice and assistance. Before my readers can understand the proof I mean to offer, they must understand the theory of currency and price. They must know that the prices of commodities are affected by two ways one by the alteration in the relative value of money, which affects all commodities nearly at the same time, – the other by an alteration in the value of the particular commodity, and which affects the value of no other thing, excepting it ent[er] into its composition.
>
> (VI, 348)

Thus his search is not for an invariable standard, but rather for a plan. He proceeds in stages, and starts with specifying the "utmost economy" – with the quantity of metal or of notes backed by metal – required for perfection. This is determined by three factors: (1) its value; (2) the amount or value of the payments to be made; and (3) the "degree of economy practised in effecting those payments."

The argument under (1) starts by noting gold is clearly preferable to silver or other metals, for 'if the denomination of a pound were given to any specific weight of these metals, fifteen times more of such pounds would be required' to meet the needs of trade at a relative value of silver to gold of 15:1.

In discussion of (2), the value of the currency relative to the value of payments to be made, Ricardo channels Einaudi's explanation of the behaviour of a unitary monetary system in which "the possibility of reaching stability in the general level of prices" requires:

> decreasing or increasing the volume of money in circulation, as prices go up or down, especially if those variations are undesirable. ... If nothing varies, except that the quantity of money is doubled, the person which has £10 instead of £5 will spend £10 instead of £5, because, if he is not willing to do so, his desire to build up monetary reserves will have

changed which is contrary to our assumption. ... Consequently, one unit of an economic good priced at £5 must necessarily go up to £10.

Einaudi (1953, p. 253)

Ricardo thus proposes that 'the quantity of money required would be in inverse proportion to the value of the metal' by analysing the impact of 'an increase in the number of transaction from an increasing opulence and industry, bullion remaining the same.' This would lead to an increase in the purchasing power of money over goods (a lower level of goods prices) and above the value of gold bullion. Restoring stability in the value of the currency would require varying (increasing) the quantity of money inversely from the direction of the change (fall) in prices. However, Ricardo does not produce a plan based on a quantity rule for the supply of money: he instead invokes the process of market arbitrage, which eventually becomes the basis for the *Proposals*, as noted above.

When 'money is more valuable than bullion or the standard, it can therefore be purchased, coined, and issued as money, with a profit equal to the difference between the market and mint prices' (IV, 57). This would automatically provide the required adjustment in the quantity of money. This

> profit, however, could not long continue; for the quantity of money which, by these means, would be added to the circulation, would sink its value, while the diminishing quantity of bullion in the market would also tend to raise the value of bullion to that of coin: from one or both these causes a perfect equality in their value could not fail to be soon restored.
>
> (IV, 57)

And at the same time restore the equilibrium general price level.

But this is not Ricardo's proposed plan – it is the argument that supports his proposal to use paper notes instead of specie. He points out that the arbitrage adjustment of the quantity of money will have a peculiar characteristic:

> if the increase in the circulation were supplied by means of coin, the value both of bullion and money would, for a time at least, even after they had found their level, be higher than before; a circumstance which though often unavoidable, is inconvenient, as it affects all former contracts. This inconvenience is wholly got rid of, by the issue of money; for, in that case, there will be no additional demand for bullion; consequently its value will continue unaltered; and the new paper money, as well as the old, will conform to that value.
>
> (ibid.)

The attentive reader will note that here Ricardo has added an additional condition to the stability property of the arbitrage process that imposes the quantity adjustment of coin and bullion, for the use of paper also requires the "judicious management of the quantity" of paper. This is where the plan emerges, as well as the discussion of the necessity of a return to convertibility.

Ricardo notes that if there is a profit incentive for a bank to borrow by issuing its own liabilities to a maximum, the maximisation of bank profits may conflict with the "judicious management" of the banks' note liabilities, and recognises the importance of convertibility in imposing limits. But again, instead of imposing some quantitative limit on the issue of notes, he reverts to the idea of the perfect currency: the need for the value of notes to be expressed in the standard, to conform to the standard, and be uniform to the standard. To this end, Ricardo reverts to his prior argument of market-based arbitrage as controlling the issue of coin. In presenting that argument, he had already pointed out that it would hold irrespective of whether the perfect money is minted coin or fully backed paper. This leads to the conclusion that this arbitrage process will operate equally well with paper and preclude the need for a "judicious management" of the issue of paper. It also then follows that the uniformity of the perfect paper standard does not depend on the convertibility of paper into coin, but only the convertibility of paper into bullion.

Thus, Ricardo's "proof" that since paper has the same stability properties resulting from price arbitrage as minted coin, and it can be varied more rapidly than using specie (which incurs the delays of dealing with the mint) paper money is preferable to gold. If there is 'judicious management of the quantity, a degree of uniformity, which is by no other means attainable, is secured to the value of the circulating medium in which all payments are made' (IV, 57–58).

And thus the Ingot Plan: As long as the Bank of England converts its notes into bullion – and vice versa – and as long as bullion can be taken to the mint in unlimited quantities to be transformed into coin, there is no need for the Bank to convert notes into coin and no need to hold coin in reserves. Notes can provide as uniform a standard as gold coin, it is more economical, as it saves on the use of gold in circulation and in bank reserves and its quantity is adjusted in the arbitrage process more rapidly than coining bullion at the mint or melting coin into bullion. The convertibility of notes into bullion is the basis of the economical and secure currency, QED.

Now since it was widely accepted that during the suspension of convertibility the market price of bullion had risen, Ricardo could argue that the reason was a failure in the operation of the automatic adjustment mechanism to limit the expansion of Bank of England notes. And the failure in the mechanism was due to the absence of convertibility. Thus, he could argue that the inflation occurred because the value of the standard had fallen below the price of bullion. The proper response was then to make it attractive to convert notes into bullion. He does this by first noting that incentives will be influenced by the bid-ask spread. This 'price ought to be so fixed as to make it the interest of the seller of gold rather to sell it to the Bank than to carry it to the mint to be coined' (IV, 66 note *).

A restoration of convertibility would then have had the effect of increasing the value of the currency and decreasing the value of bullion, as described in the arbitrage example above. The impact of restoration would then clearly be deflationary, and to offset this result an addendum to the plan called for a gradual adjustment of the spread that the Bank would charge for conversion of notes into bullion. However, when Ricardo's plan was introduced, the reality turned out to be rather different, with the existing inflation being reversed and replaced by a deflation of a magnitude much larger than Ricardo had anticipated. This was taken as evidence of the failure of the plan to stabilise the currency. Ricardo, however, countered by noting that the plan had not been faithfully observed by the Bank in that it had tried to build up gold reserves in order to prepare for eventual convertibility of notes to coin. Thus there was a much larger-than-anticipated contraction in the gold market that prevented the fall in the value of gold and impeded the operation of the arbitrage process, causing an overshooting. Ricardo thus faulted the Bank management for this failure.[10]

Recall that the main impetus for writing the pamphlet in the first place was to question the excessive profits produced by the excessive fees the Bank of England charged the government for managing the public debt. Ricardo finds them to be excessive, and suggests that they should be renegotiated, in the interest of the "economical currency," noting further that the government could itself undertake these services much more cheaply. Indeed, he goes so far as to suggest that the Bank itself could be replaced:

> It cannot, I think, be doubted, that all the services, which the Bank performs for the public, could be performed, by public servants and in public offices established for that purpose, at a reduction or saving of expense of nearly half a million per annum.
>
> (IV, 53)

As for the basis of the economical system:

> Paper money may be considered as affording a seigniorage equal to its whole exchangeable value, – but seigniorage in all countries belongs to the state, and with the security of convertibility as proposed in the former part of this work, and the appointment of commissioners responsible to parliament only, the state, by becoming the sole issuer of paper money, in town as well as in the country, might secure a net revenue to the public of no less than two millions sterling.
>
> (IV,114)

He then closes by noting that this is not a real threat since the Bank Charter was not renewed until 1833. However, as a result of the unsatisfactory implementation of the plan, Ricardo eventually built on his suggestion and produced the pamphlet calling for the creation of a national bank to replace the Bank of England.

4. Modern monetary proposals

As noted above, the modern equivalent of Ricardo's proposal to replace gold coin with bank notes is to eliminate bank notes themselves. Summers' (2016) proposal is to eliminate high-value notes to make tax evasion more difficult. Ironically, suspension required the Bank of England to issue small-denomination notes to replace gold coin that was preferred by the public. For Buiter (Buiter and Rahbari 2015) the disappearance of the physical dollar is to eliminate the protection it provides from Negative Interest Rate Policy. For both proposals, some sort of digital currency would be the solution. However, it cannot be privately provided currency such as Bitcoin or other cryptocurrency since they would not eliminate either tax avoidance or negative rates, being non-transparent systems. Thus, the only candidate to replace the "ingot" would be some sort of transaction-based use of central bank digital reserve accounts.[11]

Notes

1 References to Ricardo's works are to Sraffa's edition (Ricardo, 1951–1973). The Roman numeral indicates the volume, the Arabic numeral the pages.
2 And as an analyst, and trader in the gold market, see his 1813 letters to Malthus containing detailed calculations of arbitrage prices for various gold coinage and mint prices in foreign markets, e.g. VI, pp. 85–86 and 97–99. The authoritative description of Ricardo's activity in this area is to be found in Marcuzzo and Rosselli (1991).
3 See Marcuzzo and Rosselli (1994) and Deleplace (1994a, 1994b).
4 Trower, in a letter to Ricardo notes that the proposal "carries on the face of it so great an innovation as no doubt to startle those who have not well weighed its effects" (VII, p. 22), while Broadley objected that "the Bank should be ruined, or subjected to ruin ... is a proposition so fully fraught with injustice to that Company and the impolicy and danger to the nation itself" (VII, p. 39).
5 See Feavearyear (1931, Chapter 7) for a summary of the events leading up to the Bank Restriction Act. This also accords with Ricardo's own explanation (1952, pp. 343–344).
6 Here Ricardo follows the tradition of the external stability of the gold standard and the gold import and export points in generating profit opportunities that generate stabilising financial flows. See Keynes's *Tract on Monetary Reform* (1923), and the more extensive discussion in Marcuzzo and Rosselli (1994).
7 See Tobin's (1987) distinction between a "run" on the liabilities of a single institution and a systemic "run" from the currency.
8 I am working here from the Skinner (1966) abridged edition of 1966. Skinner notes in the Preface to volume I that "The text of books 3 and 4 of the *Principles* has been collated with Steuart's *Principles of Banks and Banking and Money*, which was published separately in 1820 and again in 1812." And must have been known to Ricardo, who only cites the former.
9 In a letter to Mill he states that "invariability of the value of the precious metals, but from particular causes relating to themselves only, such as supply and demand, is the sheet anchor on which all my propositions are built" (VI, p. 348), written just after a letter to Trower in which he admits that "I among the number (of bullionists) considered gold and silver as less variable commodities than they really are," and refers in particular to the impact of war (VI, p. 344).

10 See the discussion in Sayers (1953).
11 Indeed, Deleplace (1994c, p. 322) has already made a similar suggestion based on Ricardo's *Proposals*.

References

Buiter, W. and Rahbari, E. (2015). High time to get low: getting rid of the lower bound on nominal interest rates. *CitiBank Global Economics View*, 9 April. Available at: http://willembuiter.com/ELB.pdf.

Deleplace, G. (1994a). Les différents usages de l'étalon monétaire. *Cahiers d'Économie Politique*, 23, 101–113.

Deleplace, G. (1994b). Aux origines de la pensée monétaire moderne. *Revue Économique*, 45 (5), 1125–1136.

Deleplace, G. (1994c). Does circulation need a monetary standard? In: G. Deleplace and E.J. Nell (eds.) *Money in motion: The post Keynesian and circulation approaches*. London: Macmillan, 305–329.

Einaudi, L. (1953). The theory of imaginary money from Charlemagne to the French revolution. In: F.C. Lane and J.C. Riemersma (eds.) *Enterprise and secular change: Readings in economic history*. London: Allen & Unwin, 229–261. English translation of: L. Einaudi (1936). La teoria della moneta immaginaria nel tempo da Carlomagno alla rivoluzione francese. *Rivista di Storia Economica*, 1 (1), 1–35.

Feavearyear, A.E. (1931). *The pound sterling*. London: Oxford University Press.

Keynes, J.M. (1923). *A tract on monetary reform*. London: Macmillan.

Marcuzzo, M.C. and Rosselli, A. (1991). *Ricardo and the gold standard*. London: Macmillan.

Marcuzzo, M.C. and Rosselli, A. (1994). The standard commodity and the standard of money. *Cahiers d'Économie Politique*, 23, 19–31.

Ricardo, D. (1951–1973). *The works and correspondence of David Ricardo* (P. Sraffa, ed. with the collaboration of M.H. Dobb), 11 vols. Cambridge: Cambridge University Press. Vol. IV. *Pamphlets and papers 1815–1823*, 1951. Vol. VI. *Letters 1810–1815*, 1952.

Sayers, R.S. (1953). Ricardo's views on monetary questions. *Quarterly Journal of Economics*, 67 (1), 30–49.

Skinner, A.S. (1966). Introduction. In: J. Steuart (1767). *An inquiry into the principles of political economy* (A.S. Skinner, ed.), 2 vols. Edinburgh: Oliver and Boyd.

Steuart, S.J. (1767). *An inquiry into the principles of political economy* (A.S. Skinner, ed., 1966). 2 vols. Edinburgh: Oliver and Boyd.

Summers, L. (2016). It's time to go after big money. Blog post. Available at: http://larrysummers.com/2016/02/16/its-time-to-go-after-big-money/.

Tobin, J. (1987). The case for preserving regulatory distinctions. Available at: https://www.kansascityfed.org/publicat/sympos/1987/S87TOBIN.PDF.

Turner, A. (2013). *Helicopter money as a policy option*. Institute of New Economic Thinking, 29 May. Online. Available at: https://ineteconomics.org/ideas-papers/blog/helicopter-money-as-a-policy-option.

5 On Ricardo's measuring rod again and what Sraffa made of it

Christian Gehrke, Heinz D. Kurz and Neri Salvadori

1. Introduction

When, in 1993, two of us contributed a paper on "The 'Standard Commodity' and Ricardo's search for an 'invariable measure of value'" to the Festschrift in honour of Luigi Pasinetti (Kurz and Salvadori, 1993), we did not yet have access to Piero Sraffa's unpublished papers kept at Trinity College, Cambridge. The only sources we could use were those published by Sraffa in his lifetime: his introduction to the Ricardo edition (Sraffa, 1951) and his book *Production of Commodities by Means of Commodities* (Sraffa, 1960). We thus wrote from under a veil of ignorance as regards Sraffa's pronouncements in his papers. Things have since changed and today we are happily able to access his rich preparatory notes, manuscripts and drafts of chapters and check whether our interpretation stands up to close scrutiny. In the meantime, the three of us have spent several summers in the Wren Library in Cambridge, working on Sraffa's papers. So the two authors of Kurz and Salvadori (1993) also had the opportunity to investigate the correctness or otherwise of their earlier work. And they had the pleasure to do so in the wonderful company of Christian Gehrke, who could play the role of an independent and impartial observer, correcting any distortions on their part. The decision to involve him in this enterprise was also motivated by the fact that the three of us all were, and still are, frequently in touch with Cristina Marcuzzo and share with her a deep interest in David Ricardo's contribution to political economy and Piero Sraffa's resumption of his approach. It hardly needs to be stressed that we are full of admiration for Cristina's academic accomplishments and very fine works and wish to pay tribute to the scholar and the woman in terms of this small contribution.

The chapter is composed as follows. In Section 2 we briefly summarise the various aspects of Ricardo's treatment of the problem of the invariable measure of value. Section 3 deals with Sraffa's interpretation of these aspects in his published writings. Section 4 looks at it through the lens of Sraffa's papers. Given the huge amount of notes Sraffa left to posterity, only some of them, those we consider to be particularly important and interesting, will be referred to. Section 5 summarises our findings and relates them to Cristina's treatment of the issue of the standard of money in Ricardo's monetary thought.

2. The interpretation under scrutiny

Ricardo's search for an "invariable measure of value" in the first and second edition of the *Principles* was originally a search for a commodity that would require 'at all times, and under all circumstances, precisely the same quantity of labour to obtain it'[1] (I, p. 27 n.). In terms of such a standard of value any variation in the value of other commodities would unequivocally point towards changes in the conditions of production of these commodities. Value measured in the invariable standard Ricardo also called "absolute value." Such a measure could be used in *intertemporal* and *interspatial* comparisons: it would inform us about what has happened in a given economy in the production of any other commodity that has risen or fallen in value relative to the measure of value; and it would inform us about why the same commodity would bear different prices in different economies. If the value of a commodity has risen, or was higher, relatively more labour was necessary in its production, if it has fallen, or was lower, relatively less. The cause of any such variation or difference in the exchange ratios of commodities could thus easily and unequivocally be spotted.

Before we continue, a remark is needed here concerning the concept of "labour" in Ricardo. Ricardo was perfectly aware of the fact that labour was heterogeneous and that therefore an operator was needed to render heterogeneous kinds of labour commensurable so that quantities of them could be aggregated (I, pp. 20–22). He followed Adam Smith in this regard who had suggested using the wage structure in order to accomplish this task (see Kurz and Salvadori, 1995, Ch. 11): if labour of type i was paid twice the wage rate per hour than labour of type j, one hour of labour of type i counted as two hours of labour of type j. For intertemporal comparisons the use of the wage structure as the sought operator made sense only if that structure did not change much over time. If this condition was not met or if some kinds of labour fell victim to technical progress and entirely new kinds entered the system of production, Ricardo's search for an invariable measure of value would recur in the form of a search for an invariable kind of labour. Clearly, if one compares one and the same economy at points in time that are far apart, or economies that are far apart from each other in space (and thus climate etc.), it may turn out that they do not have in common any particular kind of labour, let alone the same set of labours. This would spell trouble for the labour-embodied approach to the problem of value along Smith-Ricardo lines of thought. An alternative would be to reckon as labour, in Marx's famous phrase, simply the 'productive expenditure of human brains, nerves, and muscles' (Marx, 1867, p. 51).[2] Marx in fact insisted that 'The labour ... that forms the substance of value, is homogeneous human labour, expenditure of one uniform labour-power' (Marx, 1867, p. 46). However, one cannot avoid asking: how can we compare the productive expenditure of labour power under consideration of a bushman in the Namib and of a computer specialist in Silicon Valley?

When, in the first two editions of the *Principles*, Ricardo put forward the above specification of the condition an invariable measure of value would have to satisfy, he was already aware of the fact that the determination of the exchange ratios of commodities in terms of the amounts of labour embodied in them was not strictly correct, because unequal proportions of profits and wages of which the various commodities were made up implied that relative prices deviated somewhat from the relative quantities of labour embodied. However, Ricardo was convinced that the labour-embodied rule involved an approximation to the correct rule that was close enough to the latter and therefore could safely be used as a makeshift solution. Its use would simplify matters considerably and not substantially affect the inferences drawn on its basis. It would allow him, or so he sought, to avoid getting lost in a "labyrinth of difficulties." In the third edition of the *Principles*, and especially in his paper "Absolute Value and Exchangeable Value," composed in 1823 shortly before his premature death, Ricardo came up with a further consideration that was already implicit in his awareness of systematic deviations of relative prices and relative quantities of labour embodied: relative prices did not only depend on the technical conditions of production reflected in the quantities of labour needed to produce the different commodities; it depended also on the distribution of income, that is, the level of wages and correspondingly of the general rate of profits. A change in the distribution of income, *given* technical conditions of production, would typically not leave relative prices unchanged. Commodities, Ricardo insisted in his paper "Absolute Value and Exchangeable Value,"

> will not vary only on account of the greater or less quantity of labour necessary to produce them but also on account of the greater or less proportion of the finished commodity which may be paid to the workman … It must then be confessed that there is no such thing in nature as a perfect measure of value.
>
> (IV, p. 404)

Now, he is mainly concerned with ascertaining the impact of income distribution on relative prices, given technology, and thus with groping towards a fully correct theory of value. Intertemporal and interspatial comparisons were, however, not completely removed from the scene (see, for instance, IV, p. 396), but were relegated to the background. Ricardo's search for a measure of value that is invariable with regard to changes in the distribution of income was a crucial part and parcel of his concern with elaborating a coherent theory of value. Or, as Sraffa perceptively remarked, this came close to "identifying the problem of a measure with that of the law of value" (Sraffa, 1951, p. xli). Ricardo was convinced that such a commodity had to exhibit a medium proportion between wages and profits: a "medium between the extremes" standard.

3. Sraffa's treatment of Ricardo's search in his published writings

In the 1993 paper, Heinz D. Kurz and Neri Salvadori argued that it is very clear that in his published writings Sraffa was only concerned with that aspect of Ricardo's search for an invariable measure of value that related to his effort to elaborate a coherent theory of value. It did not relate to Ricardo's earlier concern with intertemporal and interspatial comparisons. This is exemplified especially with regard to Sraffa's book and the concept of the Standard commodity. It is argued that Sraffa considers this device to be essentially an analytical tool capable of establishing results that can be established also with the help of other analytical tools, but also as a way to simplify the study of price changes as income distribution changes and to render transparent results that other analytical tools would have left obscure (at least to many economists). It has been shown that a few sections in Part I of his 1960 book would not be necessary for the general argument, but have been included to pay tribute to Ricardo's search for an "invariable measure of value." We know now when this problem has a solution and when it doesn't, and what the solution is when there is one. It is clear that Sraffa refers exclusively to the second aspect of Ricardo's problem that we mentioned. Against the background of his respective argument many of the opinions encountered in the literature have been shown to be difficult to sustain. The relevant sections of his book are sections 23–25, but the field is prepared already in terms of sections 17 and 21–23. These last sections are also needed in order to introduce the Standard commodity. This is so since both the Standard commodity and the "medium between the extremes" standard have in common the property of being a medium or an average. In this respect, the main difference between Sraffa and Ricardo is that Ricardo was looking for a concrete and particular commodity that actually existed, whereas Sraffa was looking for an abstract and composite commodity, that had to be constructed by a theorist.

4. The problem as it is reflected in some of Sraffa's papers

The starting point of the following consideration is Ricardo's discussion with McCulloch in their correspondence in the second half of 1821. In his letter of 21 August, Ricardo asked McCulloch, 'What means [do] you have of ascertaining the equal value of capitals?' and went on to answer himself:

> [Any two] capitals are not the same in kind – what will employ one set of workmen, is not precisely the same as will employ another set, and if they themselves are produced in unequal times they are subject to the same fluctuations as other commodities. Till you have fixed the criterion by which we are to ascertain value, you can say nothing of equal capitals, for what is equal to day may be unequal in a year.
>
> (IX, pp. 359–360)

Capitals consist of vectors of capital goods that can only be compared by using prices. Prices however depend not only on the technical conditions of production, but also on income distribution and therefore on the rate of profits. If the latter changes, prices will change and so will the values of capitals. Ricardo's formulation may be said to anticipate, in a nutshell, Sraffa's later criticism of the marginalist concept of capital.

We may broadly distinguish between two sets of documents in Sraffa's papers belonging to two different periods of his reconstructive work that are of interest to us in this short note: some documents belonging to the period that led up to his discovery of the Standard system and Standard commodity in January 1944 in a set of notes Sraffa interestingly titled "Hypothesis" (see D3/12/36, pp. 61–85); and some documents belonging to the period when Sraffa started to draft the respective sections of his 1960 book. We first have a brief look at the first period and then turn to the second.

In his papers, Sraffa variously deals with the problem of the measure of value. Interestingly, he relates it in a straightforward manner to the problem of capital in marginalist economics. Here we focus attention on this aspect.

In a note written on 6 August 1942, entitled "Measure of Capital," Sraffa insisted that capital cannot be measured in "price," because its price varies with 'the variations in the proportional distribution of the product between wages and profits' (D3/12/16, p. 10). The term "proportional distribution" echoes Ricardo's concept of "proportional" wages, that is, the *share* of wages in the social product.[3] Sraffa then specified the difficulty besetting marginalist capital theory in the following terms:

> If the quantity of capital, when measured in a variable standard, is proportional to the income of the capitalist, then the quantity of capital, measured in an invariable standard, is <u>not</u> proportional to the income of the capitalist; that is to say, the income divided by the rate of interest does not give the quantity of capital.
>
> (D3/12/16, p. 11)

Hence Ricardo's search, far from representing an antiquarian concern, outmoded and irrelevant with regard to modern (that is, marginalist) theory, implicitly pointed towards a crucial stumbling block of marginalist capital theory: the "quantity of capital," whose relative scarcity is supposed to be reflected in its marginal productivity, cannot be given independently of relative prices and the rate of profits. How then could the rate of profits be determined in a marginalist way? Ricardo's findings, we might say using Sraffa's own words, if developed coherently, 'cannot be reconciled with *any* notion of capital as a measurable quantity independent of distribution and prices' (Sraffa, 1960, p. 38; emphasis in the original).

In a note drafted in August 1942 Sraffa elaborated on his previous argument. He introduced his argument in terms of the following requirement: 'What is demanded of a Model is that it should show a constant

(constant with respect to variations of *r*) ratio between quantity of capital and quantity of product.' He concluded that the marginalist authors from Eugen von Böhm-Bawerk to Knut Wicksell and others failed to accomplish the task:

> The reason why B-B., Wicksell and Co fail to find an invariable measure of capital is their obsession with the marginal product theory of interest. For them a measure is satisfactory only if it suits the marg. prod. theory: naturally they fail to find any satisfactory. In the end W. confesses that the difficulties of a measure are "insuperable," but always clings to, and in fact never has any doubts, about the marg. prod. It never occurs to him that it is the latter problem that is impossible and has to be given up.
>
> (D3/12/16, p. 14)

And, on 17 February 1946, Sraffa emphasises that the conventional concept of capital bases its 'prestige ... on an extension of the uniform means of production' and adds that this is 'the only case in which the price measure applies accurately' and so does 'also the ton measure (and any other),' for in this case capital is 'uniform in quality, e.g. wheat' (D3/12/16, p. 27).

We now turn to the period in which Sraffa began to draft his 1960 book. In what he dubbed the "Majorca draft," because he had composed it during a stay on the Spanish island in the spring of 1955, Sraffa made the relationship of his analysis with that of Ricardo very explicit. On 18 March 1955 he wrote:

> This assumption (namely that the price relations of the N.I. [National Income] to the aggregate means of production is invariable with respect to variations of wages and profits) implies that just as the wage [share of wages] can vary between 1 and 0, so the rate of profits can vary between 0 and a maximum which is the ratio of the N.I. to the aggregate means of production. This Maximum Rate of Profit can be regarded as the magnitude that characterises an economic system. (D3/12/52, p. 16)

He continued:

> In such a world, where everything moves in every direction; where wages can increase more than profits fall; where the value and indeed the composition of the nat. rev. [national revenue] can change merely because it is divided in different ways; where the prices of commodities rise or fall, and we cannot express in simple words (or any words) the conditions under which they rise or fall; where ... one sympathises with Ricardo in his search for an "invariable measure of value." In a universe where everything moves, we need a rock to which to cling to, a horizon to reassure us when we see a brick falling that it is not we who are going up – nor that we are falling when we see a balloon rising.
>
> (D3/12/52, p. 16)

And on 19 March 1955 Sraffa added:

> Ricardo sought the solution in a commodity which should be a medium between the two extremes, which rose or fell with the fall of profits, one that should remain comparatively stable in the general upheaval. He rejected however, for reasons which are not clear, an aggregate of many commodities. This, it would seem to us, would have been an approximation to such a commodity, owing to the approximate compensation of so many divergent commodities.
>
> (D3/12/52, p. 17)

In the "Majorca draft" Sraffa referred to the Standard commodity (and the related concepts) as "newly acquired toys," thus emphasising their status as a "purely auxiliary construction" and mere "tool of analysis." On 24 March 1955 he insisted:

> Using these newly acquired toys we shall play with the economic system, seeing what happens to prices as we move the rate of profits and wages between the two extreme points where all the nat. rev. goes to labour ($r = 0$, $w = 1$) or to profits ($r = R$, $w = 0$).
>
> (D3/12/52, p. 26 (recto))

Sraffa left Majorca on 31 March and, after a trip to Spain, was back in Cambridge on 15 April. On 1 September 1955 he was drafting sections 21–25 and explained:

> We want to vary *wages and* the rate of profits and observe how the *commodity* prices vary {*move*}. Prices must *inevitably* be expressed in terms of *someone* commodity *which is* chosen to act as standard and this is the source of some *confusion*, for we shall not be able to separate the peculiar circumstances of each commodity. If we observe the movements of the price of *commodity a* in terms of *commodity b* we shall never know how much of *any* fluctuation originates in the circumstances of *a* and how much in those of *b*. The attempt to eliminate this type of disturbance lies at the basis of R[icardo]'s suggestion that we take as standard a com [modity] that is equally distant from the two extremes, those [with] much capital and those [with] much labour …. This criterion, we shall soon find, is inadequate and assumes a measurability of capital (or of time) which R[icardo] himself *elsewhere* denies (lett.[er] to McC[ulloch] measure of Cap. 1823): a commodity which at near some values of r is "intermediate" in terms of fluctuation will be extreme at others and it is only by a fluke that a single com[modity] will be found to be intermediate at all values of r (its feature would be, not only that the "q"[uantities] of direct labour & cap. are "intermediate" but that its means themselves are so). However (and here we part company with R[icardo] who rejects the mass of commod[itie]s) what is not found in one com[modity] may be found in

a crowd. In general a group of commodities taken as a whole is likely to be less variable than most of its components, since it "averages them out."

(D3/12/53, p. 4)

It deserves to be stressed that here Sraffa mentions Ricardo explicitly, whereas in the printed version of the 1960 book he is only implicitly referred to in the title of section 23, "An invariable measure of value." Even more interestingly, there is an explicit reference to the correspondence between Ricardo and John Ramsay McCulloch that two of us, in our 1993 paper, analysed in great detail. There we stressed that Ricardo considered both the problem of intertemporal and interspatial comparisons and the problem of the dependence of prices on income distribution as genuinely theoretical problems. We added that the former problem cannot be dealt with in terms of a given and unchanging socio-technical environment, which the latter problem requests. McCulloch had difficulties to understand Ricardo's point of view and was at a loss to see the rationale behind his search for an invariable measure (in the second sense). He insisted that 'The real inquiry is to ascertain what are the circumstances which determine the exchangeable value of commodities at any given period' (IX, p. 344). The other problem McCulloch qualified as 'quite insoluble' and as belonging to the 'transcendental part of Pol Economy' (IX, p. 369). Ricardo answered that despite McCulloch's misgivings even he can be expected to 'still contend for the mathematical accuracy of the measure,' and then asked:

> Is it not clear ... that as soon as we are in possession of the knowledge of the circumstances which determine the value of commodities, we are enabled to say what is necessary to give us an invariable measure of value?
>
> (IX, p. 358)

Now the specification of an invariable measure was the by-product of a correct theory of value and distribution, whilst originally the search for it had served as a device to arrive at such a theory. Close scrutiny shows that in Sraffa we encounter a similar relationship between a tool of the analysis he forged in order to elaborate a correct theory of value and distribution, the Standard commodity, and the possibility to render precise this tool in the moment in which the sought theory was found.

The drafts for Appendix D in "References to the literature" do not seem to contain any information of particular interest, except perhaps for the following one. In one of his draft versions Sraffa wrote with regard to the connection between the standard measure and the "labour commanded" concept:

> ... it is strange to find oneself led to the conclusion that it coincides with the standard suggested by his opponents, that of "labour commanded" (although this phrase, which has been given slightly different meanings by its various proponents, is here defined in yet another way).
>
> (D3/12/98, p. 15 [recto])

In the final version, the Standard commodity is no longer said to 'coincide' with 'the' "labour commanded" standard, but 'to be equivalent to something very close to the standard suggested by Adam Smith' (Sraffa, 1960, p. 94).

5. The invariable measure of value and the standard of money

Ricardo's search for an invariable measure of value and its relation to Sraffa's Standard commodity was also studied by Cristina Marcuzzo and Annalisa Rosselli in several contributions.[4] They emphasised in particular the distinction, and the connection established by Ricardo, between a standard of value and a monetary standard, and pointed out that 'Ricardo's search for an invariable measure of value has undoubtedly always been a search for both a measure of the absolute value of commodities and a good standard of money' (Marcuzzo and Rosselli, 1994a, p. 1263). They also stressed, however, that the two concepts can be analysed separately from each other, and that the properties that need to be fulfilled by the latter are quite distinct from those of the former. In fact, in Marcuzzo and Rosselli (1991), they analysed the functions of gold as a standard of money independently of its functions as a standard of value, and simply followed Ricardo in supposing that gold could be *assumed* to be a commodity that is invariable in value. In subsequent publications, they then investigated the relationship that exists between the two concepts in Ricardo's theory and noted that

> only an invariable measure of value could be a good standard of money, because only in this case is any change in money prices an unambiguous signal of a change either in the value of money or in the values of commodities.
> Marcuzzo and Rosselli (1994b, pp. 22–23)

In view of the impossibility of finding any single or composite commodity that meets the requirement of invariability with respect to both changes in income distribution *and* changes in technology, Marcuzzo and Rosselli (1994b) have discussed also the question whether an "imperfect measure" such as Sraffa's device of the Standard commodity would be a suitable candidate to perform the function of a standard of money.[5] They concluded that it 'cannot be employed to ascertain the change in the relative value of any commodity, nor to prevent changes in the price level deriving from changes in distribution' (Marcuzzo and Rosselli, 1994b, p. 27). On what grounds, then, can the superiority of a commodity standard regime be justified if neither gold nor the Standard commodity can fulfil the conditions of an invariable measure of value? Marcuzzo and Rosselli's answer is that 'in the absence of the assumption that the standard is an invariable measure of value ... the virtues of having a monetary standard vanish' (1994b, p. 30).

We may conclude by noting that in Sraffa's Papers we have not come across any documents in which the Standard commodity is related explicitly to a monetary standard.

Notes

1 From here on references to Ricardo's works will be to Sraffa's edition (Ricardo, 1951–1973); the Roman numeral indicates the volume and the Arabic numeral the pages.
2 In the German original the reference is in addition to "brain, muscle, nerve" also to "hand."
3 The upshot of the argument developed with the help of the Standard system and Standard commodity was the establishment of a simple linear relationship between the rate of profits, r, and proportional wages, w,

$$r = R(1 - w)$$

where now R is the *Standard ratio* or *Maximum rate of profits* and w is the share of wages in the net income of the Standard system.
4 See Marcuzzo and Rosselli (1991, 1994a, 1994b), Marcuzzo and Rosselli (2015); see also Rosselli (2001).
5 See Fodor (2011) for a suggestion that Sraffa's device of the Standard commodity could be adopted as "money of account" and thus serve as a monetary standard. More recently, the issue of the relationship between Sraffa's Standard commodity and the standard of money was discussed also by Deleplace (2015, 2017, pp. 85–129).

References

Deleplace, G. (2015). Monetary theory. In: H.D. Kurz and N. Salvadori, eds. *The Elgar companion to David Ricardo*. Cheltenham: Edward Elgar, 344–356.

Deleplace, G. (2017). *Ricardo on money. A reappraisal*. London: Routledge.

Fodor, G. (2011). The standard commodity and monetary theory in the first half of the twentieth century. In: R. Ciccone, C. Gehrke and G. Mongiovi, eds. *Sraffa and modern economics*. Vol. II. London: Routledge, 311–323.

Kurz, H.D. and Salvadori, N. (1993). The "standard commodity" and Ricardo's search for an "invariable measure of value." In: M. Baranzini and G. Harcourt, eds. *The dynamics of the wealth of nations: growth, distribution, and structural change. Essays in honour of Luigi Pasinetti*. New York: St. Martin's Press, 95–123.

Kurz, H.D. and Salvadori, N. (1995). *Theory of production: a long-period analysis*. Cambridge: Cambridge University Press.

Marcuzzo, M.C. and Rosselli, A. (1991). *Ricardo and the gold standard: the foundations of the international monetary order*. London: Macmillan. Revised English edition of Marcuzzo, M.C. and Rosselli, A. (1986). *La teoria del Gold Standard. Ricardo e il suo tempo*. Bologna: Il Mulino.

Marcuzzo, M.C. and Rosselli, A. (1994a). Ricardo's theory of money matters. *Revue économique*, 45 (5), 1251–1268.

Marcuzzo, M.C. and Rosselli, A. (1994b). The standard commodity and the standard of money. *Cahiers d'Économie politique*, 23, 19–31.

Marcuzzo, M.C. and Rosselli, A. (2015). Natural quantity of money. In: H.D. Kurz and N. Salvadori, eds. *The Elgar companion to David Ricardo*. London: Routledge. 370–375.

Marx, K. (1867). *Capital, vol. I*. Reprint 1954. Moscow: Progress Publishers.

Ricardo, D. (1951–1973). *The works and correspondence of David Ricardo, Vol. I. Principles of political economy and taxation* (P. Sraffa, ed. with the collaboration of M.H. Dobb). Cambridge: Cambridge University Press.

Ricardo, D. (1951–1973). *The works and correspondence of David Ricardo, Vol. IV. Pamphlets and papers 1815–1823* (P. Sraffa, ed. with the collaboration of M.H. Dobb). Cambridge: Cambridge University Press.

Ricardo, D. (1951–1973). *The works and correspondence of David Ricardo, Vol. IX. Letters 1821–1823* (P. Sraffa, ed. with the collaboration of M.H. Dobb). Cambridge: Cambridge University Press.

Rosselli, A. (2001). Sraffa's edition of Ricardo's works: reconstruction of a reconstruction. In: T. Cozzi and R. Marchionatti, eds. *Piero Sraffa's political economy: a centenary estimate*. London: Routledge, 187–206.

Sraffa, P. (1951). Introduction. In: D. Ricardo, eds. *Principles of political economy and taxation, vol. I of: the works and correspondence of David Ricardo* (P. Sraffa, ed. with the collaboration of M.H. Dobb). Cambridge: Cambridge University Press, xiii–lxii.

Sraffa, P. (1960). *Production of commodities by means of commodities: prelude to a critique of economic theory*. Cambridge: Cambridge University Press.

6 Sismondi as a critic of Ricardo

On rent, Corn Laws and methodology

Pascal Bridel

1. Introduction

Beyond the usual generalities on the Sismondi-Ricardo debate during the general glut controversy, very little has been written on Sismondi as a more general critic of some of the most cherished components of Ricardo's theoretical model. In particular, and among numerous and repeated critical warnings on various theoretical topics, Sismondi devotes specifically an entire chapter[1] in both editions of his *Nouveaux Principes* (1819 and 1827) to a systematic attack on the theoretical core of Ricardo's theory of rent. Of particular interest in this chapter is the link established by Sismondi between his attack on Ricardo's theory of rent[2] and his critique of Ricardo's price theory by way of his own price theory dating back to his own *Richesse commerciale* (1803).

Building on this theoretical discussion, Sismondi adds in his second edition an entirely new chapter devoted to the already heated discussion in England on the 1815 Corn Laws.[3] Linked of course to his life-long idea that, irrespective of its distribution between various classes, wealth can only "contribute to general happiness [but] is not the objective of society" (1991, p. 11), his central conclusion presents, with great clarity, the distributional consequences of the complete abolition of the Corn Laws suggested by "the English economists" (2015a, p. 387, 1991, pp. 204 and 228). Eventually, Sismondi's two chapters not only bring the reader back to his largely original price theory but also to some very sharp methodological remarks addressed at the "new school" of political economy, i.e. at Ricardo and his followers.

Accordingly, this chapter falls into five parts. Section 2 offers a brief chronological reminder not only of Ricardo and Sismondi's direct and indirect relationships, but also provides a short outline (in order of publication) of the various contributions of these two authors to the theory of rent and the Corn Laws debate. Using the chapters of *Nouveaux Principes* mentioned above, Section 3 concentrates on Sismondi's understanding and critique of Ricardo's theory of rent and its links with their respective price theories. Using this theoretical model, Section 4 examines Sismondi's opinion on the 1826 Corn Laws debate. Eventually, strictly within the rent/corn laws question, Section 5 recalls the various and sometimes sharp methodological critiques addressed by Sismondi at the economists of the "new school."

2. A brief chronological reminder

When discussing the Sismondi-Ricardo relationship, it is too often overlooked that though a year younger than Ricardo, Sismondi's first contribution to economics proper predates Ricardo's by nearly a decade.[4] In the field of price and rent theory, the gap is even wider. In 1803, Sismondi offers a full-blown, treatise-like, two-volume *Richesse commerciale* in which price theory and the theory of rent receive a complete treatment (see Bridel, 2011, 2017). In other words, when around 1810, Ricardo started publishing (mainly first on monetary topics), Sismondi was already a well-established economist with a substantial list of publications (see *Écrits d'économie politique 1799–1815*, Sismondi, 2012b).

In the narrower field of rent theory, while Ricardo's famous *Essay on the Influence of a Low Price of Corn on the Profits of Stocks*[5] was being published in 1815, in his 1803 book Sismondi had already discussed at length the question of the *rente foncière*. Similarly, his chapters on price theory offer an interesting continental approach very much at odds with the approach of his revered intellectual master Smith. Moreover, even if published only in 1824, Sismondi's entry for the *Brewster Encyclopaedia* on Political Economy was already sent to the publisher late in 1817. And this entry (90 per cent of which is to be found in the *Nouveaux Principes*) forms the backbone of his upcoming two volumes.

As is well known, Ricardo's theory of value only reached a publishable form in Chapter 1 of his *Principles* (1817). Thus, when attacking Ricardo two years later in his *Nouveaux Principes* (1819), Sismondi was perfectly correct in considering Ricardo as a newcomer to the field even if, he rapidly recognised him as the leader of a "new school" in political economy.

Hence, when forming his central theoretical framework (notably in his 1803 and 1817 contributions), Sismondi had obviously, no knowledge of Ricardo's still-to-come seminal contributions on value and rent. Asked by the editor of the *Brewster Encyclopaedia* to add to his 1817 draft comments on Ricardo's *Principles* (1817), Sismondi preferred to expand his entry into his *Nouveaux Principes* in which Ricardo is often mentioned and criticised. For his part, in his first edition Ricardo was well aware of Sismondi's *Richesse commerciale*[6] but, like Sismondi who never bothered to read the subsequent editions of Ricardo's *Principles*, Ricardo did not deem it fit to refer to the *Nouveaux Principes* in his own second and third editions. Finally, there is no known surviving correspondence between Ricardo and Sismondi who, however, met three times (1819, 1820 and 1822) to discuss unsuccessfully nagging questions linked to the general glut controversy.

3. "Mr Ricardo's theory of land rent" (economic theory)

Sismondi's chapter specifically devoted to a critique of Ricardo's theory of rent appears strategically in his second edition,[7] at the end of Book III, on

"Territorial Wealth." The eleven (twelve in the second edition)[8] previous chapters are basically a long, detailed and sometimes tedious discussion of one of Sismondi's favourite subjects: the various systems under which land is contracted by landowners and how the land surplus is shared between land-owners, farmers and labourers. Clearly, for Sismondi, the English farming lease system in which rent is paid (exclusively in cash and not in kind) by the farmer to the landowner is one solution – and not *the* solution to the payment of the service of the land.

In the brief opening paragraph, Sismondi qualifies Ricardo's rent theory as a "new doctrine ... absolutely opposed to that of Smith" and "which is ... far removed from ours" (1991, p. 227). Furthermore, he also calls on Say's authority and his partial refutation of Ricardo's theory of rent added in various footnotes to the 1819 translation of the 1817 edition of the *Principles* into French (Ricardo, 1819). Hence, the stage is set for Sismondi's central five-stage argument.

1 *The rate of profit is not uniform in the various sectors of the economy, and this rate is not determined in the agricultural sector irrespective of the fertility of the various types of land.* Hence, and most crucially, the rent cannot be the adjusting variable (at a maximum on the most productive land and zero on the marginal land): the rent is wrongly reduced by Ricardo "to the simple estimate of the differences in the productivity of different soils" (Sismondi, 1991, p. 228). Based on faulty premises, Ricardo's conclusions on taxation on the net and/or gross income, and/or on corn are therefore irrelevant.

From the very beginning, Sismondi's refutation is based on a dynamic disequilibrium process opposed to Ricardo's equilibrium (or long-run tendency) argument. The lumpiness of capital goods, the division of labour, the difficulty to move capital and labour from one sector to another, the demographic variable and the fact that "farmers cannot be turned at will into weavers or can be moved only with great difficulties from one county to another" imply that "equilibrium is never re-established" (ibid.). Clearly, "if there is one thing proved by experience" (ibid.), it must be the heterogeneity of the profit rate on all types of land and hence in industries. Extending his argument to free trade in corn, in his 1826/27 essay on the Corn Laws, Sismondi's irony addressed at Ricardo goes one step further when mentioning wittingly the already famous example taken from the *Principles*:

> I am aware that I shall be accused of pushing matters to an extremity; and I hear an economist of the new school [Ricardo!] observe that corn cannot be grown without a remunerating price, in the countries which are to supply England, any more than in England itself; – that if the corn lands of Poland do not return the profit which may be gained in any other business, the Polish farmers will employ their capitals in another way; – that the land n° 4, n° 5, and n° 6 will cease to be cultivated in Poland, as in

England; whilst the lands n° 1, n° 2, and n° 3, will continue to be cultivated in England, since they are cultivated in Poland.

Political economists who argue thus, and who imagine that with their eight numbers they can designate, not only every degree of fertility, but all the causes which have an influence on agricultural produce, have never reflected on the different kinds of labour, and are not aware that in cultivation by bondsmen the labour which produces corn has been paid, once for all, in anticipation, that it thenceforward continues to be due from one generation to another, so that the landowner who sells his grain, never finds that it is produced at too dear a rate, or that he cannot sell it at a price sufficient to induce him to continue to grow it. He raises corn by the application of a few hundred stripes among his serfs, at whatever price he may sell it, he finds himself sufficiently remunerated for what it cost him.

Sismondi (2015a, pp. 382–383, 1991, p. 200)

Besides the insularity, if not the ignorance, of English economists on alternative techniques of sharing the agricultural surplus,[9] Sismondi adds that Ricardo's implicit "assumption that farmers generally dictate the terms of lease to the [land]owners" (1991, p. 228) cannot be further from the truth. Given the then current situation in England (a fixed quantity of available land facing a growing population and an "indefinitely" (ibid.) growing quantity of capital), there must always be more farmers asking for land than landowners looking for farmers. Hence, a no-rent land is logically impossible.But, Ricardo's argument is even more fundamentally vitiated, argues Sismondi which raises a point linked to the property right to uncultivated lands. Ricardo's argument on rent-free land is only valid in the case of *res nullius*. If the least productive lands are privately owned (as they always are even in America), Sismondi argues that when the price of corn rises, however small the rent will be positive.[10] In his numerical example, "where [Ricardo] starts with a zero, he should have at least put a unity"[11] (p. 229). All in all, and besides the methodological rejection of equilibrium reasoning,[12] this particular critique relies mainly on a call to "real-world" arguments, not to any logical shortcomings on the part of Ricardo.

2   Sismondi's second line of argument against Ricardo's rent theory is linked to a constant leitmotiv in his writings on economics: the opposition between *gross* and *net product*. Gross product (*produit brut*) is the total value of the yearly production of a piece of land (and must be of course divided between those who contributed to the production process). Net product (*produit net*)[13] is the part of the gross product kept by the farmer/owner after all the necessary costs of production have been paid for (not including the rent if the farmer hire the land; in the English system, the net product is used as a basis to calculate the rent).[14] Sismondi lists four components to the rent – two of which Ricardo is accused of completely neglecting. They are: a) the land's own joint-contribution with labour to the value of the production[15]; b) the degree of monopoly

enjoyed by the owner of the land; c) the extensive rent proper (acquired by infra-marginal lands on the no-rent marginal land); d) the income of the sunken capital invested by landlord to improve the quality of his land.

Sismondi accuses Ricardo of neglecting a) and b) and to confuse c) with d) reducing the component of the net product to differential rent only. Here Sismondi anticipates his critique of Ricardo's love for "strong cases," which proceed by eliminating as many variables as possible in order to build simplified but revealing models of the "real world": a procedure later called by Schumpeter the "Ricardian vice," which was extensively used to build the Classical model.

3　In 1815, when discussing the question of rent with Malthus, Ricardo wrote to James Mill that "I know I shall soon be stopped by the word price" (1952, p. 348). And in his critique of Ricardo's theory of rent, Sismondi does not fail to raise precisely the question of *price/value theory*. Using his own theory of prices outlined in his *Richesse commerciale* (1803) and taken over part and parcel in the *Nouveaux Principes*, Sismondi attacks head-on Ricardo's theory of value (a critical "observation [that] concerns the entirety of Mr Ricardo's book"; 1991, p. 229).

Already discussed in details by the present author (Bridel, 2011), Sismondi's price theory is only briefly mentioned here. Breaking from Smith's approach and diverging from the still-to-come Ricardian approach, Sismondi offers a twin-theory of value: the intrinsic value determined by the costs of production of a good opposed to the relative value of the same good determined by market competition. The former, independent of any exchange, is linked to the quantity of labour necessary to bring this good to the market; the latter results from the ratio of the quantity supplied on the market with the demand actually made.

4　Using this basic price-theory distinction, Sismondi moves on eventually to the last step of his critique of Ricardo's theory of rent by working simultaneously on the priority given to gross product over net product, and by making a sharp distinction between a self-sufficient farmer owner of his land and a farmer renting his land from a landlord.

On the one hand, and using some sort of corn model[16] and with the help of a numerical example, Sismondi demonstrates that the intrinsic value of the net product is independent of any exchange and/or competitive mechanism: the surplus is expressed in physical terms and is "the labour of nature" (1991, p. 230). However, if part of this surplus (beyond the own needs of the farmer) is sold on the market, the value of this surplus will be defined by the relative price of the corn sold defined at the equilibrium between the competing forces of producers and consumers. Hence, this part of the surplus is sold not at its intrinsic price equivalent to the cost of the labour used to produce it but at its relative price equivalent to the cost of labour used to produce the goods he is offered in exchange for his corn. At this stage, Sismondi introduces the degree of monopoly the farmer enjoys when the pressure on the demand for his corn (resulting from a growing population) makes it exceed his supply. And, finally, he adds a quasi-Ricardian differential rent linked to the closeness to the market of fields of equal productivity.

On the other hand, Sismondi examines the more contentious case of the farmer renting his land from a landlord in order to solve the question of the factors determining the level of the rent. As a matter of fact, for Sismondi, after having "debated" the price of his corn with the consumers, it remains for the farmer to "debate" the level of the rent with the landlord. And to the *facilités de débit* on the market expressed by the relative price of his corn, the farmer has to add the number of his competitors offering labour and capital: if the quantity of labour and capital is higher than the quantity of land made available, the landlord will "dictate his law" (p. 231) to the farmer; and if the quantity of labour and capital is lower than the quantity of land made available, the farmer will "dictate his law" to the landlord.

All in all, the physical net product (or surplus in kind) does increase in all cases the social wealth independently of variations of the market exchange price. Hence, in this case, the rent has a "real foundation." However, the market price for corn is fixed via a "triple contest" (ibid.) which determines simultaneously the distribution of the net product/surplus between landlords, farmers, labourers and consumers.[17]

Sismondi's argument is finally summarised in the following terms:

> The work of nature, this creative labour, which she would do without man, but which she would not put in his use, is thus the source of the net product of land. Market demand, or the relation between the income of consumers and the quantity of the gross product offered for sale, determines the value of the net product, or sets its relative price. The right of ownership, or the monopoly guaranteed by society which the landlord exercises against two classes of individuals – on the one hand, those who demand provisions; on the other those who offer to work to raise them – forbids that, on the one hand, the rent of land, and on the other hand, the price of provisions, should be reduced to their lowest value. It is only after these three causes have been operative, with infinite variations depending on circumstances, that the other causes recognised by Mr Ricardo make themselves felt.
>
> (p. 231)

Clearly, Ricardo's theory of differential rent is only an appendix to a much more complicated socially and institutionally determined process. As usual, and like in most fields of economic theory, Sismondi does not suggest a new alternative theory of rent proper but attempts to demonstrate the over-restrictive character of Ricardo's own approach. In particular, the existence of property rights invalidates Ricardo's assumption of a no-rent land.

Accordingly, Ricardo's efforts to remove rent from value determination is seen as the result of a typical English insularity exclusively obsessed with the lease farming system. For Sismondi, and in perfect accordance with his 1803 theory of prices, the distribution of income is the result of a market mechanism linked to the market power possessed by the contracting parties (see Sismondi,

1803, Book II, Ch. 1). And the market power of monopolistic landlords casts serious doubts on the degree of competition behind Ricardo's model. Moreover, and this is an argument used over and over by Sismondi in connection with his grand vision of the social contract behind the working of the markets, property rights to land are not derived from the God-given Physiocratic *avances foncières*, nor are they simply assumed as they are for Ricardo. In some way, Sismondi's position is half-way between those of Ricardo and Say: the causes of rent and profits of land are based exclusively on differences of fertility for Ricardo and on property rights for Say. For Sismondi, property rights to land (and all other productive factors) are simply a "social convention" that can be altered, modified or changed to suit the purpose of the society.[18] In his own words:[19]

> The ownership of land is, indeed, not based on a principle of justice, but on a principle of public utility …. It is for society's advantage, for the poor as well as the wealthy, that it has taken the landlords under its protection …. It must be judged, as all the rest of social produce …. It is a gift of society, and in no way a natural right which pre-existed.
>
> (1991, p. 138)

5 Sismondi is then ready to deliver the punch-line against "Mr Ricardo's theory of rent":

> Therefore, far from concluding with Mr Ricardo that *the rent always falls on the consumer and never on the farmer*,[20] we see rent, or rather the net product as being born directly from the soil to the profit of the landlord; he does not take from the farmer, nor from the consumer; but we believe that, according to the state of the market, sometimes the farmer and or the consumer profit from a part of that rent; sometimes, the landlord not only receives the entire rent, but exacts a monopoly price whose loss in unequally divided between the farmer and the consumer.
>
> (1991, p. 232)

As a historian interested in comparing social and legal property arrangements as well as social and market structures, Sismondi is (as shown) rather weak on an alternative to Ricardo's *theory* of rent. However, out of such apparent weaknesses, and based on his critical chapter on Ricardo's theory of rent, he offers two sets of highly helpful comments: one to assess the then heated English debate on Corn Laws[21] (Section 4); the other on the methodological divide between his and Ricardo's theoretical apparatuses (Section 5).

4. Sismondi on the 1826 Corn Laws debate

True to his life-long methodology, in his initial 1826 article (as well as in his 1827 Book III, Ch. 10), Sismondi offers first a well-informed survey of the central questions raised by the Corn Laws debate followed by a harsh critique of the free-trade solution based on Ricardo's model.[22] In a disappointing conclusion, in which (once again) he warns of the dangers of the English system of "universal competition" (1991, p. 205, 2015a, p. 388), he does not offer any convincing alternative to "the bad English system of cultivation" (1991, p. 204, 2015a, p. 387) (short of restoring his mythical small farm system). After a full paragraph devoted, in a clearly Smithian way, to praise free markets for corn recalling anti-Physiocratic arguments used in his *Richesse commerciale*, Sismondi states that if a permanent remunerating low price of corn is to the advantage of all classes, he rightly asserts that, in England, "the [Corn] laws are enacted for the sole purpose of keeping up the price of corn" (1991, p. 198, 2015a, p. 379). And this high price of corn is a necessity to keep running this faulty system of cultivation. Clearly, in the English system of lend-lease cultivation characterised by large farms, "speculating" farmers (maximising their net product) pay their labourers in money. If the costs of production in such a system are not covered by the sale of corn, the farmer will cease to cultivate and put his capital to other use (or even emigrate to America!). The landlord will be left without income and, worst of all, the labourers will be laid off. Conversely, and particularly during the then current commercial crisis, to keep the ports shut and the price of corn high deepen the recession and increased the level of unemployment in the manufacturing sector. The manufacturers are prompt to argue that the high price of corn resulting from the Corn Laws is largely responsible for the crisis: high wages due to the high price of corn reduced their competitiveness and, hence, their export capacities. Whatever the solution adopted by the government, the working class "experience all the evils of famine" (1991, p. 199, 2015a, p. 381). Sismondi outlines thus the inherent flaws within the English system of cultivation by large farms:

> ... thus, the halves of the nation are engaged, one against the other, in a controversy on which not only profit but existence depends .... To open the market for foreign corn would probably ruin the English landowners and render farming a profitless occupation. This would be a great evil, no doubt, but it would be no injustice .... To force upon others a service which is not wanted, and then to exact their own [monopoly] price for that service, is nothing short of robbery. Society will, doubtless, be seriously impoverished, if the owners of the land lose their revenues; but it will be no less impoverished if other people's income is taken from them to fill the pockets of the landlords.
>
> (ibid.)

Without being explicitly named, Ricardo is accused again (with a reference to his famous lands 1 to 6 example), to be the victim of his insular ignorance about alternative continental agricultural systems; and that this ignorance plays a crucial role in the free trade on grain argument. However incomplete,

Ricardo's argument on rent might be partially applicable to England but certainly not to Poland where, given the compulsory labour system,[23] "the corn which the Polish labourer raises costs nothing to the Lord who sells it" (1991, p. 201, 2015a, p. 384). Hence, "the wealthy and intelligent English farmer … cannot maintain a competition with the ignorant and wretched Polish peasant, degraded by slavery and brutified by drunkenness, and whose agriculture is yet in an infant state" (1991, p. 201, 2015a, p. 386). Furthermore, Sismondi considers as unintelligible the argument in terms of taxes and/or alterations of currency invoked by "the English economists who never examine the condition of other countries" (1991, p. 204, 2015a, p. 387).

The Corn Laws issue has thus to be examined for Sismondi within a much broader framework than the narrow Ricardian rent-cum-free trade approach which, unfortunately, does not allow him to offer any practical solution but, instead, "slow remedies" linked to a complete transformation of the English cultivation system. Sismondi's strategy is simple, perfectly in line with his pessimistic vision of the future of "universal competition" (1991, p. 205, 2015a, p. 388), but largely impracticable. His argument can be summed up in three steps.

1   "Wealth, we cannot too often repeat it, is not the object of society; it is only one of the means of arriving at that object, which is the greatest good of the greatest number" (1991, p. 8). Hence maximising the net product via "universal competition" implying a "bad system of cultivation" (characterised by large farms, a land-lease system and waged agricultural labour) is the recipe to raise one half of the population against the other without even avoiding, with certainty, commercial crises.
2   Sismondi's lengthy catalogue of the dire costs of a repeal of the Corn Laws is about as long and as the catalogue of their deficiencies. In particular, whatever the solution chosen, wage labour would equally suffer in both systems: under the Corn Laws, manufacturing labour is currently "perishing of hunger" and a repeal of this legislation "would bring starvation" to agricultural labour… What should be done?" asks eventually Sismondi. Even if stating explicitly that he is "not prepared to answer this," he argues that the Corn Laws should be changed "slowly but actively" (1991, p. 204, 2015a, p. 387).
3   As expected, and leaving the modest economic policy level, Sismondi brings back to the fore no less than a complete system change to the working of the English economy. Without getting in as many details as he does in the *Nouveaux Principes*, a mere enumeration of his suggestions is enough to understand while they were hardly heard by the English economists during the Corn Laws debate. This complete transformation of the English system of cultivation would imply a) the restoration of small farms; b) the abandonment of the money wage system in agriculture; and most crucially c), the abandonment of "the universal competition for producing everything as cheap as possible" (1991, p. 205, 2015a, p. 388).

As a matter of fact, faced with what he sees as the dire future of the industrial economic system, Sismondi looks backwards to some mythical organisation of the English agricultural sector. Both Ricardo's disciple McCulloch as well as Marx understood perfectly well the unpractical and even romantic[24] side of Sismondi's solution. A particularly gifted analyst of the weaknesses of the industrial system and a formidable critic of the "economists of the new school," Sismondi was, unfortunately, the provider of rather unrealistic solutions. As he said himself in 1827 in his own defence:

> J'ai attaqué des principes qu'on disait absolus, auxquels on ne voulait admettre aucune modification; j'ai fait voir où ils mèneraient, en les prenant à la dernière rigueur; on en a conclu que je ne les admettais dans aucun cas, que je voulais les détruire. On me répond comme si j'étais l'ennemi des progrès de l'industrie, de ceux de la population, de la concurrence, de la liberté du commerce, de la production enfin. *Mais je n'ai jamais voulu montrer que les limites au-delà desquelles, dans un moment donné, ces biens peuvent se changer en maux.*
>
> (2015a, p. 439; italics added)

5. Some brief concluding methodological points

Not surprisingly, in the course of his critical assessment of Ricardo's theory of rent, Sismondi cannot escape some sharp remarks on the method adopted by Ricardo and the "English economists" adept in the new "pure political economy." One can be mercifully brief here. If some of his methodological remarks linked to the general glut controversy have already been discussed *ad nauseam*, it is not without interest to realise that some of them are also used by Sismondi in the concluding paragraphs of his critique of Ricardo's rent theory.

First, it is difficult not to read between the lines, if not Sismondi's envy, at least some irritation at Ricardo's success as a newcomer to the discipline. Sharply in opposition to the Smithian methodology (revered by Sismondi), Ricardo is very perceptively qualified as "the head of the new school" (1991, p. 599), as the harbinger of "a new era in political economy, whose numerous disciples repeat today his maxims with unquestioning belief" (p. 595).

Second, and even within the narrow field of rent theory, "strong cases" and simplifying assumptions are seen as methodological muddles. For the first time, the new Ricardian relentless, logical tactic is seen as undermining the broader and softer approach of post-Smithian economists. Strongly opposed to this new abstract approach to political economy, Sismondi complains time and again of the "unrealisticness" of wages being only made up of corn and of the absence of rent on the marginal land (p. 582), i.e. "of freeing the [rent] theory from all surroundings circumstances [in order] to make it clearer and easier to comprehend" (p. 55). For Sismondi, "the opposite has happened: the new English economists are extremely obscure and can only be understood with much efforts" (p. 55). For Sismondi, only the abstract Ricardian methodology can lead to the absurd conclusion that the rent always falls on the consumer and never on the farmer.

Third, this critical line of argument can easily be connected to his well-known more general "disequilibrium-dynamic-historical" approach. The concluding paragraph of Sismondi's chapter on "The theory of rent of Mr Ricardo" sums it all up very aptly:

> One should generally beware in political economy of absolute statements as well as abstractions. Every one of the forces destined to equilibrate each other in every market, can by itself and independently of the one with which it is supposed to be in equilibrium, experience variations. Nowhere is an absolute quantity to be found, always-equal forces are never found; and every abstraction is always a deception. Also, political economy is not a mathematical science, but a moral science. It misleads if one wants to be guided by numbers: it only leads to a goal if the feeling, the needs, and the passions of mankind are taken into account.
>
> (p. 232)[25]

What an interesting list of most elements Ricardo wanted to get rid of![26] Sismondi pinpoints even more exactly his methodological disagreement with Ricardo's technique of analysis when, later on and on a different topic, he writes: "Mr Ricardo never abandons the abstractions on which he has based his entire system, and it is difficult to bring them into conformity with the facts we have sought to lay before our readers" (p. 486).

Fourth, and eventually, this opposition to abstract economic theory is linked to Sismondi's much broader (and older) definition of political economy dating back at least to his *Richesse commerciale* (1803). Within political economy, and in opposition to Ricardo and his disciples, for Sismondi, the pursuit of wealth cannot be separated from the pursuit of "national happiness" (p. 54). In other words, a study of the "wealth of nations" cannot be separated from the distribution of that wealth among the members of society. While English economists concentrate nearly exclusively on maximising the growth rate of the economy (i.e. maximising wealth), though very much in favour of growth, Sismondi sets himself the much higher aim of maximising growth *and* both individual and social happiness. Such an ambition cannot be discussed here but underlines clearly Sismondi's entire theoretical apparatus, including his theory of rent. And the relative weakness of this apparatus when compared to Ricardo's (and the subsequent eclipse of Sismondi's intellectual influence) is no doubt the result of his extremely ambitious, if not overambitious objective. Beyond rent theory, the whole of the general glut controversy is nothing else but a variation on this central theme. Two paragraphs extracted from the "Foreword to his Second Edition" summarise vividly and better than any rewording not only his intentions but also, clearly, his disappointment at not being able to carry through with his message:

In this book ..., I have sought to establish that if wealth is to contribute to general happiness, being as it is the mark of all material enjoyments of man, its increase must be in proportion to the increase in population, and its distribution among that population must be in a proportion that cannot be disturbed without extreme danger. I intend to show that it is necessary for general happiness that income should increase with capital, that the population should not outrun the income on which it must subsist, that consumption should increase with population, and that reproduction should be proportioned to the capital which produces it as well as to the population which consumes it. At the same time, I have shown that each of these relations may be disturbed independently of the others; ... every time one or the other of these relations is disturbed, there will be suffering for society.

It is on that proportionality that my *New Principles* are founded; it is in the importance that I attach to that I differ essentially from philosophers, who, in our time, have expounded in such a brilliant manner the economic science of Messrs, Say, Ricardo, Malthus, and McCulloch. They appear to me to have constantly abstracted from obstacles, which have impeded the train of thought of their theories, and to have arrived at wrong conclusions because they never separated what was difficult for them to isolate.

Sismondi (1991, p. 11)

And the critique of Ricardo's rent theory is an excellent illustration of Sismondi's ambition and... measly theoretical results. Undoubtedly, Sismondi's appraisal of Ricardo's rent theory is certainly among the first critical appraisals of rigorous abstract theory not in terms of its internal logic but in terms of what is seen as its relevance to solve real-world issues.

Notes

1   Book III, Ch. 12 in the first 1819 edition and Book III, Ch. 13 in the second 1827 edition. For all practical and theoretical purposes, the text between the two editions is practically unchanged. All quotations in English for this chapter are from the American 1991 translation (Sismondi, 1991).
2   The nearly contemporary Ricardo-Say debate on rent theory has been recently thoroughly re-examined by Depoortère (2017, pp. 80–112).
3   Included in Book III, this Chapter 10 "On the Corn Laws" went through an earlier publication (1826) in English in the *New Monthly Magazine and Literary Journal*, and has been reproduced in Sismondi (2015a). Though attracting apparently little notice, this article bears testimony of Sismondi's contribution to the early phase of this most highly sensitive of all English political debates. In what follows, quotations from this chapter on Corn Laws are taken from the original English 1826 article (as reproduced in Sismondi, 2015a) and not from the 1991 translation. However, for the sake of completeness, page references are given to both texts.
4   Sismondi's first publication (his *Tableau de l'agriculture toscane*) dates from 1801 while Ricardo's *High Price of Bullion* only goes to print in 1810.

5 A text never mentioned by Sismondi. No mention is made either of Malthus's initial 1815 *Inquiry* or of his various pamphlets on the Corn Laws.

6 Quoted twice in the *Principles* (Ricardo, 1817, pp. 380–381 and 399). The second reference is to Malthus's critique of Sismondi's position on rent "as the sole produce of labour."

7 Sismondi explains what could appear as a belated critique of Ricardo's rent theory because he always considered it "as so far removed from ours that we have not even had an occasion to argue against it while expounding our own principles" (Sismondi, 1991, p. 227).

8 For a comparison of the two editions, see the *variorum* edition of Sismondi's *Nouveaux Principes* (Sismondi, 2015b).

9 "The English economists who have never wanted to examine what happens in other countries ..." complains Sismondi in his Corn Laws essay (Sismondi, 2015a, p. 387, 1991, p. 204).

10 Referring once again to an example, Sismondi mentions the United States (with a quasi-infinite supply of not privately owned land). The local State selling this "free" land for two dollars an acre, one cannot escape the idea that this price paid to the government is nothing but a form of... rent (Sismondi, 1991, p. 229).

11 In a footnote on p. 582, Sismondi (1991) opposes very clearly Ricardo's theoretical assumption with the opposite conclusion, which Sismondi presents "as a fact."

12 As Sismondi writes later in his *Nouveaux Principes*: "Let us beware of this dangerous equilibrium theory that re-establishes itself of its own accord! Let us beware of believing that it does not matter on which side of a scale one puts or takes away a weight, because the other will quickly adjust itself! ... It is true that a certain equilibrium will re-establish itself in the long run, but this will be by great suffering" (Sismondi, 1991, p. 487). As Joan Robinson quipped in 1973: "If only Keynes had read Sismondi instead of Malthus!" (Robinson, 1973, p. 1327, fn. 3).

13 The connection (at least in the wording) with the Physiocrats is clear (see "Les deux systèmes...," in Sismondi, 1805).

14 As discussed more fully later, Sismondi is obsessed by the demonstration that, following the industrial revolution, the principle of "universal competition for producing everything as cheap as possible" (Sismondi, 1991, p. 205) and based on a wage labour system tends (including in particular the agricultural sector) to maximise net product at the expenses of gross product: this tendency is detrimental both to employment, to the level of output and to the stability of agricultural prices. Though necessary to what Marx will call later the "primitive accumulation," the substitution of small farms by large estates might well maximise the increase of a country's wealth but certainly not the welfare, the *bonheur*, of its population.

15 Labour "draws the value from the land," but the "labour of the land" also contributes jointly to the value of the production.

16 Even if Ricardo is sharply criticised for "pushing this reasoning to its limits" by considering wages as made up of corn only (Sismondi, 1991, p. 283).

17 Sismondi suggests three generic cases: 1) the landlords keep the entire net product (even increased by his monopolistic position); 2) the farmers and the labourers share it all; 3) the consumers can profit from all or part of it.

18 Marx would indeed appreciate such a statement to its full value!

19 Sismondi adds also in his argument an explicit reference to Rousseau's famous "He who, after having enclosed a field, uttered the first *This is mine*.... (p. 138).

20 Ricardo, *Principles* (Ricardo, 1817, p. 115).

21 Though a constant political issue in England until their final repeal in 1846, English economists were particularly active in the debate during the 1820s

(notably, Malthus, Ricardo, Cobden and Torrens). Sismondi's article refers to the 1826 resumption of the parliamentary debate.

22 In 1826–27, this piece of legislation dating from 1815 was just over a decade old (*Importation Act* 1815–55 Geo. 3 c. 26).

23 Described at length in the *Nouveaux Principes* (1827).

24 To use Lenin's famous terminology.

25 On the systematic removal of all references to feeling and passions in Classical (and above all Ricardian) economics, see Bridel (2009).

26 And, incidentally, a paragraph that could be used nearly word for word by some critics of modern economic theory…

References

Bridel, P. (2009). "Passions et intérêts" revisités: la suppression des "sentiments" est-elle à l'origine de l'économie politique. *Revue européenne des sciences sociales* special issue, 47 (144), 135–150.

Bridel, P. (2011). Origines et détermination du "prix de chaque chose": la *Richesse commerciale* entre le coût de production de Smith et la "catallactique" de l'offre et de la demande de Canard. *Il pensiero economico italiano*, 19 (2), 85–92.

Bridel, P. (2017). Une économie politique dans le temps et l'espace: l'exemple de la théorie des prix. *Il pensiero economico italiano*, 25 (2), 19–24.

Depoortère, C. (2017). Say's involvement in the 1819 French edition of Ricardo's *Principles* and the issue of rent. *European Journal of the History of Economic Thought*, 24 (1), 80–118.

Ricardo, D. (1817). *Principles of political economy and taxation.* As reprinted in vol. I of: (1951) *The works and correspondence of David Ricardo* (P. Sraffa ed., with the collaboration of M.H. Dobb). Cambridge: Cambridge University Press.

Ricardo, D. (1819). *Des principes de l'économie politique et de l'impôt* (J.-B. Say, ed.). 2 vols. Paris: Aillaud.

Ricardo, D. (1952). *Letters 1810–1815. Vol. VI of: The works and correspondence of David Ricardo* (P. Sraffa, ed., with the collaboration of M.H. Dobb). Cambridge: Cambridge University Press.

Robinson, J. (1973). Unpublished letter dated 17 April 1973. In: Dupuigrenet-Desroussilles, G. (1976). Sismondi ou le libéralisme héroïque. *Economies et sociétés*, 10 (21), 1326–1338.

Sismondi, J.-C.L. Simonde de. (1803). *De la richesse commerciale.* As reproduced in: (2012a). Vol. II of: *Œuvres économiques complètes* (P. Bridel, F. Daldegan and N. Eyguesier, eds.). Paris: Economica.

Sismondi, J.-C.L. Simonde de. (1805). *Les deux systèmes d'économie politique.* As reproduced in: (2012b). *Ecrits d'économie politique 1799–1815, vol. III of: Œuvres économiques complètes* (P. Bridel, F. Daldegan and N. Eyguesier, eds.). Paris: Economica, 311–351.

Sismondi, J.-C.L. Simonde de. ([1817] 1824). Political economy. In: *Brewster Encyclopaedia.* Reprint 1966. New York: Kelley.

Sismondi, J.-C.L. Simonde de. (1819). *Nouveaux principes d'économie politique.* 2 vols, 2nd ed. 1827. Paris: Delaunay.

Sismondi, J.-C.L. Simonde de. (1826). On the Corn Laws. *New Monthly Magazine and Literary Journal*, 17, 349–356. As reproduced in: (2015a). *Ecrits d'économie politique 1816–1842, vol. IV of: Œuvres économiques complètes* (P. Bridel, F. Daldegan and N. Eyguesier, eds.). Paris: Economica, 373–389.

Sismondi, J.-C.L. Simonde de. (1827). Lettre à M. Julien, directeur de la Revue encyclopédique. *Revue encyclopédique*, 25. As reproduced in: (2015a). *Ecrits d'économie politique 1816–1842, vol. IV of: Œuvres économiques complètes* (P. Bridel, F. Daldegan and N. Eyguesier eds.). Paris: Economica, 439–441.

Sismondi, J.-C.L. Simonde de. (1991). *New principles of political economy* (R. Hyse, trans.). New Brunswick: Transaction Publishers.

Sismondi, J.-C.L. Simonde de. (2012a). *De la richesse commerciale. Vol. II of: Œuvres économiques complètes* (P. Bridel, F. Daldegan and N. Eyguesier, eds.). Paris: Economica.

Sismondi, J.-C.L. Simonde de. (2012b). *Ecrits d'économie politique 1799–1815. Vol. III of: Œuvres économiques complètes* (P. Bridel, F. Daldegan and N. Eyguesier, eds.). Paris: Economica.

Sismondi, J.-C.L. Simonde de. (2015a). *Ecrits d'économie politique 1816–1842. Vol. IV of: Œuvres économiques complètes* (P. Bridel, F. Daldegan and N. Eyguesier, eds.). Paris: Economica.

Sismondi, J.-C.L. Simonde de. (2015b). *Nouveaux principes d'économie politique. Vol. V of: Œuvres économiques complètes* (P. Bridel, F. Daldegan and N. Eyguesier, eds.). Paris: Economica.

Sismondi, J.-C.L. Simonde de. (2018a). *Etudes sur les sciences sociales. Vol. VI of: Œuvres économiques complètes* (P. Bridel, F. Daldegan and N. Eyguesier, eds.). Paris: Economica.

Sismondi, J.-C.L. Simonde de. (2018b). *Tableau de l'agriculture de la Toscane et autres écrits. Vol. I of: Œuvres économiques complètes* (P. Bridel, F. Daldegan and N. Eyguesier, eds.). Paris: Economica.

7 Roscher's metaphors and his theory of crises

Daniele Besomi and Harald Hagemann

Having worked on Keynesian and Cambridge economics for a great part of her academic life, Maria Cristina Marcuzzo is intimately familiar with writers stressing the importance of effective demand, and the implication of a monetary economy, as opposed to the assumption of a fictional barter system. In one of her latest writings, for example, she emphasises Keynes's denouncement of the "morbid instincts" of money-making individuals and the central role he assigned to expenditures on consumption-goods alike (Marcuzzo, 2018). We offer her this essay on a nineteenth-century author who had moved some steps along this line of thought: Wilhelm Roscher.

1. Introduction

It is sometimes boldly assumed that Say's Law was universally accepted after the end of the gluts debate and was only resurrected as a subject of debate when Keynes made a strawman out of it. Yet some traditions of thought – some minoritiarian, some frankly eclectic, but some with academic prestige – questioned the Law of markets (clearly attributing it to Say) and produced theories of crises that assumed at the outset that demand is the driver of production, and that there is a possibility – which in a monetary economy periodically becomes actual – that there is a significant shortage of aggregate demand causing a general crisis that affects the entire economic system.

This essay is on one of the academic writers who took such a stance in the middle of the nineteenth century, Wilhelm Roscher. As his theory of crises has already been summarised and discussed in some detail in recent literature (see, for instance, Gioia, 2001; Hagemann, 1995, 2012; Schefold, 2017; Streissler, 1995), here we take a different approach: instead of focusing on the specific mechanisms used by Roscher to explain crises, we use his metaphors as a guideline for reading his general and deepest perspective on crises. The rationale of this approach is that metaphors, far from being mere ornaments of speech, are widely recognised as often playing a heuristic role in the process of discovery.

At the time of Roscher's writing, the debate on crises was particularly lively in France, Britain and the US, as these countries had already been affected by a number of violent crises. Towards the middle of the nineteenth century, most theorists took for granted the validity of Say's law, which – following its adoption by Ricardo – was generally interpreted to mean that overproduction is logically impossible. Yet the general public was painfully aware that crises keep returning regardless of the Law of markets: at the time it was widely agreed that crises are recurrent with some approximate regularity (Besomi, 2010a) and that they share their main morphological traits: they are characterised by a phase of rapid expansion of trade accompanied by speculation in shares and/or commodities which quickly degenerates in overtrading and overspeculation giving rise to a commercial crisis or a panic, followed by diminishing prices, bankruptcies and widespread distress. How to reconcile Say's law with the actual systematic recurrence to crises, which surely could no longer be attributed to external events? The Law was silently circumvented by shifting the blame on credit and speculation. The following mechanism was widely advocated to explain the building up, the explosion and the reabsorption of crises: the availability of credit enables merchants to trade beyond their capital; this increases prices, and induces a further expansion of production, fed by even more credit; inflation eventually instigates speculative trading in goods, which in turn triggers speculation in shares of more and more adventurous companies. At some point, following any accidental event disrupting the mutual trust between merchants and shareholders, credit is restricted, prices stagnate or fall thereby falsifying the premises upon which the speculative movement was based, and a crisis ensues, sometimes accompanied by a panic. The description, in three phases – prosperity, crisis, liquidation – was centred around the crisis. Most writers understood the role of crises as that of re-establishing the conditions for the resumption of (unspecified) "normal" conditions of trade by eliminating the excesses of overtrading and speculation. This contrasts with the earlier interpretation of crises as a mere universally destructive anomaly, caused by any exogenous disturbance or political interference to the smooth working of the economic system which would otherwise be capable of self-adjusting.

Meanwhile, in Germany a different approach was taken by some writers. The general glut controversy that had developed in the early nineteenth had also been taken up intensively by German economists before Roscher (Hagemann, 1995). The great majority joined company with the classical doctrine of savings and investment, as developed by Smith, Ricardo and Say. This comes out best in the careful investigation of the macroeconomic role of saving by Hermann (1832, p. 372), who emphasised the beneficial role of savings and came to the conclusion that "on no account it has to be feared that the application of savings will have a negative impact on the economy."

In contrast to Hermann, Roscher's admired teacher Rau first had attempted to mediate between the adherents to Say's law and the dissenters in the general glut controversy.[1] In his long postscript to the German edition of the letters between Malthus and Say on the causes of the current sales stoppage, Rau (1821) agreed with Malthus that an increase of production does not necessarily lead to an equivalent increase of consumption, emphasising also the consequences of an unfavourable distribution of wealth. Five years later, however, in his *Principles of*

Political Economy, the influence of Malthusian and Sismondian ideas had disappeared and Rau considered equilibrium between production and consumption as a necessary condition of the wealth of nations and a general overproduction as "unthinkable" (Rau, 1826, p. 380).

Roscher followed in the tradition of the early Rau, and explicitly disputed the validity of Say's law for a monetary economy. This is the starting point of the main body of his theory, published as "Die Productionskrisen mit besonderer Rücksicht auf die letzten Jahrzehnte" (The production crises with particular consideration of the last decades), first published in 1849 by Brockhaus in Leipzig in a widely available encyclopaedia. The core of this article was incorporated in Sections 213–217 of his *Grundlagen der Nationalökonomie*, first published in 1854 and further edited several times (Eng. trans. 1877 as *Principles of Political Economy*).

Roscher's article was republished as Chapter 6 of "Zur Lehre von den Absatz-krisen" (On the theory of sales crises) in Roscher's 1861 *Ansichten der Volkswirthschaft aus dem geschichtlichen Standpunkte* (Views of the economy from a historical perspective). The materials were rearranged, with several modifications, and the additions of references and historical details. The core of the original theoretical arguments remained unchanged, but Roscher included a second main cause of crises, besides overproduction: the credit-overtrading-overspeculation mechanism. He also opted to change the terminology: the term *Productionskrise* was replaced by the term *Absatzkrise* as better characterising the essence of the disease, namely, the lack of sales deriving from a shortage of aggregate demand.[2]

Like Rau, Roscher pointed to the necessity of an equilibrium between production and consumption. *The proportional development of production and consumption*, of supply and demand, is one of the most important conditions of prosperity. All *disturbances* of this equilibrium belong to the most dangerous shocks, just as diseases of the great economic body, and it can hardly be said whether a temporary predominance of consumption, or of production, will have worse consequences (Roscher, 1849, p. 723, 1861, pp. 288–289). This reference to disease at the very core of Roscher's argument is not accidental. The metaphor not only recurs frequently in Roscher's texts, but helps to organise both the exposition and the foundations of the argument itself. Let us examine its deployment in detail.

2. The medical metaphor and the structuring of Roscher's argument

The medical metaphor was in the nineteenth century (and still is) one of the most pervasive uses of figurate language in the discussion of economic crises (Besomi, 2011). Like many other writers, Roscher referred to crises as a disease; like only a handful of other commentators, however, Roscher went far beyond comparing crises to an illness and referred to the medical approach as an epistemological guidance to the subject. His 1861 essay is in fact structured in sections titled "Physiological," "Pathological" and "Therapeutical"; in the 1849 version, the pathological section was divided in two parts, the first discussing general vs partial crises and the second also called "Pathology of the disease."

The presence of a section openly discussing the physiology of a capitalistic economy is by itself remarkable. The overwhelming majority of the theories of crises at this time referred to a "normal" state of the economy, characterised by the absence of disturbances and excesses, but such a state was rarely defined with precision. This reflects the absence of a definition of "health" in medical dictionaries of the middle of the nineteenth century, or a definition in terms of hygiene, or again as the absence of disease. Roscher started instead from a clear statement that the harmonic growth of the economy requires a proportionate increase of both production and consumption; the equilibrium of supply and demand is thus one of the main conditions for the prosperity of the economy. He criticised both the writers in Smith's tradition (Ricardo, Say, James and John Stuart Mill), who overemphasised the importance of production, and the critics (Sismondi and Malthus), who reversed the position and one-sidedly stressed demand, and argued instead that consumption and production are organically linked and mutually dependent, although he pointed out that need is the driving engine of every productive activity.

By characterising the physiology of the economic system in terms of equilibrium between production and consumption, Roscher established a reference point for the analysis of crises (as the pathology is understood in terms of a disturbance of equilibrium)[3], and at the same time, filled the theoretical gap left by most of his British and French contemporaries. While they claimed that the liquidation of the crisis would eliminate the excesses and bring about a return to a normal state, without specifying what this "normal" state was, Roscher characterised it as the equilibrium between consumption and production. He praised Canard's analogy between consumption and production on the one hand, and the circulation of blood in veins and arteries on the other,[4] and added (only in the 1861 version) a description of the "symptoms of a particularly healthy circulation":

> little bankruptcy; many exchanges, each of which is usually small in quantity, but as a whole sum up to a considerable amount that is paid regularly; many monetary payments; little actual speculation; no excessive supplies, and no special efforts to break them; a regular convergence of demand and supply.
>
> Roscher (1861, p. 289n)[5]

Roscher's discussion of the pathology is equally interesting. Having depicted the system's physiology in terms of equilibrium, by contrast its pathology was characterised by serious and general disturbances to the harmonious proportionality of the advance of consumption and production. Here Roscher found himself at odds with the mainstream position in French and English economic thought: after the gluts debate, the Say-Ricardo position was overwhelmingly prevalent that there cannot possibly be a divergence (other than temporary and restricted to a limited number of branches of trade) between consumption and production, because the producer immediately spends his earnings either in consumption or on investment goods, so that aggregate demand is bound to catch up with aggregate supply. In this view, general crises are logically impossible; and even partial gluts can only be temporary, because the shift in relative prices would attract capital towards the more profitable trades and bring production and demand back to equilibrium. If this position is accepted, there are only two possible ways of explaining crises: either they are attributed to significant exogenous disturbances such as wars or natural catastrophes or political interference (in particular, tariffs), or the Law of markets is circumvented by attributing crises to the excesses of speculation nourished by credit conceded too easily, either because of excessive greed and lack of prudence on the part of banks and merchants or because of incorrect monetary policies. The first solution was prevalent in the early decades of the nineteenth century, while the second was often adopted in the central decades of the century.

Roscher chose a different way: while accepting Say's law in an idealised world, he argued that in the real operation of an economic system there can be impediments permitting the creation of a gap between production and consumption. He compared his approach to the distinction between pure and applied mathematics, which respectively derive the laws of motion in a frictionless world and in the presence of air. Friction does not make the pure laws of motion false in themselves; they cannot, however, be directly applied to the actual world (Roscher, 1849, p. 725, 1861, p. 296). In economics, Say's law strictly applies to a barter system, but the presence of monetary circulation makes it possible for the vendor to postpone his purchases for some time. In this way, a gap between sales and purchases can be created, and general crises become conceivable within the economic system's own logic, with no necessity of exogenous shocks or faulty policies. This argument is essentially similar to that advanced in J.S. Mill's essay on the influence of consumption on production (written in 1829–30 but only published in 1844, p. 70, 1967 ed., p. 276), which Roscher does not quote; since he is otherwise fairly systematic in citing his sources, we can conjecture he was not aware of Mill's article and came to the same conclusion independently.

Roscher also adds that it is not easy to transfer capital from one branch of production to another, as would be required for levelling glutted trades and businesses with shortages; the process is often accompanied by losses and concerns, and sometimes it is not possible at all because of the actual form taken by capital. He cites, as examples, the industrial buildings and the tunnels of mines (Roscher, 1849, p. 724, 1854 [1877 Engl. transl.], p. 204, 1861, p. 289). This argument anticipates the concerns with the "fixity of fixed capital" that were evoked later in the century by the American writers trying to resuscitate overproduction theories of crises (Crocker, 1887; Crocker and Macvane, 1887; Smart, 1895; Wells, 1887).

While this makes for the possibility of general disequilibrium, Roscher also had to argue that small gaps can amplify to produce significant crises. His argument complements the occasional references of his contemporaries to the fact that difficulties in one branch of trade spread through the chain of its suppliers of machinery and raw materials. He argues (following in detail Léon Faucher)[6] that diminished income, whether generally or only in some trades, diffuses and amplifies via the diminished purchases of consumption goods.[7] In this passage Roscher's (1849, pp. 727–28, 1861, p. 303) emphasis is on the side of demand rather than on that of supply. He does, nevertheless, compare the economic system to a living organism, the components of which are interconnected rather than merely juxtaposed, so that the correct functioning of each of its parts is necessary to the health of the whole. Whether it is production outstripping consumption, or consumption falling behind production (Roscher is adamant that *all* divergences are dangerous and that it is hard to say whether an excess of production or of consumption implies more serious consequences: 1849, p. 725, 1861, pp. 288–289), the mutual dependency of each business upon the others spreads the disease throughout the entire economic body.

Besides a breach of equilibrium, in the 1861 version of his essay Roscher also considered the overtrading argument as identifying the second of "the two main causes of crises, commercial overproduction of goods and commercial over-speculation" (1861, p. 391; the passage is not present in the 1849 article). His formulation echoes the standard statement that can be found in dozens of writings at the time and earlier (for a particularly clear exposition, see Mill, 1848, Book III, Ch. 12, § 3). When trade is brisk, most merchants expect a rise in the price of commodities, and begin speculative buying, expanding their business beyond their own capital thanks to the facility with which credit is available. Prices therefore actually increase, which encourages increased production and, for a while, increased consumption, as people consider themselves rich. But as soon as any circumstance affects the general hope that prices will keep increasing, merchants will begin to sell in order to monetise their stores. While in the standard formulation the emphasis was on price falls right at the beginning of the crisis, to the extent that Juglar eventually defined crises as the cessation of the rise of prices (Juglar and des Essars, 1889, p. 1348), Roscher brought the emphasis back to the equilibrium of supply and demand: "everybody wants to sell, nobody to buy. How does this differ from a general sales crisis?" (Roscher, 1861, pp. 299–300).

The section on pathology essentially consists in examining the possible causes of a divergence between consumption and production, or in identifying the triggers of overspeculation.[8] In the next section we will see the metaphors he used to describe some of these disturbances. Let us remain focused here on the general structure of his essays and look at therapeutics. There, Roscher's general attitude on the relationship of crises with the working of the economic system is clearly brought out by the medical metaphor. His approach is explained as follows:

> But we must now move on to the therapy of the severe widespread disease, of which so far we have considered only the pathology. It will thereby be good to follow the model of rational physicians who explore

especially the natural healing efforts of the diseased body to then act by stimulating and mitigating it in the same direction. Bacon's great dictum is still true, that nature to be commanded must be obeyed.

We have learned that the essence of each sales crisis consists in a temporary preponderance of production over consumption. The cure must therefore be that either the supply is decreased to the level of demand, or the demand is brought up to the level of the supply. Hereupon the natural course of the disease follows its own path, although with violent pain that threatens both morally and politically.[9]

(Roscher, 1861, p. 363)

The implication is that any intervention by the government must assist, rather than interfere with, the natural course of the healing process, thus be limited to relieve the pain associated with the liquidation rather than trying to counteract it. The latter would only be expensive quackery that could only worsen the disease (1849, p. 741, 1861, p. 365). Intervention may therefore follow two paths. The first is prevention, for instance by publishing better business statistics, ensuring a smooth and uniform running of the administrative apparatus, and ensuring a consistent legal treatment of bankruptcies and defaults (Roscher considered the uncertainty of the law as more damaging than the vagaries of credit itself, which he illustrated by means of a comparison of a tree, more vulnerable to damages to the roots than to leaves and branches: 1849, p. 747, 1861, p. 386). On the other hand, the mistake of protecting domestic industry should be avoided (he illustrated the argument by comparison to plants grown in a conservatory and those grown in the wild, the latter being more resistant to storms: 1861, p. 368). The second is relieving those affected by the readjustment process, by temporarily loosening the fetters to free economic activity (he used the metaphor of a seriously sick patient who should at least be freed from oppressive garments: 1861, p. 374), helping distressed traders guaranteeing them advanced payments of their goods and organising relief works for the unemployed.

3. Metaphors on the causation of crises

While the medical metaphor offered Roscher the guiding line for structuring his interpretation of crises and also, more specifically, for organising his argument, other images were used more sparingly and only in connection with specific issues. One that recurs a few times but has little implications is the tide: Roscher refers to trade or production as ebbing and flowing, but he simply means "receding" and "advancing," without associating it to any of the connotations sometimes used at the time, such as the idea of periodicity or even predictability, or with the notion that the tide drags everything with it. Roscher's usage, however, involves the idea that the entire economy moves in the same direction, in contrast with the view held by supporters of Say's Law that overproduction in some other branch of business.

Other examples of figurate languages are specific to some precise points. For instance, Roscher takes up a metaphor by Schäffle, according to which waves are higher in the open sea than in ponds and rooms are only subject to minor air currents while in the open one can have high winds, to illustrate that internal trade is less subject to crises than international trade (Roscher, 1861, p. 306, referring to Schäffle, 1858a, p. 57). Similarly, he claimed that colonies recover from crises more rapidly than industrialised countries as a younger body heals faster from a wound than an elderly one (Roscher, 1849, p. 755, 1861, p. 312).

More meaningfully, Roscher uses some of the metaphors that were at the time associated with the description of the credit, overtrading and over-speculation relationship. Again, he did not elaborate in detail, but his usage is consonant with the prevailing metaphorical usage at the time by other writers emphasising the same mechanism. One is the very common qualification of overspeculation as "feverish" (1849, p. 734, 1861, p. 339). This image was commonly evoked at the time, yet it is interesting as it identifies the diseased state of the economy not in the crisis itself, but in the events and conditions causing it. As trade is a future-oriented activity, it was understood that some speculative activity is intrinsic to it. When, however, speculation exceeds that limit it becomes not only unhealthy, but cumulatively so. The reference to fever captures both these aspects (Besomi, 2011).

The cumulative character of speculation is also expressed by means of the image of a "fraudulent construction" piling up too high, which also conveys the idea of frailty and of a disaster looming ahead (Roscher, 1861, p. 335). Instability is stressed also by reference to the lack of solidity of the ground on which the whole edifice of speculation rests (Roscher, 1849, p. 739, 1861, p. 360), and even more forcefully by the house of cards trope, which Roscher also associated with fraud, giving it a moral connotation (1861, p. 331). These images were used in the literature of the time to emphasise the causative connection between overspeculation and the subsequent collapse. The crisis, in this view, results from the features of trade and production themselves, in contrast with the emphasis, more common in the early decades of the nineteenth century, on external or political causes of crises. The implication is on the selective character of crises: while the theories emphasising exogenous or political causes of crises described the crisis by means of natural catastrophes such as hurricanes or earthquakes, which affect everybody without discriminating, the building and house of cards metaphors directly connect the collapse to the nature of the building, and affect only those who have speculated too much, and in proportion to their excesses. While in the former view crises are just painful but accidental events, in Roscher's perspective crises perform a useful role in the working of the productive and commercial system: it eliminates the excesses that were at its origin, thereby creating better conditions for business.

Another metaphor used to the same purpose was that of the storm. The writers who considered crises as exogenously caused used the storm metaphor to emphasise their destructive character and their surprising occurrence (out of the blue sky). Proponents of endogenous theories of recurring crises saw instead storms as predictable (they can be seen "gathering"), and especially as "purifying the atmosphere." As storms cause a reduction of humidity, electricity and dust particles from the air, economic storms eliminate the impurity from the economic atmosphere – namely, the speculative excesses, – thus re-establishing "normal" conditions for production and trade (Besomi, 2014). Not only Roscher used the storm metaphor in the latter sense, but pushed it a step further. Commenting upon Marx's reference to crises not as phenomena that could be reduced to a single topical cause but as "big storms on the world market, in which the antagonism of all elements in the bourgeois process of production explodes" (Marx, 1859, Ch. 4, Note C), Roscher specifies that storms "fertilize the soil and purify the air" (Roscher, 1861, p. 361). Crises thus not only facilitate the recovery by eliminating the impurities of excessive speculation, but actively prepare the ground by fertilising it. This addition is momentous, as it paves the way to close the causal circle that the proponents of the recurrent crises approach left open: while most writers examined the premises, occurrence and liquidation of the crises, thus describing the morphology of crises in three stages centred around the event itself, Roscher rooted the premises for the next recovery in the very crisis that brought to an end the previous expansion.

It should be noted, however, that Roscher failed to explain how, precisely, the storm fertilises the ground. This did not prevent him from trying to follow his metaphor, albeit somehow confusedly. Immediately after this passage he interpreted the data on the Bank of France offered by Juglar in 1856 as indicating a growth cycle:

> If we take the discounting of the Bank of France as a measure for the French commercial transactions, the following cycle is repeated from 1799 almost every five or six years. It was only a relatively low starting point, then a rapid increase in the favorable years, a brief moment of stagnation, a striking enlargement in the year of the crisis, followed by a sudden collapse, which, however, still remains much higher than the starting point, so, with few exceptions, a regular growth!
>
> Roscher (1861, pp. 361–362)

Yet here he is using the word "cycle" to indicate a repetition of steps, rather than implying a closed causal circle. A footnote attached to this passage points in the same direction. At first, Roscher cites Wagner's characterisation of the build-up of overspeculation in three steps – one in which undertakings are really useful; one in which there are some excesses; and, finally, true swindling. Again, the emphasis is on the similarity in the morphology of the path to overspeculation, leaving out from the description the liquidation of over-speculative firms and the recovery process. Then Roscher approvingly cites an analogy suggested by Schäffle, who "compares the growth of national economy, which is continuous but subject to crises, with the growth of a tree, which also every year drops a set of new excrescences" (Roscher, 1861, p. 362n, referring to Wagner, 1857, pp. 229 ff., and Schäffle, 1861, pp. 193–194). Yet Schäffle's analogy was far more detailed, and stressed more forcefully the rhythmicity of crises thanks to the reference to the alternation of seasons:

> This whole process of interaction between money, as a means of buying all the means of production, and the movement and use value of the latter, can be exactly compared with the organic life process of the tree: a strong mass of sap increases in all branches during the spring, disseminates, deposits quickly the plastic forces everywhere, . . . and causes a thousandfold new grouping of the elements. After the rapid growth of innumerable new excrescences, there follows a time of lower flexibility, which in its entirety uses the sap, which has been sucked in for the first time and is preserved in full use. Internal diseases, or the external "accident" of the turn of the year, bring the crisis: first, a few, then more and more of the young formations die out, the crisis ends with the reflux of the sap, leaving behind the creations which have become durable. Entirely so is the described process. First the strong accumulation of the general means of exchange, then its ascent to the circulation by the mobilization of the means of production and its reallocation in all directions effected by it, its preservation in circulation by the productive process and the increased trade, then the disturbance and diminution of the latter, by leaving behind as it were annual rings in form of a number of firms which permanently gained strength, after destruction of other new and old ones, and finally, as a result of this disturbance and diminution, a sudden and strong return of the means of sale to the stockpiles, as is the case directly after every commercial crisis, in the strong accumulation of cash reserves by the banks. Only after some time of frost, the "faintness," the process begins anew. This representation can be confirmed in figures from the bank statistics.
>
> Schäffle (1861, pp. 193–194)

It should be noted, however, that the tree's rhythm is dictated not by its internal logic but by an external periodical force – the change of seasons – to which the tree reacts. At this time, then, there is no true cyclical understanding of crises; Roscher, nevertheless, was among those who laid the premises for a step in that direction.

Roscher's medical metaphors, according to which equilibrium is understood as economic health whereas disturbances of it are diagnosed as diseases requiring an appropriate therapy, have influenced the German literature on crises theory for more than half-a-century. This is best indicated by Pinkus's critical but respectful analysis of those authors "who hoped to extort 'objective truths' from economics by forcible application of methods from the natural sciences" (Pinkus, 1906, p. 224). Pinkus, who prefers to call the medical trope the "biological analogy," starts his insightful analysis (pp. 212–224) with the discussion of the authority of Roscher, whose metaphor has been taken over rather uncritically by many subsequent economists, and concludes that the biological analogy has reached its highest development with the work of Schäffle.[10]

4. Conclusion

Roscher's metaphors were not chosen lightly. The medical metaphor guided the structuring of the entire argument, while the more specific metaphors were picked from a reservoir of images shared by writers on the same issue and with similar ideas. None of these metaphors is original, but Roscher's usage of some of them is enlightening.

While comparisons of crises to a disease were rather common, Roscher's precise definition of the physiology of the economic system in terms of equilibrium growth of consumption and production explicitly sets the problem of crises with references to equilibrium conditions rather than in terms of vague notions of "exaggerations" on the one hand and an ill-defined "normal" or "healthy" state of business on the other. Roscher's faith in the self-healing capacity of the economic system is also expressed clearly by means of the therapeutics metaphor, although it remains unclear why any original disequilibrium would at first amplify and generalise and then reverse on its own into an equilibrating process.

The specific metaphors introduced in the 1861 revised version of Roscher's essay reveal that at the time of writing the encyclopedia article he was surprisingly unaware of the overtrading/speculation literature, which had by then an already long history; or, at any rate, he failed to understand its relevance; this in spite of being acquainted with the literature emphasising the recurrence of crises ("it has been observed that production crises recur fairly regularly at certain intervals": Roscher, 1849, p. 745, 1861, p. 380). The literature he cited in 1849 either referred to the gluts debate or to the debate between Currency and Banking schools (cited almost exclusively in the "therapeutics" section). The 1861 metaphors of the building grown too high and the house of cards belong instead to the literature focusing on speculative excesses as the recurrent cause of crises. Roscher's perspective seems to have changed thanks to the reading of Juglar: Juglar's 1856 essay – published in the *Annuaire de l'économie politique*, a source probably not easily available in Germany – is cited explicitly by Roscher in 1861, while Juglar's much more accessible article for the *Journal des économistes* of 1857 was quoted but not explicitly referred to.[11]

The power of metaphors emerges at its clearest with Roscher's understanding of storms not only as clearing the atmosphere, but also as fertilising the soil. Metaphors work by transferring to the target (crises, in this case) some properties belonging to the source in the original domain (the storm). The features that are selectively transferred by the writers using this metaphor reveal their understanding of the phenomenon. Storms were previously referred to for the damage they cause, and for the cleaning of the atmosphere. Everybody knew that rain also helps vegetation growth, but nobody before Roscher saw this property as pertinent to the target. Yet this property of storms was always there, only waiting to be used: the storm metaphor has thus been suggestive of a feature of crises that, after Roscher, several other writers incorporated in their understanding of the subject. What was not pertinent before was later recognised as relevant, and the new usage of the metaphor caught on, was repeated and further elaborated by others.

Metaphors can be deceptive, as they imply the risk that the target is characterised by the transferral of non-pertinent features of the source. But at the same time, they have a heuristic value precisely because they assist in the process of thought, not much by unveiling something that was already there, but by creating a similitude that did not exist before. But as historian of thought, we are more interested in what the usage of certain metaphors reveals as to their users: in the case of Roscher, they disclose a wealth of information that escaped by examining the "serious," apparently more objective and precise, non-figurate language.

Notes

1 On Rau see also Hagemann (2010).
2 In the sequel, when a passage is present in both editions both are cited.
3 On this see Pinkus (1906, p. 215).
4 Roscher (1849, p. 723n, 1861, p. 288n), with reference to Canard's "Curious parallel between the circulation of the blood and the circulation of wealth in a State," 1801 (title of the 1803 translation).
5 The passage is distilled from Tooke (1838, vol. II, pp. 242 ff.), reporting on the witnesses before the House of Commons Parliamentary Commission to inquire into the causes and remedies of agricultural distress, 1833.
6 Faucher (1844, pp. 140–141), referred to in Roscher (1849, p. 724, 1861, p. 290).
7 In a recent summary of Roscher's argument, Schefold (2017, p. 30) argued that this is a multiplier process. While of course the causal chain runs the same way, an essential ingredient of the multiplier is missing in Faucher's and Roscher's argument – namely, the fact that each decrease of consumption is smaller than the preceding one, which makes the process convergent. Whether and why the process is interrupted at some point is not clear from Roscher's argument.
8 In the surveys of the literature on crises published early in the twentieth century, Roscher was cited as the most egregious representative of the writers attributing crises to one or another *ad hoc* circumstances that happened to be present at the time of crises. See in particular Jones (1900, p. 35), who seems to have initiated this interpretative line, taken up for instance by Mitchell (1913, p. 4). This reading is unfairly reductive. Although Roscher does indeed examine in detail the material background of each crisis and singles out its occasioning causes, consistent with the method of the historical school of which he was one of the founders, the various original and generally disconnected disturbances of equilibrium he stressed with respect to each crisis can operate only on the premise that a monetary economy enables the disturbance to arise in the first place and that a spreading mechanism causes the original divergence to amplify and become general. His historicism induced him to focus on the narrative of the topical circumstances and prevented him from arguing that there are common conditions for the arising of all crises (contrary to the more theoretical approach of writers like Coquelin, Lawson, Juglar and Jevons, who stressed instead that the principle of causation requires identifying the common cause necessary to produce a similar effect: see Besomi, 2010b, pp. 208–217), yet it is clear that the premises

to all crises are rather general and that Roscher prefaced his discussion of actual crises with his reflections on their possibility and generality.

9 Similarly in Roscher (1849, pp. 740–741), using "production crisis" instead of "sales crisis."

10 Pinkus (1906, p. 219). For a more detailed analysis of Schäffle's crises theory (in particular Schäffle, 1858b), see also Bergmann (1895, pp. 393–403).

11 Roscher cited French theoreticians who believe that every 6–7 years "a general liquidation is necessary ...," a passage to be found in Juglar (1857, p. 38).

References

Bergmann, E. von (1895). *Die Wirtschaftskrisen. Geschichte der Nationalökonomischen Krisentheorieen*. Stuttgart: Kohlhammer.

Besomi, D. (2010a). The periodicity of crises: a survey of the literature before 1850. *Journal of the History of Economic Thought*, 32 (1), 85–132.

Besomi, D. (2010b). "Periodic crises": Clément Juglar between theories of crises and theories of business cycles. In: J.E. Biddle and R.B. Emmett, eds. *Research in the history of economic thought and methodology: a research annual*. Bingley, UK: Emerald, 169–283.

Besomi, D. (2011). Disease of the body politick: a metaphor for crises in the history of nineteenth century economics. *Journal of the History of Economic Thought*, 33 (1), 67–118.

Besomi, D. (2014). Tempests of the business world: weather metaphors for crises in the nineteenth century. In: R. Baranzini and F. Allisson, eds. *Economics and other branches – In the shade of the oak tree. Essays in honour of Pascal Bridel*. London: Pickering & Chatto, 291–308.

Canard, N.F. (1801). *Principes d'économie politique*. Paris: Buisson. (English translation of Ch. 6 as: Curious parallel between the circulation of the blood and the circulation of wealth in a State. *New Universal Magazine: or, Miscellany of Historical, Philosophical, Political and Polite Literature*, May 1803, 322–327).

Crocker, U. (1887). *Overproduction and commercial distress*. Boston: Clarke and Carruth.

Crocker, U. and Macvane, S.M. (1887). General overproduction. *Quarterly Journal of Economics*, 1 (3), 362–366.

Faucher, L. (1844). *Manchester in 1844: its present condition and future prospects*. London: Simpkin, Marshall.

Gioia, V. (2001). Crisi e ciclo nei dizionari economici tedeschi (1849–1925): alcuni temi di riflessione. *Storia del Pensiero Economico*, 42, 5–29.

Hagemann, H. (1995). Roscher and the theory of crises. *Journal of Economic Studies*, 22 (3/4/5), 171–186.

Hagemann, H. (2010). Karl Heinrich Rau et le débat Malthus-Say sur la possibilité des crises générales de surproduction. In: A. Tiran, ed. *Jean-Baptiste Say. Influences, critiques et postérité*. Paris: Éditions Classiques Garnier, 543–555.

Hagemann, H. (2012). Wilhelm Roscher's crises theory: from production crises to sales crises. In: D. Besomi, ed. *Crises and cycles in economic dictionaries and encyclopaedias*. London: Routledge, 197–208.

Hermann, F.B.W. (1832). *Staatswirthschaftliche Untersuchungen über Vermögen, Wirthschaft, Productivität der Arbeiten, Kapital, Preis, Gewinn, Einkommen und Verbrauch*. Munich: Anton Weber'sche Buchhandlung.

Jones, E.D. (1900). *Economic crises*. New York: Macmillan.

Juglar, C. (1856). Des crises commerciales en France de l'an VIII à 1855. *Annuaire de l'économie politique et de la statistique*, 13, 555–581.

Juglar, C. (1857). Des crises commerciales et monetaires de 1800 à 1857. *Journal des Économistes*, 14 (April and May) 35–60 and 255–267.

Juglar, C. and des Essars, P. (1889). Crises financières et commerciales. In: L. Say, ed. *Dictionnaire des Finances*. Paris-Nancy: Berger-Levrault, 1348–1355.

Marcuzzo, M.C. (2018). Consumption and money-making in Keynes: enjoyments of life or morbid instincts? In: J.L. Cardoso, H.D. Kurz and P. Steiner, eds. *Economic analyses in historical perspective. Festschrift in honour of Gilbert Faccarello*. London: Routledge, 215–223.

Marx, K. (1859). *Zur Kritik der politischen Oekonomie*. Berlin: Duncker. Engl. transl. *A contribution to the critique of political economy*. Moscow: Progress Publishers; online version: Marxists.org, 1999.

Mill, J.S. (1844). *Essays on some unsettled questions of political economy*. London: Parker. As reprinted in: *Essays on economics and society, Part 1*. Vol. IV of: *The collected works of John Stuart Mill* (J.M. Robson, ed.). Toronto: University of Toronto Press, 1967, 229–340.

Mill, J.S. (1848). *Principles of political economy, with some of their applications to social philosophy*. 2 vols. London: Parker. As reprinted in vols. II and III of: *The collected works of John Stuart Mill* (V.W. Bladen and J.M. Robson, eds.). Toronto: University of Toronto Press, 1965.

Mitchell, W.C. (1913). *Business cycles*. Berkeley: University of California Press.

Pinkus, N. (1906). *Das Problem des Normalen in der Nationalökonomie. Beitrag zur Erforschung der Störungen im Wirthschaftsleben*. Leipzig: Duncker & Humblot.

Rau, K.H. (1821). *Malthus und Say über die Ursachen der jetzigen Handelsstockung*. Hamburg: Perthes und Besser.

Rau, K.H. (1826). *Lehrbuch der politischen Ökonomie*. Vol. I, *Grundsätze der Volkswirthschaftslehre*. Heidelberg: C.F. Winter.

Roscher, W. (1849). Die Productionkrisen mit besonderer Rücksicht auf die letzten Jahrzehnte. In: *Die Gegenwart. Eine Encyclopädische Darstellung der neuesten Zeitgeschichte für alle Stände*, vol. III. Leipzig: Brockhaus, 721–758.

Roscher, W. (1854). *Die Grundlagen der Nationalökonomie: Ein Hand- und Lesebuch für Geschäftsmänner und Studierende*. Stuttgart: Cotta. (Engl. transl. of the 13th, 1877 ed., as *Principles of Political Economy*. Chicago: Callaghan, 1882).

Roscher, W. (1861). *Ansichten der Volkswirthschaft aus dem geschichtlichen Standpunkte*. Leipzig: C.F. Winter'sche Verlagshandlung.

Schäffle, A.E.F. (1858a). Die Handelskrisis von 1857 in Hamburg, mit besonderer Rücksicht auf das Bankwesen. *Deutsche Vierteljahrschrift*, 1. As reprinted in: A.E.F. Schäffle (1885). *Gesammelte Aufsätze*, vol. I. H. Laupp'sche Buchhandlung, 23–66.

Schäffle, A.E.F. (1858b). Zur Lehre von den Handelskrisen. *Zeitschrift für die gesamte Staatswissenschaft*, 14, 402–470.

Schäffle, A.E.F. (1861). *Die Nationalökonomie, oder Allgemeine Wirthschaftslehre*. 2 vols. Leipzig: Spamer.

Schefold, B. (2017). The growth of capital in business cycle theories of the nineteenth century. In: A. Alcouffe, M. Poettinger and B. Schefold, eds. *Business cycles in economic thought*. London: Routledge, 28–38.

Smart, W. (1895). *Studies in economics*. New York: Macmillan.

Streissler, E. (1995). Wilhelm Roscher. Zur Lehre von den Absatzkrisen. Oder: Gibt es in der relevanten Konjunkturtheorie und -politik in den letzten 140 Jahren etwas

Neues?. In: E. Matzner and E. Nowotny, eds. *Was ist relevante Oekonomie heute. Festschrift fuer Kurt W. Rothschild*. Marburg: Metropolis, 111–121.

Tooke, T. (1838). *A history of prices and of the state of the circulation, from 1793 to 1837.* London: Longman.

Wagner, A. (1857). *Beiträge zur Lehre von den Banken*. Leipzig: Voss.

Wells, D.A. (1887). The great depression of trade: a study of economic causes. *Contemporary Review*, 52 (Aug. and Sept.) 275–293 and 381–400.

8 The monetary education of John Hicks

Perry Mehrling

> I sometimes feel, looking back, that it ought to have been my duty, after writing "Simplifying" [(1935)], to have abandoned all other interests, and to have devoted myself entirely to pushing forward along the road on which I had taken first steps. As it was, nearly thirty years had passed before I got back to it [in "Liquidity" (1962)].
>
> Hicks (1982, p. 9)

There is no doubt that post-war American Keynesian orthodoxy – in particular what in previous work (Mehrling, 1997) I have called the "monetary Walrasianism" of Patinkin (1956), Modigliani (1944), and Tobin (1969) – took significant inspiration from Hicks' early paper "A Suggestion for Simplifying the Theory of Money" (1935), as also from his famous formalisation of Keynes' *General Theory* in "Mr Keynes and the 'Classics'" (1937). But the course of Hicks' own work traced a rather different path. Ultimately, he looked back on his formalisation of Keynes as an inadequate characterisation of what Keynes had been trying to say (Hicks, 1980). And, as we shall see, ultimately he built his own alternative edifice on the 1935 "Simplifying" foundations, in his final book *A Market Theory of Money* (1989). In the context of Hicks' own life, this last work arguably represents the culmination of his intellectual project, but it has been hard for modern economists to understand it, since they approach that work from their own context (see, for example, Hahn, 1991; Laidler, 1994). It is this problem of interpretation that we seek to remedy in what follows.

We are not the first to make such an attempt. Surveying the chronology of Hicks' thinking about money, his biographer tells a story of two quite separate attempts by the theorist to develop monetary theory appropriate for the very different circumstances of pre- and post-WWII, attempts so different as to seem the work of two different men, the early J.R. Hicks and the late John Hicks (Hamouda, 1993; see also Pasinetti and Mariutti, 2008). In this reading, Hicks "rejected his early portfolio approach" (Hamouda, 1993, p. 180, see also Hamouda 2008, p. 211) and developed instead a liquidity theory of money which, among other differences, took time seriously. More specifically, the portfolio theory of "Simplifying" (Hicks, 1935), on which Baumol (1952) and Tobin (1958) had built, was replaced by the liquidity theory of "The Two Triads"

(Hicks, 1967, Chs. 1–3), subsequently elaborated on in "The Foundations of Monetary Theory" (1982, Ch. 19) and *A Market Theory of Money* (1989).

But in fact Hicks never did reject his early portfolio approach, quite the contrary. Says Hicks himself in an essay written for a 1982 collection of his monetary essays (pp. 8–9): "I have, to this day, a much higher opinion of 'Simplifying' than of any other of these early papers; I would still stand by what I said in it, so far as it goes." What Hicks rejected was not what he himself said, but rather what others subsequently made of what he said. He continues:

> So in the end I had to go back to "Simplifying", and to insist that its message was a Declaration of Independence, not only from the "free market" school from which I was expressly liberating myself, but also from what came to pass as Keynesian economics.
>
> Hicks (1982, pp. 8–9); see also Hicks (1989, pp. 64–65)

In Hicks' mind there is continuity, not disjuncture, between his early and late work. Let us attempt to discover what he has in mind.

As a matter of intellectual biography, it seems more correct to say that Hicks left "Simplifying" aside for thirty years mainly because he thought that Keynes and his followers (perhaps specifically Dennis Robertson, who Hicks considered a mentor)[1] had adequately picked up the baton and were running with it. Instead, he turned his attention to other matters, such as *Value and Capital* (1939) and the subsequent "pioneering contributions to general equilibrium theory and welfare theory" for which he would be awarded the Nobel Prize (in 1972).

After thirty years, however, and Robertson's death in 1963, it had become apparent to Hicks that the Keynesians were running in substantially the wrong direction. And so he went back, picked up the baton himself, and began running in the direction he originally had in mind.[2] Like Keynes, he was committed to developing a monetary theory of the rate of interest; unlike Keynes, he insisted that such a theory was about the short term rate of interest, not the long term rate. But after thirty years Hicks was no longer a young man, indeed since 1952 he had been serving as the Drummond Professor of Political Economy at Oxford University, with all the duties of that office. It is perhaps significant that in 1965 he chose to take early retirement (at age 61), and so was able to devote the time and energy required to make the new start that he felt was needed.

Even so, it took him a long time to find his footing. Looking back in 1975, Hicks remarked:

> What does matter is that the Keynes theory [in *The General Theory*] and the *Value and Capital* theory were weak in corresponding ways. They both lacked, at one end, a satisfactory theory of *markets*; and at the other end, they lacked a satisfactory theory of *growth*.
>
> Hicks (1982, p. 291)

As of 1975, the majority of Hicks' published work had been on the theory of growth:

> the Harrod type, the Joan Robinson type, the Kaldor type, the von Neumann type, the Solow type – one after another. I felt that I had to learn them, and the best way to learn them is to write out one's own version.
>
> Hicks (1982, pp. 291–292)

On the theory of markets, however, he was still making a start.

The main reason for his slow progress on the theory of markets can be found in the fact that there was no similar list of contemporary authors for Hicks to learn by writing out his own version, so he could not employ his normal habit of work. Instead, he turned to economic history and the history of economic thought. In this regard, Hicks draws our attention to his 1967 essay "Monetary Theory and History: An Attempt at Perspective", a "key paper" that he suggests many readers "will find the best place at which to begin" (1967, p. vii).

I suggest that this is where Hicks himself began, placing himself now firmly within the Banking (or Credit) School of Thornton and Mill, and in opposition to the Currency School of Ricardo. Keynes' rejection of the "Classics", Hicks suggests, was in fact a rejection of the Ricardian tradition, and an embrace of the alternative (but also classical) tradition of Thornton and Mill. Thornton was himself a banker and so able to abstract theory from his own experience, but Mill was not and so had to build his analytical understanding from the accounts of others, especially Tooke and Fullarton. Hicks apparently determined to follow Mill's lead, starting from the historical and institutional account provided by his former LSE colleague Richard Sayers (1936).[3]

The central theme of Hicks' "key paper" is the historical emergence of a credit economy, already clearly apparent in the time of Ricardo, and the attempts by contemporaries to make sense of it. They all saw, as we see today, the inherent instability of such a system.

> It rests upon confidence and trust; when trust is absent it can just shrivel up. It is unstable in the other direction too; when there is too much "confidence" or optimism it can explode in bursts of speculation. Thus in order for a credit system to work smoothly, it needs an institutional framework which shall restrain it on the one hand, and shall support it on the other.
>
> Hicks (1967, p. 158)

In this respect, the great attraction of the Ricardian school was its message that instability is easily cured simply by controlling the quantity of money. The Thornton-Mill school, by contrast, frightened people by its contrary message that a credit system must be actively managed, and that such management is difficult. "It must be managed by a Central Bank, whose operations must be determined by judgement, and cannot be reduced to procedure by a mechanical rule" (1967, p. 164). Because of its greater attractiveness, the Ricardian school became official academic doctrine; because of its greater realism, the Thornton-Mill school informed actual central banking practice. That is where matters stood in the time before Keynes, and indeed where matters still stood in the time after Keynes, when monetarism emerged as the modern version of the Ricardian school.

From this perspective, the central problem for contemporary monetary theory, as Hicks came to see it, was that what had come to pass as Keynesian economics was also in effect much more Ricardo than Thornton-Mill, and some of the blame for that lay at the feet of Keynes himself.

> Keynes, for us, is *too* monetarist. What we need, as a simplified version of the monetary system, which will stress the things which for us are important, is something which will pay *less* attention than Keynes did to the Quantity of Money.
>
> Hicks (1982, p. 264)

That is what Hicks thought needed doing in 1982, and it is also what he thought he was actually doing in 1935 in "Simplifying". There he presents his own theory as an elaboration of one particular idea in Keynes' *Treatise on Money* (1930), but going beyond what Keynes had said in that book, "more Keynesian than Keynes" (1935, p. 64).

Just so, the inherent instability of the credit system, and hence the need for active management, is quite clearly a theme of "Simplifying", as also the importance of various frictions in keeping the system from being even more unstable than it is (de Cecco, 2008), and this by itself constitutes a kind of declaration of independence from the free market school. But what is most striking about the 1935 paper is Hicks' conception of agents, and the problem they face. "We ought to regard every individual in the community as being, on a small scale, a bank. Monetary theory becomes a sort of generalisation of banking theory" (1935, p. 74). When he says "bank", and "banking theory", we should understand him as having in mind what Keynes said in the *Treatise* in a passage Hicks later quoted explicitly. Bankers have, said Keynes,

> three categories [of assets] to choose from: (1) bills of exchange and call loans to the money market, (2) investments, and (3) advances to customers. As a rule, advances to customers are more profitable than investments, and investments are more profitable than bills and call loans; but that order is not invariable. On the other hand, bills and call loans are more *liquid* than investments, i.e. more certainly realizable at short notice without loss, and investments are more liquid than advances.
>
> Keynes (1930, as quoted in Hicks, 1989, p. 61)

Hicks' idea in 1935 was to extend this banking theory framework to every individual. That means thinking of each individual as a balance sheet, with both assets and liabilities, adjusting their money holding at a moment in time by spending and selling, lending and borrowing, repaying and redeeming debts, in light of their expectations about a future that is not just risky but also uncertain. In other words, Hicks is thinking of individuals as embedded in a credit economy.[4] A central problem that confronts such individuals, to varying degrees, is their inability to adjust their balance sheets continuously over time in response to changing circumstances and changing expectations, because of "the cost of transferring assets from one form to another" (1935, p. 67). Money is special because there is no such cost – it is already means of payment – and that is the fundamental reason people hold it.

This is where Hicks starts in 1935, and this is also where he starts again when he returns thirty years later, now generalising the "liquidity spectrum" to include real assets as well as financial assets, and now distinguishing three general balance sheet categories: Running Assets, Reserve Assets, and Investment Assets (1967, Ch. 3). Further, and this is new, we see the beginning of his appreciation for the importance of "middlemen".

> It is implied in the existence of financial markets that there exist financial middlemen (just as the existence of middlemen is a necessary condition for the working of any organized market) ... Surely it is in the operation of those who deal professionally upon financial markets that we have the clearest and most obvious appearance of Liquidity Preference.
>
> Hicks (1967, pp. 47–48)

In 1967, everyone is still a bank, but the liquidity preference behaviour of actual banks is especially sensitive and as such crucial for understanding how the actions of the monetary authority are transmitted to the larger economy.

Subsequently, in his *Theory of Economic History* (1969, Ch. 3), Hicks put middlemen even more at the very centre of the picture, as the origin of the distinct social arrangement he called the Mercantile Economy. Looking back in 1975, he reflected: "I am very convinced that for the purpose at hand [namely, the construction of a theory of markets], the specialized merchant is the key figure ... The role of the merchant in the development of market organization is crucial" (1982, p. 297). But he continued for a long time conceptualising merchants mainly as a source of precautionary demand for money, which is to say as leverage points and "listening points" (1982, p. 273) for central bank policy. It is not until his final book that Hicks finally conceptualised merchants more fundamentally as speculative dealers, and hence market makers, in both real and financial assets (1989, Chs. 2 and 8).[5]

What dealers do is to absorb fluctuations in demand and supply using their own balance sheets, by allowing inventories to rise and fall, setting the prices they quote so as to make a competitive profit above the interest rate cost of funding those inventories. "They introduce, in doing so, a little solidity" (1989, p. 71). Hicks does not say so explicitly, but it is easy enough to recognize dealer profits as the "cost of transferring assets from one form to another". Thus, what was an unexplained friction in 1935 became the centrepiece of his theory of markets in 1989.

In giving dealers a central importance, in effect Hicks ultimately rehabilitates Hawtrey – "It was Hawtrey's doctrine that the principal way in which interest affects trade activity is through its effects on speculative markets in commodities" (1989, p. 112) – in a more general form appropriate for the modern credit economy, with its enlarged role for speculative markets in financial assets.[6] Indeed, the interest rate itself is formed by the operations of "a special class of dealer who will discount bills for cash" (1989, p. 51). In Hicks' final formulation, the theory of markets is essentially about the operations of the dealer system, and the money rate of interest is the observable outcome of such operations in the money market.

All of this is essential background for understanding what Hicks was trying to do with his more formal modelling of the portfolio allocation decision (1962, Appendix; 1967, Ch. 6; 1982, Ch. 19, Part II; 1989, Appendix), which is to say that part of his work that most nearly resembles the Keynesian economics from which he wished to assert his independence. He is concerned in that work with establishing two "theorems". The first concerns the change in money demand as risk aversion changes. The second concerns the change in money demand as wealth changes. For Hicks, the whole reason to be interested in these matters is their bearing on the instability of a credit economy, a concern that goes back to his conjectures in "Simplifying" (1935), as he states explicitly (1982, p. 256, fn. 20). In a boom, arguably people on average become less risk averse, which causes them to demand less money, which drives down the rate of interest, so further fuelling the boom. Also in a boom, people on average become more wealthy, which causes them to demand less money, which drives down the rate of interest, so further fuelling the boom.[7] In Hicks' mature thinking, the second theorem is the more fundamental, presumably because it does not rely on shifting psychology as a free variable, but either way the important point is that a credit economy is inherently unstable.

Having come so far in rehabilitating "Simplifying" (1935) from the many hands have tried to claim it for the Ricardian Currency School rather than the Thornton-Mill Banking School, it would be remiss of me to close without reconsideration of the paper that Hicks did in fact repudiate, namely "Mr Keynes and the 'Classics'" (1937). We are now in a position to read that paper through Hicks' own eyes, rather that the eyes of the "econometrists" for whom he wrote it and the Keynesian economists who subsequently claimed it for their own. Later generations latched onto the sticky wage assumption, but Hicks himself quite clearly insists on the centrality of the monetary theory – "It is the liquidity preference doctrine which is vital" (1937, p. 133) – and on that point he never wavered.

The crucial point, as I now feel quite clear, on which the individuality of the Keynes theory depends, is the implication that there are conditions in which the price-mechanism will not "work" – more specifically, that there are conditions in which the interest-mechanism will not work.

Hicks (1967, p. 143)

It is true, as Hicks himself would recount, that in 1937 he was reading Keynes' *General Theory* through the lens of his own work that would soon appear as *Value and Capital* (1939), and it is that reading that he would eventually repudiate. But it is also true that he was reading it through the lens of "Simplifying", which is to say through the lens of his own interpretation of Keynes' *Treatise*, and this he never did repudiate. Quite the contrary, his main criticism of Keynes is that the *General Theory* insufficiently incorporates the insights of the *Treatise*.

I have been greatly helped by what Keynes said on liquidity in his *Treatise*; but in his later and more famous book he seems to have fallen into the trap just described. And how many of his monetarist followers – in this respect they were his followers! – he led into it.

Hicks (1989, p. 63)

What Hicks learned from the *Treatise*, and built into his own theory, was the central importance of liquidity preference as a rational response in a credit economy to the inescapable fact of uncertainty, a response that shows up not only narrowly in the demand for money but also much more generally in the management of balance sheet allocation as between Running, Reserve, and Investment Assets, real assets as well as financial assets. Every individual faces this fundamental management problem and, in the centre of the credit system, the central bank faces its own problem of managing the system as a whole. One might say that it is a problem of "stabilizing an unstable economy".[8] For that purpose, central bank tools are barely adequate, and anyway always chasing developments in the credit economy that eliminate frictions and so create new sources of instability. Most challenging, central banks are inherently better equipped to quash a boom than to ignite a recovery.

The Keynesian revolution, as Hicks understood it, was in the first place about broadening the set of tools available for managing the system as a whole, specifically to include fiscal policy the better to ignite recovery in the context of sustained Depression (1967, p. 170). But the shift in focus from monetary to fiscal policy also implied a shift from behind-the-scenes operation by central bankers to front-of-stage operation by elected national governments. Presciently, Hicks anticipated that this shift would have far-reaching consequences for the operation of the *global* credit economy, where

there is the same problem of the instability of credit. There is the same need that international credit should be managed, in order to be secure. . . . Can we find rules that are acceptable to national pride, and to national self-interest, and which yet give scope for some minimum of management – just enough to give the international credit structure the security it so sorely needs? It will be a narrow passage, but one must hope that there will be a way through.

Hicks (1967, pp. 172–173)

Thus Hicks in 1967 during the last days of Bretton Woods; thus ourselves fifty years later.

Notes

1 In his obituary notice for Robertson, Hicks takes pains to draw attention to Robertson's "years of partnership with Keynes" (Hicks, 1964, p. 309), up to and including Keynes' *Treatise* (1930), as background for understanding their subsequent rift and then reconciliation at Bretton Woods. In the end, it was not Keynes himself but rather the rigidity of those who adopted his system as a new orthodoxy that most distressed Robertson, and Hicks as well (Hicks, 1964, p. 314). Like Robertson, Hicks always preferred to build on the *Treatise* rather than the *General Theory*, and he specifically acknowledged Robertson's influence in this regard, stating that Robertson "converted me to my present insistence on the primacy of the Means of Payment" (Hicks, 1967, p. x). Here perhaps is the main reason that Hicks' brief sojourn at Cambridge was not a success (see Marcuzzo & Sanfilippo, 2008; Marcuzzo et al., 2008).
2 As he says himself: "'The Two Triads' is a revision and (perhaps one might venture to say) completion of Keynes's theory of money" (Hicks, 1967, p. vi); and "This book ... is mainly to be concerned with a refurbishing of monetary theory (largely Keynes's monetary theory)" (Hicks, 1989, p. 2).
3 Just so, (Hicks, 1967, p. x): "I have never been able to master the detail of monetary institutions; it has been an encouragement to me that Professor Sayers, who does understand them, has usually found that in the general way I have to talk about them, I am talking some sort of sense."
4 In 1935, Copeland's Flow of Funds accounting was not yet available (Copeland, 1952), but we can see the young Hicks groping toward something like that, not only in "Simplifying" but also in his subsequent textbook *The Social Framework* (Hicks, 1942). On this point, see Klamer (1989).
5 There is a puzzle here, since Hicks had taken great interest in Keynes' analytical account of normal backwardation in organised commodity forward markets (Keynes, 1930, vol. II, p. 143) and had adapted Keynes' argument in his own account of the term premium (Hicks, 1939, pp. 146–147). Both phenomena are presumed to arise from systematic imbalance in fundamental demand and supply in forward markets which speculators are willing to absorb for profit. But these speculators are not yet understood as a kind of middleman or dealer. See Fantacci et al. (2010); Fantacci et al., (2014).
6 The Hawtrey that Hicks cites is the Hawtrey of his textbook, *Currency and Credit* (Hawtrey, 1919) and *A Century of Bank Rate* (Hawtrey, 1938), not *The Art of Central Banking* (Hawtrey, 1932), notwithstanding Hawtrey's emphasis in the latter book on "the inherent instability of credit" (Hawtrey, 1932, p. 166). It is an interesting question to what extent Hicks' single-minded focus on Keynes prevented him from adequately appreciating the contribution of Hawtrey, until the very end.

7 For the latter, Hicks is explicitly thinking about businesses which experience ongoing cash calls, and financial firms that have existing financial obligations as well as assets.

8 The reference is to Hyman Minsky's magnum opus (Minsky, 1986). I do not suggest that either man knew or was influenced by the other. I do suggest a certain commonality of intellectual project with regard to monetary theory, on opposite sides of the Atlantic, and in very different voice. Hicks' acknowledgement of Axel Leijonhufvud "who started me off on this undertaking, convincing me that what I said on earlier occasions was not enough" (1989, p. 3) can be read as evidence that this commonality of project was recognised by at least one other American monetary economist.

References

Baumol, W.J. (1952). The transaction demand for cash: an inventory theoretic approach. *Quarterly Journal of Economics*, 66 (4), 545–556.

Copeland, M. (1952). *A study of moneyflows in the United States*. New York: National Bureau of Economic Research.

De Cecco, M. (2008). Hicks's notion and use of the concepts of fix-price and flex-price. In: R. Scazzieri, A. Sen and S. Zamagni, eds. *Markets, money and capital: Hicksian economics for the twenty-first century*. New York: Cambridge University Press, 157–163.

Fantacci, L., Marcuzzo, M.C. and Sanfilippo, E. (2010). Speculation in commodities: Keynes' "practical acquaintance" with futures markets. *Journal of the History of Economic Thought*, 32 (3), 397–418.

Fantacci, L., Marcuzzo, M.C. and Sanfilippo, E. (2014). A note on the notions of risk-premium and liquidity-premium in Hicks's and Keynes's analyses of the term structure of interest rates. *European Journal of the History of Economic Thought*, 21 (6), 1102–1108.

Hahn, F. (1991). Review of *A market theory of money*, by John Hicks. *Economica*, 58 (August), 410–411.

Hamouda, O.F. (1993). *John R. Hicks: the economist's economist*. Oxford: Blackwell.

Hamouda, O.F. (2008). Hicks: money, prices, and credit management. In: R. Scazzieri, A. Sen and S. Zamagni, eds. *Markets, money and capital: Hicksian economics for the twenty-first century*. New York: Cambridge University Press, 204–224.

Hawtrey, R.G. (1919). *Currency and credit*. New York: Longmans, Green.

Hawtrey, R.G. (1932). *The art of central banking*. New York: Longmans, Green.

Hawtrey, R.G. (1938). *A century of bank rate*. New York: Longmans, Green.

Hicks, J.R. (1935). A suggestion for simplifying the theory of money. *Economica*, 2 (5), 1–19. As reprinted in: Hicks, J.R. (1967). *Critical essays in monetary theory*. Oxford: Clarendon Press, 61–82.

Hicks, J.R. (1937). Mr Keynes and the "Classics". *Econometrica*, 5 (2), 147–159. As reprinted in: Hicks, J.R. (1967). *Critical essays in monetary theory*. Oxford: Clarendon Press, 126–142.

Hicks, J.R. (1939). *Value and capital*. Oxford: Clarendon Press.

Hicks, J.R. (1942). *The social framework: an introduction to economics*. Oxford: Clarendon Press.

Hicks, J.R. (1962). Liquidity. *Economic Journal*, 72 (288), 787–802.

Hicks, J.R. (1964). Dennis Holme Robertson, 1890–1963. *Proceedings of the British Academy*, 50, 305–316.

Hicks, J.R. (1967). *Critical essays in monetary theory*. Oxford: Clarendon Press.

Hicks, J.R. (1969). *A theory of economic history*. Oxford: Oxford University Press.

Hicks, J.R. (1980). IS–LM: an explanation. *Journal of Post-Keynesian Economics*, 3 (2), 139–154. As reprinted in: Hicks, J.R. (1982). *Money, interest and wages*. Vol. II of *Collected essays on economic theory*. Cambridge: Harvard University Press, 318–331.

Hicks, J.R. (1982). *Money, interest and wages*. Vol. II of *Collected essays on economic theory*. Cambridge: Harvard University Press.

Hicks, J.R. (1989). *A market theory of money*. Oxford: Clarendon Press.

Keynes, J.M. (1930). *A treatise on money*. 2 vols. London: Macmillan.

Klamer, A. (1989). An accountant among economists: conversations with Sir John R. Hicks. *Journal of Economic Perspectives*, 3 (4), 167–180.

Laidler, D. (1994). Hicks's later monetary thought. In: H. Hagemann and O. Hamouda, eds. *The legacy of Hicks: his contribution to economic analysis*. London: Routledge, 163–173. Reprinted in: Laidler, D. (2004). *Macroeconomics in retrospect: the selected essays of David Laidler*. Cheltenham: Edward Elgar, 343–353.

Marcuzzo, M.C., Naldi, N., Rosselli, A. and Sanfilippo, E. (2008). Cambridge as a *place* in economics. *History of Political Economy*, 40 (4), 569–593. Reprinted in: Marcuzzo M.C. (2012). *Fighting market failure: collected essays in the Cambridge tradition of economics* New York: Routledge, 11–30.

Marcuzzo, M.C. and Sanfilippo, E. (2008). Dear John, dear Ursula (Cambridge and LSE, 1935): eighty-eight letters unearthed. In: R. Scazzieri, A. Sen and S. Zamagni, eds. *Markets, money and capital: Hicksian economics for the twenty-first century*. New York: Cambridge University Press, 72–91.

Mehrling, P. (1997). *The money interest and the public interest: American monetary thought 1920–1970*. Cambridge, MA: Harvard University Press.

Minsky, H.P. (1986). *Stabilizing an unstable economy*. New Haven: Yale University Press.

Modigliani, F. (1944). Liquidity preference and the theory of interest and money. *Econometrica*, 12 (1), 45–88.

Pasinetti, L.L. and Mariutti, G.P. (2008). *Hicks's "conversion": from J.R. to John*. New York: Cambridge University Press.

Patinkin, D. (1956). *Money interest and prices: an integration of monetary and value theory*. Evanston, IL: Row, Peterson, and Co.

Sayers, R.S. (1936). *Bank of England operations, 1890–1914*. London: P.S. King.

Tobin, J. (1958). Liquidity preference as behavior towards risk. *Review of Economic Studies*, 25 (2), 65–86.

Tobin, J. (1969). A general equilibrium approach to monetary theory. *Journal of Money, Credit, and Banking*, 1 (1), 15–29.

9 Keynes's theory of rationality, the "weight of arguments" and Keynes as an investor in the financial markets

Carlo Cristiano

1. Introduction

Keynes's views on speculation and investment in financial markets as put forth in the *General Theory* (henceforth GT) are related to his concept of uncertainty, which is in turn related to the notion of weight of arguments contained in the *Treatise on Probability* (henceforth TP). The point was explicitly made by Keynes in a footnote to Chapter 12 of the GT, where he wrote that by 'very uncertain' he did not mean 'very improbable,' and that the distinction was the same as in Chapter 6 of the TP on 'The Weight of Arguments' (*The Collected Writings of John Maynard Keynes* – henceforth CWK, followed by the number of the volume – vol. VII, p. 148, fn. 1). Albeit implicitly, the same concept of evidential weight emerges in the *Treatise on Money* and in the reformulation of the GT that Keynes published in the *Quarterly Journal of Economics* in 1937 (see CWK VI, p. 322; CWK XIV, pp. 113–114).

The theory of probability that Keynes redeployed in his economic theorising during the 1930s had been born much earlier, well before its publication in 1921. It was, in fact, a generalisation of the theory of logical implication, in which probability corresponds to a relation of partial implication between a set of premises $h = h_1, h_2, \ldots h_n$ and a conclusion p. In Keynes's own notation, the theory of probability presented in the TP covers all the cases in which $0 < p/h < 1$, where the numbers 0 and 1 respectively correspond to the cases in which, given h, p is certainly false or certainly true.

The weight of arguments is a kind of second dimension of probability, which Keynes introduced to separate the rationality of an argument from the degree of confidence with which a rational agent can use it as a guide for action. While the probability that may rationally be attributed to any conclusion depends on the relevant knowledge h that is available, the weight of any argument based on this probability relation depends on the relative amount of relevant information that is available. As Keynes put it in the GT,

[t]he state of long-term expectations, upon which our decisions are based, does not solely depend ... on the most probable forecast we can make. It

also depends on the *confidence* with which we make this forecast – on how highly we rate the likelihood of our best forecast turning out quite wrong.
(CWK VII, p. 148)

This link between the TP and the GT remained unexplored for many years. After the pioneering studies by G.L.S. Shackle and H. Minsky during the 1960s and 1970s, it was only during the 1980s and 1990s that this relationship, and the wider connections between Keynes's early philosophical views and the GT, became the subject of research on a large scale. And it was with further delay that the other link, the one connecting Keynes's theoretical views on investment and speculation with his experience as a speculator and investor, began to be explored.

For a long time, in fact, Keynes's financial activities failed to attract any serious consideration in the literature. Everybody knew that Keynes had taken an active interest in financial markets since his undergraduate days. Until very recently, however, nobody had ever taken the trouble to investigate these activities in detail. For many years, Keynesian scholars had made do with the story told by Roy Harrod, of Keynes managing his portfolio by reading the financial news in the *Times* newspaper and making a couple of phone calls from his bed every morning. By introducing investments among the topics covered in vol. XII of CWK, Donald Moggridge made a much more serious effort. But the part dedicated to this topic in volume 12 is only the small tip of a large iceberg. Moreover, neither of the two major biographies of Keynes by Robert Skidelsky (1983, 1992, 2000) and by Moggridge himself (1992) has been of great help in providing a better sense of proportion. Even worse, while it had become evident that Keynes made quite a lot of money, especially in the stock market, the only explanations that were available for this (apparently) very good performance were Keynes's genius and quickness of mind (as Harrod seemed to suggest) and insider trading (e.g. Mini, 1995), the latter sounding much more plausible than the former to many a reader. Eventually, after many years of relative neglect, Keynes's investments began to attract the attention of several scholars.

A significant contribution came from David Chambers and Elroy Dimson (2013, 2015), who investigated Keynes from the point of view of the history of finance and portfolio management. These scholars are interested in Keynes above all as an institutional investor. Their main contention is that Keynes is to be credited for the innovation he brought into this field. Beginning in the 1920s, as a manager of the National Mutual Life Insurance Company, and especially in the management of King's College, Keynes pursued a substantial and systematic shift to equities, which he continued even after the crash of 1929, and which proved much more profitable than old-style investments in fixed interest securities and estate property. Based on the same evidence about King's College, together with additional evidence on Keynes as a manager of other institutions, various other works have been published offering reconstruction of the evolution of Keynes's philosophy of investment over time (see Wasik, 2013; Woods, 2013).

These studies have significantly extended our knowledge of Keynes the investor. However, their contribution to the history of economic thought (henceforth HET) and of Keynes's economics in particular, is only indirect, because none of them took a specific HET perspective. Moreover, none of them covered the wide and very complicated field of Keynes's personal investments, on which the surviving evidence is very extensive as well as being very difficult to handle.

The first systematic effort to cover this ground, and to view Keynes the investor from a HET perspective, has come from the research group coordinated by Cristina Marcuzzo. A different perspective, and the use of ampler archival resources, have widened the scope, with the inclusion of Keynes's trading in commodity futures and options as well as of Keynes's personal dealings in equities, leading to a different interpretation in which the links with theory and policy count more than the actual performance.[1]

On setting about taking stock of all the strands in the recent literature on Keynes the investor, some important conclusions clearly emerge. There seems to be a consensus, in particular, on the evolution of Keynes's strategy of investment. During the 1920s, Keynes and his associate O.T. Falk practised what they called 'credit cycle' investment, a short-term approach based on macro analysis and especially on the assumption that

> [c]hanges in the short-period rate of interest affect the value of long-dated securities to a greater degree than should strictly be the case, with the result that considerable profits can be made by changing from one class to another at the appropriate phases of the credit cycle.
>
> (CWK XII, p. 33)

Subsequently, at least beginning in the early 1930s, Keynes abandoned this strategy in favour of a long-term buy-and-hold approach based on an idiosyncratic and scarcely differentiated selection of relatively few equities that Keynes bought for keeps over very long periods. An element of continuity, in this evolution, is that from the start Keynes based his behaviour in financial markets on the best knowledge he could obtain. While this did not change, however, all the above-mentioned recent contributions on Keynes as an investor concur in affirming that the time horizon of Keynes's investments grew dramatically.

At least at first glance, there may be nothing strange about this. It looks pretty much like the natural way an investor like Keynes might evolve in the course of his life. After all, the short-term strategies of the earlier period did not turn out to be very successful, and with the 'humbling *déjà vu* of having nearly lost two fortunes' (Wasik, 2013, p. 84) it was natural to opt for a different approach. However, the story will be seen to be rather more complicated in the light of two considerations. First, Keynes shifted to a much longer-term approach during the Great Depression. Moreover, this change coincided with a significant shift to the US market, the one that had been most heavily hit by the crisis, and moreover both in his institutional investments (Chambers and Kabiri, 2016) and in his personal portfolio (Cristiano et al., 2017). Second, and probably more importantly, what Keynes went on doing during the 1930s flies in the face of what he was writing in the same span of years, especially in the GT. Here we find that '[i]nvestment based on genuine long-term expectation is so difficult today as to be scarcely practicable' (CWK VII, p. 157), along with a description, which has become standard reference, of the way short-term speculation usually prevails in stock markets. In Chapter 12, Keynes distinguished between 'speculation,' which is 'the activity of forecasting the psychology of the market,' and 'enterprise,' defined as 'the activity of forecasting the prospective yield of an asset over their whole life'; and even if 'it is by no means always the case that speculation predominates over enterprise,' he added that the more the organisation of markets improves, the more this outcome is to be expected, taking Wall Street as a good example in this respect (pp. 158–159). He observed that, in an ideal world, investment in the stock markets should be like 'marriage' (p. 160), as it is for the entrepreneur who owns her business, and as it was for every investor before the separation of ownership and management and the introduction of the stock market itself (see p. 150). But just when Keynes described this 'marriage' as next to impossible – because 'the fetish of liquidity' (p. 155) is the stock market's main attraction – Keynes presented his own strategy of investment as 'a careful selection of a few investments (or few types of investments)' and 'a steadfast holding of these in fairly large units through thick and thin, perhaps for several years, until either they have fulfilled their promise or it is evident that they were purchased on a mistake' (CWK XII, p. 107).

These apparent contradictions deserve to be investigated in greater detail, because the rationality or irrationality of investment is no trivial issue in Keynesian economics. As we learned from the literature on Keynes and probability, the irrationality of investment plays an important part in Keynes's economic theory.

2. Irrational investment

Compared to the, thus far, less copious literature on Keynes's investments, the literature on Keynes's philosophy presents many more conflicting interpretations. Nonetheless, it has produced important results that are now commonly accepted. For instance, it is now commonplace to mention Keynes, and not only Frank Knight, when uncertainty is to be distinguished from risk. It is equally commonplace nowadays to refer to Chapter 12 of the GT as a classic on herd behaviour and 'beauty contest' situations. More generally, and very importantly from a post-Keynesian perspective, the literature inaugurated by Skidelsky (1983), Carabelli (1988) and O'Donnell (1989) (to cite only the earlier monographs) must be credited for having provided masses of ammunition against hydraulic and general equilibrium/IS–LM model-based interpretations of Keynes's GT. In Roncaglia (2009), this ranks first among the main contributions offered by the literature on 'Keynes and probability.'

This tradition of thought has its roots in the works by Minsky and Shackle mentioned above. In Shackle's *Years of High Theory* (1967, p. 129), for instance, 'Keynes's whole theory of unemployment is ultimately the simple statement that, rational expectation being unattainable, we substitute for it first one then another kind of irrational expectation.' In this context, 'Investment is an *irrational* activity, a non-rational one' (p. 130, original emphasis). Winslow (1993) is a more recent exposition of a similar argument in which Keynes's economic agents are, and cannot help being, irrational. And in both Winslow and Shackle the point is crucial to economic theory. For these authors, the Keynesian revolution and the irrationality of economic agents stand or fall together; Keynes's explanation of unemployment stands or falls on investment being irrational.

Accordingly, as soon as the link between Keynes's notion of uncertainty and its philosophical underpinnings became common knowledge, the irrationality of investors became a commonplace in the post-Keynesian literature. In a paper significantly titled 'Is probability theory relevant for uncertainty? A Post Keynesian perspective,' Paul Davidson argued that,

> From this Post Keynesian perspective, decision makers either avoid choosing between 'real' alternatives because they 'haven't got a clue' about the future, or follow their 'animal spirits' for positive investment action in a 'damn the torpedoes, full speed ahead' approach. Such demands for liquidity and/or investments are 'irrational' from the standpoint of the expected utility model. Yet, people often desire to remain liquid to abstain from committing their resources even in the long run, and entrepreneurs often make spontaneous and seemingly arbitrary choices between alternate investments.
>
> Davidson (1991, p. 130)

Davidson then concluded: 'Post Keynesians believe that this behavior is sensible and understandable only in a world where uncertainty is distinguished from probabilistic concepts' (ibid.). This sounds like a stretch of Keynes's argument in which uncertainty, rather than being the second dimension of probability which is related to evidential weight, becomes an alternative to probability. In fact, what Davidson had in mind was probability calculus – namely the idea that probability can always be expressed by numbers, something that is altogether excluded in Keynes's TP – and the expected utility model, in which rational decision can always be derived from probability calculus.

The same argument can be found in Hillard (1992, especially pp. 70–71), where the impossibility of probability calculus seems to coincide with the impossibility to behave rationally. Once again, quoting from the GT (CWK VII, p. 161), 'animal spirits' and the 'spontaneous urge to action' remain the only alternatives to the kind of rational behaviour described by standard economic theory based on expected utility. Hillard favourably quoted the following passage from Hicks (1977, p. vii): 'One must assume that people in one's model do not know what is going to happen, and know that they do not know what is going to happen. As in history!' More recently, in 2011, Skidelsky has argued that, were he to rewrite his biography of Keynes, he would put more emphasis on Keynes's idea of uncertainty. And in this 'inescapable uncertainty about the future' (Skidelsky, 2011, p. 2), there seems to be no sign of any way out which is not paved with irrational conventions and arbitrariness (see also Skidelsky, 2010, p. 75). Keynes the investor as we now know him simply would not exist in this world.

3. The quest for reasonableness

The list presented in the section above could continue. Many books and papers have been published in which Keynes's theory of rational behaviour as expounded in the TP is used to show that investment cannot help being irrational. However, this list would not represent all the positions expressed, because other works point in another direction: given that perfect rationality is impossible, economic agents aim at being at least 'reasonable.'

Carabelli (2002) offers a definition of Keynes's logic of reasonableness and shows that Keynes had based his view of investment on this definition at least since his days as a young lecturer at Cambridge in 1910. Based on this evidence, Carabelli (2002, p. 170) proposes to put 'a notion of rationality which is in some way justified *a priori*, albeit very feebly,' in the place of 'the Bayesian notion of rationality as *coherence* and as a mere empirical *success* of prevision,' which prevailed in the understanding of financial markets during the last century. This weaker version of rationality, or reasonableness, is based on the idea of having 'at least *some reasons*.' Reasons that 'are always partial because our knowledge is always limited' and that provide a kind of rationality which 'is actually only *a priori* reasonableness.'

This definition is admittedly loose, but it offers a criterion upon which important distinctions can be made. In the lecture notes of 1910, Keynes himself distinguished between rational 'speculation' and pure 'gambling.' While speculation is rational as based on 'superior' knowledge, and therefore on an expectation of what the price will be that is more rational than average market opinion, gambling is simply taking a more or less calculable 'risk.' In this Keynesian perspective, it is the quantity of knowledge upon which an inference is made, i.e. the evidential weight, which makes one argument more rational than another. Moreover, as Carabelli also points out, with this criterion certain paradoxes typical of the standard Bayesian approach based on expected utility can be resolved, the typical example being that of the black and white balls in the urn, usually known as the Ellsberg paradox. Once the notion of weight is admitted, it is perfectly rational to behave differently in two situations in which the probability is the same (namely ½) but for different reasons.[2]

This brings us to what may seem contrasting views within Keynesian scholarship. On the one hand, for the arguments based on the irrationality of investment, there can be no Keynesian revolution in economic theory unless we are ready to admit that irrational agents exist. On the other hand, the reasonableness argument has it that Keynes's theory of rationality is powerful enough to explain behaviours that amount to paradoxes in terms of the expected utility/Bayesian models of rationality. In one case, economic agents are less rational than standard economic theory assumes. In the other case, we are told just the opposite: economic agents are more rational than standard economic theory suggests. The contradiction, however, is more apparent than real. Actually, it depends on the conflict between two definitions of rationality, one based on internal coherence, the other on the existence of some knowledge upon which arguments must depend if we want them to be rational. In both perspectives, the concept of weight plays the same crucial role, which is to show that a probability judgement may not be enough to take a rational decision. In fact, it does not change very much if we say either that long-term investment is *irrational* or that abstaining from long-term investment is *reasonable*.

As far as long-term investment is concerned, all the reasonableness argument seems capable of is to take us back where Keynes left us in Chapter 12 of the GT, where short-term speculation based on herd behaviour is the only rational (or reasonable) choice. If any *a priori* basis of knowledge is accepted as reasonable, then even an arbitrary one (as the arbitrary convention described by Keynes in Chapter 12) can be accepted. This is not the case of Keynes's 1910 notes on speculation as presented by Carabelli (2002), where there is a clear opposition between rational speculation based on 'superior knowledge' and average market opinion. In the same vein, Zappia (2015) takes Keynes's correspondence with Hugh Townshend after the publication of the GT as evidence that Keynes never abandoned the idea that suggestions could be made as to 'how alert agents should behave when they deliberately choose not to trust the conventional judgment' (Zappia, 2015, p. 148). Moreover, attempts have been made to use the notion of weight as an argument in favour of rational, rather than arbitrary, conduct. In Brady (1993), for instance, all the emphasis is on Keynes's attempts to combine probability and weight in a single index (see also Gerrard, 1995). In many other contributions, however, a similar idea of reasonableness creates the same kind of short circuit between reasonableness and irrationality that emerges in this passage from Meeks (1991); see also Lawson (1985, 1991, 1993):

> crucial though Keynes thought the impact of uncertainty on action and especially on the investment decision to be, he did not view the resulting behaviour as unreasonable or (in an important sense) irrational – rather the reverse. While stressing the role of some unreasoned elements in decision making, he can also be seen as offering an account of economic agents' rational response to conditions not just of risk but of gross uncertainty.
>
> Meeks (1991, p. 18)

Meeks' idea of reasonableness is merely negative, a kind of non-irrationality, like Dequech's concept of 'arationality' (1999, p. 178). It may indeed be reasonable to act on a flimsy basis, just like the market convention described by Keynes in the GT, when there is nothing more solid than that to base our decisions on. But this is a very weak argument: it cannot resolve the contradiction with Keynes's behaviour as an investor, and could even be grouped together with the hypothesis of investment as intrinsically irrational behaviour:

> adopting conventional means of evaluation, buoyed up by animal spirits as we take the plunge, represents a sensible strategy for doing as well as we can in the tight corner uncertainty condemns us to, allowing us to 'save our faces as rational, economic men.'
>
> Meeks (1991, p. 24)

As pointed out by Runde (1991, pp. 135–140), this kind of rationality is inevitably limited to the short run. Once again, this is of no great help in making sense of the contradiction between Keynes's views on investment as irrational and his behaviour as an investor.

4. Another possible way out of the contradiction

It would be hard to deny that in some respects Keynes's advice on how to invest appears to clash with the views on investment expressed in the GT. However, there are also some good reasons to hold that this contradiction is in fact more apparent than real.

It may be noticed, for instance, that when Keynes said he was buying assets with a view to keeping them for several years (see above, Section 1), he added that he was following the rule of buying 'cheap' assets, i.e. assets that were underestimated by the market. For this to be possible, there must be a great many people buying and selling on the basis of some erroneous (and possibly conventional) valuation. While in an efficient market no asset is cheap (or expensive) over long periods, this may be the case when only a few investors are in possession of knowledge which is 'superior' to that of others. A conclusion of this kind is also suggested in the closing section of Cristiano et al. (2017) as one the reasons that may have prompted Keynes's investments in the very speculative US markets during the 1930s, and does not necessarily imply that one should try to invest on the prospective yield of an asset. It is enough to bet on its price, albeit on a long-term basis.

However, there are also other, and more important reasons, to be considered. Rather than in contradiction with his statements on investment as irrational, Keynes's personal experience could be taken as the exception that proves the rule. Only a direct look at Keynes's experience as an investor, and at the ample published and unpublished evidence that has remained, can convey the sense of proportion that is inevitably missing in much of the literature on Keynes. For reasons of space, it is impossible to discuss here all the evidence that has emerged on Keynes's sources of information and his frequent discussions with other experts, impressive as it is. Nonetheless, the facts and figures now available in the new literature on Keynes the investor are sufficient evidence that finance was not just a hobby for him. It was an absorbing and time-consuming activity in which he invested not only his money, but also a great deal of his time and energy. Part of the money, and most of the time and energy, were spent on processing masses of data and voluminous information as well as acquiring high-quality analyses by a close circle of professionals whose expertise had long been tried and tested.[3]

The possibility cannot be ruled out that Keynes's early forays as a speculator in currencies as well as some of his investments in commodities (e.g. tin) were to some extent prompted by Keynes's access to privileged sources of information. But it is now clear that the remaining part of his speculation in commodities (very considerable during the 1920s) and his investments in equities from the early 1930s onwards were the result of a systematic study of information of market fundamentals as well as close scrutiny of a limited group of individual companies, which Keynes called his 'pets.' More often than not these studies were based on costly, rather than confidential, information.

In addition, we should not lose sight of the fact that during the early 1930s, precisely when he moved on from short term 'cycle investment' to a markedly long-term buy and hold strategy, Keynes was elaborating nothing short of a revolution in economic theory. It is at least plausible that, for better or worse, this may have strengthened his confidence in his own long-term forecasts compared to other people's, many of which relied, at least as Keynes saw it, on erroneous macroeconomic theory.

It has been suggested that Keynes's shift from short-term speculation based on insider trading during the 1920s to a long-run approach during the 1930s was probably determined on a moral ground (Mini, 1995). According to this interpretation, the decisive factor should have been the influence of Moore's *Principia Ethica*. However, while it is not clear how a book he read at the age of twenty only began to exert an influence when Keynes was about fifty years old, the problem with this idealised view of Keynes the investor (as well as with the classic one in Harrod's biography) is that it runs the risk of losing sight of an important conclusion that his experience suggests.

There were many elements (connections, individual skills, information, business analyses by top experts, cutting-edge economic theory) that, put together, concurred in increasing the weight of Keynes's arguments to a level that was out of reach for most of his competitors in the market. In his maturity, Keynes found himself in a state of exception. Compared to this privileged situation, pure insider trading looks like a game that could be left to those who did not belong to the very close elite that Keynes had entered. The problem, perhaps, is neither insider trading nor that Keynes's investment activity was to some extent in contradiction with his economics. To use a catchword from current politics, the point may be that Keynes was able to invest in a way that was decidedly 'for the few,' and certainly 'not for the many.'

Notes

1 On Keynes's dealings in commodities futures, see Fantacci et al. (2010), Cristiano and Naldi (2014), Foresti and Sanfilippo (2017), Marcuzzo and Rosselli (2018); on options, see Marcuzzo and Sanfilippo (2016). Cristiano et al. (2017) present an analysis of Keynes's dealing in equities in the US markets on private account, while a more specific analysis of the differences with his dealings for King's College can be found in Sanfilippo (2017). On the links with theory and policy, see also Fantacci et al. (2012), Marcuzzo (2012).
2 In Keynes's own example, an agent is asked to draw a ball from an urn which is known to contain white and black balls in equal proportions, and then from an urn containing black and white balls in unknown proportions. Even if the probability of drawing a white or a black ball is ½ in both cases, the agent might behave differently in the two situations, because 'the weight of the argument . . . is greater in the first case' (CWK VIII, p. 82).
3 More details in Cristiano and Marcuzzo (2018).

References

Brady, M.E. (1993). J.M. Keynes's theoretical approach to decision making under condition of risk and uncertainty. *British Journal for the Philosophy of Science*, 44 (2), 357–376.

Carabelli, A. (1988). *On Keynes's method*. London: Macmillan.

Carabelli, A. (2002). Speculation and reasonableness: a non-Bayesian theory of rationality. In: S.C. Dow and J. Hillard, eds. *Keynes, uncertainty and the global economy: beyond Keynes*, vol. II. Cheltenham, UK: Edward Elgar, 165–185.

Chambers, D. and Dimson, E. (2013). John Maynard Keynes: investment innovator. *Journal of Economic Perspectives*, 27 (3), 213–228.

Chambers, D. and Dimson, E. (2015). The British origins of the US endowment model. *Financial Analysts Journal*, 71 (2), 10–14.

Chambers, D. and Kabiri, A. (2016). Keynes and Wall Street. *Business History Review*, 90 (2), 301–328.

Cristiano, C. and Marcuzzo, M.C. (2018). John Maynard Keynes: the economist as investor. *Review of Keynesian Economics*, 6 (2), 266–281.

Cristiano, C., Marcuzzo, M.C. and Sanfilippo, E. (2017). Taming the Great Depression: Keynes's personal investments in the US stock market, 1931–1939. *Economia Politica*, DOI: 10.1007/s40888-017-0081-3.

Cristiano, C. and Naldi, N. (2014). Keynes's activity on the cotton market and the theory of the 'normal backwardation': 1921–29. *European Journal for the History of Economic Thought*, 21 (6), 1039–1059.

Davidson, P. (1991). Is probability theory relevant for uncertainty? A post Keynesian perspective. *Journal of Economic Perspectives*, 5 (1), 129–143.

Dequech, D. (1999). On some arguments for the rationality of behaviour under uncertainty: concepts, applicability and criticisms. In: C. Sardoni and P. Kriesler, eds. *Keynes, post-Keynesianism and political economy: essays in honour of Geoff Harcourt*. vol. III. London: Routledge, 179–195.

Fantacci, L., Marcuzzo, M.C., Rosselli, A. and Sanfilippo, E. (2012). Speculation and buffer stocks: the legacy of Keynes and Kahn. *The European Journal of the History of Economic Thought*, 19 (3), 453–473.

Fantacci, L., Marcuzzo, M.C. and Sanfilippo, E. (2010). Speculation in commodities: Keynes' 'practical acquaintance' with future markets. *Journal for the History of Economic Thought*, 32 (3), 397–418.

Foresti, T. and Sanfilippo, E. (2017). Keynes's personal investments in the wheat futures markets, 1925–1935. *History of Economic Ideas*, 25 (2), 63–90.

Gerrard, B. (1995). Probability, uncertainty and behaviour: a Keynesian perspective. In: S.C. Dow and J.V. Hillard, eds. *Keynes, knowledge and uncertainty*. Aldershot: Edward Elgar, 177–196.

Hicks, J.R. (1977). *Economic perspectives*. Oxford: Clarendon Press.

Hillard, J. (1992). Keynes, orthodoxy and uncertainty. In: B. Gerrard and J. Hillard, eds. *The philosophy and economics of J.M. Keynes*. Aldershot: Edward Elgar, 59–79.

Keynes, J.M. (1973[1921]). *The Collected Writings of John Maynard Keynes, Vol. VIII. Treatise on probability*. (E. Johnson and D. Moggridge eds.). London: Macmillan.

Keynes, J.M. (1971[1930]). *The Collected Writings of John Maynard Keynes, Vol. VI. A Treatise on money: the applied theory of money*. (E. Johnson and D. Moggridge eds.). London: Macmillan.

Keynes, J.M. (1973[1936]). *The Collected Writings of John Maynard Keynes, Vol. VII. The general theory of employment, interest and money*. (E. Johnson and D. Moggridge eds.). London: Macmillan.

Keynes, J.M. (1973). *The Collected Writings of John Maynard Keynes, Vol. XIV. The general theory and after: defence and development*. (E. Johnson and D. Moggridge eds.). London: Macmillan.

Keynes, J.M. (1983). *The Collected Writings of John Maynard Keynes, Vol. XII. Economic articles and correspondence: editorial and investment*. (E. Johnson and D. Moggridge eds.). London: Macmillan.

Lawson, T. (1985). Uncertainty and economic analysis. *Economic Journal*, 95 (380), 909–927.

Lawson, T. (1991). Keynes and the analysis of rational behaviour. In: R.M. O'Donnell, ed. *Keynes as a philosopher-economist*. London: Macmillan, 184–226.

Lawson, T. (1993). Keynes and conventions. *Review of Social Economy*, 51 (2), 174–200.

Marcuzzo, M.C. (2012). From speculation to regulation: Keynes and primary commodity markets. In: M.C. Marcuzzo, ed. *Speculation and regulation in commodity markets: the Keynesian approach in theory and practice*. Rome: Dipartimento di Scienze Statistiche, Sapienza Università di Roma, *Rapporto Tecnico* 21, 3–23.

Marcuzzo, M. C. and Rosselli, A. (2018). Trading in the 'Devil's metal': Keynes's speculation and investment in tin (1921–1946). In: M. Corsi, J. Kregel and C. D'Ippoliti, eds. *Classical economics today*. New York: Anthem Press, 167–188.

Marcuzzo, M.C. and Sanfilippo, E. (2016). Keynes and the interwar commodity option market. *Cambridge Journal of Economics*, 40 (1), 327–348.

Meeks, J.G.T. (1991). Keynes on the rationality of decision procedures under uncertainty: the investment decision. In: J.G.T. Meeks, ed. *Thoughtful economic man. Essays on rationality, moral rules and benevolence*. Cambridge: Cambridge University Press, 126–152. As reprinted in: J. Runde and S. Mizuhara, eds. (2003). *The philosophy of Keynes's economics: probability, uncertainty and convention*. London, Routledge, 18–35.

Mini, P.V. (1995). Keynes' investments: their relation to the General Theory. *American Journal of Economics and Sociology*, 54 (1), 47–56.

Moggridge, D.E. (1992). *Maynard Keynes: an economist's biography*. London: Routledge.

O'Donnell, R. (1989). *Keynes: philosophy, economics and politics*. London: Macmillan.

Roncaglia, A. (2009). Keynes and probability: an assessment. *European Journal of the History of Economic Thought*, 16 (3), 489–510.

Runde, J. (1991). Keynesian uncertainty and the instability of beliefs. *Review of Political Economy*, 3 (2), 125–145.

Sanfilippo, E. (2017). Keynes's trading on Wall Street: did he follow the same behavior when investing for himself and for King's? *STOREPapers*, WP 4-2017, available at: http://www.storep.org/wp/wp-content/uploads/2017/11/WP-4-2017.pdf.

Shackle, G.L.S. (1967). *The years of high theory: invention and tradition of economic thought, 1926–1939*. Cambridge: Cambridge University Press.

Skidelsky, R. (1983). *John Maynard Keynes: hopes betrayed, 1883–1920*. London: Macmillan.

Skidelsky, R. (1992). *John Maynard Keynes: the economist as saviour, 1920–1937*. London: Macmillan.

Skidelsky, R. (2000). *John Maynard Keynes: fighting for Britain, 1937–1946*. London: Macmillan.

Skidelsky, R. (2010). *Keynes: the return of the master*. 2nd revised ed. London: Penguin Books.

Skidelsky, R. (2011). The relevance of Keynes. *Cambridge Journal of Economics*, 35 (1), 1–13.

Wasik, J. (2013). *Keynes's way to wealth: timeless investment lessons from the great economist*. New York: McGraw Hill.

Winslow, T. (1993). Keynes on rationality. In: B. Gerrard, ed. *The economics of rationality*. London: Routledge, 64–87. Reprint 2003, pp. 91–122.

Woods, J.E. (2013). On Keynes as an investor. *Cambridge Journal of Economics*, 37 (2), 423–442.

Zappia, C. (2015). Keynes on probability and decision: evidence from the correspondence with Hugh Townshend. *History of Economic Ideas*, 23 (2), 145–164.

10 An input-output model for the *Tableau Économique*

The emergence of a theory of effective demand

Alberto Giacomin

1. Introduction

The inter-industry flows scheme, which Quesnay used in the *Tableau Économique* as a type of formula,[1] shares acknowledged similarities with the Leontief input-output model. Leontief himself recognised this resemblance and defined his own work as "an attempt to construct ... a *Tableau Économique* of the United States" (Leontief, 1941, p. 9).

Therefore, several scholars found it natural to adopt the Leontief model when formalising the *Tableau Économique*. However, by neglecting Quesnay's macroeconomic scheme, and specifically its underpinning theory of effective demand, this scholarship compromised its effectiveness as an explanatory tool.[2]

The mainstream Leontief input-output model, i.e. the open system with respect to the final demand, was designed as a tool of economic programming. Assuming constant returns to scale, it enables us to determine the level at which the production of the various industries must be set up in order to obtain given amounts of goods for the final uses.[3]

As a result, this model is primarily prescriptive and cannot be used for different purposes, unless it is opportunely reinterpreted.

The following chart shows the *Tableau* in its formula version.[4]

Quesnay aimed at determining the total output ensuing from landowners' expenditure on luxury goods within an economy in a stationary state. The model is comprised of three elements: (i) the extension of *la grande culture* (the capitalistic farming system based on tenancy) to the entire French territory,[5] (ii) the internal and external free trade of corn[6]; and (iii) the single tax on rent.[7]

Since Quesnay aimed to present the ideal situation to be expected from the combined effect of the above elements, which represent the main objectives of physiocratic economic policy, the analysis in the *Tableau* naturally leads to a prescriptive interpretation. However, the macroeconomic model at the basis of the *Tableau* remains a descriptive tool, designed to grasp the causal connections among the constitutive elements of the economic system. This is in line with the economists' habit of providing theoretical form to policy-oriented discourses. The general economic equilibrium theory, showing the outcome in terms of an

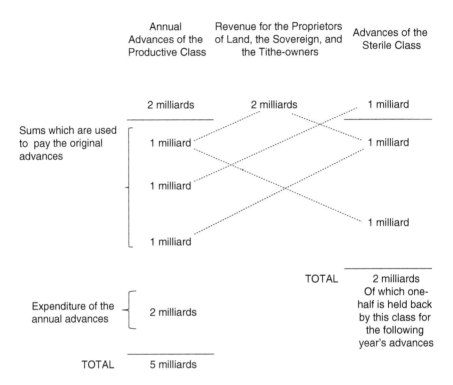

FORMULA OF THE TABLEAU ÉCONOMIQUE
Total Reproduction: Five Milliards

Figure 10.1 Meek's formula of the *Tableau Économique*.
Source: Meek (1962, p. 158).

efficient use of resources and an equitable distribution of income to be expected from a perfectly competitive organisation of markets, is also a well-known example.

To sum up, in order to correctly formalise the *Tableau Économique*, it is necessary to choose the Leontief input-output model that allows us to grasp Quesnay's macroeconomic scheme.

2. The suggestions of Phillips and Maital

2.1. Phillips

Almarin Phillips was the first to present the *Tableau* in the form of an input-output model. In his pioneering contribution,[8] Phillips stressed the existence of two versions of the *Tableau*, the so-called zig-zag and the formula. Concerning the former – specifically its 1759 third edition – he points out that it is not "an analysis of the whole of an economy," but rather "a diagrammatic representation of the regeneration of income due to the expenditure of a member of the proprietor class" (Phillips, 1955, p. 138).

Therefore, Phillips correctly identified the analysis of income determination as the theoretical core of the *Tableau*. Yet, he did not drive the necessary conclusion from such a premise. In fact, he failed to observe that the *Tableau* is based on an actual theory of effective demand and consequently adopted a closed Leontief model for its formalisation. According to this model, the landowners accounted for one of the producing sectors of the economy, which supplied land services and sourced inputs from the other sectors.

Phillips' model reads as follows:

$$(\mathbf{I}-\mathbf{A})\mathbf{x} = \mathbf{0} \qquad\qquad (10.1)$$

where the elements of vector $\mathbf{x}$ "are the rates of output of each of the three industries" and the elements a_{ij} of the matrix $\mathbf{A}$, as usual, "represent the requirements of the j_{th} industry for the i_{th} industry's product per unit output of the j_{th} industry" (Phillips, 1955, p. 140).[9] Using the *Tableau's* data, Phillips built the table (p. 141) reproduced in Table 10.1.[10]

As Phillips explained:

> Farmers produce a total of five milliards two of which they keep. One milliard is sold to proprietors and another two milliards is sold to artisans. Farmers purchase the two retained milliards of their own goods, two milliards of rental services from proprietors and one milliard of goods from artisans. Proprietors "produce" two milliards of rental services, all of

Table 10.1 Phillips' transactions table for the *Tableau Économique*

Producing Industry	Purchasing Industry			
	I	*II*	*III*	*Total*
	Farmers	*Proprietors*	*Artisans*	*Production*
I Farmers	2	1	2	5
II Proprietors	2	0	0	2
III Artisans	1	1	0	2
Total Purchases	5	2	2	9

Source: Phillips (1955, p. 141).

which is sold to farmers. Artisans produce two milliards of goods, half of which is purchased by proprietors and half by farmers.

Phillips (1955, p. 141)

Phillips was promptly criticised for recurring to the closed Leontief model as a way to represent the circulation scheme of the *Tableau*. Meek, for example, pointed out that

> Quesnay would certainly have raised his eyebrows at this model, which effectively conceals the difference between the surplus-producing capacity of the productive class and that of the sterile class, and obliges us to assume that the proprietors produce "rental services" in return for their revenue.

Meek (1962, p. 295)

Phillips' flaw consisted in interpreting the landowner class as a producing sector and, hence, in treating the varying consumption coefficients as they were production coefficients provided by techniques.

Moreover, Phillips (1955, p. 144) did not fully analyse the mechanics of Quesnay's theory and, as a result, he misrepresented Quesnay's message by stating that "the *Tableau Économique* marks the beginning of general economic equilibrium theories and well deserves mention in preface to Walras, Pareto, Cassel," to whom he also wrongfully added Leontief.

2.2. Maital

Although the limitations of a closed Leontief model had been largely acknowledged, it took some time before Shlomo Maital (1972) advanced the idea of an open model to formalise the *Tableau Économique*.

In support of his proposal, Maital (1972, p. 504) argued that "Neither the crux of Physiocratic thought (that land is the source of all value) nor the pedagogical and empirical cornerstone of input-output analysis, the inverse matrix, can emerge from a closed system." Further, Maital agreed with Meek's criticism, when rejecting a connection between rent and land services in Phillips' model (pp. 505–506).

Specifically, Maital overcame the limits of Phillips' model through a four-step design including: (i) treating "landowners' purchases as final demand rather than inputs" (p. 506); (ii) keeping the row vector of land services in the same matrix, as "the services of land, after all, do not fade away even though the old soldiers who supply them may" (p. 506). In line with these two prescriptions, Maital also suggested (iii) to shift the column vector of landowners' expenditure (inaccurately called "vector of value added")[11] to the right-hand side of the system; and (iv) to divide each element of the two (output and "value added") vectors by respective sectorial output.

The resulting input-output model reads as follows:

$$\mathbf{i} = \mathbf{v}(\mathbf{I} - \mathbf{A}*)^{-1} \tag{10.2}$$

where $\mathbf{i}$ "is a three-element unit vector" and $\mathbf{v}$ "is a vector representing value added per unit of output in each of the three sectors." According to Maital, (10.2) "can be interpreted as a system of three equations in three unknowns, the unknowns being the three elements of $\mathbf{v}$" (p. 506). $\mathbf{A}*$, the "revised 'open' matrix," is obtained by converting the flows in "Phillips' transactions table for the *Tableau Économique*" into input coefficients (Table 10.2) and then "by replacing the ½ coefficients in the landowners' column with zeros" (Table 10.3) (Maital, 1972, p. 506), as specified by points (iv) and (i) above respectively.

This way, Maital achieved the following solution:

$$\mathbf{v} = (0 \ 0 \ 1)$$

which would mean that in Quesnay's model "land is the sole source of value added (or net product, as the Physiocrats called it)" (Maital, 1972, p. 506).

Table 10.2 Maital's Table I.

Producing Industry	Farmers	Purchasing Sector	
		Proprietors	Artisans
Farmers	2/5	1	1/2
Proprietors	1/5	0	0
Artisans	2/5	0	1/2

Source: Maital (1972, p. 506).

Table 10.3 Maital's Table II.

Producing Industry	Farmers	Purchasing Sector	
		Proprietors	Artisans
Farmers	2/5	1	0
Proprietors	1/5	0	0
Artisans	2/5	0	0

Source: Maital (1972, p. 506).

As a result, Maital's model surfaced as a spurious version of the open Leontief model with respect to final demand, whose standard form is:

$$q = (I - A)^{-1} y \qquad (10.3)$$

where q is the column vector of total outputs, y the column vector of final demand and A the structural matrix of the economy. In this system, the components of q are unknown, whereas those of y are given. If $(I - A)$ is a non-singular matrix, then it is possible to determine q. In a nutshell, the model allows us to compute the sectorial outputs needed to achieve a given vector of final demand.

As previously seen, Maital divided each term of the system by its sectorial output. Consequently, the model transforms total outputs from unknowns into known terms, while the landowners' consumption (wrongly equated to value added)[12] from a known term became an unknown.

Maital's suggestion was vulnerable to various objections, concerning both the model's construction and its consistency with the author's aims. On the first point, the formulation of an open input-output model starting from Phillips' closed one was achieved through an incorrect method. Maital split up the landowners' sector into two parts: the row vector of land services that remains in the structural matrix, and the column of final demand that is moved to the right-hand side of the system and replaced with a zero vector.

In a correct transformation, the row of land services ought to be also expelled from the structural matrix and eventually laid out in a separate equation to determine "t", the amount of land services needed by the productive sector.[13] This is because land is a natural resource and hence represents an economic dimension exogenous to the model. Consequently, its services cannot enter the structural matrix of the economic system, which includes exclusively reproducible commodities.

By leaving the vector of land services within the structural matrix, Maital's model *de facto* implied that there can be an industry producing without inputs and hence at zero cost. Conveniently, this device allows to obtain a (presumed) vector of value added where the only positive element is rent and, consequently, to prove Quesnay's (imaginary) claim of the exclusive productivity of land.[14]

As for the model's consistency, it did not attain Maital's goal of yielding the inverse matrix. In fact, the set of equations (10.2) suggests that, in order to determine v, the inverse matrix is superfluous and hence the model does not highlight "the pedagogical and empirical cornerstone of input-output analysis" (Maital, 1972, p. 504).[15] The same argument applies to "the crux of Physiocratic thought," i.e. the idea that "land is the source of all value," which Maital aimed at showing with his model. However, the only result he obtained, after introducing the *Tableau*'s data, is that landowners spend a sum of two milliards, equalling to the entire net product of the economy. Surely, this fact does not imply that land is the source of all value. In contrast, it is consistent with different assumptions on income distribution and specifically with the hypothesis that landowners are the holders of a key economic resource within the power structure of the *ancien régime*.

Moreover, can the claim that "land is the source of all value" be considered "the crux of Physiocratic thought"? Despite being an established idea in the scholarship, this opinion is based on an inaccurate interpretation of the principle of exclusive productivity of agriculture. Indeed, through this statement, Quesnay meant to argue that modern agricultural techniques are more profitable than traditional ones, and that tenants, unlike craftsmen, benefited from high prices induced by bullish foreign demand for corn.[16] Moreover, Quesnay did not need the *Tableau* to have his theory accepted and, in fact he did not use it for this purpose.

To sum up, despite being consistent with the *Tableau*'s data, Maital's open model completely twists its original message, leaving Phillips's problem of presenting the *Tableau* in the form of an input-output model unsolved.

3. An alternative solution

The previous analysis showed that a satisfactory solution of Phillips' problem could not be attained without grasping Quesnay's macroeconomic scheme in the context of the French economy of the *ancien régime*. As mentioned, this scheme relies on the theory of effective demand and explains the income determination through landowners' expenditure on luxury goods as an autonomous component of global demand.[17] Therefore, Leontief open model surfaces as the most suited model for formalising the system of inter-industry flows developed in the formula version of the *Tableau*, as it determines the total output of each industry on the basis of the given vector of final demand.

According to this interpretation, the related set of equations reads as follows:

$$a_{11}\ x_1 + a_{12}\ x_2 + c_1 = x_1$$
$$a_{21}\ x_2 + a_{22}\ x_2 + c_2 = x_2 \tag{10.4}$$

$$b_1\ x_1 + b_2\ x_2 = t\ = t^* \tag{10.5}$$

or, in compact form:

$$\mathbf{x}(\mathbf{I} - \mathbf{A}) = \mathbf{c} \tag{10.6}$$

$$\mathbf{bx} = t \quad t = t^* \tag{10.7}$$

This model describes an economic system comprising: (i) a productive sector that supplies foodstuffs and raw materials (x_1); and (ii) a sterile sector that supplies manufactures and services (x_2). Production techniques are represented by $\mathbf{A}$, the matrix of input coefficients ($a_{ij;\ i,j=1,2}$) and by **b** ($b_{j;\ j=1,2}$), the vector of land direct requirements. Alongside the landowners' luxury consumption, the vector of final demand **c** ($c_{i;\ i=1,2}$) also includes the Government's and the Church's expenditure (net exports remain zero). Since landowners demand both foodstuffs and manufactures, all the components of the vector of final demand are positive.[18] Finally, t shows the land requirements of the economy, which are equal to the land available for productive purposes, t^*.[19]

Now let us consider the system (10.6). It comprises two equations with two unknowns, the amounts of x_1 and x_2 that must be produced to place the amounts of foodstuffs and manufactures c_1 and c_2 at landowners' disposal. If $(I - A)$ is a non-singular matrix, the equations can be expressed as:

$$\mathbf{x} = (\mathbf{I}\!-\!\mathbf{A})^{-1}\mathbf{c} \tag{10.8}$$

which univocally determines x_1 and x_2 as a function of landowners' consumption, given the matrix of technical coefficients. The solution of the system, once replaced into equation (10.7), yields the land requirements of the economy, t.

The full results of the system (10.8) are as follows:

$$\begin{aligned} x_1 &= \alpha_{11}c_1 + \alpha_{12}\ c_2 \\ x_2 &= \alpha_{21}\ c_1 + \alpha_{22}\ c_2 \end{aligned} \tag{10.9}$$

where α_{ij} ($_{i,j=1,2}$) are the elements of the inverse matrix $(I - A)^{-1}$ showing, by row, the total (direct and indirect) requirements of each i_{th} commodity to make one unit of commodities 1 and 2 available to the final demand. By column, the matrix shows the total requirements of the commodities 1 and 2 needed to make one unit of each j_{th} commodity available to the final demand. As a result, the amounts of product x_1, x_2 are proportional to those required for the final demand, c_1 and c_2. On the other hand, the differences ($x_1 - c_1$) and ($x_2 - c_2$) are the amounts of x_1, x_2 that the economy needs to use to obtain c_1 and c_2.

We can control the adherence of this model to the circulation scheme, displayed in the formula version of the *Tableau*, by using Quesnay's data to compute the inverse matrix of the system (10.8). Hence, we obtain:

$$\begin{aligned} x_1 &= 5/2 + 5/2 \\ x_2 &= 1/2 + 3/2 \end{aligned} \tag{10.10}$$

i.e. $x_1 = 5$, $x_2 = 2$, in line with the *Analysis*.[20]

Quesnay's "constant" price hypothesis allows us to convert univocally the milliards of *livres* of the *Tableau* into physical amounts of commodities.[21]

4. Conclusion

In this chapter we've reviewed Quesnay's macroeconomic scheme as based on the theory of effective demand. In opposition to Phillips' and Maital's solutions, it proposes an alternative interpretation of the Leontief open input-output model with respect to final demand. While Leontief originally designed his model as a tool of economic policy, this chapter instead adopts it to describe the economic theory underlying Quesnay's *Tableau*.

The model is informed by Quesnay's own assumptions, including (i) luxury consumption is the autonomous component of global demand, while (ii) the dependent components are the productive investments comprising amortisation, working capital and producers' means of subsistence. This distinction lies in the fact that rent represents a freely disposable income, as it largely exceeds land-owners' needs. Landowners can spend these rents at their discretion in terms of both amount and composition. Conversely, other classes' income is unavoidably bound to ensure the maintenance of labour force and the prosecution of the productive process.

If these assumptions are accepted the Leontief open model, with respect to final demand, becomes descriptive rather than prescriptive. This shows the positive role of landowners' class in the context of the *ancien régime*. If landowners spend the whole rent, farmers and craftsmen, after producing luxury goods for their consumption, will be able to restore the means of production and subsistence needed by the producing sectors, securing the reproduction of the system and hence the regular running of institutions (the Government and the Church).

This conclusion requires some further explanation. First, Quesnay, as a classical economist, understood the working of the economy as a circular flow that, through time, reproduced the commodities employed as a means of production and subsistence and yielded a surplus or net product. Given the power structure during the *ancien régime*, the entire net product accrued to landowners. According to Quesnay, the *Tableau* was meant to illustrate that it was possible to reach the full exploitation of productive resources, even when the institutional order of society and, in particular, the rules that determine income distribution remain unchanged, under the condition that landowners spent the entirety of their rents.

Second, Quesnay adopted a macroeconomic approach based on the theory of effective demand, whose elements can be clearly traced in his writings.[22] Namely: (i) the distinction between the autonomous and dependent components of global demand; (ii) landowners' expenditure as a major trigger of production; (iii) the income multiplier.[23]

Unlike Quesnay's, Keynes' model introduced investments instead of luxury consumption as autonomous components of effective demand, reflecting the different historical and institutional conditions of modern industrial economies as opposed to those of the *ancien régime*. Among these conditions the most significant were: (i) the landowners' loss of political weight ensuing from the decreased importance of agriculture as a share of income; (ii) the crucial role of bank credit in determining the level of firms' productive investments; (iii) a more equal income distribution, as workers are assigned a higher share of total output via increased wages.

In sum, the preceding analysis suggests that Quesnay used the *Tableau* to stress the political and economic implications of his theory of effective demand. In his view the landowners' expenditure on luxury goods determines the level and composition of total output and hence the allocation of the economic resources in the context of the *ancien régime*. If landowners spent their whole revenue, farmers and craftsmen, after having produced the same revenue, will be able to restore the means of production and subsistence needed by the producing sectors, securing the reproduction of the system and the continuation of the social structure and institutions underpinning the French *ancien régime*.

Notes

1 This version of the *Tableau*, which replaces the previous zig-zag one, can be found in Quesnay's *Analysis of the arithmetical formula of the* Tableau économique *of the distribution of annual expenditure in an agricultural nation* (henceforth referred to as *Analysis*). This version was originally published in the *Journal de l'agriculture, du commerce et des finances*, the official Physiocracy outlet, in June 1766: see Meek (1962, pp. 150–167), which contains some English translations of Quesnay's works in *Part One*. On the reason of the shifting from zig-zag to formula version of the *Tableau*, see Giacomin (1995, pp. 204–215).

2 See on this point Section 3.

3 See on this point Pasinetti (1975, pp. 78–86).

4 See Quesnay's *Analysis* in Meek (1962, p. 158). Meek, followed by Phillips, translates "propriétaires des terres," used by Quesnay, with "proprietors of land"; we have opted for the most common "landowners."

5 Quesnay compared *la grande culture* with *la petite culture* (traditional farming based on the Metayage system) in his *Farmers* and *Corn* articles, originally published in Diderot's and D'Alembert's *Encyclopédie* in 1757–58.

6 In his *Analysis*, Quesnay recognises international trade relations, but he does not factor them in the *Tableau*, where he assumes a constant equilibrium in the trade balance:

> But there is no kingdom whose territory produces all the kinds of wealth suitable for the enjoyment of its inhabitants: thus there must be external trade, by means of which a nation sells abroad a part of its products in order to buy from abroad those which it needs [...] in a situation where there is free competition in external trade there is simply an exchange of value for equal value, without loss or gain on either side.
>
> (Meek, 1962, p. 162)

7 In the *Extract from the royal economic maxims of M. De Sully*, following the "Third Édition" of the *Tableau Économique*, Quesnay points out that: "taxes ... are laid directly on the net product of landed property, and not on produce, where they would increase the costs of collection, and operate at the detriment of trade" and that "they are also not taken from the advances of the farmers of landed

property; for the advances of a kingdom's agriculture ought to be regarded as if they were fixed property which should be preserved with great care in order to ensure the production of the taxes and the revenue of the nation" (Kuczinsky and Meek, 1972, pp. 4–5). In line with this proposal, Quesnay's *Analysis* includes the King and the Church as part of the landowner class, whose total revenue accrues to the former for two sevenths and to the latter for one seventh: "with a total revenue of two milliards the sovereign's share would be 572 millions; that of the proprietors would be *four seventh*, or one milliard 144 millions; and that of the tithe-owners would be … 286 millions, taxes included" (Meek, 1962, p. 153).

8   Phillips, 1955. However, according to Samuels (1969, p. 112, 117), in 1946 George Malanos "under the supervision of Joseph Schumpeter and Wassily Leontief" included "in his doctoral dissertation at Harvard an exposition of Quesnay's *Tableau Économique* in an input-output form anticipating and reducible to that published by Phillips."

9   Phillips specified that, for example, "$a_{12} = x_{12}/X_2$ where the x_{12} is the amount of the first industry's product which the second industry purchases" and X_2 the output of the second industry.

10 On the basis of the dimensions of this table, Phillips (1955, p. 141) computed the technical coefficients of the *Tableau*:

$$a_{11} = .4 \qquad a_{12} = .5 \qquad a_{13} = 1.0$$
$$a_{21} = .4 \qquad a_{22} = 0 \qquad a_{23} = 0$$
$$a_{31} = .2 \qquad a_{32} = .5 \qquad a_{33} = 0$$

11 For further information on this point see note 12.

12 Equating **y,** the vector of final demand, to **v**, the vector of value added, is incorrect because **v** takes its place in a different model, namely the Leontief open model with respect to prices:

$$\mathbf{p} = \mathbf{v}\,(\mathbf{I} - \mathbf{A})^{-1}$$

This is a dual equation system of (10.3) where **v** has the role of known term to determine the vector of unknown prices.

13 See, for a correct statement of the problem, equations (10.6) and (10.7).

14 For further information on this point see Giacomin (1995, pp. 190–197).

15 Actually, **v** can be obtained by solving the system **i** $(\mathbf{I} - \mathbf{A}^*) = \mathbf{v}$. If $\mathbf{A}^*$ is the matrix of techniques represented in Maital's "Table II" (Table 10.3), then:

$$(\mathbf{I} - \mathbf{A}^*) = \begin{bmatrix} 3/5 & -1 & 0 \\ -1/5 & 1 & 0 \\ -2/5 & 0 & 1 \end{bmatrix}$$

By pre-multiplying this matrix with **i** = (1 1 1), we obtain **v** = (0 0 1).

16 See note 15.

17 Quesnay used "luxury in the way of subsistence" and "luxury in the way of ornamentation" to refer to luxury consumption of foodstuffs and manufactures by landowners respectively (Kuczinsky and Meek, 1972, p. 12).

18 Below the heading "*CLASS OF PROPRIETORS*," in his *Analysis*, Quesnay added: "A *revenue of two milliards* accrues to this class. It spends *one milliard* in

purchases from the *productive class* and *the other milliard* in purchases from the *sterile class*" (Meek, 1962, p. 151).

19 In his *Analysis*, Quesnay specified that the large kingdom considered in the *Tableau* had a territory, whose extent "is about *130 million arpents* of lands of different qualities …; and the population consists of about *30 million* people, who can subsist comfortably, in accordance with their positions, on the annual product of *five milliards*" (Meek, 1962, p. 151, note 2). The *arpent*, which Quesnay refers to, is an ancient measure of land area equivalent to 5107.2 sq m (see Quesnay, 2005, p. 164, note 3).

20 The structural matrix of the formula version of the *Tableau* reads as follows:

$$\mathbf{A} = \begin{bmatrix} 2/5 & 1 \\ 1/5 & 0 \end{bmatrix}$$

Hence, it shows:

$$(\mathbf{I} - \mathbf{A}) = \begin{bmatrix} 3/5 & -1 \\ -1/5 & 1 \end{bmatrix}$$

21 After having specified that the value of agricultural product resulting from using "the best possible methods" of cultivation (namely the large-scale agriculture or *la grande culture*) is *"five milliards,"* Quesnay's *Analysis* points out that: "the permanent maintenance of that value is ensured by the constant prices which are current among trading nations, in a situation where there is unremitting free competition in trade and complete security of property in the wealth employed in agriculture" (Meek, 1962, p. 151).

22 For further information on this point see Giacomin (1995, pp. 216–219).

23 The presence of the income multiplier in the *Tableau* results from the expenditure flows in Figure 10.1. Landowners' initial expenditure for luxury goods, equal to 2 milliards livres, triggers cycles of expenditure by the productive and sterile classes. The former purchases manufactures and services, while the latter goes for food and primary goods. The resulting total expenditure amounts to 5 milliards, which implies a multiplier of 2.5. As described in system (10.10), the total output is 7 milliards, which comprise 5 milliards for agricultural products and 2 milliards for manufactures and services. The 2 milliards surplus after expenditure occurs because part of the expenditure ("Expenditure of the annual advances" in Figure 10.1) is directed towards the agricultural sector. Thus, it does not show among the demand flows triggered by the initial landowners' expenditure.

References

Giacomin, A. (1995). *Il mercato e il potere. Le teorie della domanda effettiva di Boisguilbert, Cantillon, Quesnay*. Bologna: Clueb.

Kuczinsky, M. and Meek, R.L. eds. and trans. (1972). *Quesnay's Tableau Économique*. London: Macmillan. New York: Augustus M. Kelley Publishers.

Leontief, W.W. (1941). *The structure of American economy: 1919–1939*. New York: Oxford University Press.

Maital, S. (1972). The *Tableau économique* as a simple Leontief model: an amendment. *Quarterly Journal of Economics*, 86 (3), 504–507.

Meek, R.L. (1962). *The economics of Physiocracy. Essays and translations.* London: Allen & Unwin.

Pasinetti, L. (1975). *Lezioni di teoria della produzione.* Bologna: Il Mulino.

Phillips, A. (1955). The *Tableau économique* as a simple Leontief model. *Quarterly Journal of Economics*, 69 (1), 13–144.

Quesnay, F. (2005). *Œuvres économiques complètes et autres textes.* Paris: Institut National d'Études Démographiques, Paris.

Samuels, W. (1969). The *Tableau économique* as a simple Leontief model: a precursor to Phillips. *Indian Economic Journal*, 17 (1), 112–117.

Part II

Perspectives on macroeconomics in our century

11 The Clearing Union as Keynes's intellectual testament

Mario Cedrini and Luca Fantacci

Introduction

The international monetary system was a prominent and permanent interest of Keynes from his first essay on *Indian Currency and Finance* (Keynes 1971[1913]), *The Collected Writings of John Maynard Keynes* – henceforth CWK, followed by the number of the volume – vol. I) to his *Proposals for an International Clearing Union* (1943, CWK XXI, pp. 21–33, 40–66, 68–94, 108–139, 168–195, 233–235). Still, as Moggridge (1986, p. 57) once remarked, Keynes's work in international economics "exhibits several changes of views," which are usually and obviously portrayed as reflections of the varying historical circumstances in which Keynes advanced proposals of international reform. The traditional perspective wherewith scholars approach this evolution induces to retrace *the* fundamental change in the Great Depression, which is also seen as the main driver of Keynes's revolution in macroeconomics (accomplished in *The General Theory*). It becomes an easy step then to assume, however implicitly, that Keynes's international economics logically follows, rather than co-evolves with, his theory about how national economies should be managed. The main risk that this perspective entails is to lose sight, first, of the substantial continuity, despite the various positions that Keynes assumed over three decades on the ideal form of an appropriate international monetary system concerning the principles on which it should be built; and, second, of the logical impossibility to treat the "closed" and "open" dimensions of Keynes's macroeconomics as if they had an independent existence.

The present chapter wants to throw light on these aspects. We thereby try to document the "sort of order" (to borrow again from Moggridge, 1986, p. 57) to which Keynes's numerous and somehow heterogeneous contributions in international economics can effectively be reduced. Our main claim, with respect to other reconstructions of this kind (among the most systematic and synthetic, at the same time, are Williamson, 1983; Moggridge, 1986; Cesarano, 2001), is that the focus should be on the Clearing Union plan. This chapter argues that Keynes's Clearing Union represents the coherent and accomplished result of his lifelong speculation on how national economies should approach the complexity of their interconnectedness, as well as on how they can be helped by a supportive international architecture to achieve their targets. The thesis is supported by tracing the distinctive features of the Clearing Union plan, and of the international money that it envisaged (bancor), not only in Keynes's major theoretical writings, but also in some earlier and less known contributions.

The Keynes plan: objectives and features

There are evidently many possible ways of investigating the theoretical premises of Keynes's plan for Bretton Woods, depending on the peculiar perspective adopted. The Clearing Union plan is, in any case, the architrave of an international *monetary* system, and "the monetary system," as Bergsten (2013, p. 3) recently remarked, using Joseph Nye's famous dictum on the security system, "is like oxygen: you never notice it until its absence poses serious, even existential, problems." This helps to focus the attention on the specific circumstances in which the plan originated – or, that is, on the need to revamp multilateral free trade, after 1945, on bases quite different from those that had sustained it during the gold standard epoch, given the disasters of the interwar period. Yet, that the lack of a veritable international monetary system can pose "existential" problems is necessarily connected to the nature and functioning of money, which brings us to monetary theory and, in this case, to Keynes's own theory of money. The two elements, circumstances and theory, are both at the bases of the Clearing Union proposal. The plan, it has been remarked (Carabelli and Cedrini, 2010a), was explicitly designed to prevent a repetition of the "competitive struggle for liquidity" (CWK XXI, p. 40) of the interwar period. Keynes's response to the generalisation of mercantilism as nations' *modus vivendi* in the Thirties has firm theoretical roots in his theory of money. The new supranational money, bancor, is in truth, as we will argue, an international unit of account distinct from national currencies that responds to the primary aim of attenuating the characteristic feature of "money as we know it,"[1] that is, its liquidity, its store-of-value function, in favour of an encounter between debtors and creditors.

To develop our argument, we here attempt to retrace the somehow hidden structure of Keynes's reform plans, by enumerating the primary objectives they were intended to achieve, and their prominent features.

Objectives

Bearing in mind that they are not separate goals, but the constituent, and somewhat overlapping elements of a coherent integrated view, the primary objectives of Keynes's proposal for an international monetary system may be summarised in the following terms:

1   to promote free trade of goods against goods
2   to prevent the build-up of persistent global imbalances
3   to avoid the need for protectionism (*alias* mercantilism)
4   to reconcile monetary autonomy and openness to foreign trade, by allow-ing individual countries to freely set interest rates in accordance with the needs of the domestic economy.

Features

The distinctive features of Keynes's proposal consisted in:

A capital controls to stave off speculative short-term capital flows
B an alternative source of funding for temporary current account imbalances in the form of overdraft facilities provided by an international clearing institution and denominated in an international unit of account
C an international money deprived of the store-of-value function by the application of artificial carrying costs on positive balances
D an equal distribution of the burden of readjustment between creditor and debtor countries
E a system of adjustable pegs to redress persistent imbalances.

The plan, and Keynes's previous work

The seeds of Keynes's plan were sown over the previous thirty years. The main ideas that eventually gave shape to the proposal can be detected throughout his previous works, in significant passages of Keynes's theoretical writings, correspondence, articles, and proposals to reform the international monetary system. Here we consider in succession the distinctive objectives and features of the plan, not as separate, let alone independent elements (and without pretension to exhaustivity) but in view of tracing back their genealogy to a common root that is firmly grounded in the core of Keynes's monetary thought.

Objectives

1 Free trade

Free trade was established as a fundamental principle of the postwar economic order by the Atlantic Charter. For Britain, it implied renouncing the Imperial preference. Keynes was quite aware that his country could not afford to make such a commitment, without adequate guarantees that it would not create unbearable imbalances. He designed the Clearing Union as a framework capable of ensuring that free trade, on a multilateral basis, maintained its promises. Now, it was Keynes himself to observe that everything in his plan was ancillary to the re-establishment of multilateralism (CWK XXV, p. 270), which was tantamount to posing an end to the generalised trade controls of the interwar period. Contrary to appearances, as Dimand (2006) maintains, Keynes's position as regards trade is consistent over time, with the "lost paradise of pre-1914 globalization" sketched in the opening pages of *The Economic Consequences of the Peace* as the star to follow.

The "end of laissez-faire" predicated by Keynes since 1926 should certainly not be understood as an abjuration of the principles of free trade. What

Keynes's oft-quoted (perhaps seldom read) pamphlet proposes is, instead, a solution to the crucial problem of the fallacy of composition, which affects both national economies and the international environment. Broadly speaking, Keynes suggests a restriction of individual self-interest to the spheres where it has proved to be compatible with, and indeed favourable to the common interest, while envisaging public intervention in the sectors where it is necessary. It is worthwhile noting that here, Keynes mentions specifically "the deliberate control of the currency and of credit by a central institution" (CWK IX, pp. 291–292).While his plea for "National Self-Sufficiency" in 1933 is to be interpreted (see below) as an illustration of the caveat made in *Am I a Liberal*, of 1925, when describing free trade, "*in the long run and in general*" (emphasis added), as "the only policy which is technically sound and intellectually tight" (CWK IX, p. 298). The main problem with free trade, rather (to anticipate objectives 2 and 3), is that, with "laissez-faire in foreign exchange" (CWK XXV, p. 8), the analogy with barter proves to be an illusion.

2 Prevention of global imbalances

Ever since the beginning of his involvement in postwar planning, in 1941, Keynes identified in global imbalances a major factor of social turmoil and political instability, both at national and at an international level:

> The problem of maintaining equilibrium in the balance of payments between countries has never been solved, since methods of barter gave way to the use of money and bills of exchange. .... [T]he failure to solve this problem has been a major cause of impoverishment and social discontent and even of wars and revolutions.
>
> CWK (XXV, p. 27)

The reference was, more specifically, to the financial imbalances that had characterised the interwar period and that represented the burdensome legacy of the ill-conceived peace after World War I. In fact, the need to reduce international debts, and particularly war debts between the Allies, instead of imposing the onus of their repayment entirely on the shoulders of the defeated enemy in the form of reparations, had been the main argument set forth by Keynes in *The Economic Consequences of the Peace*:

> The war has ended with everyone owing everyone else immense sums of money. Germany owes a large sum to the Allies; the Allies owe a large sum to Great Britain; and Great Britain owes a large sum to the United States. .... The whole position is in the highest degree artificial, mislead-ing, and vexatious. We shall never be able to move again, unless we can free our limbs from these paper shackles. A general bonfire is so great a necessity that unless we can make of it an orderly and good-tempered affair in which no serious injustice is done to anyone, it will, when it

comes at last, grow into a conflagration that may destroy much else as well.

CWK (II, pp. 177–178)

But Keynes's argument is, more generally, one against mercantilism (see Carabelli and Cedrini, 2015; Kregel, 2015). German reparations can only be paid through net exports, which, however, require creditors (the United States, the only net creditor at the end of the conflict, and European countries themselves, at the risk of scrapping their own export industries) to open markets, eliminate trade barriers, and run external deficits.

3 Avoidance of protectionism

The Clearing Union was explicitly designed by Keynes to "make unnecessary those methods of restriction and discrimination which countries have adopted hitherto, not on their merits, but as measures of self-protection from disruptive outside forces" (CWK XXV, p. 449). Keynes viewed mercantilism as a *pis-aller*, an expedient adopted by governments to defend the domestic economy in the context of an international monetary system that set national interests against one another. This position was held consistently by Keynes throughout the decades (see Carabelli and Cedrini, 2015). Already in 1913, in *Indian Currency and Finance*, he denounced "the original sin of mercantilism" (CWK I, pp. 125–126). In the interwar period, Keynes criticised mounting mercantilism since the early Thirties. He accused creditors of having created an environment where each government was trying "to make its international balance sheet more liquid by restricting imports and stimulating exports by every possible means, the success of each one in this direction meaning the defeat of someone else" (CWK XXI, p. 40). True, in *The General Theory*, Chapter 23, Keynes praised the virtues of mercantilists, whose correct analysis of the tensions inherent to "monetary economies of production," to use Keynes's own words, provides theoretical support to policies ultimately aiming at exporting unemployment, as an expedient against the shortcomings of "golden fetters" of excessively rigid systems like the gold standard. Yet, as the pragmatic philosophy of "practical protectionism" (Radice, 1988) exposed in *National Self-sufficiency* makes sufficiently clear, mercantilism is a *national* solution to an *international* problem: a means to safeguard the policy autonomy required by each state to pursue full employment (CWK XXI, pp. 233–246), in a fundamentally anarchic environment (Cairncross 1978) that makes it otherwise impossible to achieve this result.

4 Reconciliation of autonomy and openness

To preserve the autonomy of monetary policy, without renouncing the benefits of free trade, is one of the explicit goals of the Keynes plan: "the whole management of the domestic economy depends upon being free to have the appropriate rate of interest without reference to the rates prevailing elsewhere in the world" (CWK XXV, p. 149). The international system presents a "dilemma," as Keynes called it in *A Treatise on Money*, (CWK V, p. 325) to individual countries, under the form of a choice to be made between the stability of local currencies in terms of the international standard and national autonomy over the interest rate. Already in the *General Theory*, Keynes had claimed the need to allow each country to pursue the latter policy and had condemned the gold standard for putting the interest of one country against those of its neighbours (CWK VII, p. 349). The Clearing Union was designed precisely to achieve the conditions envisaged in the *General Theory*, by establishing an international framework where the interests of member states would not be in contrast with the balance of the world economy as a whole. Nations can "learn to provide themselves with full employment by their domestic policy" and international trade can be what it should, namely "a willing and unimpeded exchange of goods and services in conditions of mutual advantages" (CWK VII, p. 382).

> It is the policy of an autonomous rate of interest, unimpeded by international preoccupations, and of a national investment programme directed to an optimum level of domestic employment which is twice blessed in the sense that it helps ourselves and our neighbours at the same time. And it is the simultaneous pursuit of these policies by all countries together which is capable of restoring economic health and strength internationally, whether we measure it by the level of domestic employment or by the volume of international trade.
>
> CWK (VII, p. 349)

Keynesian policies cannot work properly "in one country," and need a supportive international architecture, to the contrary of the "progress towards negation" policies (CWK XXI, p. 40) employed during the economic juggernaut of the Thirties (when nations, if we are to follow the logic of *The End of Laissez-Faire*, were playing the zero-sum game of mercantilism, with malign neglect for the system's general interest). The following enumerates the main features of Keynes's desired reform.

Features

A Capital controls

The Clearing Union was intended to finance temporary current account imbalances, while restricting movements on capital account. To be sure, at the time, Keynes was not alone in advocating capital controls. In fact, this was perhaps the major point of agreement (and one of the main traits of the miracle that favoured the creation of the new order; see Ikenberry, 1993; Rodrik, 2011) between the US and UK delegations throughout the bilateral negotiations leading to Bretton Woods. And capital controls were indeed the most distinctive feature of the international financial system that was eventually established.

However, Keynes's scepticism towards the virtues of free capital flows can be traced back at least to the *General Theory* (and, in truth, to *A Treatise on Money*: see Dimand, 2006). In Chapter 12, Keynes identifies in short-term financial flows a major cause of instability in the level of investments and outputs, and suggests that the evil effects of speculation could be overcome by reducing, and ideally even abolishing, the liquidity of investments:

> The spectacle of modern investment markets has sometimes moved me towards the conclusion that to make the purchase of an investment permanent and indissoluble, like marriage, except by reason of death or other grave cause, might be a useful remedy for our contemporary evils. For this would force the investor to direct his mind to the long-term prospects and to those only.
>
> CWK (VII, p. 160)

The restriction of international capital flows to foreign direct investments, and the exclusion of liquid portfolio movements, responds to the same intention of favouring long-term commitments over short-term speculation.

B Overdraft facilities

Everything is ancillary to multilateralism, in the Clearing Union plan. And multilateralism serves the purpose of free trade – whose "virtue ... depends on international trade being carried on by means of what is, in effect, barter" (CWK XXV, p. 8). The Clearing Union seems to be designed along the lines of the description of commerce that Keynes (1914) had found thirty years before in the article "What is money?" by Mitchell-Innes that he had reviewed for the *Economic Journal*:

> By buying we become debtors and by selling we become creditors, and being all both buyers and sellers we are all debtors and creditors. As debtor we can compel our creditor to cancel our obligation to him by handing to him his own acknowledgment of a debt to an equivalent amount which he, in his turn, has incurred. For example, A having bought goods from B to the value of 4100, is B's debtor for that amount. A can rid himself of his obligation to B by selling to C goods of an equivalent value and taking from him in payment an acknowledgment of debt which he (C, that is to say) has received from B. By presenting this acknowledgment to B, A can compel him to cancel the debt due to him. A has used the credit which he has procured to release himself from his debt. It is his privilege.
>
> Mitchell-Innes (1913, p. 393)

This is also the basis of the "overdraft facilities" principle of the Clearing Union. Keynes developed it after recognising the merits of the general philosophy underlying the system of bilateral payments agreements with capital controls established by

Germany between 1934 and 1937 with European and Latin American countries to conduct trade without foreign exchange, as an international barter centred on Berlin. It was the very "simple idea," says Kregel (2015, p. 7), of the banking principle invoked by Keynes – "the necessary equality of debits and credits, of assets and liabilities" (CWK XXV, p. 44) – : "financial stability [is] predicated on a balance between imports and exports" (Kregel, 2015, p. 7). After all, as Keynes observed, "the one trading transaction must necessarily find its counterpart in another trading transaction sooner or later" (CWK XXV, p. 18). The creation of a Clearing Union

> eliminated national currency payments for imports and exports; countries received credits or debits in a notional unit of account fixed to the national currency. Since the unit of account could not be traded, bought, or sold, it would not be an international reserve currency. The implication was that there would be no need for a market for "foreign" currency or reserve balances, and thus no impact of volatile exchange rates on relative prices of international goods, or tradable and non-tradable goods.
>
> (ibid.)

C Artificial carrying costs

It follows from what precedes that, if overdraft facilities are not a possibility for debtor countries to circumvent discipline, they "do not involve particular indebtedness between one member-State and another" (CWK XXV, p. 74), exactly because they are conceived as a (temporary) means of reaching the balance between exports and imports. This also means that they cannot be "a real burden to others" creditors (ibid.): they simply represent "those resources which a country voluntarily chooses to leave idle ... a potentiality of purchasing power, which [creditor countries are] entitled to use at any time" (ibid.). Provided they use it, thereby easing international adjustment. Positive bancor balances accrued by surplus countries would be subject to charges (and indeed to an outright expropriation for the part exceeding the country's quota, in the early drafts of the proposal). Unlike other international currencies – such as gold, sterling, dollar, or even IMF's Special Drawing Rights – bancor cannot be considered, strictly speaking, a reserve asset. In fact, it was not intended to perform the store-of-value function. On the contrary, the charges imposed on positive bancor balances would act as a sort of artificial carrying cost, designed to discourage the accumulation of idle balances by surplus countries and to incentivise the expenditure of bancor in support of global demand.

This may be regarded as the truly distinctive feature of Keynes's proposal: departing from the ordinary banking principle, which was otherwise taken as the explicit source of inspiration for the plan, the Clearing Union imposed a sort of negative interest rate on creditors, and not just on debtors.

This feature may be understood as a way of addressing the crucial flaw of the economic system that Keynes had detected in *The General Theory*, namely the characterisation of money as a "safe asset," capable of diverting savings from finding an outlet in real investments. In Chapter 17, Keynes explained that the tendency of the rate of interest to exceed the level required to attain full employment was due to the fact that money, unlike other assets, could be accumulated indefinitely without loss. And he concluded with one of the rare policy recommendations of *The General Theory*:

> Thus those reformers, who look for a remedy by creating artificial carrying-costs for money through the device of requiring legal-tender currency to be periodically stamped at a prescribed cost in order to retain its quality as money, or in analogous ways, have been on the right track; and the practical value of their proposals deserves consideration.
>
> CWK (VII, p. 234)

The reference is, in particular, to Silvio Gesell and to his proposal of a stamped money, on which Keynes returns with expressions of appreciation in Chapter 23: "The idea behind stamped money is sound" (CWK VII, p. 357). Bancor may be seen as an international money incorporating the principle underlying similar proposals: an artificial carrying cost, in the form of charges on positive balances, aimed at relieving world trade from the contractionary pressures produced by the accumulation of credits by surplus (mercantilist) countries.

It is interesting to note, as a confirmation of this intuition, that the article of the Clearing Union plan prescribing such charges was dubbed by Keynes and Harrod in their correspondence the "Gesell clause." The Clearing Union was, truly, an antidote to diseases like the one affecting the international environment in the Thirties, when each government tried "to make its international balance sheet more liquid by restricting imports and stimulating exports by every possible means," and had "to stop capital development within its own borders for fear of the effect on its international balance" (CWK XXV, p. 40).

D Symmetry and creditor involvement

In the Clearing Union, a credit always involves a debt. Bancor is not a mere purchasing power, but also an obligation to purchase:

> a country finding itself in a creditor position *against the rest of the world as a whole* should enter into an obligation to dispose of this credit balance and not to allow it meanwhile to exercise a contractionist pressure against the world economy and, by repercussion, against the economy of the creditor country itself. This would give us, and all others, the great assistance of multilateral clearing.
>
> (CWK XXV, p. 47; emphasis in the original)

The idea of contrasting the contractionist pressure exerted on the economic system by creditors accumulating idle balances is in line with the "euthanasia of the rentier" advocated by Keynes in the *General Theory*: "the euthanasia of the cumulative oppressive power of the capitalist to exploit the scarcity-value of capital" (CWK VII, p. 376). Bancor is not a scarce currency, lent by creditors to debtors at a price, but a currency created by the Clearing Union in proportion to the requirements of international trade, and with a built-in reminder for creditor countries of their obligation to dispose of their credit, and thereby sustain global demand.

Remarkably, a similar conception of money may be found in a manuscript note among the preparatory writings for *A Treatise on Money*: "Characteristic of money that each man is at the mercy of his neighbours" (Keynes Papers TM/2/302). In 1932, writing on Inter-Allied indebtedness, Keynes had warned that the "sanctity of contract" (CWK XVIII, p. 384) is valid only if "creditors are reasonable ... Internationally, contract has nothing to support it except the self-respect and self-interest of the debtor" (ibid.). It is a specific "duty of the creditor not to frustrate payment": debtors cannot be asked to sacrifice their "self-respect and self-interest" in favour of "narrow calculations of financial self-interest" on the part of the creditor (p. 385). This line of reasoning already permeated both the *Tract on Monetary Reform* and, as known, *The Economic Consequences of the Peace* (see Carabelli and Cedrini, 2010b; Marcuzzo, 2010). The legitimate interest of the creditors to see their credits repaid, in Keynes's vision, is always subordinated to the superior, collective interest of ensuring the actual possibility for debts to be repaid.

It is Keynes himself who presents the Clearing Union as the concrete – and radical – realisation of this reasoning, when he observes that "the substitution of a credit mechanism for hoarding would have repeated in the international field the same miracle already performed in the domestic field of turning a stone into bread" (CWK XXV, p. 114). By eliminating the possibility of hoarding, Keynes transforms credit positions into a powerful engine for expansion, encouraging nations to pursue full-employment policies (see Davidson, 2009).

E   Adjustable pegs

The choice of the most appropriate exchange rate regimes appears to be an issue where Keynes shows less consistency. "By the time Keynes came to draft his proposals for the post-World War II monetary system, he had at one time or another recommended almost every exchange rate regime known to modern analysts except completely freely floating exchange rates" (Moggridge, 1986, pp. 66–67). Cesarano (2015) has recently elaborated on the apparent (and maybe more than so) contradiction between Keynes's strenuous defence of national autonomy in monetary policy and his advocacy of various forms of fixed exchange rates in his reform proposals since *Indian Currency and Finance*. Building on the influence of the latter on Keynes's subsequent work, Cesarano suggests that the tension might be caused by less than full appreciation on the part of Keynes of "the epoch-making transition to fiat money" (Cesarano, 2015, p. 265). In the first draft of the International Clearing Union plan, Keynes applauds the pre-war gold standard regime for the pattern of peaceful international relations intrinsic to the classical adjustment mechanisms. Yet, Keynes's response to a German student's question, in 1936, on his own preferences about currency regimes provides both a striking illustration of pragmatism, and an example of his capacity to conflate different objectives into a coherent whole. Here, Keynes declared to be in favour of fluctuating exchange rates – but not "constantly" fluctuating, since stability – "so long as there are no fundamental grounds for a different policy" – has its own advantages. "The practicability of stability" (CWK XI, p. 501), he emphasised, depends on capital controls, as well as on similar wage movements in different countries.

At Bretton Woods, Keynes proposed an adjustable pegs regime, as a kind of intermediate solution between fixed and flexible exchange rates. And, as it is often the case with Keynes, it is truly a "middle course" solution. It is, in other words, another example of Keynes's peculiar way of addressing the complexity and interdependence characterising international economic relations, based on an "extraordinarily clear understanding of how pieces of the global economy interact, driven by the policies of autonomous nations, in an only partly coherent manner" (Vines, 2003, p. 339). One should also note that this *ante-litteram* "middle course" approach to the dilemma of the international system exposed in *A Treatise on Money* dates back to the *Tract on Monetary Reform*. There, Keynes rejected both freely fluctuating exchange rates and a return to the pre-war gold standard (Meltzer, 1989, p. 109), and suggested, instead, that the exchange rate ought to be made a policy instrument in the hands of the central bank, just like the rate of interest:

> I believe that we can go a long way in this direction [of reconciling domestic and international concerns] if the Bank of England will take over the duty of regulating the price of gold, just as it already regulates the rate of discount.
>
> (CWK IV, p. 149)

Conclusions

The proposal for an International Clearing Union was the consistent result of three decades of reflections on money. It interlaces the ultimate theoretical and political implications of Keynes's thought: any received view that assigns logical priority to Keynes's "closed" macroeconomics or sees the Clearing Union plan as the international prolongation, so to speak, of his theoretical achievements about the management of domestic economies should be reconsidered in this light. As we have tried to demonstrate, the Clearing Union plan is truly to be regarded as Keynes's intellectual testament. The attention that Keynes's new international currency, bancor, has recently received, in the times of the crisis (and tensions within the so-called "Bretton Woods II" regime), is in itself a tell-tale sign of the drastic novelty of Keynes's international macroeconomics, but the discussion, in which bancor is usually considered as a supranational reserve currency, signals a certain degree of misunderstanding. It is the radical difference of Keynes's economics, of his theory of money, also in relation to international trade, that – embedded in the Clearing Union plan – provides the true alternative to today's disorder. And it is thus by elaborating upon this radical difference of vision that one can hope to reconstruct, on more solid bases, the myth of the Bretton Woods regime. As Rodrik (2011, p. 72) claims, during the Glorious Thirty, "national policies promoted globalization mostly as a byproduct of widely shared economic growth … the success of the Bretton Woods era suggests that healthy national economies make for a bustling world economy." As surprising as this may seem to modern eyes, Keynes would have found it pretty obvious.

Note

1   To borrow an expression that Keynes uses repeatedly throughout Chapter 17 of *The General Theory*, where he discusses the essential properties of interest and money (CWK VII, pp. 230, 236–237).

References

Bergsten, C.F. (2013). Currency wars, the economy of the United States and reform of the International Monetary System. *Stavros Niarchos Foundation Lecture*, 16 May. Available at: https://piie.com/publications/papers/bergsten201305.pdf.

Cairncross, A. (1978). Keynes and the planned economy. In: A. Thirlwall, ed. *Keynes and laissez-faire*. London: Macmillan, 36–58.

Carabelli, A.M. and Cedrini, M.A. (2010a). *Indian Currency* and beyond: the legacy of the early economics of Keynes in the times of Bretton Woods II. *Journal of Post Keynesian Economics*, 33 (2), 255–279.

Carabelli, A.M. and Cedrini, M.A. (2010b). Keynes and the complexity of international economic relations in the aftermath of World War I. *Journal of Economic Issues*, 44 (4), 1009–1027.

Carabelli, A.M. and Cedrini, M.A. (2015). On "fear of goods" in Keynes's thought. *European Journal of the History of Economic Thought*, 22 (6), 1115–1148.

Cesarano, F. (2001). *Gli accordi di Bretton Woods. La costruzione di un ordine monetario internazionale*. Laterza: Roma-Bari.

Cesarano, F. (2015). *Indian Currency and Finance*: John Maynard Keynes's prismatic view of the International Monetary System. *History of Political Economy*, 47 (2), 241–269.

Davidson, P. (2009). *The Keynes solution: the path to global economic prosperity*. New York: Palgrave Macmillan.

Dimand, R.W. (2006). Keynes and global economic integration. *Atlantic Economic Journal*, 34 (2), 175–182.

Ikenberry, J.G. (1993). Creating yesterday's new world order: Keynesian "New Thinking" and the Anglo-American postwar settlement. In: J. Goldstein and R.O. Keohane, eds.

Ideas and foreign policy: beliefs, institutions, and political change. Ithaca: Cornell University Press, 57–86.

Keynes, J.M. (1971[1913]). *The Collected Writings of John Maynard Keynes, Vol. I. Indian currency and finance* (E. Johnson and D.E. Moggridge, eds). London: Macmillan.

Keynes, J.M. (1914). "What is money?" Review article. *Economic Journal*, 24 (95), 419–421.

Keynes, J.M. (1971[1919]). *The Collected Writings of John Maynard Keynes, Vol. II. The economic consequences of the peace* (E. Johnson and D.E. Moggridge, eds). London: Macmillan.

Keynes, J.M. (1971[1923]). *The Collected Writings of John Maynard Keynes, Vol. IV. A tract on monetary reform* (E. Johnson and D.E. Moggridge, eds). London: Macmillan.

Keynes, J.M. (1971[1930]). *The Collected Writings of John Maynard Keynes, Vol. V. A treatise on money: the pure theory of money* (E. Johnson and D.E. Moggridge, eds). London: Macmillan.

Keynes, J.M. (1973[1936]). *The Collected Writings of John Maynard Keynes, Vol. VII. The general theory of employment, interest and money* (E. Johnson and D.E. Moggridge, eds). London: Macmillan.

Keynes, J.M. (1972[1931]). *The Collected Writings of John Maynard Keynes, Vol. IX. Essays in persuasion* (E. Johnson and D.E. Moggridge, eds). London: Macmillan.

Keynes, J.M. (1983). *The Collected Writings of John Maynard Keynes, Vol. XI. Economic articles and correspondence: academic* (E. Johnson and D.E. Moggridge, eds). London: Macmillan.

Keynes, J.M. (1978). *The Collected Writings of John Maynard Keynes, Vol. XVIII. Activities 1922–32: the end of reparations* (E. Johnson and D.E. Moggridge, eds). London: Macmillan.

Keynes, J.M. (1982). *The Collected Writings of John Maynard Keynes, Vol. XXI. Activities 1931–39: world crisis and policies in Britain and America* (E. Johnson and D.E. Moggridge, eds). London: Macmillan.

Keynes, J.M. (1980). *The Collected Writings of John Maynard Keynes, Vol. XXV. Activities 1940–44: shaping the post-war world: the clearing union* (E. Johnson and D.E. Moggridge, eds). London: Macmillan.

Kregel, J.A. (2015). *Emerging markets and the international financial architecture.* Public Policy Brief, no. 139. Annandale-on-Hudson, NY: Levy Economics Institute of Bard College. Available at: http://www.levyinstitute.org/pubs/ppb_139.pdf.

Marcuzzo, M.C. (2010). Reason and reasonableness in Keynes: lessons from *The Economic Consequences of the Peace* 90 years later. In: A. Arnon, J. Weinblatt and W. Young, eds. *Perspectives on Keynesian economics.* Berlin: Springer, 35–55.

Meltzer, A.H. (1989). *Keynes's monetary theory: a different interpretation.* Cambridge: Cambridge University Press.

Mitchell-Innes, A. (1913). What is money? *The Banking Law Journal*, 30 (5) May, 377–408.

Moggridge, D.E. (1986). Keynes and the International Monetary System 1909–46. In: J. S. Cohen and G.C. Harcourt, eds. *International monetary problems and supply-side economics: essays in honour of Lorie Tarshis.* London: Macmillan, 56–83.

Radice, H. (1988). Keynes and the policy of practical protectionism. In: J. Hillard, ed. *J.M. Keynes in retrospect: the legacy of the Keynesian Revolution.* Aldershot: Edward Elgar, 152–171.

Rodrik, D. (2011). *The globalization paradox: democracy and the future of the world economy.* New York: W.W. Norton.

Vines, D. (2003). John Maynard Keynes 1937–1946: the creation of international macroeconomics. A review article of *John Maynard Keynes 1937–1946: fighting for Britain* by Robert Skidelsky. *The Economic Journal*, 113 (488), 338–361.

Williamson, J. (1983). Keynes and the international economic order. In: D. Worswick and J. Trevithick, eds. *Keynes and the modern world.* Cambridge: Cambridge University Press, 87–113.

12 Keynes as a planner and negotiator

*Toshiaki Hirai**

In July 1940, the Chancellor of the Exchequer's Consultative Council was set up to help and advise the Chancellor on special problems arising from war conditions. Keynes accepted Council membership and was soon to find himself engaged in a range of important assignments.

I have already dealt elsewhere (see, for example, Hirai, 2011, 2013) with Keynes's activities in the 1940s, as a planner and negotiator in the international spheres in relation to the Relief and Reconstruction problem and the Commodity problem. The present chapter focuses only on the role of Keynes as a planner and negotiator of a new international monetary system.[1]

As a result of my previous work, (for further information, see "Addenda" below), I have come to the following conclusion: initially Keynes designed and put forward plans permeated with the spirit of internationalism. As the political and economic situations changed, however, he came to show a more pragmatic approach, giving priority to protecting the interests of the British Empire. In both cases, his original plans were foiled at an early stage.

These features are also clearly recognisable in the sphere concerned, as will be shown below.

1. The starting point

At an early stage of the Second World War the problem of how a new international monetary system should be constructed for the post-war world came under the attention of the UK cabinet and, quite separately, of the US administration.

In the UK it started with Harold Nicolson of the Ministry of Information asking Keynes, in November 1940, to counter Funk–Schacht's proposal for a German "New Order." Keynes, however, actually approved of the German idea of substituting barter with an international currency (gold), and eventually proposed a more elaborate monetary system than the Gold Standard, as can be seen in Keynes's two memoranda (8 September 1941).[2]

In the US, meanwhile, it started with Henry Morgenthau, Treasury Secretary, asking Harry White, then Assistant Director of Research, to prepare a memorandum on an inter-Allied stabilisation fund, in December 1941. White quickly drew up a 12-page memo, "Suggestions for Inter-Allied Monetary and Banking Action."

The UK, as leader of the Allied Forces, had been waging a gruelling war with Germany since September 1939, and suffered a near-fatal defeat at Dunkirk in May 1940, subsequent to which France was forced to surrender to Germany. In order to continue to fight in the war, the UK, which had endured tremendous losses of foreign reserves and accumulated huge debts, desperately needed the financial assistance of the US, on which Churchill, a staunch defender of the British Empire, was to put a high priority since he became Prime Minister on 10 May 1940.

Contrastingly, the US was a new world power with huge economic and military resources. In December 1941, it finally entered the war in response to the Pearl Harbour attack by the Japanese navy, and became an ally of the UK. However, the top politicians in the Roosevelt Administration – including Roosevelt himself, Morgenthau, Harry White and Lauchlin Currie – were averse to UK Imperialism and hoped to play a leading role, together with the Soviet Union, in the post-war world.[3]

As the war proceeded, the UK's financial situation went from bad to worse. Given this state of affairs, the US enacted the "Lend-Lease Act" (March 1941), which allowed the US to send armaments to the UK only if the President regarded them as indispensable for the defence of the US. This was an act mainly designed with the UK in mind. Thus Anglo-American financial negotiations set in. Based on the Lend-Lease Act, the two sides put forward proposals, and went on with discussions until they finally reached the "Anglo-American Mutual Aid Agreement" (February 1942). Keynes was a leading figure for the UK in these negotiations.[4]

In the course of the negotiations, the US asked for "considerations" as quid pro quo for aid to the UK. The most heated debate occurred around "Article 7" in the US plan, which contained terms like "against discrimination in either the US or the UK against the importation of any produce originating in the other country." Some in the UK (including Keynes)[5] suspected that the US was aiming at dismantling the Sterling Bloc, composed of the Imperial Preferential Tariff and exchange control, as a symbol of the British Empire.

Immediately after the War, the Lend Lease Act was terminated. The UK, faced with abrupt financial difficulties, endeavoured to obtain financial aid from the US, the result of which was the "Anglo-American Financial Agreement"[6] (December 1945). Keynes was also a leading negotiator.

2. The International Clearing Union (the Keynes Plan)

2.1. *The process up until the Keynes Plan*

Keynes's plan for a new international system started with the "First Draft" ("Post-War Currency Policy", 8 September 1941; CWK XXV, pp. 21–40) for circulation within the Treasury. Then came the "Second Draft" ("Proposals for an International Currency Union", 18 November; CWK XXV, pp. 42–66), which became the most important for discussion in the Treasury-Bank of England meetings. This was followed by the – greatly rewritten – "Third Draft" ("Proposals for an International Currency Union", 15 December; CWK XXV, pp. 68–94), and the "Fourth Draft" ("Plan for an International Currency [or Clearing Union]", January 1942; CWK XXV, pp. 108–139), which made up paragraphs 61–134 of a memorandum by the Treasury on External Monetary and Economic Problems.[7]

It is worth briefly taking a look at how Keynes's plan was treated in Whitehall.[8] The official who criticised it most harshly and continued to do so to the end was Hubert Henderson who supported "managed trade and bilateral barter agreements," at the Treasury. The Bank of England at first went along with Henderson, but later on – with figures including Thomas Catto, Harry Siepmann and George Bolton – came round to supporting Keynes's plan. Within the Treasury, together with Hubert Henderson, Ralph Hawtrey and Robert Brand were critical of Keynes's plan. But the Treasury as a whole came to regard it as a proposal worth presenting to the ministers.

Meanwhile, keen support, albeit with strong pressure for certain amendments, came from Lionel Robbins and James Meade of the Economic Section, as well as Roy Harrod (Admiralty) and Dennis Robertson (the Treasury).

In May 1942, Keynes's plan, entitled "Proposals for an International Clearing Union" (CWK XXV, pp. 168–195) was finally approved by the War Cabinet. It was sent to White, now Director of Monetary Reserch, by Frederick Phillips (28 August). As this is a de facto UK official plan, it is worth showing its main features. Let us call this plan "the Keynes Plan" hereafter.

2.2. Principal features of the Keynes Plan

i To set up an International Clearing Union (ICU), in which each central bank of a member country is to open an account. The account is to be kept in terms of bancor,[9] an international currency used only among these accounts. All the international transactions[10] are to be carried over to the bancor accounts concerned, and cleared – an "international version" of a domestic banking system (Banking Principle).

ii To allow for overdraft facilities as well as credit creation. The ICU permits a member country to use overdraft facilities subject to an agreed rule based on the "quota," and a member country that keeps the account in persistent credit to grant credit to a country in need of some capital.

iii To keep each account within the prescribed range. The plan emphasises the prevention of persistent unbalances in the balance of payments of a member country, either in surplus or in deficit. If the sum should exceed a prescribed figure, a penalty should be imposed.

iv To aim at attaining growth in the world economy. The plan aims at facilitating growth in the world economy through the above-mentioned mechanism.

v To aim at a new type of international monetary system. It should aim at a new system free from the defects of the Gold Standard as well as the de facto US dollar system and a flexible exchange rate system.

vi Parity and its change. The "parity" of a member country defined as a rate between its currency and the bancor is fixed on agreement. Thereafter, when fundamental disequilibrium occurs, the country concerned is allowed to change the parity through consultation.

vii To provide funds for the primary commodity problem and the relief/and reconstruction problem. The institutions concerned should be allowed to open their bancor accounts.

3. The International Stabilization Fund (the White Plan)

White continued to revise his plan, and put forward Preliminary Draft Proposal for a 'United Nations Stabilization Fund' (hereafter UNSF or the White Plan [Ia]) and a 'Bank for Reconstruction and Development of the United and Associated Nations' (hereafter BRD or the White Plan [Ib]) in April 1942. (This was the document that Keynes was mainly to review before the publication of White's revised version of 7 April 1943). Then the US Treasury, after discussions with nearly thirty governments, announced "Preliminary Draft Outline of a Proposal for an International Stabilization Fund of the United and Associated Nations" (10 July 1943.[11] Hereafter referred to as the White Plan [II]).[12]

Let us now take a look at the White Plan [Ia] and [Ib].

3.1. UNSF: the White Plan [Ia]

Its principal aim is to maintain the stability of exchange rates among the member nations, their volatility having been the main cause of the unstable world economy in the interwar period. For this (especially, addressing the fundamental disequilibrium in the balance of payments) the UNSF, with quotas subscribed by the member states, should buy and sell currencies, gold and government bonds with them. It could also make loans to them or issue bonds to acquire currencies or invest currencies into short-term securities.

The exchange rates among members' currencies are fixed, any change being allowed only to correct fundamental disequilibrium. The total balance of the UNSF should remain the same, and many decisions are made subject to four-fifth majority votes.

There are other features worth noting, designed to serve the following purposes: (1) to liberate "blocked balances" – although the US is mentioned, very much in mind here is the UK (the "Sterling Balances"); (2) to reduce controls over foreign exchange and foreign trade, and to eliminate bilateral clearing arrangements, albeit the White Plan [Ia] does not pursue a "Free Trade" policy, arguing that any such policy is based on unreal and unsound assumptions (see Horsefield, 1969, p. 70). Its basic stance is: "The task before us is not to prohibit instruments of control but to develop those measures of control ..., as will be the most effective in obtaining the objectives of world-wide sustained prosperity" (ibid., p. 64).

The Plan [Ia] strongly encourages participation on the part of the Soviet Union, stating that the Soviet Union "despite her socialist economy could both contribute and profit by participation" (ibid., p. 72).

3.2. BRD: the White Plan [Ib]

The main objectives of the BRD are to provide long-term capital for economic reconstruction, to supply short-term capital for foreign trade and to eliminate the danger of worldwide financial crises. It also aims at addressing issues regarding commodities and raw materials – it could organise and finance an "International Essential Raw Material Development Corporation" and an "International Commodity Stabilization Corporation."

The BRD has the powers to make short-term and long-term loans, to guarantee loans made by private investors, to issue its own demand currency ("international unit"[13] appears for the first time in the White Plan [Ib]).

It could make loans, dividing them into two parts: local currency and international units. It could buy, sell, hold and deal in gold as well as the obligations and securities of any government.

4. The two plans compared

4.1. Awkward relationship

By August 1942, the Keynes Plan and the White Plan [Ia and Ib] had been sent to the counterparties. On 3 August, Keynes sent a memo on the White Plan to Sir Frederic Phillips (Joint Second Secretary) and Harry Hopkins (Adviser to Roosevelt), remarking that the general attitude of mind is helpful, while the actual technical solution is quite hopeless – a version of the Gold Standard.[14] In October, Keynes and White met unofficially in London. Keynes suggested holding a direct meeting between the two countries in advance of an international conference, but in vain.

Instead, October and November saw the UK discussing post-war planning with the Dominions and India. Keynes grew suspicious of the US attitude, and asked Phillips to hold a sort of Anglo-American commission, to which Phillips responded that Washington would not accept it.

In February 1943, the State Department sent the (eighth draft) of the White Plan (which dropped the plan for the Bank for Reconstruction and Development)[15] – without consultation with the UK – to Britain, Russia and China as a "basis of discussion," proposing to invite thirty-seven experts individually.

The UK, in return, sent the Keynes Plan to Russia and China, and initiated discussion with the finance ministers of the West European Allies. The US sent a representative, but turned down the UK suggestion that the US should send the White Plan for comparison.

Then, on 7 April the Stabilization Fund Plan ([I]SF Plan) and the ICU Plan ("Proposals for an International Clearing Union"; Cmd. 6437) were publicised.

4.2. The ICU Plan as publicised

Keynes wrote the preface to the ICU Plan (CWK XXV, pp. 233–235), stating that there were four international spheres to be provided for: (1) a currency and exchange mechanism; (2) a framework for commercial policy, (3) primary commodities and (4) aid to investment.

As important conditions in setting up international economic institutions for these spheres, the following needs are mentioned:

i to minimise interference with domestic spheres;
ii to devise a planning technique applicable irrespective of the types of member countries;
iii to ensure that administration and management of the international institutions be genuinely international;
iv to give the member countries a withdrawal option;
v to gear planning to the overall interests and particular benefits of the member countries.

The preface contains four important points. Firstly, Keynes reveals his vision of international economic systems. Secondly, he gives priority to the ICU plan which should provide a desirable currency and exchange mechanism. Thirdly, the ICU should be regarded as an institution for promoting economic growth. Fourthly, he might contemplate something like the Bank for Reconstruction and Development.

4.3. The two plans reviewed

Keynes wrote "Notes on C.U. and S.F." (16 April; CWK XXV, pp. 245–249) in which he reviewed the [I]CU Plan and the [I]SF Plan. The following, except for the headings, is a summary.

i *Voting Power.* The CU Plan does not take a rigid stance on voting powers, while the SF Plan does.
ii *Gold.* The SF Plan makes no provision for changing the gold value of unitas, unlike the CU Plan. Unitas needs, somehow or other, to be activated.
iii *Multilateral Clearing.* The SF Plan, unlike the CU Plan, makes no provision for multilateral clearing, and should therefore be revised.
iv *The Scale of Quotas.* The fundamental difficulty with the SF Plan is that the demand for the currencies of certain creditor countries might far exceed the Fund's capacity to provide for them.

v *The "Abnormal War Balances" Problem.* As the war proceeded, the UK, for example, came to owe huge debts to, among other countries, India. If India were to sell them for dollars, the UK would come up against serious financial difficulties – the "Sterling Balances Problem."[16]

vi *The Rationing of Scarce Currencies.* Without this provision, the logic of the SF Plan would collapse.

vii *Subscribed Capital vs Banking Principle.* If the latter (of the CU Plan) were to be adopted rather than the former (of the SF Plan), compromise would be possible in other matters.

The most essential points of contention were focused on the Banking Principle and Multilateral Clearing.

5. The integration process between the two plans

In May 1943, an informal monetary meeting was held between the two Treasuries in Washington. Robertson, who was present, sent a suggestion to Keynes in London that it should be reasonable to accept the SF Plan, and then persuade the US to turn "unitas into a real medium of exchange"[17] – i.e. preserve "some of the elegance of C.U." In fact, Keynes himself had written to Harrod: "I fully expect that we shall do well to compromise with the American scheme and very likely accept their dress" (CWK XXV, p. 268), for he thought that "The real risk, ..., is that they will run away from their own plan, let alone ours. By continuing to press ours, there is at least a little chance that they may develop some patriotic fervour for their own" (CWK XXV, p. 268). It was agreed in the meeting that the CU Plan would be a non-starter.[18]

The integration process can be divided into two phases: the "monetisation of unitas" and the final phase of the negotiations.

5.1. Monetisation of unitas

Keynes prepared a memorandum entitled "The Synthesis of C.U. and S.F." (29 June 1943; CWK XXV, pp. 308–314). Far from reflecting the title, it was based on the SF Plan, putting the CU Plan on the shelf, and yet advocating that the SF Plan should adopt unitas as genuine "international money".

Reading the SF Plan of 10 July (this should be the White Plan [II] – a revised version of the White Plan [7 April]),[19] Keynes sent a letter to Wilfrid Eady (CWK XXV, pp. 316–320). Firstly, he was prepared to "accept the substance of White's essential conditions" (subscription principle, the limitation of liability, the general shape of S.F., etc.). Secondly, he argued that the SF Plan should be revised by replacing the "entirely unacceptable features of... [the SF Plan]" (CWK XXV, p. 318) with the UK's three essential conditions as follows:

  i to make change in the value of a member's currency more elastic;
  ii that the Fund should monetise unitas and perform multilateral clearing;
 iii gold subscription for a member should not be 25% but 12.5% of the quota.

    In a letter to White (21 September), Keynes sent a memo, "Suggestions for the Monetisation of Unitas" (CWK XXV, pp. 342–344). The gist was an attempt to transform unitas into bancor. Each member country would be allowed to open an account within the Fund. Although the quota remained, the banking principle would be introduced as the main framework. More precisely, each country would obtain unitas, initially, by subscribing the quota with gold and securities, but thereafter would be allowed to sell their currency to other members and buy their currency in exchange for a transfer of unitas subject to certain conditions. The Fund would be able to buy gold from a member at its par value in exchange for unitas, which would induce a member holding a large amount of gold to sell to the Fund. He stated that "[t]his appears to me to get over the objection you raised the other day, . . . since gold obtained under this clause would be *free* gold it would be available . . . to deal with the scarce currency problem" (CWK XXV, p. 341).

    In September, meetings of the two nations were held at the US Treasury. Keynes argued that, although several points were "translatable into S.F. terminology," the following were not so easily addressed:[20]

  i unqualified multilateral clearing;
  ii the duty of members to maintain exchange stability (management of foreign exchange markets remained important in the SF Plan);
 iii the passivity of the Fund.

    In a letter to Eady (3 October; CWK XXV, pp. 352–357), Keynes reported the situation in Washington, pointing out the problems difficult to agree upon, namely:

  i the British claim that gold subscription should be regarded as collateral;
  ii the US claims that the Fund should be given more discretion in members' way of using it (the British claims that the Fund should act passively);
 iii the US opposition to unitas monetisation.

In particular, (iii) was a major point of contention.[21]

    From late September to early October, Keynes grew distrustful of this US attitude. A dismal atmosphere was in the air.[22] Keynes's "explosions," however, finally brought about a "new American draft."[23]

5.2. *The final phase of the negotiations*

In the meeting held in October 1943 it was agreed to "prepare directives for the Drafting Committee that would meet to draw up finally the details of the Fund and to draft in terms of a Stabilisation Fund" (CWK XXV, p. 365). After the meeting Keynes wrote a letter to White explaining the view of the British Government (pp. 366–368), stressing:

i   preference for a system under which an alteration in the exchanges requires only consultation;
ii to aim at unitas monetisation;
iii subscription in gold should be regarded as collateral.

On point (ii), Keynes stated that: "London emphasises that they are not at present prepared to release us from our instructions to aim at the monetisation of unitas ..." (p. 367).

Work on the draft proceeded, resulting in the "Anglo-American Draft Statement of Principles" (12 October; CWK XXV, pp. 379–392). An odd feature of the main text (pp. 379–389) was that it was virtually the SF Plan minus "unitas". Before presenting "the main text," the following paragraph was inserted as the "UK reservation": "[The following draft] ... is expressed in terms of a Fund which holds members' currencies. This ... expression has been used to meet the convenience of the United States Treasury and in no way commits the British representatives ..." (pp. 379–380).

Then "the main text" by the American group is stated. Following it, there comes "The Draft Statement of Principles in terms of a monetised unitas" (CWK XXV, pp. 389–392) by the British group, beginning with the following paragraph: "In order to express the substance of the Draft Statement of Principles in terms of monetised unitas, the following paragraphs should be substituted for those carrying the same number in the Draft discussed with the American group" (p. 389).

In his letter to Opie (7 December; CWK XXV, pp. 393–394), astonishingly, Keynes toned down his stance, stating that there was no need to stick to the monetisation of unitas and that the need was, rather, to be clear "about what happens during the transitional period." Keynes wrote that, although he "vastly" preferred the monetised version, the difference with the non-monetised version was not *"really such as to make it a justifiable reason for an ultimate breach. The emphasis on the transitional period, on the other hand, ... [seems to be] ... justified and important"* (pp. 393–394; emphasis added.

Keynes thus approved the US plan fully in the section drafted by him "II. The Main Objects of the Plan" (7 February 1944; CWK XXV, pp. 399–408), and yet stated:

we cannot enter into this scheme [IMF system] unless there is an assurance of our not being expected to use its facilities prematurely, and that we cannot have any such assurance until they have given us some indication of the financial régime succeeding the lend lease phase ... (p. 407)

It should be noted that he even held that the two set-ups should be the same in substance (See p. 405) – quite contrary to the view strongly expressed so far.

Furthermore, Keynes showed "some ardour in favour of the new institution (the IMF system)," stating that it was "a concrete example of international agreement for post-war economic policy" and "not mere words" (p. 408).

What all this adds up to is that Keynes fully supported the SF Plan, putting priority on the assurance of financial assistance from the US in the transitional period (See Section 1). His activities as a system designer came to an end. From now on, he was to act as a supporter of the Bretton Woods system as well as defender of the interests of the British Empire.

Concerning the situation of the Treasury, Lord Cherwell reported to the Prime Minister, on 9 February 1944, that there were two rival factions: one headed by Keynes with most of the Treasury, the Economic Section and the Board of Trade, the other by Henderson and Eady, supported by the Bank of England (p. 408).

During the first 5 months, Keynes was forced to fight virtually single-handed to protect the "Anglo-American Draft Statement of Principles" from the rival faction within the Treasury, the Bank of England and other widespread political hostilities.[24]

The Bank of England, for example, strongly opposed the Draft for the following reasons: the power of discretion which it had enjoyed might be greatly reduced; the sterling balances problem; refusal of the "passiveness" of the Fund; the method of management of the Fund might be implemented by the US.

On 11 February, the War Cabinet agreed to set up a "Committee on External Economic Policy" to determine how it should issue an instruction "on the assumption that Britain would proceed with the scheme" (CWK XXV, p. 408). The Committee allowed deliberations to proceed "on the basis that Britain eventually would see its way clear to enter into the proposed post-war arrangements" (p. 409).

Keynes's stance was a pragmatic one, seeking to establish an "Anglo-American Bloc Offered as an International Scheme" (p. 411). With it the UK could maintain the dignity of the British Empire as a central player together with the US, and yet it could be proposed as an international scheme.

In a letter to White (18 March), Keynes wrote that he would not make the unitas problem a condition for concluding an agreement[25] (on 22 April he publicly stated in Cmd. 6519 that there was no need for either bancor or unitas[26]– which meant a total defeat for the CU Plan).

From October 1943 to April 1944, the Draft was revised seven times. Moggridge (1992, pp. 728–733) sums up the negotiation process, which clearly shows that almost all the points of revision came from the US side and were accepted by the British side.

On 14 April, the British Cabinet agreed to make public announcement of the "Joint Statement by Experts on the Establishment of an International Monetary Fund" (CWK XXV, pp. 469-477). On 23 May, Keynes made a speech in the House of Lords (CWK XXVI, pp. 9–21), in which he emphasised that the Joint Statement Plan was superior to either the CU Plan or the SF Plan.

6. The Atlantic City, Bretton Woods and Savannah conferences

Keynes's activities from the Atlantic City Conference between the US and the UK (June) to the Bretton Woods Conference (July 1944)[27] were characterised by flexibility on his part; that is, Keynes emerged as a political pragmatist. The principal task there was to breed a "dog of mixed origin"[28]– born from the SF Plan and the CU Plan and agreed upon in the Joint Statement.

Points of dispute and the claims made by each side in Atlantic City ran as follows: (i) To what degree is the IMF plan a return to the Gold Standard? (ii) Where should authority be endowed? (iii) The size of the Fund, and (iv) the length of the transitional period.

Keynes and White were able to determine the essential matters between them, so the Bretton Woods Conference was a formal rather than a substantial occasion.[29] And yet the most contentious and difficult issues were the Sterling Balances, the transitional period and the amount of quota allocated.[30]

On 7 June 1945, the US House of Representatives passed the Bretton Woods Agreement Act. Then, at the Savannah Conference (March 1946) the final agreement was concluded among the participating countries.[31] On 9 March, Keynes's speech at the inaugural meeting of governors of the IMF and the IBRD concluded with irony and cynicism, using the story of Sleeping Beauty. Keynes issued a warning:

> I am hoping that Mr Kelchner [the convenor] has not made any mistake and that there is no malicious fairy ... whom he has overlooked and forgotten to ask to the party. For if so the curses which that bad fairy will pronounce will ... run as follows: "You two brats shall grow up politicians; your every thought and act shall have an *arrière-pensée*".
>
> (CWK XXVI, p. 216)

If that should happen, the best is "for the children to fall into an eternal slumber, never to waken or be heard of again in the courts and markets of Mankind" (pp. 216–217).

7. Keynes's stance shown in the international monetary system

How should we evaluate Keynes's stance over the whole process. First Keynes put forward the ICU Plan permeated with internationalism. As the negotiation proceeded, however, his stance began to change. Around April 1943 Keynes agreed that the White Plan should be a starter, so he prepared a memorandum in June based on it. In the meeting in Washington in October, Keynes made a great effort, pressing for the monetisation of unitas, but in vain. However, in December he expressed the view that there should be no need to stick to monetisation; the need was, rather, to think about the transitional period (in April 1944 the UK gave up the idea of monetisation). Moreover, Keynes came to appreciate the IMF system not only as a concrete example of international agreement (February 1944), but also as a "dog of mixed origin" (May).

Thus Keynes failed to have the essential elements of the ICU Plan incorporated into the White Plan. Keynes's strategy dramatically shifted to focus on how the UK could get financial assistance from the US in the transitional period. White summarised what had been achieved in Washington thus: "It is a part compromise, but much more like the American plan" (Skidelsky, 2000, p. 320).

Keynes might have been hoping for some sort of international monetary system after the failed Rescue/Reconstruction and Commodity Plans. His temperament was such that, when his ideal plans failed to get through, he tried to revise them, getting advice from various quarters. But once his efforts proved unavailing, he then changed his strategy and was able to work as a pragmatist as well as defender of the British Empire[32] through the negotiations, putting his failure as a theorist aside.

Keynes had been much concerned that, without help from the US, the British Empire might collapse.[33] He himself was, in fact, a leading figure in the loan negotiations with the US subsequent to abrupt termination of the Lend-Lease Act in 1945 (See CWK XXIV, Ch. 4).

Let us take an example of Keynes's grasp on world geopolitics in the draft for "The Savannah Conference on the Bretton Woods Final Act" (27 March 1946). He emphasises affirmation of the position of the British Empire relatively to the US "by making use of" international institutions.

> Nothing can suit us better, therefore, than that international institutions, where we are free to play a very important part, should administer what will be largely American funds for the succour of these regions. . . .
>
> I firmly believe that the whole of the British Commonwealth and the Sterling Area and of Europe stood closer to us than to the Americans and looked to us, rather than to them, for leadership.
>
> (CWK XXVI, pp. 230–231)

8. Addenda

8.1. Relief and reconstruction

In October 1941, Keynes put forward the Central Relief and Reconstruction Fund (CRRF) Plan permeated with internationalism, tasked to manage a joint fund comprising money donations or contributions in kind from various countries. The basic principle behind the CRRF was to create an ideal international organisation to distribute commodities, efficiently and with humanitarian criteria, among countries in need of relief.

In February 1942, however, he abruptly abandoned the Plan and took a pragmatic line mainly dependent on the newly concluded "Anglo-American Mutual Aid Agreement" (February), due to the severe economic decline weighing on the British Empire, which threatened to embroil it in the humiliating situation of having to provide figures on gold and foreign resources, showing that the UK could not pay cash for what it needed. (See CWK XXVII, p. 65)[34]

8.2. Commodity problem

Keynes put forward the Fifth Draft of International Buffer Plan (April 1942), which was very clear and excellent in that it enhanced price stabilisation through a buffer stock management system named "Commod Control." However, as the Sixth, Seventh and Eighth Draft followed, due to criticism from various governmental departments, restriction on output came to be increasingly emphasised to the extent that the first principle of the Fifth Draft was lost.

And yet we have no evidence of Keynes's dissatisfaction with this transformation. He seems, rather, to have gone on working in the spirit of a political pragmatist.

Although the Eighth Draft was accepted by the War Cabinet (May 1944), the US took a negative stance on the buffer stock plan in the Anglo-American Conference in September. The agreed document itself came in for staunch opposition from the Ministry of Agriculture and the Bank of England.[35]

Notes

* The author gratefully acknowledges Prof. Annalisa Rosselli's invaluable suggestions for revision.
1 Fundamentally based on Hirai (2015).
2 As reprinted in *The Collected Writings of John Maynard Keynes*, henceforth CWK followed by the Roman numeral of the volume: CWK XXV, pp. 23–24 and 32.
3 For Roosevelt, see Wolfe (1995), and for White, see Skidelsky (2000, p. 242), and Steil (2013, Ch.10, which details White's espionage for Soviet, firstly revealed in 1948 and confirmed by the FBI's Venona Project in 1995).
4 Keynes drew up a draft for the Chancellor (CWK XXIII, pp. 137–140).
5 See CWK XXIII, pp. 175–177.
6 See CWK XXIV, Ch. 4.
7 In the three earlier drafts the viewpoints from the UK side are more striking than in the Fourth, which reveals his political stance.
8 See Skidelsky (2000, Ch. 6, V).
9 "S.B.M." in Keynes (1930, Ch. 38) was to be a precursor of bancor.
10 All the current balances and capital balances for secure investment only are considered. Speculative capital movement and capital flight should be controlled, the method being left to each member country.
11 The White Plan went on to be revised to meet the opposition from the State Department and the Federal Reserve Board. This was mainly done by E.M. Bernstein. See Mikesell (1994, p. 16).
12 For the White Plan [Ia] and [II], this chapter refers to Horsefield (1969), while for the White Plan [Ib], to Office of the Historian (1942).

13 This is to be named "unitas" in the White Plan [II]. White himself was, in fact, critical of this idea, believing that the dollar should be an international money. The idea comes from Morgenthau and Roosevelt. See Steil (2013, p. 148).

14 See Moggridge (1992, p. 687). For Keynes's confused view on the Gold Standard, see Steil (2013, pp. 137–139).

15 For how the Bank Plan evolved after the White Plan [Ib], see Mikesell (1994, pp. 36–39).

16 Keynes took this seriously in 1941. For June 1942, and for May 1943, see CWK XXIII, respectively, p. 233 and p. 267.

17 See CWK XXV, p. 292.

18 See Skidelsky (2000, p. 301).

19 In the White Plan [Ia], the term, "new international unit" appears without explanation, while in the White Plan [Ib], the term is explained very roughly as international money. The White Plan [II] is, contrastingly, unique in "III. Monetary Unit of the Fund" where unitas is introduced (albeit as a unit of account).

20 See CWK XXV, p. 348.

21 See CWK XXV, p. 359.

22 See CWK XXV, pp. 364, 370–372.

23 See CWK XXV, pp. 370–371.

24 Eady's note (19 January; CWK XXV, pp. 395–398) describes the situation vividly. He points out that the attitude and technique behind the White Plan consistently reflect the principles of the Equalization Fund (see p. 397).

25 See CWK XXV, pp. 427–428.

26 See CWK XXV, p. 438.

27 Just before it, New York bankers tried to offer a huge loan to the UK in return for opposition to a new international system. See Steil (2013, p. 153).

28 See CWK XXVI, p. 10.

29 See CWK XXVI, p. 61 and p. 70.

30 See CWK XXVI, pp. 77–83.

31 Hawtrey (1946) harshly criticises the Bretton Woods Agreement which fatally neglects the fundamental theme that "the money units linked by the rates of exchange should themselves be stabilised in their wealth-value" (p. v) while he values positively the ICU plan because it embodies the theme, which is embodied in the Jenoa Plan (see pp. 26, 28 and 29).

32 Skidelsky (1983) states that "[Keynes] assumed the Empire as a fact of life" (p. 91). Contrastingly, Hawtrey (Hawtrey Papers 12/2, Churchill College, Cambridge University) criticised Imperialism on ethical grounds, as resting on "false ends." Leonard Woolf, advocating an idea of the international government for the Labour Party, took a critical stance on Imperialism (see Wilson, 1995, p. 83). Turnell (2002) interprets Keynes's ICU Plan as a truly liberal adjunct to his realism in the sense of E.H. Carr.

33 For Keynes's view (23 April 1944) on Anglo-American co-operation, see CWK XXV, pp. 446–447.

34 For details, see Hirai (2013).

35 On this, see Hirai (2011).

References

Hawtrey, R. (1946). *Bretton Woods for Better or Worse*. London: Longmans, Green and Co.

Hirai, T. (2011). Keynes and the transmutation process of the plan for commodity control scheme. Paper presented at the XV Annual Conference of the European Society for the History of Economic Thought (ESHET), Boğaziçi University, Istanbul, 19–22 May.

Hirai, T. (2013). International design and the British Empire: Keynes on the relief problem. *History of Economics Review*, 57 (1), 63–83.

Hirai, T. (2015). Keynes's battle over international monetary system. Paper presented at the XIX Annual Conference of the ESHET, Roma Tre University, Rome, 14–16 May.

Horsefield, J.K., ed. (1969). *The International Monetary Fund 1945–1965: twenty years of international monetary cooperation, Vol. III. Documents*. Washington, DC: International Monetary Fund. Available at: http://www.elibrary.imf.org/staticfiles/IMF_History/IMF_45-65_vol3.pdf.

Keynes, J.M. (1930). *A treatise on money*. London: Macmillan.

Keynes, J.M. (1980). *The Collected Writings of John Maynard Keynes, Vol. XXIII. Activities 1940–1943: external war finance* (E. Johnson and D.E. Moggridge, eds.). London: Macmillan.

Keynes, J.M. (1980). *The Collected Writings of John Maynard Keynes, Vol. XXIV. Activities 1944–1946: the transition to peace* (E. Johnson and D.E. Moggridge, eds.). London: Macmillan.

Keynes, J.M. (1980). *The Collected Writings of John Maynard Keynes, Vol. XXV. Activities 1940–1944: shaping the post-war world: the Clearing Union* (E. Johnson and D.E. Moggridge, eds.). London: Macmillan.

Keynes, J.M. (1980). *The Collected Writings of John Maynard Keynes, Vol. XXVI. Activities 1941–1946: shaping the post-war world: Bretton Woods and reparations* (E. Johnson and D.E. Moggridge, eds.). London: Macmillan.

Keynes, J.M. (1980). *The Collected Writings of John Maynard Keynes, Vol. XXVII. Activities 1940–1946: shaping the post-war world: employment and commodities* (E. Johnson and D.E. Moggridge, eds.). London: Macmillan.

Mikesell, R. (1994). *The Bretton Woods debates: a memoir*. Essays in International Finance Series, no. 192. Princeton, NJ: Princeton University, Department of Economics, International Finance Section.

Moggridge, D. (1992). *Maynard Keynes: an economist's biography*. London: Routledge.

Office of the Historian (1942). *Foreign relations of the United States: diplomatic papers, 1942, General; the British Commonwealth; the Far East, Volume I, Document 148*. Available at: https://history.state.gov/historicaldocuments/frus1942v01/d148.

Skidelsky, R. (1983). *John Maynard Keynes: hopes betrayed, 1883–1920*. London: Macmillan.

Skidelsky, R. (2000). *John Maynard Keynes: fighting for Britain, 1937–1946*. London: Macmillan.

Steil, B. (2013). *The battle of Bretton Woods: John Maynard Keynes, Harry Dexter White and the making of a new world order*. Princeton, NJ: Princeton University Press.

Turnell, S. (2002). *Keynes, economics and war: a liberal dose of realism*. Macquarie Economics Research Papers, no. 7. Sydney: Macquarie University, Department of Economics.

Wilson, P. (1995). Leonard Woolf and international government. In: D. Long and P. Wilson, eds. *Thinkers of the Twenty Years' Crisis: inter-war idealism reassessed*. Oxford: Clarendon Press, 122–160.

Wolfe, L. (1995). The other war. FDR's battle against Churchill and the British Empire. *The American Almanac*, August 28.

13 Keynes, the Labour Party and Central Bank Independence

Carlo Panico and Marco Piccioni

1. Introduction

The issue of Central Bank Independence (CBI) has been at the centre of literature in recent years. The topic was raised after WWI, when financial markets grew in size and complexity as a result of the debt supplied to finance the war. At that time, the banks of issue fully acquired the functions of central banks, and a forceful demand for their independence emerged. The new situation led to the examination of how to integrate CBI with the working of democracy, a subject intensely disputed within the Labour Party. In 1932, Keynes published an essay titled "The Monetary Policy of the Labour Party" in *The New Statesman and Nation*, examining the relation between different forms of CBI and democracy. Only recently, however, have his views on this topic attracted attention.[1]

In what follows we examine some elements that most of this literature has underplayed. We stress that Keynes maintained that CBI must guarantee that authorities operate in the interests of society as a whole, rather than those of private or public groups. Keynes did not assume the simplistic position of some recent literature, namely that misguided policies only come from the pressures of unreliable political authorities. He did not overlook the fact that institutional relations depend on the formal content of legislation and on the actual interactions among the subjects involved, both of which reflect the historical evolution of a country and the concrete participation of society in the life of democratic institutions. In all these cases, we highlight the relevance of Keynes's views for current debates.

The chapter is organised as follows: Section 2 classifies the meanings of CBI and recalls the diverse institutional organisation of policy existing in the USA and UK. Section 3 describes how banks of issue fully acquired the functions of central banks and demanded independence after WWI. Section 4 points out how the Labour Party discussed this topic. Section 5 assesses how Keynes intervened in this dispute and Section 6 concludes.

2. Different forms of "CBI"

Central banks can enjoy different forms of independence and possess them to varying degrees (see Panico and Piccioni, 2016; Panico and Rizza, 2004). In what follows we focus on four forms that are discussed in Keynes's work.

The first form is "personnel independence". This depends on the norms regulating the appointment, the dismissal and earnings of the monetary authorities, and the development of personnel careers during and after service. The content of these norms affects the capacity of authorities to resist the pressures of economic and political groups demanding the introduction of policy measures convenient for them.

The second form, "financial and administrative independence", refers to the capacity of a central bank to earn and administer its resources. Long-lasting discussions have been held in literature as to whether the property of the central bank should be private or public and whether it is better for society to have a central bank influenced by the interests of private shareholders or by the parties leading the "government of the day". Central banks in rich countries earn such a large number of resources from their activities that they are protected from shareholders' pressures.[2] This may not occur in poor countries where the central bank may not be able to resist external pressures if the norms on the transfer of funds from other entities are not well devised.

The third form is "technical independence", which is the power of central banks to decide how to achieve objectives by applying the tools of monetary policy at their discretion. With the exception of monetarism,[3] all schools of thought have recognised that this form of independence should be conceded to central banks.

The fourth form is "goals and priorities independence", which is the power of central banks to define the value of the variables that represent the objectives of monetary policy, for instance the rate of inflation that policy must achieve, and the priority that is assigned to different goals. Past legislation hardly attributed this kind of independence to central banks. It entrusted this power to democratically elected bodies, moving from the view that these must take the most important decisions for the life of a society. These bodies can learn what society's preferences are in terms of policy goals and priorities, through the electoral mechanism. Achieving these goals is a complex activity that democratic representatives can rarely carry out effectively, for they often lack the necessary expertise. The activity is consequently delegated to technical authorities. According to the Radcliffe Report (1960, paragraph 767), the central bank is "a highly skilled executant in the monetary field of the current economic policy of the central Government". The bank should be given technical, financial, administrative and personnel independence, but not address goals and priorities. Recent literature has instead considered it convenient to hand this power to central banks (see Rogoff, 1985, and the related "institutional design literature"). It has proposed attributing power to central banks to decide the goals and priorities of monetary policy, assuming it is beneficial for society that the preferences of technical authorities prevail systematically over those expressed by citizens in the electoral process. This position has had a remarkable impact on literature, but has also generated strong reactions. To introduce the 1997–98 reform of the Bank of England, the Labour majority had to find a compromise solution that attributed the power to Parliament to make formal decisions on the objectives of monetary policy.

Several experts say that institutional design literature offers limited understanding of the phenomena considered and is incompatible with the functioning of democracy. Blinder (1998) criticised this literature for giving a false representation of the working of central banking.[4] Tobin (1994) claimed that the functioning of democracy is based on respect for procedures and not on the achievement of results defined by some theorists as socially optimal. When Greenspan (1996) was President of the Federal Reserve (Fed), he expressed concerns as to the way society could perceive the role of the central bank in the political context. For him, "it cannot be acceptable in a democratic society that a group of unelected individuals are vested with important responsibilities, without being open to full public scrutiny and accountability". These positions have led the Fed to adopt an organisation of policy that differs from that of the Bank of England. Both institutions recognise that the efficacy of monetary policy depends on the ability of the central bank to shape the operators' expectations. Yet, the Bank adopts a "credibility" strategy of communication, which implies complementing technical discretion with transparency in order to persuade the operators that the central bank is not involved in "dynamically inconsistent" behaviours and in the demagogy of the political authorities. The 1997 reform prescribes detailed rules that the Bank of England must obey to improve transparency. The Fed, on the other hand, adopts a strategy of communication aiming at reinforcing the "confidence" of the public in its ability to correctly interpret the movements of the markets and to represent a reliable guide for investment decisions.[5]

These analyses of the institutional organisation of monetary policy and of the strategies that can be adopted in central bank communication raise questions on the formal and actual functioning of a representative democracy. The reform of the Bank of England formally restored the principle that democratically elected bodies must make the most important decisions for the life of a society. However, the definition of goals and priorities also requires expertise that members of Parliament do not often possess. The competent technicians of the central bank can thus intervene in the decision process, directing Parliament on what must be done. The questions of the actual functioning of democracy and of the space occupied by the central bank in decision-making processes were considered by Keynes in his 1932 essay on CBI.

3. Central banking after WWI

A forceful demand for CBI emerged after WWI when the tasks of monetary authorities grew in complexity.[6] According to Sayers (1976), although "the Bank of England was not a central bank according to mid-twentieth-century usage of this term" before 1914 (p. 1; see also p. 66), it had performed functions implying public responsibilities and had gradually given priority to these responsibilities over its commercial interests. The Bank had been operating in three spheres of activities. Regarding the funding of financial institutions, "central banking was already recognisably in operation before 1914 ... the Bank after 1918 was most like the pre-war Bank" (Sayers, 1976, p. 272). The funding of the government sector was instead less developed. Until 1914, the supply of Treasury Bills, which were introduced in 1877, was small and irregular and the Bank did not keep them in portfolio (see Sayers, 1976, pp. 37, 42). The Bank had finally considered its primary responsibility the protection of gold reserves and the smooth working of the gold standard, which the political authorities had judged beneficial for the country (see Sayers, 1976, p. 28). The Bank had been protecting its gold reserves through the manipulation of the Bank Rate, for which it had developed effective techniques before 1914. The international capital flows had proved sensitive to changes in this rate. Its handling had been successful and there had been scarcely any complaint on the negative effects on trade and industrial activity (see Sayers, 1976, pp. 111–112). Moreover, there had been no interference with the funding of the government sector because "though rarely spoken between them, both Governor and Chancellor knew that the Treasury's needs ought not to get in the way of measures to protect the gold reserve" (Sayers, 1976, p. 8).

During the war, there were changes in the operation of monetary policy in relation to the funding of the government sector and the management of the international financial system. The support of the war effort enlarged the monetary powers of the Treasury. At the same time, the Bank of England had to favour the government's use of its gold reserves[7] and, for the first time, had to participate as technical advisor in the international meetings organised by the government to secure the supply of commodities to the national economy and to the Allies during the war.[8]

After WWI, the operations concerning the funding of the government sector and the consolidation of the British position in the international financial system underwent new variations. The state of public deficits transformed the funding of the Treasury into the main source of monetary issues and the large amount of trading in Treasury Bills dominated the determination of short-term interest rates. "The Bank had to accept the fact that the key short interest rate in London was none of its own fixing but was the rate fixed by the government for tap Treasury Bills" (Sayers, 1976, p. 112).

At the beginning of the 1920s, the Bank of England firmly advocated that the government discipline itself if the gold standard had to be restored, a standard the political authorities still considered beneficial for the country. By 1923, however, the Bank had taken advantage of the enlarged size of the market for Treasury Bills to control the short-term interest rates through open market operations, which Keynes (1930, vol. II, p. 208) considered the best device hitherto evolved to conduct monetary policy. From mid-1923 onwards, through these operations, "the Governor was in one way or another keeping rates pretty well where he wanted them in relation to Bank Rate" (Sayers, 1976, p. 301). When in 1924 he "told the Committee of Treasury that this was his channel, he was informing them of a practice that had already become permanent" (Sayers, 1976, p. 302).

The operations concerning the consolidation of the British position in the international financial system also underwent important variations. First, the need to restore the gold standard and to reconstruct the financial structures impaired by the war, in some European nations, led the Bank to take on new tasks, whose execution implied the adoption of political aims. Second, the enlarged amount of debt freely floating through Europe and USA trimmed down the ability of the central banks to control international capital flows. Changes in the interest rates lost effectiveness in directing these flows and the probability that they could interfere with the funding of the business and the government sectors rose, making the management of the Bank Rate a sensitive political issue.

During the war, the Bank of England had already established cooperative relations with the New York Federal Reserve Bank and its President Benjamin Strong. When the war was over, the unsettled state of the international financial system reinforced the need to cooperate with the US authorities. The Bank and the Fed became leading actors of the reorganisation of the international financial system. Strong and Norman, the Governor of the Bank of England, had a common objective "to bind [central bankers] together in a professional caste of mutual support and comfort" (Sayers, 1976, p. 156). They believed that independent central bankers "had more chance than any politicians of guiding the peoples of the world, both nationally and internationally, in the adoption and maintenance of policies needing time and patience" (Sayers, 1976, pp. 154–155).

The financial conferences held in Brussels (1920) and Genoa (1922) set the road for the development of cooperation among the monetary authorities and for the attribution to them of formal and substantial independence. The principle of autonomy

> was embodied ... in the new central banking statutes that formed part of the reconstruction schemes sponsored by the League of Nations, in Austria and Hungary, and the British Delegation had no difficulty in securing its inclusion in the formal Resolution of the Genoa Conference.
>
> Sayers (1976, p. 159)

The financial reconstruction of Europe led the Bank of England to direct, together with the Financial Committee of the League of Nations and the Fed, the process leading to the re-establishment of the financial system in Austria, Hungary, Germany and Poland and to the design of central banks in those countries and in the Dominions. Norman and Strong also piloted the agreements over the Italian war debt, asking independence for the Bank of Italy. These activities led the Bank of England to take initiatives that had no parallel in its history. The Bank gave a loan to the Austrian government on a non-commercial basis in order to persuade the international operators to channel funds to this country. It was an effort that the Bank made "to facilitate any support the Government wished to give ... Fortunately in this instance there was no difference between the Bank and Treasury as to the overriding political aims" (Sayers, 1976, p. 169).

The need for international cooperation generated by the enlarged size of financial transactions led the monetary authorities to develop stable links among them based on confidence, understanding and support. These elements promoted the institution of the Bank for International Settlements, which was conceived as a "club" for central bankers, i.e. as a place where the financial problems of the world economy were discussed, and as a "non-political central bank for central banks", i. e. as an institution complying with the principle that it had to be independent of governments and able to analyse and regulate the international payments system (see Sayers, 1976, p. 353). These aspirations were realised in 1930 when the Bank for International Settlements started to operate.

The Bank of England also played a leading role in the return to the gold standard. However, the international financial system had become difficult to control. Capital flows could now move among different financial centres in Europe and USA. The greater number of directions that these capital flows could take reduced the ability of the Bank to control them. The changes in the Bank Rate required to manage them were so large as to affect the funding of the business and the government sectors. These were not changes tolerated by society, which increasingly considered this aspect of monetary policy a sensitive political issue. The view that the gold standard had sacrificed the interests of industry and trade was widely held among industrialists, trade unionists and politicians of different parties. It led to initiatives like the Conference on Industrial Reorganisation and Industrial Relations and the request of a government inquiry into monetary policy (see Sayers, 1976, p. 360). These discontents were present in the 1928 programme of the Labour Party and were at the centre of the inquiry of the Macmillan Committee (1929–31). The Governor and the Directors of the Bank were preoccupied with the consequences on the Bank's independence with the accession to power of the Labour Party in June 1929 and with the recommendations of the Macmillan Report (1931). The actions of the government and the content of the Report, however, proved these preoccupations unjustified (see Sayers, 1976, pp. 211, 362, 371–372).

4. Keynes's activity in journalism and politics and the issue of CBI

Keynes discussed the issue of the independence of the Bank of England in public debates, in part published in literary-political media. He was guided by two convictions. First, he believed that political action could "make the private property system *work better*" (Keynes, 1939, p. 493; author's emphasis). Second, he thought that the main obstacle towards achieving this objective did not lie in overcoming conflicts of interest among social groups, but in devising the "techniques" that could solve problems and put them into practice by persuading public opinion (see Keynes, 1925, p. 329).

To favour the adoption of valuable policies, he considered it crucial that there be communication between the "opinion of the politicians, the journalists and the civil servants ... expressed in limited circles" (Keynes, 1921, pp. 48–49; see also Moggridge, 1992, p. 370) and the public. He thought that the views of the "limited circles" have to percolate, through open discussions, "to wider and wider circles" and "gradually affect" public opinion (Keynes, 1921, pp. 46–48 and 50).

The importance Keynes attributed to affecting public opinion led him to maintain contact with newspapers and magazines. After successfully editing some supplements to the *Manchester Guardian* (1922–23), he chaired and collaborated with a liberal journal, *The Nation* (see Graham, 1930, pp. 317–320; Moggridge, 1992, pp. 389–392; Skidelsky, 2009, p. 154). In subsequent years, the electoral weakness of the Liberal Party led Keynes to revise his strategy and to devote attention to the Labour Party (see Moggridge, 1992, p. 465). To this aim, a new vehicle for interventions was found in *The New Statesman*. In 1931, *The Nation* and *The New Statesman* merged and Kingsley Martin, highly esteemed by Keynes, was appointed editor. Keynes became chairman of the combined board and held the post until his death (see Moggridge, 1992, p. 508).

Another occasion for relations with the Labour Party arose when Snowden, as Chancellor of the Exchequer, appointed Keynes as a member of the Macmillan Committee (see Moggridge, 1992, pp. 481–482). Unlike those with Bevin, who had also been designated as a member of the Committee, the relations with MacDonald and Snowden were lukewarm. When the *Macmillan Report* was ready in spring 1931, Keynes signed it "without reservation" but, feeling that it was incomplete, appended an *Addendum* with his "Proposals Relating to Domestic Monetary Policy" (Moggridge, 1992, p. 510). Bevin and Allen signed the *Report* and the *Addendum*, presenting *Reservations* to both of them.

Although they were not focussed on the issue, the *Report* and the *Addendum* contained opinions on the role and legal position of the Bank of England. Some of these opinions reflected Keynes's conception of an institutional setting as a network of bodies in which the independence of each should be balanced by coordination based on reciprocal cooperation and deliberate division of labour. Bevin's views, advocated in his *Reservations*, were not far from this conception. They seem to differ from Keynes's position mainly for the kind of involvement of society that they envisaged – Bevin focusing on "popular confidence" and Keynes on "inner circles" of experts.

Bevin's position is connected with a moderate line of the Labour Party that prevailed in the formulation of the 1928 programme. This plan proposed that the Bank of England should be controlled by a public corporation (Labour Party, 1928, p. 27; see also Miliband, 1964, pp. 154–156).

Important developments in the Labour's analyses and proposals occurred after the fall of the second MacDonald Government in 1931. In August, MacDonald had formed a new government in coalition with Conservatives and Liberals and with the exclusion of former Labourite Ministers. This was seen as a betrayal by the National Executive, which expelled MacDonald and his supporters (see Pimlott, 1977, pp. 11–13). In the subsequent general election (October 1931) the Labour Party tried to reconstruct its identity and the reaction against the National Government led to a daring electoral manifesto. This differed from the 1928 programme for advocating the "national ownership" of the whole "banking and credit system" and the formation of a "National Investment Board for the control of domestic and foreign investment" (Dale, 2000, pp. 39–44). The election resulted in one of the worst defeats for Labour and the consequent shock triggered a search for a new strategy (see Pimlott, 1977, p. 17; Toye, 2003, p. 33). The Party set up a "Policy Committee" and a "Finance and Trade Subcommittee", both chaired by Hugh Dalton. They were fed with ideas and information from unofficial research groups, like the New Fabian Research Bureau[9] and the XYZ Club[10] (see Miliband, 1964, p. 196; Pimlott, 1977, p. 36; Toye, 2003, p. 53). Keynes had no direct role in these groups, but many of their members had close links with him (see Moggridge, 1992, p. 464).

While the New Fabian Research Bureau reviewed the intellectual background of the new Labour's strategy, the 1932 *Policy Report No. 1, Currency, Banking and Finance* of the Finance and Trade Subcommittee was prepared with the assistance of the XYZ Club (see Toye, 2003, p. 54). The *Report* included four resolutions that the National Executive submitted to the upcoming Conference of the Party. It reflected the moderate views of the XYZ Club and proposed that "the Bank of England should be brought under public ownership and control", without however involving the nationalisation of the joint-stock banks that had been required by some previous documents of the Party (see Toye, 2003, pp. 54–56). However, during the October 1932 Conference, the Left of the Party succeeded, in spite of Dalton's and Bevin's opposition, in having an amendment approved, asking for the nationalisation of joint-stock banks (see Miliband, 1964, pp. 202–203).

5. Keynes's 1932 essay on CBI and its relation with some modern disputes

On the 17th and 24th of September 1932 Keynes published a comment in *The New Statesman and Nation* on the Labour *Policy Report*, where he stated that its resolutions deserve attention "for they set forth a moderate and quite practicable monetary policy" (Keynes, 1932, p. 128). This remark gives more support to Toye's (2003, p. 55) view that Keynes's attitude towards the *Report* was one of "guarded approval" than to that of Bibow (2002, pp. 772–773), which concludes that Keynes strongly opposed it.

The first part of Keynes's (1932, pp. 130–131) comment contains a short but articulated discussion of the role and legal position of the Bank of England. Keynes reviewed the *Report* by laying down "five propositions as embodying the essentials". The first three deal with "personnel" and "financial and administrative independence". As to the former, Keynes (1932, p. 131) stated that "the higher appointments should require the approval of the Chancellor of the Exchequer" and that "the directorate should be elected on public grounds and should not stand for the interests of the City any more than for other nominal interest" (Keynes, 1932, p. 131). Regarding the latter, he underlined that the Bank, as a "national institution", must be free from the pressures of private groups and work in the interest of the whole society. These remarks are noteworthy given that some authors dealing with the origin of the recent financial crisis recognise that current literature has overlooked the pressures of private groups on financial authorities to focus on those of the political authorities (see Levine, 2010).

The fourth proposition deals with "goals and priorities independence". Keynes (1932, p. 131) stated that elected bodies in a representative democracy must make the fundamental decisions on the objectives that society wants to achieve. According to him, these decisions establish "the main lines of policy, the choice of which, as distinct from the execution, was not properly [the Bank's] affair at all" (*ibid.*, p. 132). This standpoint has some elements in common with that expressed by Greenspan (1996) as a reaction to the proposal of Rogoff (1985) and of the institutional design literature to attribute this form of independence to central banks.

To further clarify the roles of elected and non-elected authorities, Keynes (1932, p. 131) added a sixth proposition dealing with "technical independence". For him, "the less direct the democratic control and the more remote the opportunities for parliamentary interference with banking policy the better it will be". He added: "If the Bank of England is to carry out the monetary policy which is proposed in [the Labour Party's] pamphlet, it will be engaged in the practice of a very difficult technique, of which Parliament will understand less than nothing".

This separation of competence among elected and non-elected bodies does not imply absence of communication, cooperation and coordination among them. The question of cooperation and coordination was considered in the second part of Keynes's comment (1932, pp. 133–136), where he stated that if we want to carry out a monetary policy that effectively controls the fluctuations of employment and the value of the sterling, "what we need is a coordinated policy to determine the rate of aggregate investment by public and semi-public bodies". Keynes had raised this problem in previous writings[11] and he "warmly" welcomed the resolution of the *Report* in his comment, providing several additional elements on its content.

The importance that Keynes (1932, p. 131) attributed to communication is reflected in the fifth proposition presented in his comment. He stated that information about the Bank's activities "should be as public as possible and should be deliberately exposed to outside criticism". This remark is in line with what he had stated in previous work. Keynes (1926, pp. 315 and 318) had pointed out that an effective measure to improve the results of monetary policy is to enhance "the collection and dissemination on a great scale of data relating to the business situation" and submit the policy decisions to public discussions with the "involvement of Societ". This position is also connected to his convictions that the authorities should not be involved in any social or political conflicts and should clarify the reasons for the adoption of technical decisions.

Keynes's position on communication is close to that recently adopted by the Fed, which underlines the need to establish intense interchanges with society in order to develop a high degree of confidence in its technical ability. This position differs from that implied by the last reform of the Bank of England, which attempts to increase the credibility of this institution by implementing a high degree of transparency in order to persuade the operators that the central bank is not involved in "dynamically inconsistent" behaviours and in the demagogical attempts of the political authorities to deviate from the "natural rate of unemployment" (see Le Heron, 2007). Unlike the institutional design literature, the analyses of Keynes and the Fed do not move from the standpoint that democracy is harmful for society because the political authorities are unreliable. The works that have recently examined Keynes's view on CBI have underestimated this point.

Keynes (1932, pp. 132–133) concluded his analysis of the roles of elected and non-elected authorities with a clarification of the influence of formal legislation and of the actual interactions among the subjects involved in the policy decision-making process. This is another point that recent literature on Keynes's view on CBI has underplayed. Keynes started with a defence of the Bank of England, saying that "its independence and its prestige are assets" for the whole society and "its public spirit over the last decade" cannot be called in question. According to Keynes, the Bank should be criticised for its policy rather than for the powers that legislation assigns to it. There had however been a problem, he stated, with the peculiar way policy decisions had been taken after WWI. Parliament had failed to identify the detailed objectives that the monetary authorities had to achieve, leaving the Bank free to exercise powers that it should not have:

> The demand for its subjection to the democracy largely arises, I think, out of peculiarities of recent years which will not characterise a normal regime. More often than not since the War the country has possessed no defined standard and not even a defined monetary policy laid down by Parliament; with the consequence that the Bank of England has been left free to exercise, though it has not been loath to exercise, a wider discretion than it ought to have ... on matters which go far beyond the practice of a technique for the attainment of a purpose, the general character of which has been laid down by higher authority.
>
> Keynes (1932, p. 132)

For Keynes, the solution to this problem requires improving Parliament's actual participation in decisions on the main lines of policy.

In spite of its relevance, which Keynes lucidly perceived,[12] the distinction between the influence of formal legislation and the actual interactions among the subjects involved, has often been overlooked in recent literature. However, some essays recognise the importance of this distinction. Describing his experience as a component of the Council of Economic Advisors of President Clinton, Stiglitz (1998) points out that, even when there were significant divergences with the Fed,[13] the Council avoided debating them in public:

In the Clinton Administration, we adopted a policy of not commenting on Fed policy, not because we did not have strong views – at certain critical stages, many in the Administration thought their policies were seriously misguided – but because we thought a public debate would be counter-productive. We thought the Fed would not listen, the newspapers would love the controversy, and the markets, worried by the uncertainty that such controversy generates, would add a risk premium to long-term rates, thereby increasing those rates, which was precisely what we did not want to happen.

Stiglitz (1998, p. 200; see also p. 201)

For Stiglitz, the Fed, aware of the reactions of the markets, took advantage of this situation to ignore the President's requests to reconsider its position. He wrote:

Presidents have not been shy about expressing to the Fed what they think it should do, but the Fed has not been shy about ignoring these messages.

Stiglitz (1998, p. 200; see also pp. 201 and 209 fn. 9)

6. Conclusions

In an essay examining the 1932 *Policy Report* that the National Executive submitted to the Labour Party Conference, Keynes presented a proposal on how to organise relations between the central bank and other private and public institutions.

The proposal clarifies that CBI must protect policy decisions from the pressures coming from both private and political groups. This view is relevant today given the institutional design literature's neglect of the pressures of private groups and its insistence on the need to free central banks from political pressures. The ideas of Levine and Goodhart reveal that Keynes's views still shed light on present disputes: Levine (2010) elucidates that the neglect of the pressures of private groups has had an important bearing on the occurrence of the recent financial crisis and Goodhart (2008) makes the specious statement that the Bank of England became independent in 1997, when it was isolated from the demagogic pressures of the political authorities.

Keynes did not hold the political authorities in contempt. The communication strategy currently utilised by the monetary authorities in the USA (see Le Heron, 2007) indicates that his respectful attitude towards the political authorities can still lead to a satisfactory institutional organisation. Moreover, he did not argue, as some recent literature does (see Panico and Vazquez Suarez, 2008), that enlarging the powers of central banks and restraining those of the other authorities can avoid misguided policies. He maintained instead that an institutional setting prompting coordination between monetary and fiscal policies is necessary to attain a proficient use of all available instruments. In the face of the disappointing results achieved by the recent restraint of discretionary fiscal policies, Keynes's conclusions are to be warmly welcomed.

Notes

1 See Arestis, 2006; Arestis and Sawyer, 2006; Bibow, 2002, 2010; Panico and Piccioni, 2016.
2 Sayers (1976, p. 290) and Keynes (1932, p. 131) point out that after 1914, the earnings of the Bank of England were so large as to make the pressures of its private shareholders ineffectual.
3 Arguing against technical independence, Friedman (1962, pp. 50–51) claimed: "To paraphrase Clemenceau, money is too serious a matter to be left to the Central Bankers". For him, discretion leads central banks to errors and abuses. They should follow a fixed rule of monetary issue instead.
4 Recalling his experience in the Federal Reserve, Blinder denies that central bankers suffer from "inflation bias". On these points, he says, this literature "is barking at the wrong tree" (1998, p. 24).
5 For an analysis of the difference between "credibility" and "confidence" strategy, see Le Heron (2007).
6 See Sayers (1967, pp. 66–67). Sayers (1976, p. 272) says that "the 1914–18 war is a watershed in the history of the Bank of England".
7 There were conflicts between the Bank of England and the Treasury regarding the use of gold reserves in 1915 and 1917. These conflicts, which are analysed by Sayers (1976, pp. 88–89 and 99–105), can be seen as the first fights over CBI. Sayers also points out the existence of conflicts between the Bank of England and the London commercial banks during the same period.
8 De Cecco (2003, pp. 34–35) notices that in April 1915, before Italy entered WWI, the Italian and the British governments met in Nice to organise the funding of the imports that Italy needed for the war effort. On that occasion, the Governors of the central banks accompanied the political authorities. According to De Cecco, this was perhaps the first time that the official delegations were composed in this way. It was an acknowledgement that the central bank was an integral part of the powers of a nation at its highest level.
9 Cole formed the New Fabian Research Bureau in 1931, out of frustration with both the old Fabian Society and the Labour government. The Bureau included several young Keynesians, like Colin Clark, James Meade, Roy Harrod, Richard Kahn (see Miliband, 1964, p. 196 note 2). In January 1932, it organised a Conference on the Socialisation of Banking.
10 The Club was formed by sympathetic City experts (including some former Keynes's students and Nicholas Davenport, financial columnist of *The New Statesman*). Dalton acted as the group's main liaison with the Party (see Toye, 2003, p. 53).
11 In his *Addendum* to the *Macmillan Report* (*Addendum I*, pp. 190–192), Keynes had acknowledged that the gold standard regime "strictly limited" the ability of the Bank of England "to diminish the rate of interest" in order "to stimulate the volume of investment", and had suggested a close coordination with the Government in order to enhance investment at home through a Board of National Investment. This measure had also been proposed in the 1928 Report of the Liberal Industrial Inquiry and in the electoral pamphlet supporting Lloyd George (see Keynes and Henderson, 1929).
12 Kaldor (1970) too perceived this distinction. He pointed out that central bankers are like "constitutional monarchs". Their policy decisions must take into account the powers that legislation formally attribute to them, their influence on society and the reactions of political authorities to them. As Stiglitz (1998, p. 222) pointed out by recalling the views of two US central bankers, Volcker and Burns, central bankers must be considered "political actors" participating in the life of society.

13 "We shared data with the Fed. We even shared models. We had the same data describing what was happening to wages and prices. But we frequently made different inferences about what was likely to happen in the future" (Stiglitz, 1998, p. 217). This was because "value judgments often assert themselves even in what should be purely 'positive' discussions of the trade-off between inflation and unemployment" (Stiglitz, 1998, p. 218).

References

Arestis, P. (2006). New monetary policy and Keynes. *European Journal of Economics and Economic Policies: Intervention*, 3 (2), 245–262.

Arestis, P. and Sawyer, M. (2006). Inflation targeting and CBI: we are all Keynesians now! *Journal of Post Keynesian Economics*, 28 (4), 639–652.

Bibow, J. (2002). Keynes on central banking and the structure of monetary policy. *History of Political Economy*, 34 (4), 749–787.

Bibow, J. (2010). *A Post Keynesian perspective on the rise of CBI: a dubious success story in monetary economics*. Levy Economics Institute Working Paper, no. 625. October. Annandale-on-Hudson, NY: Levy Economics Institute of Bard College.

Blinder, A.S. (1998). *Central banking in theory and practise*. Cambridge: MIT Press.

Dale, I., ed. (2000). *Labour Party general election manifestos 1900–1997*. London: Routledge.

De Cecco, M. (2003). L'Italia e il sistema finanziario internazionale, 1860–1936. In: F. Cotula, M. de Cecco and G. Toniolo, eds. *La Banca d'Italia: sintesi della ricerca storica, 1893–1960*. Roma-Bari: Laterza.

Friedman, M. (1962), *Capitalism and Freedom*. Chicago: The University of Chicago Press.

Goodhart, C.A.E. (2008). Bank of England. In: S.N. Durlauf and L.E. Blume, eds. *The New Palgrave Dictionary of Economics*. 2nd edition. London: Palgrave Macmillan.

Graham, W. (1930). *English literary periodicals*. New York: Thomas Nelson & Sons.

Greenspan, A. (1996). The challenge of central banking in a democratic society. In: *Remarks by Chairman Alan Greenspan at the Annual Dinner and Francis Boyer Lecture of the American Enterprise Institute for Public Policy Research*. Washington, DC. 5 December 1996. Available at https://www.federalreserve.gov/BOARDDOCS/SPEECHES/19961205.htm.

Kaldor, N. (1970). The new monetarism. *Lloyds Bank Review*, 97 (July), 1–18.

Keynes, J.M. (1921). *The revision of the treaty*. London: Macmillan. Reprinted in Keynes (1931) *Essays in persuasion*. London: Macmillan.

Keynes, J.M. (1925). Am I a liberal? *The Nation and Athenaeum*. August 8 and 15. Reprinted in Keynes (1931) *Essays in persuasion*. London: Macmillan.

Keynes, J.M. (1926). *The end of laissez-faire*. London: Hogarth Press. Reprinted in Keynes (1931) *Essays in persuasion*. London: Macmillan.

Keynes, J.M. (1930). *A treatise on money*. 2 vols. London: Macmillan.

Keynes, J.M. (1932). The monetary policy of the Labour Party. *The New Statesman and Nation*, Sept. 17 and 24. As reprinted in (1982) *Activities 1931–1939: world crises and policies in Britain and in America*, vol. XXI of: *The Collected Writings of J.M. Keynes* (D. Moggridge, ed.). London: Macmillan, 128–137.

Keynes, J.M. (1939). Democracy and efficiency. *The New Statesman and Nation*, Jan. 28. As reprinted in (1982) *Activities 1931–1939: world crises and policies in Britain and in America*, vol. XXI of: *The Collected Writings of J.M. Keynes* (D. Moggridge, ed.). London: Macmillan, 491–500.

Keynes, J.M. and Henderson, H.D. (1929). *Can Lloyd George do it?* London: The Nation and Athenaeum.

Labour Party. (1928). *Labour and the nation.* London: Labour Party.

Le Heron, H. (2007). The new governance in monetary policy: a critical appraisal of the Fed and the ECB. In: P. Arestis, E. Hein and E. Le Heron, eds. *Aspects of modern monetary and macroeconomic policies.* London: Palgrave Macmillan, 146–171.

Levine, R. (2010). *The governance of financial regulation: reform lessons from the recent crisis.* BIS Working Papers, no. 329. November. Basel: Bank of International Settlements.

Miliband, R. (1964). *Parliamentary socialism: a study in the politics of Labour.* New York: Monthly Review Press.

Moggridge, D.E. (1992). *Maynard Keynes: an economist's biography.* London: Routledge.

Panico, C. and Piccioni, M. (2016). Keynes on Central Bank Independence. *Studi Economici,* 118-119-120, 190–216.

Panico, C. and Rizza, M.O. (2004). CBI and democracy: a historical perspective. In: R. Arena and N. Salvadori, eds. *Money, credit and the role of the state: essays in honour of Augusto Graziani.* Aldershot: Ashgate, 445–465.

Panico, C. and Vazquez Suarez, M. (2008). Policy coordination in the Euro Area. *Studi Economici,* 96 (3), 5–31.

Pimlott, B. (1977). *Labour and the left in the 1930s.* Cambridge: Cambridge University Press.

Radcliffe Report. (1960). *Committee on the working of the monetary system: report,* Cmnd. 827. London: Her Majesty's Stationary Office.

Report of [Macmillan] Committee on Finance and Industry. (1931). *With addenda and reservations.* London: His Majesty's Stationary Office.

Rogoff, K. (1985). The optimal degree of commitment to an intermediate monetary target. *Quarterly Journal of Economics,* 100 (4), 1169–1189.

Sayers, R.S. (1967). *Modern banking.* 7th edition. Oxford: Oxford University Press.

Sayers, R.S. (1976). *The Bank of England: 1891–1944.* 2 vols. Cambridge: Cambridge University Press.

Skidelsky, R. (2009). *Keynes. The return of the master.* New York: Public Affairs.

Stiglitz, J. (1998). Central banking in a democratic society. *De Economist,* 146 (2), 196–226.

Tobin, J. (1994). Panel discussion: how can monetary policy be improved? In: J.C. Fuhrer. ed., *Goals, guidelines, and constraints facing monetary policymakers. Proceedings of a Conference held at North Falmouth, MA,* June, Federal Reserve Bank of Boston, Conference Series, no. 38, 232–236.

Toye, R. (2003). *The Labour Party and the planned economy 1931–1951.* Woodbridge: Boydell Press.

14 "New Liberalism" the Italian way: 1918–1947

Marco Dardi

1. Introduction

According to a widespread historiographical convention, the term "New Liberalism" (NL) indicates an intellectual movement precisely circumscribed in space and time: the authors – the most common references are to Green, Bosanquet, Hobson and Hobhouse – who emphasised the need to update the liberal political doctrine in the face of the social issues emerging in Britain in the decades around the turn of the twentieth century. But NL was also a response to a more general historical trend, one that was not limited to Britain and was variously described as the "crisis," or "failure," or "end" of liberalism – in short, a crisis involving the two cornerstones of the doctrine, i.e. the idea of natural personal rights and the restriction of the role of the State to the mere sanction of the pact of reciprocal respect of such rights. The evolution of British and American capitalism during the course of the nineteenth century was seen as evidence that that particular eighteenth-century doctrine was essentially flawed. Since the free interplay of economic rights, identified with basic personal rights, had led to the formation of big capitalistic conglomerates that competed with the State for political power and enjoyed privileges from which most people were barred, the existence of internal contradictions in the doctrine was apparent. To get rid of these, basic rights would need to be reshaped and the State would have to disown the position of indifferent custodian that it had been assigned.

While by convention NL is typically British, the crisis of liberalism and the attempts to respond to it are not. It does not seem strained, therefore, to extend the label NL to cover other historical cases, in particular the Italian case that is our concern here. The fact of using the same label is not meant to suggest that the Italian NL, chronologically later than the British original, was influenced by the latter. De Ruggiero, the philosopher and well-known historian of European liberalism, made it clear that, in the early years of the period covered here, the British NL was still unknown in Italy and the main cultural and political references were continental.[1]

Although the reasons for the liberal crisis were understood to lie in the economy, British NL originated in ethical and political thought, with comparatively minor attention being paid to economic aspects. Of the founding fathers of NL mentioned above, only Hobson was an economist, and one whose credentials were not above suspicion. Recent historiography, however, has emphasised how leading British economists, although not openly adhering to NL, immediately responded to it. The birth and development of welfare economics at the hands of Cambridge economists Marshall and Pigou can be seen as a sign that the process of revising the foundations of liberal thought involved also the headquarters of British economic theory (see Backhouse and Nishizawa, 2010).

The Italian case was quite different for obvious reasons of context. The social question that besieged *soi-disant* "liberal" governments at the turn of the century was not the outcome of the excesses of an industrial development of the Manchesterian type – an unknown phenomenon in Italy. Rather, it resulted from a policy of enforced industrialisation, supported by strong doses of State interventionism and protectionism, imposed on a country in which backward economic and social conditions prevailed.[2] The élite group of liberal economists that, in 1890, took over the management of the *Giornale degli economisti* – De Viti de Marco, Pantaleoni, Pareto and Mazzola – insisted that the social conflicts of the period were not to be imputed to defects in the implementation of liberal policies, because no such policies had ever been carried out in Italy. The crisis was interpreted as the exclusive effect of misconceived measures taken by a sequence of governments that were neither liberal nor democratic. And while in Britain the new field of welfare economics provided economic remedies for some of the most evident market failures, the Italian liberal economists still advocated traditional measures of privatisation and liberalisation, together with political reforms aimed at breaking the links between government and old or newly established privileged classes. Liberals did not represent the majority of Italian economists, however, and in any case they lacked any sort of political influence. Thus, nothing much changed from their point of view until the aftermath of WWI, when the sense of a radically new start after the mayhem led new generations of liberals to doubt that the old couple liberalism-cum-democracy was still what was needed for the future of the country.

This is why 1918 is taken here as the beginning of the Italian NL. In the violent clash between a socialist movement with a strong Marxist component and an authoritarian blend of nationalism soon to be merged with fascism, liberals of the traditional kind[3] seemed to hesitate between embracing the anti-socialist faction or siding with an emerging liberal-reformist movement that was trying to constitute a "third position" between the conflicting parties. This movement relied on prominent intellectual figures, such as the ex-socialist historian Gaetano Salvemini or the liberal legal scholar Francesco Ruffini, and also on a small number of young energetic intellectuals among whom Piero Gobetti and Carlo Rosselli unquestionably stood out. It was around these two figures that a laboratory for redefining the meaning of liberalism was formed. Eventually, fascism came out as the political winner, and made the lives of its opponents difficult if not impossible, but this did not prevent a few of them from continuing their struggle in clandestinity. Paradoxically, fascism itself, however anti-liberal, in boasting that it had surpassed the old dichotomy between liberalism and socialism, felt the need to elaborate a response of its own to the issues raised by the new-liberals: a task that a minority of "left-wing fascists"[4] interpreted in directions not overly distant from NL. Apparently, the contrast between liberalism and authoritarianism did not hinder the convergence of the two sides on the same knots in trying to identify ways out of the problems of the epoch.

Around 1942, a group of survivors of the new-liberals of the 1920s, together with younger newcomers, managed to set up a clandestine political formation called Partito d'Azione (PdA), an anti-Fascist, non-communist and non-Catholic organisation that was to become one of the protagonists of the Italian "Resistenza." The social and economic views of the different components of the PdA were far from coherent, and indeed the party survived the end of the war for only two years until its final split in 1947. That is also the final date of this reconstruction. The story of the metamorphoses of liberal thinking in Italy certainly does not stop there, but the coordinates after WWII belong to an entirely different historical phase.

This chapter does not intend to reconstruct the positions of the several individuals and currents of thought involved – a volume would not suffice for such a task. The much less ambitious aim is to identify a few conceptual dichotomies that can be used as coordinates of a simplified conceptual space in which it is virtually possible to locate individuals and political movements. I took the idea of a conceptual map of this sort from the first chapter of that splendid book on British NL, Collini (1979), although Collini's coordinates, which refer to a different country and epoch, inevitably differ from mine. The result is a graphic rendering that may help us in understanding the conceptual closeness or distance behind the smoke of contingent political battles. It also helps us to make sense of the relatively modest impact of this long phase of intellectual unrest on the Italian economic profession.

2. Social liberalism vs left–wing corporatism

This section presents a synthetic view of the main issues debated in the first part (approximately 1918–1925) of the interval to which this chapter refers, and of how the debate was successively suffocated by the fascist regime, to be rekindled only after 1942 inside the PdA. As hinted in Section 1, in the years immediately after WWI the need for renovating Italian liberal thinking did not come from a direct experience with failures in a liberal economic order that had never materialised in this country. Severe social strife, however, made it easy for a number of politically committed young intellectuals to think of the historical moment in terms of the classical "new force against old resistance" pattern typical of the golden age of the birth of liberalism. Differently from the eighteenth century, the progressive force was now represented by the socialist movement, the agenda of which was not an extension of the traditional economic rights to the working class, but the latter's seizure of political control over the entire productive process of the economy. Resistance, in turn, was represented not so much by a despotic State – governments of the period up to the fascist *coup d'état* of 1922 were fragile and irresolute – but by the concentration of economic power in the hands of industrial and financial capital and *ancien-régime* landed property. It is understandable that, confronted with this evidence, the young liberals adopted the widespread view according to which socialism was the next step to liberalism or, better still, the interpreter of liberalism for the contemporary age.[5] This was the frontier in which liberalism had to position itself if it wanted to return to playing a progressive role in society.

Embracing socialism meant embracing its agenda and identifying the same enemies. With regard to the agenda, a common trait of new-liberal authors such as Rosselli, Gobetti and others who contributed to the most vivacious liberal and socialist journals of the period,[6] was the reclamation of liberty as an instrument of political action, a means to enhance the individual's capacities by granting him/her enough autonomy from material needs to develop a moral and political conscience. The classical emphasis on economic liberties was correspondingly deflated. The main target was not the addition of a belated new bourgeoisie to the old one, but the access of the working class to self-government, i.e. to participating in the formation of the aims and values of the entire society. As for the common enemy, there was no question that this was capitalism, the degenerate son of the economic liberties. But here, a discriminant between new-liberals and certain currents of socialism came to light: for liberals, replacing capitalism with a different economic order could not mean one-class dominance and socialisation of all the means of production as the final solution to the social conflict. Politically, for them liberty meant "method," not "system," and if liberty had to remain the historical progressive force, final solutions could not even be conceived. The new-liberals' view of history was that of an open-ended process characterised by incessant struggle, mediation, creativity: nothing that could be predicted in advance, and in particular nothing in common with "Second International" doctrines of socialism. For some new-liberals, adhesion to socialism as the heir to liberalism was explicitly conditional on a divorce between socialism and Marxism, at least Marxism in its most mechanistic interpretations.[7]

The latter aspect reveals the imprint of the philosophical culture of the times, characterised by that merger of anti-positivism and idealism that in Italy was represented by the Neo-Idealism of Benedetto Croce and Giovanni Gentile. Anti-positivism was reflected in the distance from Marxism seen as a social theory based on a sort of naturalistic determinism. Croce's liberalism – a highly abstract and philosophical doctrine – differed from Gentile's at least as much as their respective versions of idealism did,[8] but a feature they shared was the emphasis on a positive notion of liberty as opposed to the negative liberty of classical economic liberalism. This aspect was well expressed by De Ruggiero, another philosopher of the idealist ilk:

Liberty is not indetermination and arbitrary will, but the capacity of the individual to determine himself, hence to redeem himself from the subjection to practical necessity and constraints by means of a spontaneous adhesion of his own conscience … Being free coincides with being *sui iuris*.

De Ruggiero (1925, p. 339)

This philosophical notion of autonomy as the "conscience of necessity" equated liberty with a moral task, that of being an active member of society and contributing to the creation of its destiny. The instruments for such a task, in particular the personal rights that provide the conditions for performing it adequately, were related to the prevailing cultural sensitivity of the historical moment: they could not be specified once and for all. The result was the reduction of personal rights to historical incidents, in accordance with the idea of fluidity of the liberal political order discussed in the previous paragraph.

Positive liberty and the historicisation of personal rights had a deep impact on the legal foundations of liberalism, as Ruffini – an acknowledged master for many young new-liberals – was quick to realise (Ruffini, 1926). First, all ties with *jus naturale* were definitely severed. Ruffini elevated personal rights to the status of essential components of the constitution of a State – "public" personal rights, rooted in the same cultural ground as the authority of the State, i.e. in the juridical conscience of the people, 'a spontaneous psycho-collective phenomenon' (ibid., p. 124). Twenty years later another jurist and PdA member, Piero Calamandrei (1946), in commenting on Ruffini would theorise the principle of the "open list" of personal rights, a list destined to change with changes in political culture, as opposed to the "closed list" of the economic rights of classical liberalism. He also pointed out that, with many personal rights, the State's obligation to guarantee their actual universal enjoyment amounted to a program of positive action of an economic and discretional nature. Thus, also the ties with the principle of the minimal State were severed.

The twenty years that divided Calamandrei's comments from Ruffini's text were those in which the first generation of Italian new-liberals was either physically eliminated, imprisoned or in any case reduced to silence by the fascist regime. That story does not need to be repeated here. In this interval, however, the regime did not limit itself to repression. Since it boasted that it had gone beyond liberalism and socialism by opening up a "third way" to the solution of social problems, it needed ideas to give some substance to the formula. Corporatism was the only asset that could be brought to bear on the issue, although an exact interpretation of what it actually consisted in was always in dispute even inside the fascist party. It was within this context that a "left-wing" fascist current, the main exponents of which were the two philosophers Ugo Spirito and Arnaldo Volpicelli,[9] outlined an interpretation of corporatism that encroached on themes that had been the typical reserve of new-liberal speculations. According to Spirito and Volpicelli, the corporative system had to be based on the corporations' taking over the ownership of capital from private hands; the management of capital was to be entrusted to a technocracy recruited from the highest layers of the labour force; trade unions were to be abolished, since the collective proprietary structure had removed all reasons for labour conflicts; and, at the top of the hierarchy, the State had to coordinate the whole system and indicate national strategic targets. In spite of the anti-liberal tirades found in almost all their writings on the subject, this technocratic dream ("dream" because nothing like that was ever near enough to be realised by the regime) paralleled arguments that are found in new-liberal literature although not with the same authoritarian flavour, as will be seen in the next section.[10]

The last episode of our story is less neat. The PdA took up the inheritance of Gobetti's and Rosselli's movements together with other anti-fascist groups formed independently in later years, not all of whom however shared the same inspiration as the new-liberals. Even the "Liberalsocialismo" movement promoted in 1937 by the philosopher Guido Calogero and the non-conventional Catholic thinker Aldo Capitini differed in various respects from Rosselli's "Socialismo liberale," notwithstanding the similarity in names.[11] Other components of the party were nearer to classical economic liberalism or to more left-wing versions of socialism. The maximum effort at a synthesis of the various souls of the PdA was produced in 1942 with a scheme for the post-war reconstruction of the economy of the country according to a mixed private-public institutional architecture split into two sectors, with partial socialisation of the means of production and labour's participation in the management and profits of firms.[12] Consensus within the party was always fragile, however, and at the first post-war elections of 1946 the PdA also suffered a total lack of popular support, revealing itself for what it was, more an élite movement run by a highly intellectual coterie than a true political force. Perhaps the fittest comment came from one of its members, the economist Alberto Bertolino, who in a posthumous evaluation of the PdA defined it as 'the most demanding political experiment of Italian historicism' (Bertolino, 1951, p. 778).

3. The concept-space of the debate

If we now reconsider the previous survey from the point of view of the main stress lines underlying the relations between new-liberals and the other players in the game – classical liberalism, socialism, fascism – we can envisage a sort of concept-space with two coordinates that seem to capture all the crucial issues. One is the role assigned to subjective intentionality in determining social and economic trends; the other is the kind of relationship established between individuals and collective agencies.

The new-liberals' historicism was naturally opposed not only to the most deterministic versions of Marxism, but also to the utilitarian foundations of the economic theories that supported classical liberalism, such as e.g. Pantaleoni's economic hedonism or the mathematical models of competitive equilibrium. It was easy to reframe these tensions in terms of a contrast between two extreme philosophical positions that here we can call "mechanicism" (sometimes described also with the term "naturalism") and "historicism," defined by the emphasis laid on freely formed subjective intentionality as an agent of social transformation. This emphasis was clearly non-existent in the former extreme, with history being viewed as not being substantially different from the unfolding of a natural process regulated by known and unchangeable impersonal laws. Emphasis was instead a maximum in the latter extreme, in which "history" was just another name for "liberty in process," as Croce had it: the external projection of ideas operating as creative forces through a human agency. Between the two, one can of course think of a continuum of virtual intermediate positions, depending on the extent to which intentionality is made to operate under constraints set by objective factors.

Also the second coordinate of our space can be identified by defining two opposite extremes that, to use a terminology of the time, we can call "organicism" and "individualism." The former refers to collectivities seen as something distinct from the collections of individuals who contingently happen to constitute them. An organic group is an abstract collection of past, present and future individuals linked to each other by some kind of biological, cultural and institutional continuity extending through time: an entity that remains equal to itself, although individuals flow through it like drops in a stream. Typically, such a group is attributed personhood and interests of its own, distinct from those of the individuals who temporarily provide it with a physical body. Each individual may internalise the group's interests, making them coincide with his/her own, or refuse them.[13] At the opposite extreme, the essence of the individualistic point of view consists in seeing a collectivity as nothing more than an empirical collection of individuals who share certain characteristics. For the individualist, the group is a non-person, and has no other interests than those that can be constructed through some kind of combination of its members' individual interests.

The new-liberals, with their idea of the individual as a conscious and active interpreter of society's needs, naturally belonged to the organicist field. In this, they polemically opposed classical liberalism, which they identified with an essentially individualistic social theory. Their relationship with socialism was more complex, however. Socialism too was organic, in their view, but with a tendency to drown the individual's moral tension in the collective effort of the working class as an independent whole, first to gain and then to administer complete control of the economy. This was more organic than the new-liberals were willing to accept, as we saw in Section 2. There was thus a hierarchy of organicisms, and the new-liberals' one was not at the top of it. On a legal plane, this was clearly theorised by Ruffini (1926, pp. 13–22) with the notion of "organic representation" – the right of organic groups, as legal persons, to have a representation of their own in government – which he separated into partial and total representation. The former corresponds to the organicism of the liberal State, which leaves the individuals free to form and/ or join organised groups that, in turn, contribute through their interaction to the formation of social will. The latter characterises the authoritarian State, which forces the individuals to adhere to groups pre-established by the State itself for special purposes: practically organs of the State. This was the case of the Soviet State according to Ruffini, and also of the fascist corporate order that was beginning to be outlined in the 1920s. In new-liberal thought, the partial organic representation took the shape of decentralisation of power, federalism, trade-unionism, workers associations and the like – all recurring themes in the 1920s and later at the time of the PdA.[14]

If for graphic convenience we combine the two conceptual coordinates just discussed in a bi-dimensional diagram we obtain the square represented here below as Figure 14.1, our virtual conceptual space. Take the horizontal side to represent the gap between mechanicism (point 0) and historicism (point 1), and the vertical side that between individualism (0) and organicism (1). In the Figure, the points marked with L and S indicate the positions occupied, respectively, by classical liberalism and socialism according to their adversaries on both the left and the right political sides.[15] In fact, none of the great liberal economists of the time – neither Pantaleoni, nor Pareto, nor Einaudi, to limit ourselves to some of the biggest names – as the complex social thinkers that they were, could be cornered to L; neither could a sophisticated socialist and later communist political thinker such as Gramsci be forced in S. But this is how they were often represented for polemical reasons. The position of the new-liberals, marked with NL, is instead clearly understandable in the light of the previous discussion.

The ubiquity of Gentile in the survey of Section 2 above, and the presence of a left-wing fascist minority that seemed to appropriate the themes typical of NL, suggest that locating these two intellectual positions in our concept-space might turn out to be interesting.

Still in 1923, just before being appointed an honorary member of the Fascist party, Gentile titled a short programmatic paper of his "My Liberalism" (Gentile, 1923). What kind of liberalism was that? As idealist as he was, Gentile had strong reasons for rejecting mechanicism in all its forms. The Hegelian brand of his idealism led him directly to conceive the State as an organic entity embodying all the highest manifestations of spirit: his State was

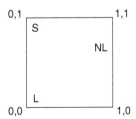

Figure 14.1 Diagram 1

the Ethical State, and as such it had the duty to educate its citizens. The problem of the individual rights of liberty of the citizens disappears at this point because, if it performs its mission successfully, the will of the State becomes the citizens' will, and in consciously submitting to it their "subjective" liberty comes to coincide with "objective," absolute liberty. This doctrine of the identification of the individual with the State was not too far from De Ruggiero's definition of liberty as the "conscience of necessity" recalled above. But in identifying necessity with the expression of the will of an ethical State, Gentile prepared the ground for arguing that even Mussolini's authoritarian State was an instance of a liberal State. Indeed, he did not say so, but the identification of individual and State may well be the result of inculcation. In any case, Gentile's so-called liberalism, indicated with GG in Figure 14.2 here below, must occupy the north-east corner of our concept-space, distinct from NL simply by being further north.

Although promptly disowned by Gentile, the radical corporative proposals of Spirito and Volpicelli did in fact continue his line with only a slight reduction in the emphasis on the centralisation of power in the hands of the State. Workers were forced to adhere to their corporation, but the expropriation of private capital was supposed to reinforce their spirit of collaboration and to foster identification of the individual with the corporation. The task of the State was to arbitrate between the interests of different corporations with a view to the national interest. Ruffini might perhaps have defined this scheme as one of partial organic representation: certainly less liberal than the new-liberals would have wanted it, but also more liberal than Gentile's, thanks to the intermediate step – the corporation – introduced in the process of identification between individual and State. The result is the conceptual position indicated by point C in our Figure 14.2, competing for space in the interval between NL and GG.

The crowding of NL, GG and C towards the north-eastern corner of the box obviously depends on the rather rough-grained definition of our concept-space, which cancels out other relevant dimensions. Centralisation or decentralisation of power, voluntary or coercive adhesion to organic groups, and top-down or bottom-up creation of the same, all these are no small differences. Not by

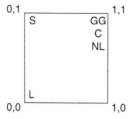

Figure 14.2 Diagram 2

chance, NL will result in the mixed-economy 1942 scheme of the PdA, full of decentralisation, while in the same years Spirito was to participate in discussions on fascist planning. Democracy and decentralisation versus centralisation and authoritarianism, but in all cases a strong role was assigned to the State as the coordinating authority, true to the anti-capitalist spirit of both NL and left-wing fascism. Besides, for different reasons, both disregarded the original economic rights of classical liberalism, now become irrelevant (Gentile, left-wing corporatism) or replaced by an open list of public personal rights (Calamandrei).

4. The economists' aloofness

In the previous reconstruction we did not have many occasions for meeting members of the Italian economic profession of the period. In the new-liberal group, and among their strange bedfellows left-wing corporatists, we found plenty of jurists and philosophers but very few economists or people with a specific training in that field. Of the four economists of the 1890 liberal club mentioned in Section 1, De Viti de Marco was the only one who followed a path – from "scienza delle finanze" to welfare economics – that looked like a new-liberal path. For a brief period in the early 1920s, also Einaudi was very close to new-liberal circles, winning Gobetti's admiration for his "anti-dogmatism" and his habit of searching for "truth in praxis" (Gobetti, 1922). But as far as economic theory was concerned, Einaudi was also the man who would never miss an occasion to reaffirm the classical doctrine whenever he saw it at risk of being disputed.

Reasons for the economists' aloofness are not difficult to find. Although some of the new-liberals gave signs of vague dissatisfaction (see, e.g., Bertolino, 1934), and Spirito repeatedly exhorted economists to trash the entire existing theory, the issues that these scholars were trying to settle revolved around theses of political philosophy with scarce direct impact on the normal work of economists. It was already widely accepted at the time that what we nowadays call "situational determinism" and the focus on individual economic agents do not involve philosophical options *per se*, but methodological hypotheses that could be validly applied only to inquiries of a limited scope. Rosselli tried to go beyond these limits, and explored the theories of bilateral exchange with an eye to their application to trade union bargaining; however, this did not lead him to challenge the foundations of currently accepted economics. He probably did not find anything to object to in the arguments with which Pasquale Jannaccone, at the time one of the deacons of the Italian economic profession, refuted Spirito's rantings. What does it mean, Jannaccone asked, that the economic agent is not an individualist and internalises common interests? Translate this into precise hypotheses and show us what the implications for prices, income shares, trading, etc., are (Jannaccone, 1930, p. 524 ff.). If NL with its social radicalism was a parenthesis that closed soon after WWII, for most Italian economists it remained a parenthesis that had not even been opened.

Notes

1 De Ruggiero (1946, p. 240). Of the other authors who will be mentioned in this chapter perhaps only Carlo Rosselli and Guido Calogero were directly exposed to the influence of British NL.

2 The summary reconstruction that follows draws on research carried out by a host of Italian historians: see the classical works by Lanaro (1979), Vivarelli (1981), Cardini (1981, 1993).

3 The Italian language makes a useful distinction between "liberalismo," liberalism intended as a political and economic doctrine, and "liberismo" intended as the exclusively economic part of that doctrine, i.e. the principles of intangibility of property rights, free trade and minimal State. Here, I shall use "traditional" or "classical" liberalism for "liberismo" when that distinction is relevant.

4 On the use of the category "left-wing fascism" see Parlato (2000) and Santomassimo (2006). On the trends of the recent historiography of fascism, see Carlesi (2016).

5 See Furiozzi (2001) for a reconstruction of the origins of this liberal-socialist tradition in Italy.

6 The most remarkable was *Rivoluzione Liberale* (1922–1925), the centre of a group of politically involved intellectuals founded and edited by Gobetti. The complete collection is now available online at www.erasmo.it/liberale. Other journals include Gramsci's *L'Ordine Nuovo* (1919–1925), Turati's *Critica sociale* (suspended in 1926), the young socialists' *Libertà* (1924–1925), and for a brief spell in 1926 in Rosselli's *Il Quarto Stato*.

7 An early discussion of the concept of liberty as method can be found in articles by N. Papafava in *Rivoluzione Liberale* from 1922, later collected in Papafava (1924). The divorce between socialism and Marxism was argued by Rosselli in his "Socialismo liberale" manifesto, reproduced in Rosselli (1973). Gobetti's ideas with respect to Marxism were clearly in a transition phase when sudden death after violent fascist aggression interrupted his elaboration (on this controversial phase see, among others, Sbarberi, 1999, pp. 25–53).

8 In the abundant literature on Croce's political thought, Bobbio (1974) remains a valuable reference. Gentile's own personal version of liberalism will be briefly discussed in the next section.

9 Both were pupils of Gentile, but Spirito had also attended Pantaleoni's classes at the University of Rome and deemed himself competent enough to scathingly criticise the economic mainstream of the time. They were close to the *gerarca* Giuseppe Bottai and until 1935 could rely on a vivacious journal of their own, the *Nuovi Studi di Diritto, Economia e Politica*.

10 Although silenced by the regime after 1935, the left-wing corporatism of Volpicelli and Spirito had a follow-up in the early 1940s thanks to Camillo Pellizzi, a fascist ideologist close to Spirito, who tried to redirect corporatism towards an explicit system of fascist economic planning. For the history of this attempt, see Melis (1997).

11 Both Calogero and Capitini had connections with Gentile in their early years. Calogero was also a close friend of Spirito's in spite of the divide in their political allegiances, respectively anti- and pro-fascist. As regards Calogero's references to the British NL, see Cavallari (2005). The text of the first "Manifesto del liberalsocialismo" (1940) is reproduced in Calogero (1972).

12 See the classic history of the PdA by De Luna (1997) and, on the 1942 and later programmes, Aga Rossi (1969).

13 Of the many formulations of this concept available in the literature, one of the most precise is due to the nationalist (and later fascist) jurist Alfredo Rocco (1914).

14 For the presence of these themes in Gobetti and Rosselli, see for example Sbarberi (1999). An influential text in this regard was that by Romano (1909), who set the stage for discussions extending to very recent times.

15 With exceptions: for example, the above-mentioned nationalist Rocco (1914) would place S in the same south-west corner as L, considering Marxism to be a covert form of utilitarianism.

References

Aga Rossi, E. (1969). *Il movimento repubblicano Giustizia e libertà e il Partito d'Azione*. Bologna: Cappelli.

Backhouse, R.E. and Nishizawa, T. (2010). Towards a reinterpretation of the history of welfare economics. In: R.E. Backhouse and T. Nishizawa, eds. *No welfare but life: welfare economics and the welfare state in Britain, 1880–1945*. Cambridge: Cambridge University Press, 1–21.

Bertolino, A. (1934). Postille corporativistiche. *Studi Senesi*, 48 (1–2, 5), 195–225, 478–508.

Bertolino, A. (1951). Inchiesta sul Partito d'Azione. *Il Ponte*, 7 (7), 778–781.

Bobbio, N. (1974). Benedetto Croce e il liberalismo. In: *Politica e cultura*. Torino: Einaudi, 211–268.

Calamandrei, P. (1946). L'avvenire dei diritti di libertà. In: F. Ruffini, *Diritti di libertà*. 2nd edition. Firenze: La Nuova Italia, vii–lvi.

Calogero, G. (1972). *Difesa del liberalsocialismo ed altri saggi*. In: M. Schiavone and D. Cofrancesco, eds. Milano: Marzorati.

Cardini, A. (1981). *Stato liberale e protezionismo in Italia (1890–1900)*. Bologna: Il Mulino.

Cardini, A. (1993). *Le corporazioni continuano ... Cultura economica e intervento pubblico nell'Italia unita*. Milano: Franco Angeli.

Carlesi, F. (2016). La storiografia sul corporativismo fascista dal dopoguerra a oggi. *Nuova Rivista Storica*, 100 (1), 277–288.

Cavallari, G. (2005). Guido Calogero e il neoidealismo inglese (1940–49). *Il Pensiero Politico*, 38 (3), 417–432.

Collini, S. (1979). *Liberalism & sociology: L.T. Hobhouse and political argument in England 1880–1914*. Cambridge: Cambridge University Press.

De Luna, G. (1997). *Storia del Partito d'Azione. 1942–1947*. 2nd edition. Roma: Editori Riuniti.

De Ruggiero, G. (1925). *Storia del liberalismo europeo*. Bari: Laterza. As reprinted (1962). Milano: Feltrinelli.

De Ruggiero, G. (1946). *Il ritorno alla ragione*. Bari: Laterza.

Furiozzi, G.B. (2001). *Dall'Italia liberale all'Italia fascista*. Napoli: Edizioni Scientifiche Italiane.

Gentile, G. (1923). Il mio liberalismo. *La nuova politica liberale*, 1 (1), 9–11.

Gobetti, P. (1922). Il liberalismo di Luigi Einaudi. *La Rivoluzione Liberale*, 1 (10), 37–38.

Jannaccone, P. (1930). Scienza, critica e realtà economica. *La Riforma Sociale*, 41, 521–528.

Lanaro, S. (1979). *Nazione e lavoro. Saggio sulla cultura borghese in Italia 1870–1925*. Venezia: Marsilio.

Melis, G. (1997). *Fascismo e pianificazione: il convegno sul piano economico (1942–43)*. Roma: Fondazione Ugo Spirito.

Papafava, N. (1924). *Fissazioni liberali*. Torino: Gobetti Editore.

Parlato, G. (2000). *La sinistra fascista*. Bologna: Il Mulino.

Rocco, A. (1914). Economia liberale, economia socialista, ed economia nazionale. *Rivista delle Società commerciali*, 4 (4), 293–308.

Romano, S. (1909). *Lo stato moderno e la sua crisi: discorso per l'inaugurazione dell'anno accademico nella R. Università di Pisa letto il 4 novembre 1909 dal prof. Santi Romano.* Annuario della R. Università di Pisa per l'anno accademico 1909-1910. Pisa: Tipografia Vannucchi. As reprinted in: (1969). *Lo stato moderno e la sua crisi. Saggi di diritto costituzionale.* Milano: Giuffrè, 4–26.

Rosselli, C. (1973). *Socialismo liberale e altri scritti* (J. Rosselli, ed.). Torino: Einaudi.

Ruffini, F. (1926). *Diritti di libertà.* Torino: Gobetti editore.

Santomassimo, G. (2006). *La terza via fascista: il mito del corporativismo.* Roma: Carocci.

Sbarberi, F. (1999). *L'utopia della libertà eguale. Il liberalismo sociale da Rosselli a Bobbio.* Torino: Bollati Boringhieri.

Vivarelli, R. (1981). *Il fallimento del liberalismo. Studi sulle origini del fascismo.* Bologna: Il Mulino.

15 Learning from the past

Two stories of successful state intervention in capitalism

Fernando J. Cardim de Carvalho† and Julio López G.

Hyman Minsky used to joke that "there are as many varieties of capitalism as Heinz has pickles". In stark contrast, today's mainstream economics would have us believe that the single type of capitalism that can exist, or at least the only viable capitalism, is the one where state intervention is minimal. Given the dominance of the mainstream view, the danger exists that the achievements of previous experiences of successful state intervention under capitalism be underestimated and their lessons forgotten. The danger is real because widespread dissatisfaction with the current state of the economy and proposals for the future are seldom accompanied by efforts to learn from the past. Thus, for example, immediately after the recent world crisis, in the US many authors, following different ideological inclinations, revisited the ways the Roosevelt administration had coped with the crisis of the 1930s. But as it became clear that the recent crash would not repeat the collapse of the 1930s, interest in the subject fell substantially. Another glaring (negative) example: France recently experienced a disputed presidential election, and candidates, as well as pundits, put forward many proposals to reduce the huge rate of unemployment (about 10% of the active population) that has plagued the country for over 30 years. Lacking in the debate, however, was any reference to the ways the country successfully reconstructed itself, with practically no unemployment, during the 30-odd years that followed the end of World War II. In both cases, Roosevelt's US and post-war France, economic recovery and the fall in unemployment resulted, to a decisive extent, from active intervention by the state in the operation of the economy.

This "amnesia" motivates the present chapter. We recall here those two historical episodes of effective and efficient state intervention in advanced capitalist economies. Our aim is not to propose novel interpretations of processes that have already been extensively studied. Rather, it is a matter of rediscovery, recalling some salient aspects of those two experiences which we see as highly relevant to the issues before us today.

1. The New Deal and the role of the state in the United States economy

The New Deal is generally acknowledged as the starting point of the Era of Big Government in the US.[1] However, contrary to a popular narrative, its birth was neither immediate nor easy. It is, of course, a myth that until then the state had played no significant role in American economic development. Nevertheless, one might argue that the state acted mostly through the creation of a context favourable to development rather than through direct participation. From the times of the first Treasury Secretary, Alexander Hamilton, to those of President Abraham Lincoln, governmental initiative usually consisted in creating a legal context favourable to development, rather than intervening directly in production or capital accumulation.

The restricted scope granted to the federal government seemed to have been the Founding Fathers' design. Resulting from the voluntary union of thirteen former British colonies, political power in the United States was to remain primarily with the states. At the federal level, Congress was the primary channel for the voice of the people. Executive power was the power to *execute*, not to *formulate*, policies designed by Congress in the areas where the states' manifold interests could be involved. In modern terms, the federal government had had limited jurisdiction, with few direct responsibilities. Small and balanced budgets seemed to define the appropriate fiscal policy in such a framework (Kimmel, 1959).

Franklin Roosevelt, running for president for the first time in 1932, seemed largely to agree that the scope for federal government policies should remain limited. The electoral campaign developed when the US economy was reaching its lowest point. Unemployment was at its peak, production at rock bottom. Roosevelt seemed to be torn between the perception that the main contribution to be given to recovery was to seek to balance the federal budget, "to restore confidence" among private businessmen, and the perception, developed while he governed New York state, that there was very little states could do to relieve, let alone overcome, the depression. Most states were at the limit of their capacity to give support to the unemployed and their families. They had no financial resources to develop any serious attempt to promote recovery through public investment.

As is frequently noted in the literature, Roosevelt actually criticised Hoover for his inability to control budget deficits and stop the growth of the public debt. Although it was, in part, politically expedient to air such criticisms, there is little doubt that his deepest instincts did in fact move Roosevelt in this direction. At least twice he publicly supported the platform approved in the 1932 Democratic convention proposing an immediate 25% cut in federal government expenditures. After his inauguration, among his first decisions was a cut in the salaries of federal employees.

The President counted among his closest collaborators proponents of at least three major views of the causes of the depression and the appropriate remedies to overcome it. In the "Brains Trust", created during the electoral campaign, Rexford Tugwell and Raymond Molley blamed imbalances between profits and wages, and between the purchasing power and productive capacities of the major sectors of the economy for the depression. The remedy was what Tugwell (1968) called "collectivization", the introduction of planning mechanisms to promote a "concert of interests", by coordinating production and investment plans of businesses in all sectors, wage policies and labour conditions, price support schemes, etc.[2] Planning targets should be set through tripartite negotiations involving businessmen and workers under the leadership of the federal government. A second group had the sympathies of business and proposed the traditional path of fiscal restraint to restore the confidence of producers and investors. As observed, Roosevelt instinctively seemed to lean toward this group, and would in fact frequently return to this policy, at least until the recession of 1937, when the line was definitively abandoned (May, 1981). The view was strongly defended by Lewis Douglas, a fiscal conservative appointed by Roosevelt as budget director, and a little later, when he took over the post of Treasury Secretary, by Henry Morgenthau. The third group, were the remnants of the Progressives, who blamed the emergence of mono-polies for the depression (and many other weaknesses of the economy) and thought that only the restoration of free competition would, by breaking down monopolies and conglomerates, set the economy on the road to recovery. The view was championed by Supreme Court Justice Louis Brandeis and shared by the surviving Wilsonians that supported Roosevelt on the assumption that he was one of them. Felix Frankfurter, later appointed by the President to become a Supreme Court Justice, was the main member of this group advising Roosevelt.

There were no proto-Keynesians among Roosevelt's closest senior advisors in this period.[3] They would join the administration later, particularly when Marriner Eccles was appointed chairman of the Federal Reserve. Many, like Tugwell, defended some immediate expansion of federal spending because there seemed to be no agent capable of breaking through the impasse other than the federal government. But apart from implicit rejection of "crowding out" notions, the proposals did not rest on a more sophisticated view of the way autonomous public investment can impact the economy. Even if they had, we should remember that Roosevelt himself never accepted concepts like the Kahn/Keynes income multi-plier, when they eventually became known (Stein, 1990, p. 57).

Nevertheless, emergency situations call for emergency action. President Roosevelt moved along several paths at the same time. The above-mentioned reduction in government salaries was designed to satisfy balanced-budgeters. Unemployment relief initiatives were taken through the Temporary Relief Administration, headed by Harry Hopkins and, later in 1933, through the creation of the Civilian Works Administration to help unemployed workers survive the winter.

The "concert of interests" by planning proposed by Tugwell entered, in diluted form, into the creation of the National Recovery Administration (NRA), a framework to establish sectorial codes of conduct and fix prices to prevent "destructive competition". The Progressives, of course, were not pleased. More consequentially, perhaps, the same National Industrial Recovery Act (NIRA) that generated the NRA also instituted a public works program, to be managed by a new public entity, the Public Works Administration (PWA), under the authority of Interior Secretary Harold Ickes.

1.1. The public works administration

NIRA established that the PWA, under the authority of the President,

> shall prepare a comprehensive program of public works, which shall include among other things the following: (a) construction, repair, and improvement of public highways and parkways, public buildings, and any publicly owned instrumentalities and facilities; (b) conservation and development of natural resources, including control, utilization, and purification of waters, prevention of soil or coastal erosion, development of water power, transmission of electrical energy, and construction of river and harbor improvements and flood control ...; (c) any projects of the character heretofore constructed or carried on either directly by public authority or with public aid to serve the interests of the general public; (d) construction, reconstruction, alteration, or repair under public regulation or control of low-cost housing and slum-clearance projects; (e) any project (other than those included in the foregoing classes) of any character heretofore eligible for loans.
>
> Hosen (1992, p. 202)

according to an emergency act passed in 1932.

Let us briefly dwell upon some important features of the initiative.

First, a public works program with such an ambitious scope certainly requires careful planning and setting of priorities. However, planning was not to be extended to private businesses other than by signalling future demands. Private contractors would more commonly be responsible for execution, although in some cases the Army Corps of Engineers would take on direct responsibility for a project. Planning, therefore, was confined to the government sphere. Private production and investment plans were to continue to be drawn up as before. Second, even though NIRA was proposed as an *emergency* measure, to expire or be renewed in two years, given the very nature of public investment in the areas that were listed, much longer time horizons were in fact being considered. And this is in fact what happened: PWA became a permanent entity of the federal government. It was not shut down, as was the case with other entities created to fight the depression, but succeeded by an institution with an even larger scope, the wartime National Resources Planning Board, in 1939. Third, the creation of

PWA was not inspired by the idea that public investment was just an excuse for reviving demand. Public investment still had to be justified in terms of the usefulness of each individual project. Besides, projects that were able to pay for themselves were generally preferred because it could be argued that any fiscal deficit created by this type of expenditure would eventually be covered by the revenues it was expected to generate.

Could such a program be said to make of the New Deal state a "developmental state"? Of course, the answer depends on how one chooses to define developmental states. If they are defined as states that play a part in driving economic growth up, or contribute to capital accumulation, the answer is certainly yes. The PWA not only contributed decisively to recovery in key industries like construction, but also created infrastructure facilities that are in use even today. But the concept of developmental state was inspired mostly by Western Europe's experience with supporting development, before and after World War II. It also refers to the type of state strategy to promote development that was implemented in parts of Latin America and Asia in the past century. As already stressed, the New Deal did not steer *private* activities towards anything in particular. The relation between the federal government and the private sector remained "external": government expenditures required the engagement of businesses as producers and suppliers but in no way committed them to any progressive path or development strategy.

Section 203 of NIRA authorised the federal government "to construct, finance, or aid in the construction or the financing of any public-works project" included in the list reproduced above (Hosen, 1992, p. 203). It also allowed the federal government "to make grants to States, municipalities, or other public bodies" to implement those projects (ibid.), releasing semi-bankrupt subnational administrations from the obligation of borrowing from the federal government to finance both relief and public works, as demanded by the Hoover administration. Let us recall that Treasury officials in Great Britain made a lot of this point in their opposition to Keynes's demands for an expansion of British government spending (Middleton, 1985). Central government spending would trespass on local responsibilities, coordination between government levels would be all but impossible – these were some of the arguments raised by the British Treasury to oppose Keynes's expansionary proposals. The Roosevelt experience was empirical proof that reaching such coordination was much less of a problem than it was assumed to be in the orthodox "Treasury View".

Finally, it is also worth noting that a quid pro quo demanded by the Roosevelt administration from private firms and local political leaders was the modernisation of labour relations. The first part of NIRA, creating the NRA, already imposed conditions on private participation in the program in the form of compliance with labour regulations. To qualify for participation in the programs supported by the PWA, private contractors were also to commit to paying minimum wages (Hosen, 1992, p. 205).

It is true that the American economy did not fully recover until the war. Critics of the New Deal in general, and of expanding public investment in particular, raise this point to reject fiscal expansion as a recovery strategy.[4] It can certainly be argued, on the other hand, that expanding public investment permanently was a result of a fundamental change in the way the Federal Government saw its own role in the economy. Roosevelt, for the first time in American history, stated explicitly that supporting the level of activity and fighting unemployment was a responsibility of the federal government. This responsibility was later to become the law of the land, through the Employment Act of 1944. On the other hand, it is undeniable that public investment in improving infrastructure in the United States economy after 1933 contributed decisively not only to allowing for the extraordinary economic expansion occurring during the war but also to supporting economic growth in peace time.

In designing PWA strategies, the Roosevelt administration started from a clear distinction between *relief* and *recovery* policies. It was recognised that arriving at a workable large-scale public works plan would take too long to offer relief to the millions of unemployed workers in 1933. Relief policies had to be designed to create jobs immediately. Public expenditure, therefore, would flow through two relatively independent channels. One was designed to create as many jobs as possible per dollar of fiscal expenditure. These programs were left under the responsibility of Harry Hopkins. The other channel, public works investment, was to support economic growth. The investment projects selected for implementation would not necessarily be those ranked by the number of jobs they created.

As Smith remarked in his excellent study of public investment in the Roosevelt era:

> The PWA, created in 1933, received an initial appropriation of $3.3 billion (about $45.8 billion in 2002 dollars), which it mainly applied to heavy construction and large-scale building. To put this figure in context, this amount was just over 165% of the federal government's revenues in 1933, or 5.9% of the 1933 US gross domestic product (GDP). Relying on private contractors, the PWA deployed its funds in 3,068 of the nation's 3,071 counties, while helping to pay for projects like the Tennessee Valley Authority and Boulder Dam.
>
> Smith (2006, p. 2)

Smith observes that the PWA represented more than just a government program, important as it may be seen to have been from 1933 to 1939, when it was liquidated. The PWA not only established the view that the government had taken on responsibility for large-scale investments in infrastructure to support growth and prosperity. It also created the structures that allowed the federal government to develop methods and techniques to continuously implement ambitious investment programs in parallel with private investments. In a sense, it helped, along with other institutional changes taking place during the New Deal, to change the rules of operation of the American economy through a fundamental change in the way the government accepted and met its obligations in peacetime.

Approached from this angle, the PWA was a success, independently of its actual contribution to recovery in the period. The PWA was succeeded by a more inclusive planning apparatus, as one might expect in the context of total war. After the war, planning was downsized again, but the federal government never returned to its pre-depression scope and relative powerlessness.

The PWA, of course, ran into the problems one would expect. A large expenditure program sponsored by the federal government had to face the opposition of conservatives and, at best, an ambiguous reception from business-men. Creating new markets for privately produced goods and services was welcome, of course, but the fear that this would result, as it actually did, in encroachment by the state on areas traditionally left to private discretion was received with suspicion. As Kalecki (1943/1971) observed, capitalists always try to preserve their power and dominance in the determination of the ways a capitalist economy operates. When the state enlarges its responsibilities, it necessarily reduces the political power of businessmen. In the context of a depression, businessmen were certainly feeling that power was slipping through their fingers and were eager to impose some "discipline" on government. The goal was to restore their political influence and social prestige as leaders of the country, at least in respect to economic matters. If we bear in mind that this is also a period when more radical ideas met with an increasingly sympathetic audience based on the perception that the Soviet regime was free from unemployment, it is not so very surprising that businessmen mounted such ferocious opposition to President Roosevelt.

The PWA also had to develop methods to deal with the drive by politicians to distribute those resources among their supporters. Both the PWA and the WPA (see below) were noted for having been singularly nonpartisan federal initiatives, but one can imagine how the politicians, especially those associated with the Democratic Party, responded to such an approach. Methods to curb the obvious opportunities offered by programs on this scale to corrupt admin-istrators, politicians and contracts were also developed.[5]

1.2. The job creation program: the WPA

While the investment projects sponsored by the PWA tended to be more capital-intensive, the Works Progress Administration (WPA) tended to support more labour-intensive initiatives. The WPA, however, was not just a relief agency, ready to create unneeded and unskilled jobs just to guarantee a subsistence wage for unemployed workers, even though its detractors tried to ridicule its programs as promoting "boondoggling", that is, fake jobs that were just a pretext to give away money to the unemployed.

The WPA effectively not only supported public works but also developed a very original approach to the matter, supporting not only those projects that included menial jobs or produced some material result, but also blue collar jobs and the arts. Theatre, music, literature – all found ways to benefit from the WPA's willingness to support them.

As summarised by Smith:

> Created in 1935, the WPA did lighter construction work [than the PWA] and avoided private contracting. Its initial appropriation of $4.88 billion (about $64 billion in 2002 dollars) was about 135% of the federal government's revenues in 1935, or about 6.7% of GDP in that year. Although primarily intended as a vast relief effort for employing the unskilled, the WPA built an impressive range of projects, including over 480 airports, 78,000 bridges, and nearly 40,000 public buildings.
>
> Smith (2006, p. 2)

2. France's developmental state

We now turn to discussion of France's experience after World War II. This is also a particularly interesting case study for several reasons. First, the rate of growth achieved by this country was outstanding: between 1950 and 1970 it averaged almost 5% per annum, and the rate of unemployment hovered around 1.8%. It is true that in those years the European growth rate was also very high (just below 5%), and that France lagged behind Germany and Italy. Still, France's growth rate was well above that achieved in the UK and the USA in the same period (at about 2.5% in the two countries). It was also higher than it had reached in the interwar years (between 1920 and 1938 the growth rate averaged 1.8%). Second, France's high growth lasted about thirty years (which became known in the country as "Les trente glorieuses"). Third, during those years France put into place a very effective *developmental state*, and constructed an efficient *mixed economy* ("économie concertée"), two institutional innovations few capitalist countries have been able to bring successfully into being under democratic conditions. And, last but not least, most of this took place under extremely difficult political conditions, inter alia because France had come off worst in two Liberation Wars, first in Indochina and then in Algeria.

2.1. The background

For a long time before World War II, French public opinion was extremely critical of what many saw as the decline of their country's international and economic standing.[6] Concurrently, the notion was widespread that redressing and modernising the economy was a responsibility of the state, not only because this fitted well with French historical experience of state intervention but also because recent history had shown that the liberal economy could not fulfil that function.

To the right of the political spectrum, a rather large group was attracted by the way the Nazi government had reorganised and was steering the German economy and especially by the way it had reduced unemployment, though few seemed to have noted that higher employment came along with stagnant or declining real wages and that the whole economy was organised around the goal of rearmament. But the German experiment also had some influence on the left of the political spectrum. Left-wing groups rejected the emphasis on rearmament and the totalitarian nature of the regime, but many seemed also to be mesmerised by the impressive economic recovery Germany achieved in the 1930s.

For an appreciable part of the French intelligentsia, the notion that demand expansion-cum-state intervention was necessary under capitalism was also strengthened by the Roosevelt experience in the US.[7] However, before the war only a minority fully endorsed aggregate demand management. Moreover, the intellectual influence of Keynes among French progressive economists was scant, and in particular the series of papers Keynes wrote for *The Times* in 1933, later published as "The Means to Prosperity", where he put forward his most eloquent and popular proposal for government large-scale loan-financed expenditure, had little impact.[8]

When Leon Blum's socialist government (June 1936–June 1937) came to power, it brought in a set of long-lasting social measures that are still greatly appreciated today, but it did not implement resolute government-led demand expansion (see Kalecki, 1938). A new Blum government, elected in April 1938, proposed a much more radical economic program.[9] The project included large-scale government spending, such that "The English press, and notably the *Financial Times*, considered this the first attempt to implement Keynesian ideas" (Rosanvallon, 1989, p. 183). But it would perhaps be more correct to trace the inspiration for this project to Nazi Germany, as Blum himself later explained.[10] Indeed, the main objective of the proposed increase of government spending was to support the war effort, and the project also included complete control over foreign trade and capital movements. The bill was defeated in the Senate and Blum resigned.

Besides the enormous human and material losses France suffered during World War II, the defeat in 1940, and the war itself, changed the country profoundly and played an important role in postwar development. On the one hand, an ample segment of the largest industrial firms and the banking system, as well as the political right, collaborated with the Vichy Government and the German occupant. Therefore both the "haute bourgeoisie" and the political right came out of the war not only materially but also politically weakened in the eyes of public opinion after Liberation.

On the other hand, the state of public opinion underwent a radical change during the war. There were expectations that once the conflict was over, the economic situation should improve visibly, with mass unemployment eliminated. To a large extent this change of public opinion responded to the call of left-wing political forces, which had played an important role in the fight against the occupant. An important actor in this camp was the French communist party, which had abandoned its previous extremely radical stance and was now aligned into a Popular Front-type strategy, which emphasised the role of the state in ensuring mass assistance, and indeed in economic recovery.[11]

Also, during the war, the group that accompanied De Gaulle in the United Kingdom, and De Gaulle himself, were able to learn from the experience of demand management, and also from the lively debate the country saw in the heyday of the Keynesian revolution. When de Gaulle returned to liberated Paris in September 1944, members of this group occupied the top positions in his government. Such was the case of Mendès-France, whose economic vision had already been influenced by Keynes's theory. Mendès was appointed Minister for National Economy in the provisional government. However, he disagreed on many issues with the Finance Minister, René Pleven, who favoured free market policies. When de Gaulle sided with Pleven, Mendès-France resigned.[12]

2.2. Economic growth and state intervention

Immediately after the end of the World War II, and in spite of De Gaulle's rather right-of-centre proclivity, his government nationalised several large industrial firms, such as Electricité de France, Charbonnages de France, SNCF (railroads), and Renault, as well as the Banque de France and the four leading commercial banks. The Banque de France, which was not independent but a branch of government, would strictly supervise the destination of credit and the operation of private banks, and administer a stringent exchange control mechanism (which lasted until 1967). Last, but not least, De Gaulle's government inaugurated French Indicative Economic Planning, on which more later.

This alleged series of attacks against the principle of private property and the free market did not bring about chaos or economic collapse: recovery followed soon after the war and, as said, between 1950 and 1973 the annual rate of growth averaged almost 5%, while the unemployment rate stood at 1.8%.

Investment was the leading demand component behind this outstanding performance, with an annual growth rate of 9% between 1950 and 1973. Massive investments were carried out first of all in the large nationalised firms, but private investment did not lag behind. Note, however, that the high rate of growth of output achieved did not require a high share of investment in GDP: the latter averaged just a bit over 22% in the 1950–1972 period. Fast economic growth was achieved rather cheaply in terms of capital expenditure. High degrees of capacity utilisation, a consequence of fast growing demand, probably account for this remarkable performance.

Consumption also rose rapidly, at 5.2% annually, with private consumption stimulated above all by strongly and continuously rising wages. The latter led to inflationary pressures, and France's inflation rate, at about 4% annually between 1955 and 1970, stood above the European average. Nevertheless, cost pressures were not excessive because labour productivity was also rising at a phenomenal rate: 5% per annum between 1950 and 1973. Real wages grew faster than labour productivity, and thus the wage share rose: from about 42% in 1950 to about 50% in 1973 (and then to about 55% in 1980). Accordingly, the profit share was declining. But this did not negatively affect total profits and investment, because higher wages stimulated consumption and demand. Paraphrasing former German Chancellor Schmidt's famous motto, one might have said at the time: today's high wages create today's demand, and thus tomorrow's investment and employment.[13]

Of course, the foreign trade constraint may limit the speed of growth of any country. The French experience is worth studying also in this respect, because the country's exports grew at the phenomenal rate of about 8.5% between 1950 and 1973. Imports also grew, though not too fast, and the trade balance was kept more or less in check. Of course, the fast growth of world markets contributed to French export success. However, the country's export performance is exceptional all the same, not only because competition in those markets was intense but also, and most importantly, because it was achieved concurrently with fast growth in real wages. Thus the country neither needed to, nor indeed could, enter into cutthroat price competition, which would have implied a worsening of its terms of trade. Fast growth of exports (and moderate growth of imports), came about mostly because new investments were massively channelled to the tradable goods sector and especially to lines of production promising fast-growing markets, or indispensable to secure domestic production of the requisite intermediate inputs. Now, it is important to note that new investments were adequately channelled not exclusively, and perhaps not even mainly, thanks to the signals shown freely by the market. State command, indicative planning, and selective credit, all parts of a well-designed industrial strategy, played a prominent role. Let us now discuss the role of the state during "les trente glorieuses".

Government spending, which grew annually at 6% on average, played a key role in the French experience, and fast-growing government consumption brought France's generous Welfare State ("l'état providence") into being. Along with this, and as part of it, resolute application of the "automatic stabilizers" as well as discretionary counter-cyclical fiscal and monetary policies combined to soften the cyclical recessions that accompany capitalist development.

Indicative planning was as important for France's performance in demand management, if not indeed more so. It began with (Jean) *Monnet's plan* immediately after the war. Starting from the first plan, to democratise procedure and to base the main economic choices on knowledge and anticipation of the real actors, the definition of objectives and means of the several plans enacted brought together high government officials, and representatives of entrepreneurs and workers.[14]

It is hard to tell to what extent the plans contributed to guiding private investment and the action of the private sector in general. The planners certainly wanted to achieve this, and for this purpose they developed a very comprehensive system of economic information, including input-output accounts to ascertain the sectorial impacts of growth and induce private investment toward where it was most needed. There was also frequent consultation with leading entrepreneurs and trade union leaders. In fact, a special study conducted on the subject found that "about 80% of French industrial firms knew the expansion objectives of the Vth Plan, two thirds of them also knew the economic perspectives of their branches, and half of them both the growth and investment prospects of their branches" (Carré et al., 1972, p. 577). Maybe James Tobin was not off the mark when he speculated: "[p]erhaps Jean Monnet's postwar 'indicative planning' in France, where government sponsored a coordinated raising of sights to overcome pessimism and lift investment, is an example of what Keynes had in mind ..." (Tobin, 1983/1987, p. 8).

Anyway, the democratic procedure adopted to establish the main objectives and means of the plans did not diminish the role of the government, which had the upper hand due to its direct control over investment in large nationalised firms, and in banks, and thus over credit availability. Indeed, as reported by Szeworski,

> In 1954 about 35% of productive and unproductive investment was financed by the government, especially by investment credits to the private sector by the nationalized banks ... All in all, in 1954 over 50% of fixed capital investment depended directly or indirectly on the State.
>
> Szeworski (1959, p. 127; English trans. by J. López)

Together with its overall governance of the developmental process through planning and its different instruments to guide the action of the private sector, the state participated directly in the development of supply capacities and technical progress. On the one hand, thanks to massive public investment the infrastructure expanded considerably, first to respond to the needs of reconstruction after the devastation caused by the war and later in response to and anticipation of the future needs arising from fast economic growth.

Together with the above, the state directly invested as an entrepreneur. Stoffaës gives a detailed account of state direct intervention in the industrial area. In his words

> The large project policy [was] linked to both national defense (nuclear, space and aeronautics, information and electronics), and ensuring supply of basic inputs (petroleum, oil, uranium, etc.....). "Big projects" were supported by a large variety of means and industrial policy actors, the "national champions". They could be either research laboratories or large public entities such as the "Commissariat à l'Énergie Atomique", the "Centre Nationale d'Études Spatiales", the "Centre Nationale de la Recherche Scientifique", the "Centre Nationale pour l'Explotation des Oceans".
>
> Stoffaës (1991, p. 454)

He goes on to say that the "champions" could also be public firms: arsenals from the Ministry of the Army, firms from the oil industry, or also private or mixed firms. In fact, the entrepreneurial state, so vividly described by Mazzucato (2014) in her study of experience in the USA today, had played a much larger and more central role throughout the French immediate postwar economic scene.

3. Conclusions

The New Deal brought to the American economy a new view of the role of government investments in capitalist economies. The famous "first hundred days" of Roosevelt's first term in office included initiatives in the area of public investment that outlived by far the program they were part of. The New Deal is, in many senses, history now, but the activist view of the role of the state in maintaining and enlarging the infrastructure on which private production and investment depend seems deeply rooted in the political imagination of the United States, even in times of neoliberal dominance such as these (Block and Keller, 2011). Initiatives such as the PWA were certainly important to support aggregate demand, but even some of Keynes's most ferocious critics in the country would now admit that there is a need for public initiative when dealing with infrastructure investments. This change of mind is among the most durable legacies of the New Deal, and indeed the New Deal may well be signalled as a landmark in the emergence of a developmental state in the United States.

As for French macroeconomic development during the "trente glorieuses", it might be tempting to identify the strategy followed as a successful implementation of Keynesian principles. However, as shown before, this would not give a complete picture of what took place in France. It is true that demand management was a defining and essential feature of this country's economic strategy. But this was only one component of that strategy, which comprised many other crucial elements. Amongst those elements, we have called attention to planning, the entrepreneurial functions of the state, and the close association between the state and the private sector. It was this ample set of constitutive elements, by themselves and in their interaction, which made up the successful growth model and which ultimately explains why France was able to achieve such an exceptional economic feat during the three-odd decades immediately following World War II.

Notes

1 "In 1929 total federal expenditures were about 2.5% of the gross national product, federal purchases of goods and services about 1.3%, and federal construction less than .2%. In 1965, for comparison, these figures were 18%, 10%, and 1%" (Stein, 1990, p. 14).

2 For readers familiar with the terms "collectivisation" or "collectivism", it may sound unusual in this context. In fact, collectivisation here means simply that economic decisions should not be taken by isolated individuals on the basis of their exclusive individual interests. Instead, decisions should be taken collectively, with the participation of other stakeholders, including government authorities. In the

view of the supporters of planning participating in Roosevelt's Brains Trust, private property was not the problem, as long as decisions were taken collectively. As stated by Tugwell (1968, p. xxv), "[w]e were on the side of those who would collectivise." Complaining that President Roosevelt later somewhat lost his faith in the type of planning he was advocating, Tugwell (1968, p. 307) observed: "I told them that Roosevelt still listened when I argued for a collectivised progressivism, even sometimes mentioned it himself." Of course, soviet-style collectivisation, the sense that eventually prevailed, had nothing to do with it.

3 Let us recall that Keynes had been advancing the notion that expansion of public investments was the solution to the crisis at least since 1929, and the proposal had an especially important impact on American economists when he visited the country in 1931.

4 The British Treasury often referred to the failure of FDR's investment policies to support their own position, cf. Peden (2004).

5 Smith (2006) supplies an excellent discussion of the two problems and the ways they were dealt with.

6 France's economy was certainly less advanced than that of the UK and the USA. For example, "a statistical survey on the conditions of the nation's stock of industrial equipment discovered that the average age of French machinery was twenty-five years in 1939 and for the modern sector it was twelve years … In comparison, officials calculated, the average for the British was seven years and for America five years" (Kuisel, 1981, p. 140). However, the available data do not support the notion of a marked French decline, except when compared with the USA. In 1900, France's GDP per capita stood at 4214 (Real GDP per capita in 2011 US $) and in 1930 at 5502. The respective figures for the UK were 5608 and 7301, for the USA 6252 and 9490, and for Germany 4596 and 4624 (Maddison International Database).

7 Georges Boris, a journalist-economist, closely associated with Pierre Mendès-France and to play an important role in the future, wrote a fine book on that experience (Boris, 1934). Boris also introduced Keynes's ideas to Leon Blum in 1937.

8 Arena (2011) and Rosanvallon (1989) give evidence about Keynes's lack of favour among French academic economists, which probably explains why few French economists made important contributions to the Keynesian revolution. But Keynes also found scant favour with French public opinion, because his book *The Economic Consequences of the Peace* was seen by many as an attack on France, especially because there was the widespread conviction that France, which had suffered most among all the belligerents during World War I, had not received just compensation in the Versailles Treaty.

9 The bill was drawn up by Pierre Mendès-France, Under Secretary of State for the Treasury, and by Georges Boris (Rosanvallon, 1989).

10 In 1947, Leon Blum explained that this plan would have made it possible "to furnish assistance to the war industry within a closed economy, by means analogous to those Dr. Schacht implemented in Germany" (Rosanvallon, 1989, p. 183).

11 The Parti Communiste de France was practically absent in the struggle against the occupant until Germany invaded the Soviet Union, but from that moment on it committed itself completely to the struggle. In the legislative elections of 1945, it won 26% of the vote, becoming the most voted party in France, and in November 1946 it obtained its best score in the legislative elections, at 28.3% of the vote.

12 An anecdote may be useful here to illustrate both the extent of the Keynesian influence on De Gaulle's following, as well as the contradictions within this group. In December 1944, Mendès-France invited Michal Kalecki, who had written extensively on the subject, to propose a rationing system. Kalecki wrote a short memorandum on rationing of expenditure during the post-war reconstruction in France (Kalecki, 1997). Kalecki later recollected that upon reading his memorandum and

discussing with him Mendès said: "Why are we debating all that? They won't do anything that you suggest" (Osiatynski, 1997, p. 493).

13 Considering this major peculiarity of the French experience, it is not surprising that the French Regulationist School considered the type of wage arrangements as a key element to differentiate between alternative growth regimes. Nor is it surprising that Robert Boyer, a leading member of that school of thought, co-authored a paper proposing the possibility of a regime where higher wages stimulate output and investment growth (Bowles and Boyer, 1990). The paper was published contemporaneously with the oft-quoted Bhaduri and Marglin (1990), which inaugurated a whole line of research on wage- and profit-led growth regimes.

14 French indicative planning generated widespread interest. "In May 1962, faced with an economic slump at home, Kennedy marveled at the performance of the French economy and considered transposing aspects of French dirigisme to the United States. The president sent Council of Economic Advisers Walter Heller and James Tobin to Paris … for a study of the French economic planning process … To generate interest in economic planning in the United States, Kennedy arranged for French officials to speak to labor and business groups" (Trachtenberg, 2003, p. 107).

References

Arena, R. (2011). *French forms of Keynesianism and Keynesian economic policies in the immediate post-WWII period (1945–1955): historical contents and contemporary legacy.* Contribution to the conference 75 ans de la Theorie Generale. Paris: Maison des Sciences Economiques.

Bhaduri, A. and Marglin, S. (1990). Unemployment and the real wage: the economic basis for contesting political ideologies. *Cambridge Journal of Economics*, 14 (4), 375–393.

Block, F. and Keller, M., eds (2011). *State of innovation: the U.S. government's role in technology development.* Boulder, CO: Paradigm Publishers.

Boris, G. (1934). *La revolution Roosevelt.* Paris: Gallimard.

Bowles, S. and Boyer, R. (1990). A wage-led employment régime: income distribution, labour discipline, and aggregate demand in welfare capitalism. In: S.A. Marglin and J. Schor, eds *The golden age of capitalism.* Oxford: Clarendon Press, 187–217.

Carré, J.J., Dubois, P. and Malinvaud, E. (1972). *La croissance française. Un essai d'analyse économique causale de l'après guerre.* Paris: Seuil.

Hosen, F.E. (1992). *The great depression and the New Deal: legislative acts in their entirety (1932–1933) and statistical economic data (1926–1946).* Jefferson: McFarland and Company.

Kalecki, M. (1938). *The lessons of the Blum experiment.* As reprinted in: (1990). *Collected works of Michal Kalecki* (J. Osiatynski, ed.). Vol. I: *Capitalism: business cycles and full employment.* Oxford: Oxford University Press, 326–341.

Kalecki, M. (1943/1971). Political aspects of full employment. In: *Selected essays on the dynamics of the capitalist economy: 1933–1970.* Cambridge: Cambridge University Press, 138–145.

Kalecki, M. (1997). Rationing of expenditure. As reprinted in: *Collected works of Michal Kalecki* (J. Osiatynski, ed.). Vol. VII: *Studies in applied economics: 1940–1967. Miscellanea.* Oxford: Oxford University Press, 493–505.

Kimmel, L.H. (1959). *Federal budget and fiscal policy 1789-1958.* Washington, DC: The Brookings Institution.

Kuisel, R.F. (1981). *Capitalism and the state in modern France.* New York: Cambridge University Press.

May, D. (1981). *From New Deal to New Economics: the American liberal response to the recession of 1937*. New York: Garland Publishing.

Mazzucato, M. (2014). *The entrepreneurial state: debunking public vs. private sector myths*. London: Anthem Press.

Middleton, R. (1985). *Towards the managed economy: Keynes, the treasury and the fiscal policy debate of the 1930s*. London: Routledge.

Osiatynski, J., ed (1997). *Collected works of Michal Kalecki: Vol. VII: Studies in applied economics: 1940–1967. Miscellanea*. Oxford: Oxford University Press.

Peden, G.C., ed (2004). *Keynes and his critics: treasury responses to the Keynesian revolution 1925–1946*. Oxford: Oxford University Press.

Rosanvallon, P. (1989). The development of Keynesianism in France. In: P. Hall, ed *The political power of economic ideas: Keynesianism across nations*. Princeton, NJ: Princeton University Press.

Smith, J.S. (2006). *Building New Deal liberalism: the political economy of public works, 1933–1956*. Cambridge: Cambridge University Press.

Stein, H. (1990). *The fiscal revolution in America*. Revised edition. Washington, DC: The AEI Press.

Stoffaës, C. (1991). La restructuration industrièlle, 1945–1990. In: M. Levy-Leboyer and J.C. Casanova, eds *Entre l'État et le marché. L'économie française des années 1880 à nos jours*. Paris: Editions Gallimard, 445–472.

Szeworski, A. (1959). Sytuacja gospodarcza Francjii w porównania z okresem Przedwojnym (The economic situation of France in comparison with the pre-war period). *Ekonomista*, 1, 117–132.

Tobin, J. (1983/1987). Keynesian policies in theory and practice. In: *Policies for prosperity: essays in a Keynesian mode*. P. Jackson (ed) Cambridge, MA: MIT Press, 4–13.

Trachtenberg, M., ed (2003). *Between empire and alliance: America and Europe during the cold war*. New York: Rowman & Littelfield.

Tugwell, R.G. (1968). *The Brains Trust*. New York: The Viking Press.

16 Engines of growth and paths of development in the Euro-area

Annamaria Simonazzi

1. Introduction

Since 2008, the EU has been suffering from a steep fall in demand: businesses, households, and governments have been deleveraging simultaneously. Tight fiscal policies, belated monetary stimulus, and perverse adjustment policies have created profound crisis in the European periphery and stagnation throughout the euro area. Given the severity and scale of the crisis, it is threatening the very survival of the monetary union, urging radical change in EU policies. At the global level, the spectre of "secular stagnation" has revived interest in long-forgotten theories. After the liberal phase of the last decades, economists now seem to agree on the need for expansion of domestic demand and a "new" industrial policy, required to tackle the regional divide in the level of development within the Eurozone and, indeed, to respond to the challenges of globalisation and technical change.

While there is agreement on the goal, views differ widely on how to achieve it. In the mainstream approach the crux of development lies mainly in achieving static efficiency, allocating resources more productively by responding to market failures. In contrast, the network theory of development stresses the need for a multilevel policy aimed at capturing the interactions between firms and institutions and stimulating the interdependence between aggregate demand and supply of products and capabilities. In a short, acute review of a book by Sebastiano Brusco, a dear friend from the Modena University days, Cristina Marcuzzo recalls how his research was dedicated to finding a way to "contaminate" the Italian Southern regions with those elements that made a success of the development model for Italy's northern regions (Marcuzzo, 2004). The way has not been found yet, hampered also by the prevalence of the neo-liberal consensus on economic theory and policy. Worse, the gulf has spread to the entire European Union, with increasing divergence between the northern and southern regions of the Eurozone.

The first part of the present chapter outlines the historical evolution of the theory of development that helps interpret the development of core-periphery relations within the EU (Sections 2 and 3). The following sections investigate the policies needed to sustain balanced growth within the EU, arguing that the EU must "find a way" to ensure a rebalance between the core and the periphery. This calls for an overhaul of the institutional framework governing the Eurozone and a new role for industrial policy.

2. The vicissitudes of a concept[1]

'The development ideas that were put forward in the forties and fifties – argues Hirschman (1981, p. 3) – shared two basic ingredients in the area of economics'. The first was rejection of the *monoeconomics* claim: claiming universality, traditional economics extended analysis appropriate to the "special case" of a minority of developed economies to the underdeveloped countries. This new body of research was far from unified. It was still the monoeconomics view that inspired Rostow's five stages of development, 'with identical content for all countries, no matter when they started out on the road to industrialization' (ibid., p. 11). Gerschenkron's analysis of the process of industrialisation of latecomers, such as Germany and Russia, with respect to the British industrial revolution, by contrast, showed that there could be more than one path to development (Hirschman, 1981). For latecomer countries, industrialisation represented a formidable undertaking that could not be left to market forces. Development economics therefore endorsed a stronger steering role for the State in the developing countries than did the mainstream, and new rationales were developed for protection, planning, and industrialisation itself. "Industrial policy" came to identify the set of policies aiming to change the structure of the economy with a deliberate, intensive, and guided effort.

The second ingredient was the mutual benefit claim, namely the assertion that economic relations between the two groups of countries 'could be shaped in such a way as to yield gains for both' (Hirschman, 1981, p. 3). In contrast with this view, the doctrine of unequal exchange proposed by Prebisch and Singer lent support to the argument for protection and industrialisation, while Myrdal and Hirschman's principle of cumulative causation urged the need for public policy to counteract polarisation.

The difficulties encountered on the path of development, the many failures and dramatic reversals in many countries, exposed the naiveté of the idea that progress 'would be smoothly linear if only [the developing countries] adopted the right kind of integrated development program' (Hirschman, 1981, p. 24). Criticism came from two opposite fronts: from the neo-Marxist camp (the dependency theory), and from the neoclassical camp, which stressed the risk of misallocation of resources. As from the early 1980s, development economics – as articulated by what in 1989 John Williamson called the Washington Consensus, namely the World Bank, the International Monetary Fund (IMF), the US Treasury, and economics departments in western universities – changed direction and more or less merged its priorities with those of the mainstream, dragging in industrial policy and public intervention in the economy with them. According to the new conventional wisdom, public intervention is only justified when (1) markets fail to produce social optima (due to some form of "externalities"), and (2) the intervention can be presumed to move the outcome closer to the social optima at a cost less than the gain. It then asserts that in the real world, both conditions are rarely satisfied. With several more steps in between, the conclusion is drawn that, 'Governments cannot pick winners, but losers can pick governments'

Wade (2012, p. 225)

The demise of the original principles of development economics marked a similar fate for industrial policy. True to these developments, as from the 1980s the European industrial policy came to be conceived of mostly in terms of market selection mechanisms, achieved by enforcing EU competition policy and reinstating the monoeconomics claim. In fact, ignoring the peculiar problems of countries at different stages of development, the institutions of the EU were shaped on the premise that all its members were on a level playing field, except for "less modern" ("anti-competition") institutions, individual values and attitudes. The implicit assumption was that an austerity regime, associated with institutions close to those assumed to be prevailing in the "core" countries, would create the "right" environment for growth in the periphery (Simonazzi and Ginzburg, 2015).

It should be noted, however, that, even if shunned by academia and the EU, industrial policy continued to enjoy a very concrete and lively existence within the industrial countries, although often "under the radar", as documented by an increasing number of studies. Eventually, the neoliberal conception that had been the near-consensus for the previous three decades was challenged by various circumstances including, notably, at least in Europe, the widening divide between the core and periphery within the Eurozone which the crisis finally brought out.

One of the side effects of the current economic crisis has been the rediscovery of the terms centre and periphery to analyse the dynamics of the European integration processes in the second half of the twentieth century (Simonazzi and Ginzburg, 2015; Celi et al., 2018). The divergent trajectories of the core and the peripheral European countries can be interpreted in terms of interdependent economies with different productive capabilities. Two concepts follow: the first is the distinction between first-comer industrialisers (the "centre"), latecomers (Italy), and late-latecomers (Spain, Portugal, and Greece) in the periphery, with the related concept of level and quality of productive structures; the second concerns competition, and specifically the distinction between price and product competition.

The differences in the production structure between centre and periphery were very considerable at the start of the Europeanisation process, but decreased up to the beginning of the 1970s. All the countries in the periphery recorded high-income growth, led first by investment and consumption, and then by exports. They all placed special emphasis on basic industry, deemed necessary for the creation of an industrial sector. The state supported accumulation either directly, through publicly owned companies, or indirectly, through subsidies and incentives to domestic and foreign capital.

The crisis of the 1970s, which was associated with the saturation of the major mass consumer goods in the advanced countries and the onset of globalisation, marked a sharp break in the history of relations between the centre and periphery of Europe. It led to profound transformation in demand, production, and competition. Demand for substitution and quality competition (vertical diversification) favoured the transition from price to product competition. Since the early 1970s, the international market system has been increasingly dominated by competition in differentiated products. This evolution has affected the core and peripheral econo-mies in different ways. The "centre" succeeded in restructuring its industry, enhancing its ability to remain in the market thanks to processes of "creative destruction" and reconstruction undertaken with the support of industrial policies.[2] The restructuring of the core deeply affected the countries of the periphery which, in reorganising their economies, struggled to adapt to the new environment, dominated by disinflation and quality competition. The restrictive monetary policies of a centre country exert asymmetric effects on the periphery because of both its mono-specialisation in commoditised products and the rapid return of capital to the safe-haven centre countries – a phenomenon observed time and again (Ginzburg and Simonazzi, 2011), most recently in the current sovereign crisis (the "sudden stop"). In a context of fixed exchange rates, austerity measures in the periphery are assigned the task of implementing a "flex-price" policy through domestic devalua-tion. In the 1980s, the fall in the relative prices of flex-price items hit the countries in the periphery harder. Their basic industries and "mature" production faced the competition of the developing countries, calling for drastic cuts in production. The new situation would have required innovation in the state's capabilities in order to guide and facilitate the reorientation of investment to respond to a rapidly weaken-ing economic structure. However, as from the beginning of the 1970s, the countries of Europe were caught up between two different levels of deregulation, global and European. Thus, precisely when the state should have been taking on new tasks to ease the process of restructuring, diversification, and quality upgrading, these countries adopted across-the-board liberalisation policies, implementing what might be called "plain destruction" of their capabilities to create new products, market niches, and markets.

Over the thirty years of European integration as from the early 1980s, the Southern peripheral countries were exposed to macroeconomic and industrial policy measures that, although apparently neutral, generated increasing regional disparities, both between centre and periphery and within countries. Early liberalisation policies in the periphery prevented public investment guidance: industrial policies were redefined as policies to guarantee competition. Thus, partly as a consequence of their policies, their growth fell behind in the 1980s, and the crisis associated with deregulation opened a gap in aggregate demand that was eventually filled by welfare and construction expenditure. This "pre-mature deindustrialisation" – restructuring without industrialisation – exposed the peripheral countries to stunted growth and persistent fragility in the face of external changes even before the formation of the Monetary Union (Ginzburg and Simonazzi, 2017).

The institutional features of the euro area were not such as to sustain the capacity of the Southern European countries to achieve a sufficient level of diversification and specialisation in their productive structures; indeed, they may even have contributed to worsening it (as seems to be the case with Southern Italy). In contrast, the increasing integration of the Central and Eastern European economies into the supply chain of German industry speeded up their process of diversification and specialisation. The eastward integration of German industry, combined with the persistent containment of the internal demand of the major economies of the euro area, has gone hand-in-hand with an impoverishment of the productive matrix of the southern regions less connected with Germany, while at the same time seeing a general redirection of trade flows (Simonazzi et al., 2013; Celi et al., 2018).

As in the 1970s and 1980s, the outbreak of the current crisis coincided with the development of a new phase in the paradigm of international production and technology. On the one hand, the new emerging countries entering the scene have put pressure on the lower end of the product range. On the other hand, there has been a growing commoditisation of knowledge. Supported and extended world-wide through international agreements,[3] the role of closed science and closed markets is expanding at the expense of open science and open markets, favouring exclusive ownership of the knowledge used in production and the global monopolisation of knowledge (Pagano, 2014). Different competition regimes thus coexist: price competition for commoditised products at the lower end of the product scale, quality competition for products and services increasingly bound up with monopolised knowledge along the value chain.

The current crisis has amplified the divergence within the Eurozone, where two different industrial models coexist: a solid industrial basis in the core, which is export-oriented and commands a strong position on the global markets, and a less diversified industrial sector in the periphery (with appreciable differences across and within countries). The export-oriented model has managed to offset the fall in domestic demand by increasing its exports, but the widening divergence between core and periphery is jeopardising the sustainability of the Economic and Monetary Union (EMU).

3. Short- and long-term policies for EMU sustainability

There is, by now, an increasing consensus on the need for macroeconomic policies able to (to absorb the shocks of the sovereign crisis and fight recession. Recognition of the need to act through fiscal policy has been reinforced with the consideration that quantitative easing, though helpful, has reached its limits as an instrument to create demand. Public investment in infrastructure has been indicated as a measure that, given the extremely expansionary monetary policy, could be carried out at almost zero cost to the public budget – hence the call for countries with fiscal space to expand public investment in infrastructure. The expansion of demand, it is argued, would benefit deficit countries through the action of the foreign trade multiplier.

Two considerations are in order. The first concerns the differential effects of an expansionary policy. Expansion on the part of the surplus countries, though helpful, does not respond to the problem of closing the gap in productive capabilities between the deficit and surplus countries, for two good reasons. Its effects will depend on the productive abilities of the peripheral countries to match the demand from the expanding countries (which has been estimated to be fairly small for some countries) and, even more importantly, the composition of demand that trickles down to the periphery will reflect the priorities of the expanding countries, which do not need to respond to the competitiveness and growth problems of the periphery.

The second point concerns the consistency of the policies pursued at the EU level. The recent endorsement of an "industrial compact", which sanctions the need for action in support of industrial upgrading for the member states, clashes with both the austerity policies and the "structural reforms" that are strongly advocated by the European institutions. A strategic policy of industrial development is incompatible with cuts in public budgets, and more generally in aggregate demand. Fiscal consolidation hinders implementation of a more comprehensive developmental approach at the national level. Similarly, labour market deregulation can provide a perverse incentive to firms hindering quality innovation (Guarascio and Simonazzi, 2016). Finally, two decades of labour market reforms have resulted in greater income inequality and impoverishment of families in the core and periphery countries alike. Combined with the external challenge of globalisation and competition from the emerging economies, they have oriented the process of reorganisation and innovation of firms against expansion of capacity, thereby reducing the economy's rate of growth.

4. National industrial policy

The periphery needs to implement a policy that responds to its problems of reindustrialisation and growth. The arguments in favour of a national industrial policy rest on the observation that the process of development is far from linear. It consists in moving towards more complex, less ubiquitous products, broadening the range of activities and capabilities, and not, as the theory of comparative advantage would have it, in specialising in what the country does best (Hausmann and Hidalgo, 2011).[4] Changes in a country's productive structure can thus be understood as a combination of two processes: (i) the process by which countries find new products as yet unexplored combinations of the capabilities they already have, and (ii) the process by which countries accumulate new capabilities and combine them with other, previously available capabilities to develop yet more products. Since development occurs through diversification into products that are "near" to those that are already being successfully produced and exported, a country's ability to add new products to its production depends on having many near products and many capabilities that are being utilised in other, potentially more distant, products.[5] The mainstream approach hypothesises a continuum in the product space that ensures the achievement of dynamic efficiency, moving up in the product space by shifting resources to the more efficient production. Thus, the problem of development is mostly to achieve static efficiency: to better allocate resources by responding to the market failures caused by monopolies, asymmetric information, and externalities. In contrast, the existence of discontinuities in the product space and the need to develop and coordinate those capabilities that growing industries demand prove a formidable obstacle to the process of development. Countries with a low diversity of capabilities can become stuck in "quiescence traps", which make catching up more difficult. This is why government policy is called upon to coordinate the dispersed actions of firms, to help them identify new opportunities for differentiation and upgrading, and to contribute to developing the capabilities required for the production of more complex products (Ginzburg and Simonazzi, 2017).

Innovative countries rely on the presence of innovative businesses that compete on the basis of new products or processes and/or more effective use of new technologies (and not primarily on the basis of price). Firm performance crucially depends on both the structured interrelationships (the linkages) that they can establish upstream and downstream, and the support received from the material and immaterial infrastructures, development agencies, and financial institutions that sustain the process of innovation in the long term (Ginzburg, 2012).[6] As argued above, these features were (and still are) asymmetrically distributed between the countries of the centre and the Southern periphery of Europe. With the fast rate of technical change and globalisation, and the increasing commodification and private appropriation of knowledge, the EU latecomers can be caught in the "middle-income trap", no longer (price) competitive because of the developing countries catching up, and not yet capable of entering into worldwide (quality) competition.

However, the notion of product-led competition is a relative concept. It relates to the creation of new products and new markets in a given productive system. Thus, it does not concern only countries and markets at the technological or organisational frontier of knowledge but, on the contrary, takes on special importance in the peripheral countries. Rodrik's distinction between *cost discovery* and innovation (or R&D), with its emphasis on "self-discovery", suggests that: 'What is involved is not [only] coming up with new products or processes, but "discovering" that a certain good, already well established in world markets, can be produced at home at low cost' (Rodrik, 2004, pp. 7–8). The focus on potential markets can reveal opportunities also in fields less obvious than exports or manufacturing. Imports, for instance, can signal the existence of unexploited opportunities – final demand for products or bottlenecks to development – that well-integrated policy action can help to seize. The provision of public goods for the productive sector can offer new opportunities for innovative firms, while exerting a strong activating capacity. Public services exhibit rapid growth in demand in cities and metropolitan areas. The focus on welfare as an engine for growth calls for systemic action at different levels of governance (national, regional, municipal) and institutions to coordinate the supply and demand of innovative services (Cappellin et al., 2015).

State intervention is needed not because 'the government officials [are] omniscient or cleverer than businessmen but because they [can] look at things from a national and long-term point of view, rather than sectional, short-term point of view' (Chang, 2009, pp. 16–17). Since market prices cannot reveal the profitability of products that do not exist yet, and dynamic externalities can limit firms' readiness to embark upon risky projects without public incentive and support, promising innovations may not be taken up by firms. Public action can support firms in their innovation processes and provide guidance for development strategies that promote products (and capabilities) as a way to create incentives to accumulate capabilities (and develop new products) in a cumulative, virtuous circle. Moreover, the transfer and adaptation of technologies, forms of organisation, business strategies, and products originally designed in other socio-economic systems raise specific challenging problems in both the supply and demand domains that public policy can help solve. Thus, although concern about government inefficiencies should be taken seriously, it should not justify inaction.

5. European industrial policy

There have been three phases in European industrial policy: from product market intervention (1950s–70s), through laissez-faire policies (1980s–90s), to interventions aiming at facilitating coordination. After the first phase, industrial policy came to be conceived solely as competition policy, with greater reliance on market forces, as epitomised by the Single European Act of 1986. Assuming all member countries to be alike in terms of productive capability and degree of development, priority was given to horizontal measures instead of targeted ones, and industrial specialisation was left to the market forces. The result, as was argued in the previous sections, has been increasing divergence within the European Union. Since 2000, and especially since the crisis, the laissez-faire policies of the 1980s and 1990s have given way to a "soft" kind of industrial policy: governments should take on a coordinating role, facilitate innovation, and focus on correcting "systemic failures". In January 2014, the European Commission introduced a new policy initiative called the Industrial Compact, which established the target of restoring industrial activities from the present 16 per cent to 20 per cent of GDP by 2020. In November, the Commission launched the Investment Plan for Europe (IPE, known as the Juncker Plan). Conceived as a response to the drop in investment within the EU (by 15 per cent since the 2007 peak), it envisaged that, by catalysing investment, in particular private investment, and by increasing companies' access to financing, the investment gap could be reduced, boosting growth, competitiveness, and job creation in the European Union. Implementation of the European Fund for Strategic Investment (EFSI), which is the financial pillar of the IPE,[7] has been entrusted to the European Investment Bank (EIB) Group. The Fund provides an EU guarantee amounting to 21bn euros[8] and aims to mobilise additional investments in the order of 315bn euros over three years with a multiplier, or leverage effect estimated at 15 times). In his 2016 State of the

Union address, President Juncker announced the Commission's proposal to extend the EFSI, increasing its firepower and duration as well as reinforcing its strengths. To improve the working of the EFSI, the Commission plans to address the issue of geographical coverage by placing stronger emphasis on providing local technical assistance to those who wish to apply for funding and to further simplify the possibility to combine EFSI funding with other EU sources, such as the European Structural and Investment (ESI) funds.

The success of the new approach depends on three factors: sufficient funding, coordination across all levels of governance, and ensuring that latecomer countries can participate on an equal footing, which may imply preferential treatment. In all these respects, it still falls far short of what is needed to kick-start rebalanced growth in the Eurozone (Pianta and Lucchese, 2014; Celi et al., 2018). In fact, it seems fair to say that the IPE project does not meet the requirements discussed in the previous Section 1) It does not respond to the immediate need to support recovery. In fact, the plan is underfinanced, and the total amount (even taking the multiplier at its maximum level) is largely insufficient for the task of supporting innovation and infrastructure and stimulating growth. Moreover, it is biased towards projects with low and/or deferred employment impact. The Social Investment Package, launched in 2013 by the EC with high hopes of a paradigm shift in social investment, failed to find adequate room in the project. 2) It does not respond to a clear development strategy. The allocation of funds is demand-driven (by firms), within a very broad range of targets. The requisite of "additionality" for investment projects, finalised to create and finance new investment opportunities, is difficult to assess. The requirement that the projects be profitable constrains the scope of its policy to projects promising immediate commercial success, leaving out projects that could generate new, interesting and potentially enabling capabilities (Ciuriak, 2016). 3) Finally, there is no sectorial or geographic pre-allocation, which can leave weaker firms in weaker countries at a disadvantage. Although the financial guarantee is likely to be more valuable for firms in countries subject to a credit-crunch (as demonstrated by the larger share of the Southern countries in the first year), investment opportunities, or capability barriers could penalise these firms more. All considered, it is doubtful that IPE can perform the twofold role of sustaining recovery and reducing divergences between countries.

6. Conclusion

After the neo-liberal phase of the last few decades, economists now seem to agree that exiting the current recession requires a mix of macroeconomic and industrial policies designed in such a way as to enable latecomer countries to overcome their structural disadvantage. There is far less agreement on the ways to achieve this. Indeed, the view stressing competition and market mechanisms as the best ways to rejuvenate and innovate the industrial structure still prevails in many quarters. Yet its main tenets – that success stories are never the result of a coherent design, devised by an enlightened planner, but are the outcome of individuals' actions in the market – is increasingly challenged by the evidence (Mazzucato, 2013). Analysis of the main phases of development in the Southern European countries since the aftermath of World War II provides further evidence against "market fundamentalism". Similarly, the views that allocative efficiency requires that low productivity firms be forced out of the market, that well-designed structural reforms of product and labour markets, albeit entailing costly adjustments in the short run, ensure greater productivity through a more efficient allocation of resources in the long run, are increasingly challenged, theoretically and empirically. The introduction of a "protective" element – that is, "helping losers" by temporarily shielding them from the full forces of the market – may be indispensable to preserve the productive and employment capacity of a country and help its firms to enter technological fields, while reducing the costs of restructuring. This policy should not be confused with the traditional industrial policy that often tried to preserve existing structures. Support for declining sectors may be needed to encourage and sustain the process of structural change and productivity growth, and preserve existing firms and capabilities while allowing time to develop new ones, developing new products also within "mature" sectors (Chang et al., 2013).

A more balanced form of European economic integration requires a common undertaking to reduce the gaps between and within countries. This strategy is lacking in the present economic programme, which reiterates the aim to combine financial stability and growth, but is too concentrated on the (necessary) supply side, efficiency-enhancing measures, in a void of strategic vision.

Notes

1 This section draws on Celi et al. (2018).
2 Although the exact extent and details of Germany industrial policy are hard to ascertain, given the multiplicity of measures and actors (at the federal, *Länder*, and municipality level), Chang et al. (2013) rate German industrial policy among the most active in Europe.
3 For instance, the 1994 Trade-Related Aspects of Intellectual Property Rights agreements within the World Trade Organization (WTO).
4 'Countries do not become rich by making more of the same thing. They do so by changing what they produce and how they produce it. They grow by doing things that are new to them; in short, they innovate' (Hausmann, 2013).
5 Chang and Andreoni (2016) observe that apparently distant products can be produced with relatively similar technologies and suggest a transition from a product-based taxonomy to a production technology-based taxonomy.
6 See also the study by Brusco (2004) quoted in Marcuzzo (2004).
7 There are two more pillars. The second, the European Investment Advisory Hub and the European Investment Project Portal, provides technical assistance and greater visibility for investment opportunities. The third focuses on removing regulatory barriers to investment both nationally and at the EU level (EIB, 2015).
8 It consists of an EU Guarantee (16bn euros) complemented by an EIB contribution (5bn euros) provided from its own resources (http://europa.eu/rapid/press-relea se_IP-16-3002_en.htm).

References

Brusco, S. (2004). *Industriamoci. Capacità di progetto e sviluppo locale*. Roma: Donzelli.

Cappellin, R., Baravelli, M., Bellandi, M., Camagni, R., Ciciotti E. and. Marelli E., eds. (2015). *Investimenti, innovazione e città: una nuova politica industriale per la crescita*. Milano: Egea.

Celi, G., Ginzburg, A., Guarascio, D. and Simonazzi, A. (2018). *Crisis in the European monetary union: a core-periphery perspective*. Abingdon: Routledge.

Chang, H.-J. (2009). Industrial policy: can we go beyond an unproductive confrontation? In: *Annual World Bank Conference on Development Economics*, Seoul, 22–24 June.

Chang, H.-J. and Andreoni, A. (2016). Industrial policy in a changing world: basic principles, neglected issues and new challenges. In: *Cambridge Journal of Economics 40 Years Conference*, Cambridge, 12–13 July.

Chang, H.-J., Andreoni, A. and Kuan, M.L. (2013). International industrial policy experiences and the lessons for the UK. Future of Manufacturing Project: Evidence Paper 4. London: Foresight, UK Government Office for Science.

Ciuriak, D. (2016). Rebooting Europe. McKinsey Global Institute Prize Essay Competition: Opportunity for Europe. Available at SSRN: https://ssrn.com/abstract=2851329

EIB (European Investment Bank) (2015). *EFSI Report. From the European Investment Bank to the European Parliament and the Council on 2015 EIB Group Financing and Investment Operations under EFSI (European Fund for Strategic Investment)*. Available at: http://www.eib.org/attachments/strategies/efsi_2015_report_ep_council_en.pdf

Ginzburg, A. (2012). Sviluppo trainato dalla produttività o dalle connessioni: due diverse prospettive di analisi e di intervento pubblico nella realtà economica italiana. *Economia & Lavoro*, 46 (2), 67–93.

Ginzburg, A. and Simonazzi, A. (2011). Disinflation in industrial countries, foreign debt cycles and the costs of stability. In: R. Ciccone, C. Gehrke and G. Mongiovi, eds. *Sraffa and modern economics*. Abingdon: Routledge, 269–296.

Ginzburg, A. and Simonazzi, A. (2017). Out of the crisis: a radical change of strategy for the euro zone. *The European Journal of Comparative Economics*, 14 (1), 13–37.

Guarascio, D. and Simonazzi, A. (2016). A polarized country in a polarized Europe: an industrial policy for Italy's renaissance. *Economia e Politica Industriale*, 43 (3), 315–322.

Hausmann, R. (2013). The conglomerate way to growth. www.project-syndicate.org, 25 July 2013. Available at: http://www.project-syndicate.org/commentary/big-companies-and-economic-growth-in-developing-countries-by-ricardo-hausmann.

Hausmann, R. and Hidalgo, C. (2011). The network structure of economic output. *Journal of Economic Growth*, 16 (4), 309–342.

Hirschman, A.O. (1981). The rise and decline of development economics. *Essays in trespassing: Economics to politics and beyond*. Cambridge, UK: Cambridge University Press, 1–24.

Marcuzzo, C. (2004). Lo sviluppo locale come vera risorsa. Recensione di S. Brusco, Industriamoci. Capacità di progetto e sviluppo locale, Roma, Donzelli, 2004. *Il Sole-24 Ore*, 29 August. Available at: https://www.donzelli.it/reviews/383.

Mazzucato, M. (2013). *The entrepreneurial State: debunking public vs. private sector myths*. London: Anthem Press.

Pagano, U. (2014). The crisis of intellectual monopoly capitalism. *Cambridge Journal of Economics*, 38 (6), 1409–1429.

Pianta, M. and Lucchese, M. (2014). Una politica industriale per l'Europa. *Economia & Lavoro*, 48 (3), 85–97.

Rodrik, D. (2004). Industrial policy for the twenty-first century. *HKS Working Paper Series*, no. RWP04-047, November. Cambridge, MA: Harvard Kennedy School of Government.

Simonazzi, A. and Ginzburg, A. (2015). The interruption of industrialization in Southern Europe: a center-periphery perspective. In: M. Baumeister and R. Sala, eds. *Southern Europe? Italy, Spain, Portugal, and Greece from the 1950s until the present day*. Frankfurt: Campus, 103–137.

Simonazzi, A., Ginzburg, A. and Nocella, G. (2013). Economic relations between Germany and Southern Europe. *Cambridge Journal of Economics*, 37 (3), 653–675.

Wade, R.H. (2012). Return of industrial policy? *International Review of Applied Economics*, 26 (2), 223–239.

17 The flaw in 20th century macroeconomic thought

The general equilibrium benchmark

Elisabetta De Antoni

1. Introduction

This chapter starts with the Swedish Flag, a metaphor introduced by Leijon-hufvud (1983, 1992) in order to depict the course of macroeconomic thought in the twentieth century. The result is a faithful and stimulating fresco whereby the Flag is a useful teaching aid, as well as providing stimulating food for thought. Leijonhufvud's conclusion is that macroeconomics started with Keynes but ended with repudiation of the Keynesian revolution.

As shown in the next Section, the success of Leijonhufvud's metaphor descends from an ace in the sleeve: implicitly and uncritically, the Flag adopts the same presuppositions as the mainstream theory. We refer to the use of competitive general equilibrium as a benchmark. This implies referring to a competitive economy whose state of health is characterised by (i) perfect individual rationality, (ii) perfect correspondence of macroeconomics with microeconomics and (iii) perfect collective rationality. As shown in Section 2, the realism and validity of these presuppositions are highly questionable. Analogous considerations apply to the two corollaries of the aforementioned benchmark represented respectively by (*a*) the "shock plus maladjustment" approach to economic fluctuations, and (*b*) the dichotomy between nominal and real variables. The issue under examination is of crucial importance: an unrealistic and groundless benchmark risks distorting and misleading the analysis. The geocentric approach of Aristotle and Ptolemy could never have allowed us to understand the solar system. The problem is also relevant today, since mainstream theory generally keeps referring to the general equilibrium benchmark.

In light of these considerations, Section 3 will retrace Leijonhufvud's description of the course of the debate, highlighting its main turning points. Section 4 will then show that the presuppositions of the mainstream represent "blinkers" which have distorted its representation of the world, directing it towards an artificial world which − *ex ante* and *a priori* − excludes uncertainty, the non-neutrality of money, the active role of effective demand, "unnatural" involuntary unemployment, endogenous instability, the inefficiencies of finan-cial markets, and so on. As if this were not enough, the same presuppositions have also affected the evolution of dominant macroeconomic theory, pushing it further and further away from reality. It is thus hardly surprising that, at the beginning of the new century, the profession proclaimed that it had acquired "full control of the rudder" (see, e.g., Blanchard, 2000, 2008) just as the crisis was coming and even when it was exploding under the profession's feet.[1]

With regard to the increasing gap between theory and reality, moreover, Section 4 highlights that the various imperfections introduced by the various schools to explain deviations from general equilibrium and observed economic fluctuations were ephemeral. In the light of past experience, the research strategy based on general equilibrium plus maladjustments seems thus doomed to failure. This result is not surprising: being incompatible with the neoclassical Olympus, maladjustments represented an easy theoretical shooting target. As a consequence, they ended with being systematically criticised and then removed, leaving the field free for full coordination. In light of these considerations, general equilibrium may be likened to a mermaid who attracts sailors without leaving them any escape route. Put otherwise, if general equilibrium has magnetic properties, they are of an ideological and intellectual (rather than economic) kind. On these bases, Section 5 will draw some lessons about the future.

2. The Swedish Flag and its questionable presuppositions

Let us therefore start with Leijonhufvud's metaphor. The basic presupposition of the Swedish Flag is the benchmark represented by competitive general equilibrium, i.e. the assumption that it represents the state of an economy's health. In the absence of imperfections, we would consequently have a perfectly competitive regime in which optimal individual choices are perfectly coordinated by the price mechanism. This benchmark has in turn two corollaries of remarkable importance. The first is the impulse plus propagation mechanism (or shock plus maladjustment) approach to economic fluctuations. If general equilibrium were hit by a shock, the price mechanism would instantaneously clear all markets. To justify deviations from general equilibrium and observed economic fluctuations, it is then necessary to introduce a propagation mechanism, i.e. a maladjustment able to prevent the price mechanism from adequately performing its role. The second corollary ensues from the neoclassical dichotomy and implies the possibility of sharply distinguishing between nominal and real variables.

By associating the nature – real or nominal – of the variables affected by the possible shocks and maladjustments, Leijonhufvud obtains four cells and overlaps them with the blue squares of the Swedish Flag in Figure 17.1. On those bases, he shows that the macroeconomic debate of the past century moved from one square of the Flag to another, finally returning to the starting point, i.e. to Keynes' square. At the end of its circular path, however, the debate disowned the revolutionary contribution of *The General Theory*, above all the crucial role of effective demand.

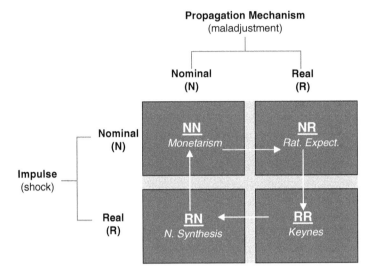

Figure 17.1 Leijonhufvud's Swedish Flag

Leijonhufvud presents the Flag without dwelling on it. Between the lines, however, his metaphor hides an ace in the sleeve which explains its effectiveness in synthesising the evolution of dominant macroeconomic thought: the Flag acritically adopts the same presuppositions as the mainstream. We essentially refer to the assumption of perfect competition and to the three pillars of general equilibrium represented by (i) perfect individual rationality, (ii) perfect correspondence of macroeconomics with microeconomics, and finally (iii) perfect collective rationality. These presuppositions cannot be taken for granted. As we shall see below, their realism and their validity is highly questionable.

To start with perfect individual rationality, this assumption presupposes optimising agents with rational expectations. This means referring to Olympic demigods, who possess perfect information and the cognitive skills required by perfect foresight and optimisation. For poor flesh-and-blood human beings, however, the future is mostly unknown: each day may be their last one. The continuous evolution and complexity of the world in which they live prevent them from identifying the model (assuming it exists, is unique, and so on) that rules the economy and from formulating rational expectations on those bases. Even if perfect foresight were possible, moreover, it cannot at all be said that they have the cognitive skills required by optimisation. Even if they had the cognitive skills, it is not said that problems are tractable. Not by chance – as shown by Behavioural Economics and in line with Keynes's "animal spirits" – the behaviours of ordinary mortals reflect psychological considerations which have not much to do with rational calculations.

Turning to the correspondence of macroeconomics with microeconomics, the assumption is that aggregate behaviours represent the sum of individual ones, being consequently traceable to them: in other words, macroeconomics has to be microfounded. This, however, means excluding *ex ante* and *a priori* phenomena like Keynes's paradox of thrift or Fisher's debt paradox that some European countries seem to have concretely experienced firsthand. On the other hand, the literature (for instance, Lavoie, 2014, pp. 17–18) highlights several fallacies of composition according to which aggregate results do not correspond to the sum of individual behaviours. These fallacies match with our daily experience, according to which the same ingredients may be combined in different ways to produce different dishes.

Let us finally consider perfect collective rationality, i.e. the assumption of full coordination of the system by virtue of the price mechanism. As highlighted by Samuelson (1947, p. 5), in physics there is the force of gravity, whereby an egg does not stand on its tip but tends to settle on its side. Analogously, in economics there is the invisible hand, whereby prices instantaneously clear all markets. The pathologies that systematically afflict the real world show the irrealism of this assumption. In addition, its theoretical underpinnings are questionable as well. For instance, the existence of a positive interest rate able to align full-employment saving and investment cannot be taken for granted (Krugman, 2011). The same holds for the assumption of an imaginary auctioneer able to coordinate the whole system. As shown by Velupillai (2006), any *tâtonnement* process would amount to solving the halting problem of a Turing machine, known to be undecidable.

No less questionable are the two corollaries of the benchmark under examination. Starting with the first, the shock plus maladjustment approach reflects the *ex ante* and *a priori* exclusion of endogenous instability. This assumption is again questionable. Postwar historical experience shows that growth may lead either to an increase in the prices of raw materials followed by inflationary spirals or to speculative waves leading to financial crises. From the theoretical point of view, Minsky (1986) teaches us that stability is destabilising. The general equilibrium benchmark *ex ante* and *a priori* rejects this eventuality. The system is intrinsically stable: economic fluctuations consequently require not only a shock but also a maladjustment able to propagate it to income and employment.

Let us now move to the second corollary, i.e. to the distinction between nominal and real variables. In the absence of imperfections, money is neutral. Financial markets are so efficient in coordinating intertemporal saving and investment decisions that they can be ignored. All of this implies the irrelevance of the Flag's yellow stripes, where nominal and real variables are so closely interconnected that they cannot be separated. The realism of this exclusion, however, is again not granted. If money were neutral, the reasons why it replaces barter would be mysterious. With regard to the efficiency of financial markets, the recent sub-prime crisis is an evident demonstration of its irrealism. Even admitting the dichotomy, and consequently focusing on the blue squares of the Flag, however, the distinction between nominal and real variables is not univocal but depends on the theory taken into account. According to the neoclassical conception, for instance, the interest rate is a real variable determined by the forces of productivity and thrift. In *The General Theory*, by contrast, the interest rate is a nominal variable: "Interest has been usually regarded as the reward of not-spending, whereas in fact it is the reward of not-hoarding" (Keynes, 1936, p. 174). As far as money is concerned – insofar as it increases the liquidity and thus reduces the riskiness of wealth[2] instead of representing a mere medium of exchange – it proves difficult to consider it as a nominal variable.

To conclude, the common benchmark of the Flag and the mainstream seems highly questionable both in its realism and in its theoretical underpinnings. The point is not necessarily irrelevant, since a wrong benchmark risks being distortive and misleading. To check this, the following Section will retrace the evolution of dominant macroeconomic theory. On those bases, Section 4 will analyse the influence of its benchmark.

3. The evolution of dominant macroeconomic theory in the twentieth century

The macroeconomic debate starts with *The General Theory*, which Leijonhufvud places in the RR square of the Flag. As known, every economist has her/his own interpretation of Keynes. In Leijonhufvud's Keynes,[3] both shock and maladjustments concern variables that general equilibrium theory classifies as real. Specifically, the shock is represented by the fall in the marginal efficiency of capital (and consequently of investment) caused by a worsening of expectations. The maladjustment consists in the only partial fall of the interest rate to its lower natural level. Unlike entrepreneurs, speculators ignore the fall of the marginal efficiency of capital and consequently of the natural interest rate. Expecting the market rate to return to its former level, they sell securities, thus sustaining their yield. Out of this incorrect interest rate level, the fall of investment triggers quantity adjustments that lead to an amplified contraction of income and employment.

One year after the publication of *The General Theory*, Hicks (1937) introduced the IS–LM model as a synthesis of Keynes's book. By amputating the innovative contribution of the Keynesian revolution,[4] Hicks's model sets the premises for the subsequent neoclassical developments of the Synthesis. The Neoclassical Synthesis moves to the RN square of the Flag. The shock is still represented by the fall of the marginal efficiency of capital and thus of investment; it consequently remains real. This time, however, the maladjustment concerns the money wage (instead of the interest rate) and consequently becomes nominal. The change is triggered by Modigliani (1944) and comes to completion with Patinkin (1956). The conclusion of the Neoclassical Synthesis is that – if involuntary unemployment turned into the fall in money wages and prices – real money balances would rise, stimulating the economy to full employment even under a liquidity trap, i.e. even in the presence of downward rigidity of the interest rate. Consequently, a wrong interest rate does not represent an obstacle.

The only imperfection able to justify deviations from full employment (Keynes's economics) is represented by money wage rigidity. More generally, according to the Neoclassical Synthesis, Keynesian theory holds only in a short run defined by money wage rigidities. In the long run, money wages become perfectly flexible, and general equilibrium theory is the proper one. Given the duration and the staggering of wage contracts, however, the short run of the Synthesis tends to last years and years. This justifies the state's intervention in support of the economy, even though – according to Phillips (1958) – such support implies higher inflation. On this last issue, however, the Neoclassical Synthesis clashed with the stagflation of the 1970s, when the simultaneous increase in unemployment and inflation disavowed the trade-off envisaged by the Phillips curve.

The subsequent school of thought is represented by Monetarism Mark I,[5] which brings us to the NN square. This time, both the shock and the maladjustment become nominal. The leader of this school, Milton Friedman, is a staunch supporter of the free market and firmly believes in the effectiveness of the price mechanism. In his view, Keynes's liquidity preference[6] is a sacrosanct theoretical acquisition. Practically, however, it is irrelevant, since the interest rate is determined by the real sector's equilibrium. In the presence of an exogenous increase in money supply, therefore, the clearing of the money market can be only carried out by nominal expenditure and income. Friedman (1956, 1971) thus restates the Quantity Theory. In his view, instability has a monetary origin, and consequently shocks become nominal. As far as maladjustments are concerned, Friedman (1968, 1977) rejects the money wage rigidity of the Neoclassical Synthesis. Firstly, the latter presupposes an unjustified money illusion; what matters in the labour market are real (not money) wages. Secondly, since equilibrium represents the optimal situation, money wage rigidity is inefficient and as such theoretically unjustified.[7] Friedman then assumes labour market equilibrium and introduces the concept of "natural unemployment", incorporating the phenomenon into general equilibrium. At this point, however, he still has the problem of justifying observed economic fluctuations. In this regard, Friedman points out that – if money wages are anchored to expected inflation and the latter is the same for firms and workers – the traditional labour demand and supply curves as functions of real wages remain unchanged, keeping unemployment at its natural level. Friedman then focuses on information asymmetries. Contrary to firms, workers do not have sufficient information to anticipate the price level. Being unable to foresee the increase (fall) in prices, they keep their requested money wage unchanged, accepting the fall (rise) in real wages. Workers' money illusion consequently implies a temporary increase (fall) in the traditional labour supply curve which stimulates (depresses) income and employment above (below) their full-employment levels. To sum up, Friedman's maladjustment concerns inflationary expectations (instead of money wages) and consequently remains nominal.

The next square of the Swedish Flag (NR) is occupied by Monetarism Mark II, or the School of Rational Expectations, also termed New Classical Economics. This school represents a refined version of neoclassical macroeconomics, according to which every aggregate relationship has to be based on intertemporal optimisation by individual agents (specifically, of the representative agent). The leader of this school, Robert Lucas, shares Friedman's faith in the price mechanism. He too consequently adheres to the Quantity Theory according to which money supply (by assumption exogenous) determines nominal expenditure and income. In Monetarism Mark II, instability thus continues to have a monetary nature, and consequently shocks remain nominal. With regard to the propagation mechanism, by contrast, Lucas rejects Friedman's information asymmetries. Because information is a source of utility, it is a good which spreads through learning, imitative behaviours, consulting, and so on. Lucas then focuses on incomplete information: agents know the deterministic component of reality but do not know the random one. Specifically, Lucas adopts the assumption of rational expectations: by avoiding systematic errors, agents succeed in formulating expectations coherent with the model which rules the working of the economy, i.e. with general equilibrium solutions. To surprise them are random changes in the rate of inflation arising from stochastic changes in the growth rate of money supply. To have real effects, however, these surprises have to affect relative prices (those which determine individual behaviours). In Lucas's Monetarism Mark II, the maladjustment consequently becomes real. Specifically, inflationary surprises pose a problem of signal extraction: firms/workers mistake the increase in the general price level for an increase in the relative price of (in the demand for) their products/services and consequently increase their supply of goods/labour. In the short run, inflationary surprises thus exert expansionary effects on the real economy. In line with the policy ineffectiveness proposition (Sargent and Wallace, 1976), to sustain – even only in the short run – income and employment, monetary policy has to be unanticipated. By contrast, an anticipated monetary restriction can eradicate inflation without any real cost.

There is, however, a contradictory aspect of Monetarism Mark I and II that seems to pave the way to subsequent developments. The essence of both kinds of Monetarism consists in tracking economic fluctuations back to a money supply, which – according to the Quantity Theory inspiring them – should instead be neutral. This explains the transition to the Real Business Cycle Theory. In Prescott's (1986) view, the business cycles experienced by industrialised countries in the postwar period reflected random changes of productivity due to technological progress. As in Keynes's case, this time shocks become real. As regards the propagation mechanism, the promptitude characterising the publication of data concerning the money supply belittles the relevance of Lucas's inflationary surprises and of the related explanations of economic fluctuations. This time consequently maladjustments disappear: information is perfect, and the system is always in general equilibrium. Economic policy authorities need not worry: economic fluctuations are efficient ones.

Leijonhufvud's conclusion is that the return of the macroeconomic debate to Keynes' square is associated with radical repudiation of the Keynesian revolution. For our purposes, by contrast, the Flag represents a tool to analyse the influence of the mainstream's presuppositions on its vision and on its evolution (of which the increasing distancing from Keynes is only one aspect).

4. The misleading effects of the general equilibrium benchmark

In light of the foregoing analysis, the general equilibrium benchmark, first of all, focused the mainstream view on an artificial and counterfeit representation of the world with which it had very little in common. The neoclassical Olympus (with its Olympic demigods) *ex ante* and *a priori* excludes ignorance of the future and the boundedness of human rationality. Moreover, it relegates financial markets and their possible destabilising role to behind the scenes. Its perfection banishes real phenomena such as irrational exuberance. Its omnipotent auctioneer prevents endogenous instability, the insufficiency of effective demand, involuntary unemployment, and consequently banishes the need for intervention by economic policy authorities. All of this, however, is at odds with our concrete experience. We recently had a sizeable real estate bubble followed by a devastating financial crisis with considerable real effects, and it is thanks to Keynesian economic policies that we have overcome the crisis. As far as the assumption of perfect competition is concerned, it sweeps under the rug the iniquity and inefficiencies of income distribution that are so heavily afflicting our time, putting our democracies themselves at risk.

According to the previous Section, however, the general equilibrium benchmark not only misled the mainstream viewpoint: it also affected its evolution. Specifically, our survey of dominant macroeconomic theory shows that the several maladjustments adopted from time to time by the various schools of thought were all ephemeral. As a consequence, the several general equilibrium plus imperfections strategies did not resist long. This result is not surprising. Being incompatible with the neoclassical Olympus, maladjustments represented an easy target; from the beginning, they were consequently destined to be criticised and then removed. According to Section 3, this has been the case of the interest rate rigidity in Leijonhufvud's Keynes, of money wage rigidity in the Neoclassical Synthesis, asymmetric information in Friedman, and inflationary surprises in Lucas. As a result of these progressive exclusions, the benchmark of the mainstream finally came to dominate the scene entirely.

At the beginning of the new century, the gap between theory and reality consequently became so wide as to prevent the economics profession from grasping the evident symptoms of the crisis and from arranging in time the countermeasures that might have avoided, or at least mitigated, the disaster. On the other hand, before the crisis, Lucas himself admitted that:

> The problem is that the new theories, the theories embedded in general equilibrium dynamics of the sort that we know how to use pretty well now – there's a residue of things they don't let us think about. They don't let us think about the US experience of the 1930s or about financial crises and their real consequences in Asia and Latin America. They don't let us think, I don't think, very well about Japan in the 1990s.
>
> Lucas (2004, p. 23)

Put otherwise, mainstream economics is like a medical science devoted to Olympic demigods that are immune to any pathology. With hindsight, however, Lucas should also recognise that neither has the mainstream approach been neutral. It has actively contributed to the crisis, for instance by legitimating the financial deregulation that facilitated its occurrence (and that Trump has recently reproposed).

5. Some lessons concerning the future

One way to solve the current divergence between theory and reality consists in returning to the real world without any "blinkers", i.e. by abandoning the general equilibrium benchmark. The state of the real economy's health does not imply an invisible hand, but presupposes a balanced relationship between antigens and antibodies.[8] In light of past experience, moreover, any general equilibrium plus imperfections strategy seems destined to represent an only temporary expedient to justify observed deviations from full employment and economic fluctuations. Should we give up the crutch represented by the mainstream benchmark, the authors that admitted the limits of coordination like Keynes (together with his most authentic followers, like Minsky and other Post Keynesians)[9] could help us.

Our Keynes, however, cannot be located on the Swedish Flag as Leijon-hufvud does. Instead of adopting general equilibrium as a benchmark, he rejects its pillars one by one. According to *The General Theory*, ignorance about the future precludes optimisation justifying behaviours or laws of a psychological nature. To quote Keynes:

> ... human decisions affecting the future ... cannot depend on strict mathematical expectation, since the basis for making such calculations does not exist; and ... it is our innate urge to activity which makes the wheels go round, our rational selves choosing between the alternatives as best we are able, calculating where we can, but often falling back for our motive on whim or sentiment or chance
>
> Keynes (1936, pp. 162–163)

In the presence of fallacies of composition like Keynes's paradox of thrift, macroeconomic aggregates do not represent a simple sum of individual behaviours and consequently have to be considered independently from the latter. As far as collective rationality is concerned, general equilibrium is only one of the infinite possible cases: the price mechanism does not grant it a magnetic property. The concept of underemployment equilibrium is itself questionable: the alternation of waves of optimism and pessimism may generate endogenous business cycles around an underemployment growth path.

In light of these considerations, it does not seem possible to locate *The General Theory* on the Swedish Flag. After all, Keynes himself feels the need to express his rejection of orthodoxy with unprecedented vehemence from the first chapter of his book (not by chance, a short and incisive page entitled "The General Theory"). To quote Keynes:

I shall argue that the postulates of the classical theory are applicable to a special case only and not to the general case, the situation it assumes being a limiting point of the possible equilibrium positions. Moreover, the characteristic of the special case assumed by the classical theory happen not to be those of the economic society in which we actually live, with the result that its teaching is misleading and disastrous if we attempt to apply it to the facts of experience

Keynes (1936, p. 3)

Considering the responsibilities of the profession in allowing the sub-prime crisis, the quotation takes on a prophetic connotation.

As regards finance, Chapter 12 of *The General Theory* seems to be equally prophetic. In that context, Keynes presents the Stock Exchange as a secondary market where existing capital goods may be sold, consequently becoming more liquid and less risky for their owners. This result, however, is only an individual illusion; for the economy as a whole capital goods continue to be as illiquid and risky as before. This fetish of the liquidity of investment is not without consequences. Firstly, it leads to a more sustained – but also riskier – capital accumulation and economic growth. Secondly, it allows entrepreneurs to transform themselves into speculators who buy capital goods with the sole aim of selling them at a higher price.

We thus come to the casino capitalism that the recent financial crisis has brought into the limelight. Keynes's rejection is again without remission:

> Of the maxims of orthodox finance, none, surely, is more anti-social than the fetish of liquidity ... It forgets that there is no such thing as liquidity of investment for the community as a whole. The social object of skilled investment should be to defeat the dark forces of time and ignorance which envelop our future. The actual, private object of the most skilled investment today is "to beat the gun", as the Americans so well express it, to outwit the crowd, and to pass the bad, or depreciating, half-crown to the other fellow.
>
> Keynes (1936, p. 155)

Now, what else is the securitisation of loans but the creation of a secondary market where they can be sold, consequently becoming more liquid and less risky for the individual bank that granted them, despite remaining just as liquid and risky for the system as a whole? This mirage fed the unprecedented increase in the volume and in the riskiness of loans that led to the sub-prime crisis. To sum up, the recent financial crisis seems to be a re-edition of Keynes's liquidity fetish. Given its adherence to reality, Keynes's auctioneerless economics might have helped us to prevent the crisis.

With regard to the future, a rethink in the aforementioned directions might be more appropriate now than ever. As an example, let us consider the surprising technological progress underway. According to the supply-side approach of the mainstream, the phenomenon represents manna from heaven:

as a consequence of higher productivity, it will turn into an increase of real wages, labour supply, employment, and income. In Keynes's demand-constrained economy, by contrast, the result would be a fall in employment, which in turn would trigger a cumulative contraction of the real economy. If Keynes were right this time too, the crisis would again catch the profession unprepared and off guard.

Notes

1 In recent times, mainstream economists have begun to discuss the real interpretative capacity and utility of general equilibrium models (see, e.g., Solow, 2010; Romer, 2016; Blanchard, 2016; Stiglitz, 2018). The prevailing opinion, however, seems to be that general equilibrium keeps representing a key analytical apparatus, although it requires a greater alignment with reality.
2 We refer to Tobin (1958).
3 As an example, see Leijonhufvud (1981).
4 The IS–LM model presupposes two simple simultaneous equations implying a stable equilibrium based on given expectations. In *The General Theory*, by contrast, relationships among macroeconomic aggregates are sequential rather than simultaneous. The transition from one step of the sequence to the other is not ruled by cosmic laws, but depends on the circumstances and thus on expectations. According to the latter, money may affect the interest rate but it also may not; the interest rate may affect investment but it also may not; the price mechanism may trigger the "Keynes effect" thus absorbing involuntary unemployment but it also may not; the system may tend to an under-employment equilibrium but it may also fluctuate systematically around it.
5 The definition comes from Tobin (1980, 1981).
6 As known, the term "liquidity preference" refers to the dependence of the demand for money on the interest rate arising from the conception of money as a store of value.
7 As if this were not enough, in an inflationary context like that of the 1970s, the downward rigidity of money wages has no empirical relevance.
8 The main task of our immune system consists in protecting us from harmful substances of both endogenous (cancer) and exogenous nature (bacteria and viruses). The lack of balance between antigens and antibodies may give rise on the one hand to immunosuppression (insufficient antibodies reaction) and on the other hand to hyperactivation (antibodies attack healthy cells, as in the case of autoimmune diseases). As far as the choice of the benchmark is concerned, the analogy between economics and the human body seems more fruitful than the analogy between economics and celestial bodies.
9 With regard to this issue, Marcuzzo's works represent a landmark.

References

Blanchard, O. (2000). What do we know about macroeconomics that Fisher and Wicksell did not? *The Quarterly Journal of Economics*, 115 (4), 1375–1409.
Blanchard, O. (2008). *The state of macro*. NBER Working Paper Series, no. 14259, August. Cambridge, MA: National Bureau of Economic Research. Available at: http://www.nber.org/papers/w14259.pdf.

Blanchard, O. (2016). *Do DSGE models have a future?* PIIE Policy Brief, no. PB16-11, August. Washington, DC: Peterson Institute for International Economics. Available at: https://piie.com/system/files/documents/pb16-11.pdf.

Friedman, M. (1956). The quantity theory of money: a restatement. In: M. Friedman, ed. *Studies in the quantity theory of money.* Chicago, IL: Chicago University Press, 3–21.

Friedman, M. (1968). The role of monetary policy. *American Economic Review*, 58 (1), 1–21.

Friedman, M. (1971). A monetary theory of nominal income. *Journal of Political Economy*, 79 (2), 323–337.

Friedman, M. (1977). Nobel lecture: inflation and unemployment. *Journal of Political Economy*, 85 (3), 451–472.

Hicks, J. (1937). Mr Keynes and the classics: a suggested interpretation. *Econometrica*, 5 (2), 147–159.

Keynes, J.M. (1936). *The general theory of employment, interest and money.* London: Macmillan.

Krugman, P. (2011). Mr Keynes and the moderns. Paper presented at the Cambridge Conference commemorating the 75th anniversary of the publication of *The General Theory of Employment, Interest and Money.* Available at: https://www.princeton.edu/~pkrugman/keynes_and_the_moderns.pdf

Lavoie, M. (2014). *Post-Keynesian economics: new foundations.* Cheltenham, UK: Edward Elgar.

Leijonhufvud, A. (1981). The Wicksell connection: variations on a theme. In: A. Leijonhufvud, ed. *Information and coordination: essays in macroeconomic theory.* New York: Oxford University Press, 131–202.

Leijonhufvud, A. (1983). What would Keynes have thought of rational expectations? In: G. Worswick and J. Trevithick, eds. *Keynes and the modern world.* Cambridge: Cambridge University Press, 179–204. Republished in A. Leijonhufvud, ed. (2000). *Macroeconomic instability and coordination: selected essays of Axel Leijonhufvud.* Cheltenham, UK: Edward Elgar, 3–32.

Leijonhufvud, A. (1992). Keynesian economics: past confusions, future prospects. In: A. Vercelli and N. Dimitri, eds. *Macroeconomics: a survey of research strategies.* Oxford: Oxford University Press. Republished in A. Leijonhufvud, ed. (2000). *Macroeconomic instability and coordination: selected essays of Axel Leijonhufvud.* Cheltenham, UK: Edward Elgar, 33–51.

Lucas, R. (2004). My Keynesian education. In: M. deVroey and K. Hoover, eds. *The IS-LM model: its rise, fall and strange persistence, Annual Supplement to History of Political Economy, 36.* Durham, NC: Duke University Press, 12–24.

Minsky, H. (1986). *Stabilizing an unstable economy.* New Haven, CT: Yale University Press.

Modigliani, F. (1944). Liquidity preference and the theory of interest and money. *Econometrica*, 12 (1), 45–88.

Patinkin, D. (1956). *Money, interest and prices: an integration of monetary and value theory.* Evanston, IL: Row Peterson.

Phillips, A. (1958). The relation between unemployment and the rate of change of money wage rates in the United Kingdom, 1861–1957. *Economica*, 25 (100), 283–299.

Prescott, E. (1986). Theory ahead of business cycle measurement. *Federal Reserve Bank of Minneapolis Quarterly Review*, 10, 2–11.

Romer, P. (2016). *The trouble with macroeconomics.* Delivered as the *Commons Memorial Lecture of the Omicron Delta Epsilon Society.* Available at: https://paulromer.net/wp-content/uploads/2016/09/WP-Trouble.pdf.

Samuelson, P. (1947). *Foundations of Economic Analysis.* Cambridge, MA: Harvard University Press.

Sargent, T. and Wallace, N. (1976). Rational expectations and the theory of economic policy. *Journal of Monetary Economics*, 2 (2), 169–183.

Solow, R. (2010). Building a science of economics for the real world. Congressional Testimony, Hearing before the Subcommittee on Investigations and Oversight, Committee on Science and Technology, House of Representatives 111th Congress, Second Session, July 20, no. 111–106. Washington, DC: U.S. Government Printing Office, 12–15. Available at: https://www.gpo.gov/fdsys/pkg/CHRG-111hhrg57604/pdf/CHRG-111hhrg57604.pdf.

Stiglitz, J. (2018). Where modern macroeconomics went wrong?. *Oxford Review of Economic Policy*, 34 (1/2), 70–106.

Tobin, J. (1958). Liquidity preference as behavior towards risk. *The Review of Economic Studies*, 25 (2), 65–86.

Tobin, J. (1980). *Asset accumulation and economic activity: reflections on contemporary macroeconomic theory.* Chicago: University of Chicago Press and Blackwell.

Tobin, J. (1981). The monetarist counter-revolution today: an appraisal. *Economic Journal*, 91 (361), 29–42.

Velupillai, K. (2006). Algorithmic foundations of computable general equilibrium theory. *Applied Mathematics and Computation*, 179 (1), 360–369.

18 History of economic thought and mainstream economics

A long-term analysis

Marcella Corsi, Alessandro Roncaglia and Giulia Zacchia

[The] *history of economic thought may help to enhance the ability to speak the same economic language, a necessary requisite of any scientific communication, with awareness of the variety and diversification in approaches to economic ideas and problems*

Marcuzzo (2008, p. 114)

1. Introduction

The aim of our contribution is, overall, to shed some light on the increasing difficulties experienced by historians of economic thought in having their role recognised both in terms of research activity and in their contribution to economic debate. By contrast, we strongly believe that 'economics without [the] history of economic thought is a body without soul' (Roncaglia, 2014, p. 8).

That is why, after a preliminary introduction to the role of the history of economic thought (HET) in economics, we concentrate on the new challenges stemming from the bibliometric evaluation of research in economics.

In this context, we refer to the results of the Italian national research assessments (held in 2011 and in 2016), analysing the biases in the evaluation of HET journals, and HET articles in general. Moreover, we seek to show how poorly designed indicators, such as journal impact factors (JIFs) and citation counts, can have negative consequences mainly in terms of pluralism. In doing so, we link our analysis to many contributions made by Cristina Marcuzzo during her career, both as researcher and as ambassador of the economic profession, at the national and international level.

2. Why is HET a core field in economics?

Mainstream views of HET rely on a hidden assumption: a "cumulative view" according to which the provisional point of arrival of contemporary economics incorporates all previous contributions in an improved way.

Indeed, explicitly or – more often – implicitly, a sort of positivist attitude dominates: economic knowledge grows over time, through accumulation of new theories and new empirical knowledge; the personalities of the economists, their ethical values or their fundamental vision of the world are external to the field of economic science and should, rather, be considered as belonging to the field of cultural history, together with the history of mathematics or physics.

As a matter of fact, viewing HET as belonging to the general field of the history of culture (or the history of sciences) rather than the broad field of economics is an attitude taken by some contemporary historians of economic thought.[1] This viewpoint was taken to its extreme with the removal (by the European Research Council in 2018) of HET from economic research classifications in the European Union.[2] Our view is that HET belongs to both fields: a good practitioner of HET should be knowledgeable both in economic theory and in the history of culture.[3] As for the partition of academic careers, an opening to HET should be left in both fields, depending on the individual researcher's specialised contributions, as is the case in many other bridge disciplines.

Moreover, if we recognise the existence of different (and contending) paradigms,[4] the history of economic thought takes on a new role.

In the first pages of his *History of Economic Analysis*, Schumpeter (1954, pp. 41–42) makes his well-known distinction between various stages in economic research: i) the "pre-analytic cognitive act" or "vision", meaning by this a vague vision of the issue to be considered and some tentative hypotheses as to the direction of research; ii) conceptualisation, namely 'to verbalise the vision or to conceptualise it in such a way that its elements take their places, with names attached to them that facilitate recognition and manipulation, in a more or less orderly schema or picture'; iii) model building and, finally, iv) the application of such models to the interpretation of economic reality. What matters to us here is the second stage, quite often overlooked, although Schumpeter himself attributes great importance to it.

Conceptualisation, in fact, becomes an essential aspect of the economist's work when the vision that the researcher is trying to develop differs from the visions adopted/developed by other theoreticians. It is in this stage of work that the theoretician can clarify the distinct character of her/his own representation of the world: not only the relative importance attributed to different aspects of the real world, but also, and especially, the perspective from which each aspect is viewed. Conceptualisation is a complex activity where, for instance, the requirement of consistency (which of course still holds) has a different, broader meaning as compared with the formal coherence required of mathematically framed theories; in any case, conceptualisation represents the (explicit or implicit) foundation for clarifying the connection between such mathematically framed theories and the real world.

It is not unusual for mainstream theoreticians to overlook the role of this stage in economic research. This is clearly due to the fact that the underlying vision of the economy is common to all of them (albeit with different nuances) and is considered the only possible one. Supply and demand reasoning reigns supreme; differences between streams of mainstream economics are a matter of the framework to which supply and demand analysis is applied, as for instance when introducing market forms other than perfect competition, imperfect and asymmetric information, and the like. Thus, it is only these latter aspects that are considered when illustrating the conceptual foundations for the activity of model-building.

On the other hand, there are profound differences in the visions of the economy underlying Classical, Keynesian and neoclassical-marginalist economics. In order to understand them, recourse to the history of economic thought is necessary: it is only when seeking through HET a direct understanding of the visions of the world of a Smith, a Ricardo, a Keynes, a Jevons, or a Walras that we can perceive these differences, and the true content of the different concepts referred to in formal analyses of the economy.[5]

All this does not mean that HET is only useful from a non-mainstream point of view. A better understanding of the meaning of the concepts utilised in economic theorising is essential whatever the researcher's own preferred approach. It is also essential – but this is a different, additional element – for serious debate between contending approaches.[6]

3. HET and economics in research assessments: the Italian case

During the years of austerity, the growing pressure for audit and evaluation of public spending on higher education and research has increased the use of metrics and quantitative indicators to promote a more "transparent" evaluation approach. Bibliometric indicators have been used not only for the purposes of selection of researchers and their career promotion, but also for the allocation of public resources to universities and public research institutions.

The increased adoption of standard metrics to measure research "quality" and the consequent creation of academic journal rankings, generally computed looking at the number of citations received (mainly proxied by Thomson Reuters Web of Science's Impact Factor[7] and Scopus' Scimago Journal Rank),[8] has created an increasingly competitive environment, heavily founded on rigid standardised indexes of scientific productivity.

Many studies – carried out in the Anglo-Saxon world (in the UK, Lee et al., 2013; Lee and Elsner, 2008; in Australia, Bloch, 2010), in France (Chavance and Labrousse, 2018) and in Italy (Corsi et al., 2010, 2018a) – show that identification of "quality" with citations in research assessments systematically tends to rate heterodox and even pluralist departments, journals and researchers lower.

The consequences of such an approach is that HET courses are increasingly removed from the core economics curricula to the periphery of optional courses. Economics departments are no longer training historians of economics with PhD courses, so that optional HET courses risk dwindling away over time with the retirement of the older scholars.[9]

The empirical evidence shows that, in the last ten years,[10] there has been a 30.4% decrease in professors (full and associate professors plus researchers) qualified as experts in HET in Italian universities; moreover, while 59% of them where employed in economics departments in 2006, the share fell to 50% in 2016, because they are increasingly being appointed in fields adjacent to economics, such as philosophy and political sciences. Even in terms of the visibility of historians of economic thought among the broader national classification of economists and statisticians (the so-called area 13) there is evidence of a negative trend: in 2006 they accounted for 0.98% of all professors, while in 2016 the share was significantly lower (0.67%).

However, a contrary trend can be observed in HET courses offered to undergraduate students: according to the latest available data,[11] the number of HET courses has increased by almost 75% in the last few years (from 39 in 2009 to 68 in 2011, the latest available data), including courses held in economics departments.

The contradictions revealed by this evidence – recognising HET's pedagogical importance (more undergraduate courses) but denying its research dignity (no PhDs and less academic staff) – bear out, in our view, the premonition that new attacks on HET are likely to come and practitioners of this field must be prepared to resist.[12]

In Italy, the major battlefield is currently research evaluation practice since it is reshaping the "identity" of economics from a social science, similar to other "moral" sciences like philosophy, sociology, politics, and history, to a "hard" science, like physics, chemistry, biology, and so on. Basically, the threat from mainstream economists to HET in Italian research assessments arises on two sides:

i   from the mainstream cherished ambition to recognise economics as "hard science";[13]

ii from the denial of research assessments' basic principle of neutrality among different research fields, which is effectively reshaping the research habits and interests of Italian academic economist.[14]

Before analysing the evidence of the increasing call for standard bibliometrics in Italy, it is useful to outline the evolution of the research assessments for the allocation of public funds to universities in Italy.

Originally in 2006, the Ministry of Education, University and Research (MIUR) launched the first research evaluation assessment, the "eValuation of Triennial Research" (VTR), designed to evaluate the excellence of research activities carried out by universities and public research institutions. Only *ex post* was the real purpose of the VTR revealed: to restructure the system of allocation of public funds to universities and public research institutions.[15] Inspired by the UK RAE, the VTR evaluated, through peer review, 18,500 papers published in 2001–2003, involving 6,661 experts. It cannot be considered a massive university research assessment, because it involved only a sample of research output selected by the research institutions participating (not by the researchers).

Each research product was evaluated by at least three experts according to four criteria: i) *quality*, ii) *importance/relevance*, iii) *originality/innovation*, iv) *internationalisation*. The results of the VTR have been criticised mainly for the economic area, since the benchmark judgements on the quality of research were identified with the mainstream paradigm of neoclassical economics, penalising research areas that did not achieve sufficient visibility in mainstream journals (see Pasinetti, 2006; Corsi et al., 2010).

In 2011, the National Agency for the Evaluation of University and Research (ANVUR)[16] started its largest-scale evaluation assessment, known as the "eValuation of the Quality of Research" (for short, I VQR), across 95 universities, 12 public research institutions and 16 voluntary organisations, for the research outputs published in 2004–2010. The aim was to create a national ranking of universities and public research institutions that could be used to allocate public funds[17] to institutions that showed superior performance. Fifty per cent of the overall evaluation was based on the quality of the research products submitted, while the remaining 50% referred to a composite score based on six indicators.[18] There were mainly two differences with the 2006 VTR:

– the "top-down" selection of research outputs submitted was abandoned and replaced by a massive bottom-up selection, in the sense that, all researchers made and submitted their own selection of articles to be evaluated;
– a mixed assessment system was introduced. Each panel could choose one or both of the following two evaluation methods:

1   bibliometric analysis that implied the use of two indicators: a measure of the impact of the journal (i.e. Impact Factor by Web of Science and Scimago Journal Rank by Scopus) and the number of citations received by each article;
2   informed peer review carried out by external experts.

Bibliometric analysis was used in the hard sciences, whereas for social sciences and humanities it was decided to adopt only informed peer review. The only exception was economics (Area 13), which tried out a mixed approach: all journals articles were evaluated, where possible, only by bibliometric indexes that measured the impact of the journal where the article was published – Impact Factor (IF) and Article Influence Score (AIS) by Web of Science (WoS), and H index by Google Scholar. All other outputs (books, book chapters, journal articles not indexed in WoS or Google Scholar) were evaluated by peer review.

Using the 5-year Impact Factor (IF5) and the Article Influence Score (AIS) by WoS, the panel of evaluators ranked in four merit classes – from "excellent" to "limited" – 1,903 economic journals in the four research areas:

A – Business, Management, and Finance: 767 journals (40%);
E – Economics: 643 journals (34%);
H –Economic History and the History of Economic Thought: 48 journals (2%);
S – Statistics and Applied Mathematics: 445 journals (23%).

Italian journals represented just 5.7% of the total number of journals, and no Italian journal was ranked in class A. Ten per cent of the journal articles, randomly selected, were also sent for peer review evaluation in order to verify the correlation between these two methodologies.

For economics, the final evaluation report concludes that bibliometric and informed peer review tend to concur, although peer review assigns a lower number of papers to the top class than does bibliometric analysis. Nevertheless, analysing the processed data – the microdata are not available – the principal evaluators found different levels of agreement between informed peer review and bibliometric analysis for different subfields in economics[19]; in particular, for economic history and the history of economic thought the degree of agreement (measured by Cohen's kappa)[20] is close to zero (0.28) and lower than the average of all the other economic subfields. Moreover, the lower frequency of "A" articles and the higher frequency of "B" in the informed peer review, as compared to bibliometric analysis, occur for all sub-areas except economic history and the history of economic thought. Thus bibliometric analysis does not yield the same results as peer review in all the subfields of economics, and certainly not for HET.

Notwithstanding, in the second and last national research assessment (for short, II VQR), run in 2016 for the research outputs published in the period 2011–2014, the quality of articles was still proxied by measures of journal citations (journal impact indicators from ISI WoS, Scopus and Google Scholar). The procedure ranked all research output within 5 classes of merit: "excellent", "good", "fair", "acceptable", and "limited". For economics, journal articles were evaluated with an updated ranking similar to that used in the I VQR. For the research area H (Economic History and the History of Economic Thought), the number of journals ranked increased from 48 to 71 but the number of those classified as "A journals" remained the same (10 journals, none Italian).

Concentrating on HET (subfield SECS-P04) alone, the scenario is even more alarming: only 2 "A journals" out of the 10, listed for research area H, in the I VQR published more than 50% of articles about HET, though HET researchers represented 17.8% in area H. In the II VQR, although the share of historians of economic thought remained almost the same (16.5% of area H), no journal listed in the A class for History has published more than 3% of articles about HET.[21]

In terms of products submitted, the differences between HET and other economic fields (for comparison we used the subfield that had the higher number of publications evaluated, SECS-P01 – political economy) are evident.

In general, there has been a decrease in the number of publications presented in the second round of VQR due to both the reduction of the maximum number of publications that each researcher could present (although this applied only to full and associate professors since, the criteria remained the same for researchers) and the different time frame of the evaluations (seven years for the I VQR and just four years in the II VQR). HET has seen a decrease in the number of professors and a sharper reduction of publications presented for evaluation (46.6% fewer HET publications were presented in 2016) identifying the peculiarities affecting this research field in the last few years: i) the decrease in historians of economic thought employed in Italian universities (as described previously in the chapter);

ii) an international trend to reduction in the share of HET articles published in academic journals, which delays the publication processes (for a complete analysis, see Marcuzzo and Zacchia, 2016).

As clearly shown in Table 18.1, since bibliometrics became a key element for the second round of VQR, there has been a general increase in journal articles presented for evaluation and a decrease in publications that could entail peer review judgement (e.g. books and articles in collective volumes).

Moreover, 91.15% of the publications presented in the II VQR were written in English and only 8.71% in Italian, underlining how the absence of Italian journals at the top of the journal ranking is shaping the direction and practices of research in economics in Italy.

As Table 18.2 shows, historians of economic thought can be considered the "black sheep" of the economic field in this trend to converge to a "more visible" way of doing economics. In fact, they increased – from 8.57% in I VQR to 23.21% in II VQR – the share of books presented for evaluation, while reducing the share of journal articles (from 55.24% to 46.43%). Even the share of publications written in Italian remained high (39.29%). That is why, in the II VQR, for HET there has been an increase in the use of peer reviewing for evaluation of research products, in contrast with other economic fields.Considering the results of the assessments (once more, we were only able to analyse the aggregate results for research fields since microdata are not available), we can confirm that the use of standard bibliometrics, as proxy of research quality, tends to create distortions and disadvantages for historians of economic thought, even if they have been evaluated according to a specific journal ranking for Economic History and the History of Economic Thought.

Table 18.1 Research products presented for the I VQR and II VQR

	Economics SECS-P/01		History of economic thought SECS-P/04	
	I VQR	*II VQR*	*I VQR*	*II VQR*
Number of publications evaluated	1,966	1,378	105	56
Number of professors evaluated	754	776	38	32
		By type (%)		
Journal articles	80.11	84.83	55.24	46.43
Conference papers	0.61	0	0	0
Collective volume articles	13.73	10.45	33.33	30.36
Books	4.78	3.56	8.57	23.21
Other	0.76	1.16	2.86	0
		By language (%)		
English	73.91	91.15	51.43	58.93
Italian	17.24	8.71	40.00	39.29

Table 18.2 Results of I VQR and II VQR

	Economics (SECS-P/01)						History of economic thought (SECS-P/04)					
	I VQR			II VQR			I VQR			II VQR		
	E	G	L	E	G	L	E	G	L	E	G	L
Evaluation type (%)												
Peer review	34.70			18.03			62.86			64.81		
Results (%)												
Total	**32.37**	**14.68**	**30.17**	**34.67**	**24.72**	**6.35**	**9.26**	**20.37**	**45.37**	**6.56**	**26.23**	**11.48**
Publication type (%)												
Journal articles	**42.58**	16.93	23.68	**44.14**	30.97	3.68	**13.79**	27.59	41.38	**3.85**	38.46	19.23
Conference papers	0	18.18	72.73	0	0	0	0	0	0	0	0	0
Collective volume articles	1.13	10.15	65.41	0.69	4.17	29.86	0	5.71	65.71	5.88	11.76	11.76
Books	**3.23**	10.75	67.74	**4.08**	4.08	18.37	**12.5**	33.33	0	**15.38**	30.77	0
Other	0	7.69	92.31	0	0	0	0	0	0	0	0	0

Note: E = excellent; G = good; L = limited (we ignore all other scores).

First of all, we wish to stress that, in general, the share of publications classified of "limited quality" decreased, but concentrating on excellence, just for HET, the share of top-ranked research products decreased in the II VQR (from 9.26% in I VQR to 6.56 in II VQR). It also needs stressing that, while in economics 34.67% of the publications presented have been declared "excellent", for HET the share is over five times lower (just 6.56% of all HET products have been evaluated as excellent research outputs). When we consider journal articles alone, where the journals' bibliometric indexes are used to evaluate the articles, these differences are even more evident: the share of excellent HET journal articles decreases from 13.79% in I VQR to just 3.85% in the II VQR, while for economics the numbers are completely different: 42.58% in I VQR and 44.14% in the II VQR. Instead, for books, where bibliometrics is not applied, the scenario is completely different: the share of excellent books is much higher for HET than in other economic fields (in the VQR II 15.38% for HET and just 4.08% for economics), and the share increases from the first to the second round of the national research assessment. The same evidence can be found for articles in collective volumes, where citation indexes are not available.

In our view, the data reported in Tables 18.1 and 18.2 provide a clear picture of the evolution of research assessment procedures in economics, and how a massive use of bibliometrics penalises HET. Indeed, a reversal in research assessment procedures in economics is needed to counteract the current incentives for researchers to flatten their research methods and interests so as to be more visible in terms of citation indexes and thus to the research assessment evaluators.

4. Final notes

Our contribution deals with the importance of HET within economics and considers how its role is increasingly under attack and downgraded in national research assessments, in particular in Italy.

An incidental consequence of the (mainstream) economists' failure to foresee and forecast the recent (and old) financial crisis has been a new boost to the concept of diversity in the economic profession, underlying how diversity is an enriching factor for the development of economic theory and a better understanding of economic realities. This is a great opportunity to give more centrality to HET in economic debate. HET is a vital key to connect ideas, preserving identity and schools of thought; it shows that there are different ways and means to establish a multi-dimensional rather than univocal discipline.

A new "renaissance" for HET could derive from a critical approach to research evaluation based on bibliometrics, highlighting the negative conse-quences poorly designed indicators can have, above all in terms of lack of pluralism and diversity.[22] Identification of responsible metrics that could account for diversity, using a range of indicators to reflect and support pluralism and anticipate the systemic and potential effects of indicators by updating them in response, could give a new boost to HET and new incentives to researchers involved in the field. Restoring HET to a position at the centre of economic debate is essential to preserve ideas from oblivion and avoid the risks of their misuse when extrapolated from their original context. But it is also important to introduce new perspectives in contemporary economic discourse, as in the case of the gender perspective,[23] where:

> HET could be an important tool in the work of exposing an impossible neutrality and pervasive gender blindness. A gender-sensitive reading of past works and theories could open our eyes to the gradual shifts in meaning of the terms, the slow movement of the boundaries of the discipline
>
> Marcuzzo (2008, p. 120).

Notes

1 Cf. for instance Schabas (1992).
2 Despite the protests, culminating in a letter addressed to Professor Jean-Pierre Bourguignon, President of the European Research Council, signed by the presidents of the major HET associations, including Maria Cristina Marcuzzo (as president of STOREP, Associazione Italiana per la Storia dell'Economia Politica), HET has been shifted from sub-panel SH1 (= Individuals Markets and Organisations) to sub-panel SH6 (= The Study of the Human Past). For more details, please see http://www.aispe.eu/wp-content/uploads/2017/09/ERC-panels-HET-societies-170920.pdf
3 On this point see also Marcuzzo (2008).
4 It is beyond the scope of this chapter to discuss the critiques of positivism and the alternative methodological views (Kuhn, Popper, Lakatos, McCloskey and so on). For a very concise survey of some of these views from the point of view of the history of economic thought, see Roncaglia (2005), from where we have taken some material for our contribution.
5 Cf. Corsi et al. (2018b).
6 Confrontation between contending approaches is useful for the scientific community at all levels, from the international community at large down to the individual university department level. So much can be maintained on three counts: as a stimulus to demonstrate through research that the viewpoint adopted amounts to a progressive scientific research programme; as a drive to greater clarity in presenting research results; and as a source of criticism essential to a conjecture-confutation scientific process. Departments in which different approaches coexist are livelier than departments where one single faith reigns supreme; this liveliness attracts bright students and constitutes a fundamental element in their formation as researchers. Of course, it calls for strong moral sentiments and scientific openness on the part of researchers.
7 The journal impact factor (JIF), computed by Thomson Reuters, measures the average number of citations received by recent articles published in that journal.
8 Scimago Journal Rank, created by Scopus, measures the scientific influence of journals, accounting for citation count and importance of journal citation.
9 Cf. Marcuzzo and Rosselli (2002).
10 Data by the Ministry of Education, University and Research (MIUR) from 31/12/2006 to 31/12/2016.
11 Data by the Ministry of Education, University and Research (MIUR) updated to 31/12/2009 and 31/12/2011.
12 Kates (2013) stresses the risks that HET is running and proposes a sort of guidelines to develop actions in defence of HET's role within the economics field in research and teaching.

13 This tendency is revealed in the conclusions of the Final Area Report of the last National Research Assessment (VQR 2016): 'there is evidence of a generalised evolution of the Area (Economics) toward increased internationalisation and, at the same time, a choice of publication outlets gradually getting closer to that of the 'hard' sciences' (Anvur, 2016, p. 48).

14 This is not an Italian peculiarity. Lee et al. (2013) empirically tested the consequences of a recursive use of bibliometrics in research assessments in UK: since 1992, there has been evidence of a progressive decline in variability in approaches and an increasing convergence of research towards the mainstream paradigm.

15 The results were used to allocate about 2% of public funding.

16 Anvur is a public institution supervised by MIUR, established in 2006 in order to assess the activities of universities and public research institutions in Italy.

17 The results of the VQR have been used by MIUR to award 540 million EUR in "prize funds" for universities with the highest rates.

18 Capacity to attract resources (10%); mobility of research staff (10%); internationalisation (10%); PhD programs (10%); ability to attract research funds (5%); and overall improvement from the last VQR (5%).

19 Cf. Bertocchi et al. (2015).

20 Cohen's kappa is defined as $k = [Pr(a) - Pr(e)]/[1 - Pr(e)]$, where $Pr(a)$ is the relative observed agreement among referees, and $Pr(e)$ is the probability of random agreement. It ranges from 1 (complete agreement) to 0 (no agreement among the referees and bibliometric analysis).

21 We have considered the articles (published from 2004 to 2010 for the first VQR and from 2011 to 2014 for the second one) recorded in Econlit with a JEL code characterised by the letter B, with the exception of B5 "Current Heterodox Approaches".

22 See the recent research and dissemination activities carried out by the Institute for New Economic Thinking (INET).

23 Cf. Marcuzzo and Rosselli (2008).

References

Anvur (2016). Evaluation of research quality 2011-2014 (VQR 2011–2014). Final area report group of evaluation experts for area 13 (GEV13). Available at: http://www.anvur.org/rapporto-2016/files/Area13%20-%20eng/VQR2011-2014_Area13%20-%20eng_RapportoFinale.pdf.

Bertocchi, G., Gambardella, A., Jappelli, T., Nappi, C.A. and Peracchi, F. (2015). Bibliometric evaluation vs. informed peer review: evidence from Italy. *Research Policy*, 44 (2), 451–466.

Bloch, H. (2010). Research evaluation down under: an outsider's view from the inside of the Australian approach. *American Journal of Economics and Sociology*, 69 (5), 1530–1552.

Chavance, B. and Labrousse, A. (2018). Institutions and science: the contest about pluralism in economics in France. *Review of Political Economy*, DOI: 10.1080/09538259.2018.1449472

Corsi, M., D'Ippoliti, C. and Lucidi, F. (2010). Pluralism at risk? Heterodox economic approaches and the evaluation of economic research in Italy. *American Journal of Economics and Sociology*, 69 (5), 1495–1529.

Corsi, M., D'Ippoliti, C. and Zacchia, G. (2018a). A case study of pluralism in economics: the heterodox glass ceiling in Italy. *Review of Political Economy*, DOI: 10.1080/09538259.2018.1423974

Corsi, M., Kregel, J. and D'Ippoliti, C., eds. (2018b). *Classical economics today*. London: Anthem Press.

Kates, S. (2013). *Defending the history of economic thought*. Cheltenham: Edward Elgar.

Lee, F.S. and Elsner, W. (2008). Publishing, ranking, and the future of heterodox economics. *On the Horizon*, 16 (4), 176–184.

Lee, F.S., Pham, X. and Gu, G. (2013). The UK research assessment exercise and the narrowing of UK economics. *Cambridge Journal of Economics*, 37 (4), 693–717.

Marcuzzo, M.C. (2008). Is history of economic thought a "serious" subject? *Erasmus Journal for Philosophy and Economics*, 1 (1), 107–123.

Marcuzzo, M.C. and Rosselli, A. (2002). Economics as history of economics: the Italian case in retrospect. *History of Political Economy*. 34 Annual Supplement, 98–109.

Marcuzzo, M.C. and Rosselli, A. (2008). The history of economic thought through gender lenses. In: F. Bettio and A. Verashchagina, eds. *Frontiers in the economics of gender*. London: Routledge, 3–20.

Marcuzzo, M.C. and Zacchia, G. (2016). Is history of economics what historians of economic thought do? A quantitative investigation. *History of Economic Ideas*, 24 (3), 29–46.

Pasinetti, L.L. (2006). *A note on points of dissent*. Appendix 4 to the CIVR Final Report for Area 13, Available at: http://vtr2006.cineca.it/pubblicazioni/Area_13.pdf.

Roncaglia, A. (2005). *The wealth of ideas*. Cambridge: Cambridge University Press.

Roncaglia, A. (2014). Should the history of economic thought be included in undergraduate curricula? *Economic Thought*, 3 (1), 1–9.

Schabas, M. (1992). Breaking away: history of economics as history of science. *History of Political Economy*, 24 (1), 187–203.

Schumpeter, J. (1954). *History of economic analysis*. E. Boody Schumpeter, ed. New York: Oxford University Press.

Index

Note: Locators in **bold** refer to tables.

For Product Safety Concerns and Information please contact our EU
representative GPSR@taylorandfrancis.com
Taylor & Francis Verlag GmbH, Kaufingerstraße 24, 80331 München, Germany

www.ingramcontent.com/pod-product-compliance
Ingram Content Group UK Ltd.
Pitfield, Milton Keynes, MK11 3LW, UK
UKHW021009180425
457613UK00019B/874